SCREENING AND DIAGNOSIS
OF CHILDREN WITH
LEARNING DISABILITIES

SCREENING AND DIAGNOSIS OF CHILDREN WITH LEARNING DISABILITIES

By

RONALD A. BERK

Associate Professor of Education
The Johns Hopkins University
Baltimore, Maryland

CHARLES C THOMAS • PUBLISHER
Springfield • Illinois • U.S.A.

Published and Distributed Throughout the World by
CHARLES C THOMAS • PUBLISHER
2600 South First Street
Springfield, Illinois 62717

© *1984 by* CHARLES C THOMAS • PUBLISHER

ISBN 0-398-04925-4

Library of Congress Catalog Card Number: 83-17895

With THOMAS BOOKS *careful attention is given to all details of manufacturing and design. It is the Publisher's desire to present books that are satisfactory as to their physical qualities and artistic possibilities and appropriate for their particular use.* THOMAS BOOKS *will be true to those laws of quality that assure a good name and good will.*

Printed in the United States of America
Q-R-3

Library of Congress Cataloging in Publication Data

Berk, Ronald A.
  Screening and diagnosis of children with learning disabilities.

  Bibliography: p.
  Includes indexes.
  1. Learning disabilities.   2. Ability testing.
I. Title.
LC4704.B474 1984   371.92   83-17895
ISBN 0-398-04925-4

To Professor Charles "Paper Chase" Kingsfield,
for inspiring the maintenance and
attainment of high standards of performance

INTRODUCTION

Purposes of the Book

As the professor to whom this book is dedicated would say,

The contents of this volume will be new and unfamiliar to most of you, unlike anything you have known before. Its purpose is to train your mind; you can teach yourself the specific procedures. As you enter these pages with a skull full of mush, remember, that if you succeed in understanding the concepts presented, you will exit thinking more systematically and critically about the assessment process.

THE book has three major purposes: (1) to evaluate what has been done, (2) to recommend what should be done, and (3) to suggest what still needs to be done in the screening and diagnosis of children with learning disabilities. This trinary orientation is linked directly to the federal guidelines promulgated in P.L. 94-142 and the related rules and regulations for its implementation (U.S.O.E., 1977a, 1977b).

Specifically, a critical examination of current screening and diagnostic practices is conducted in order to bring into sharp focus the important issues that have been resolved and those that need resolution. This examination served as the foundation for proposing a strategy for screening and diagnosis that is effective and efficient and can be executed easily by classroom teachers, learning disability specialists, and school psychologists. The review also furnished ideas for proffering alternative approaches to tackling the diverse problems typically encountered in the assessment process.

This text attempts to address systematically some of the most pressing practical problems and thorny technical issues that decision makers must confront. These include appraising the curricular and instructional relevance of standardized tests, setting mastery standards on criterion-referenced tests, scoring tests that are administered below grade level, defining a severe discrepancy between ability and achievement, and determining the effectiveness of a screening procedure and a diagnostic test. Interestingly, none of these concerns have been examined in any available volumes on assessment or learning disabilities.

Quantitative Versus Qualitative Paradigm

There are two categories of information that can serve as the bases for screening and diagnostic procedures: quantitative and qualitative. The quantitative information often consists of the scores from formal and informal data-gathering instruments, especially tests and scales. In contrast, the qualitative information is derived from clinical experience, case studies, and direct observation. Conceptually, these two categories provide the boundaries of a continuum, where the anchors at the extremes designate the use of qualitative data only and quantitative data only. This continuum is depicted as follows:

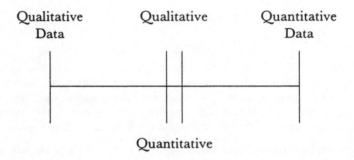

The various approaches to screening and diagnosis can be located at particular points along this continuum. Where the midpoint indicates an equal weighting of qualitative and quantitative data, the other points represent greater emphasis on one or the other type of data. The position advanced in this book is the *quantitative paradigm*, where valid and reliable quantitative data are stressed over qualitative data. The importance of the decisions makes it imperative that technically defensible instruments constitute the core of both screening and diagnostic procedures.

This quantitative paradigm has been given legal sanction at the federal level by P.L. 94-142, the *Procedures for Evaluating Specific Learning Disabilities* (U.S.O.E., 1977b), and court cases such as *Frederick L. v. Thomas* (1976). Moreover, the recent findings of the National Research Council's panel on the selection and placement of children in special education (Heller, Holtzman, & Messick, 1982) emphasized the value of technically adequate norm-referenced and criterion-referenced tests as part of a comprehensive assessment battery.

Major Theses

The assessment of learning-disabled children is viewed as a two-stage process:

1. *Screening — to determine a severe ability-achievement discrepancy.* The first stage involves the use of standardized, norm-referenced ability and achievement test batteries to determine whether severe individual discrepancies in performance exist. A severe discrepancy is defined as a discrepancy

so large that it is real, not a chance occurrence due to errors of measurement. This reliable discrepancy, however, must also be valid so that those children who exhibit severe discrepancies are, in fact, learning disabled.

2. *Diagnosis — to pinpoint specific skill-development weaknesses.* The second stage consists of diagnostic testing with criterion-referenced tests to pinpoint specific skill-development weaknesses in the previously identified area(s) of severe discrepancy. The results of this testing can be used to guide the development of individualized education programs (IEPs) and to verify the accuracy of the screening decisions.

Within the context of this process, a deliberate effort has been made to devise screening and diagnostic procedures that are psychometrically and conceptually sound and also satisfy all of the pertinent legal requirements of P.L. 94-142 and the subsequent rules and regulations.

Organization of the Book

The book is divided into eight chapters. The topics covered are arranged sequentially and correspond to many of the key steps in developing and using a screening procedure and a diagnostic test. The balanced treatment of screening and diagnosis necessitated a similar weighting of norm-referenced tests and criterion-referenced tests in the assessment process.

The first seven chapters and one section in Chapter 8 suggest answers to seven fundamental questions:

1. What is the definition of learning disabilities?
2. What is the most appropriate battery of tests?
3. What type of test scores should be used?
4. What is wrong with current screening procedures?
5. How can the effectiveness of a screening procedure be evaluated?
6. How can the validity and reliability of diagnostic tests be measured?
7. What is the role of the multidisciplinary team in the assessment process?

The final chapter synthesizes the material presented in the preceding chapters into a set of step-by-step procedures for screening and diagnosis that practitioners can follow. Concrete examples are also provided to illustrate particular procedures, especially those requiring computations.

Intended Uses of the Book

Consistent with its structure, contents, and orientation, this book is intended for an introductory course in measurement or assessment for upper level undergraduate and graduate students majoring in special education, learning disabilities, or reading. It can also serve as a handbook and resource for the following audiences: (1) classroom teachers, (2) reading and learning disability specialists, (3) school psychologists, (4) counselors, and (5) school, district, and state level administrators of special education programs. The presentation of the topics throughout the book presumes the reader has had at least one course in learning disabilities or comparable practical experience. No previous course work in measurement or statistics is needed.

References

Frederick L. v. *Thomas,* 419 Supp. 960 (E.D. Pa. 1976), *aff'd,* 557 F.2d 373 (3d Cir. 1977).

Heller, K.A., Holtzman, W.H., & Messick, S. (Eds.). *Placing children in special education: A strategy for equity.* Washington, DC: National Academy Press, 1982.

Public Law 94-142. Education for All Handicapped Children Act, S.6, 94th Congress [Sec 613(a) (4)] 1st session, June 1975. Report No. 94-168.

U.S. Office of Education. Education of handicapped children: Implementation of Part B of the Education of the Handicapped Act. *Federal Register,* 1977, *42*(163), 42474 – 42518. (a)

U.S. Office of Education. Assistance to states for education for handicapped children: Procedures for evaluating specific learning disabilities. *Federal Register,* 1977, *42*(250), 62082 – 62084. (b)

FOR PRACTITIONERS ONLY

GIVEN the vast array of textbooks and guidebooks on measurement techniques now available, why must you plod through this additional volume? One reason might be that it is used in a course required for a degree. A better reason is the information it provides, which is unobtainable from the other books on the market.

This book was written expressly for professionals who are involved directly in the assessment of learning-disabled children and in the decisions that affect their educational future. If you are a regular classroom teacher, a resource teacher, a diagnostic-prescriptive teacher, a learning disability specialist, or a school psychologist, then you can benefit from the ideas presented (some of the ideas are listed in the Introduction).

Unlike most measurement texts, this text is structured according to the specific decisions you make and the types of information that must be gathered to guide and substantiate those decisions. In view of the time constraints under which you operate, explicit recommendations and Memory Joggers are presented in the chapters (see List of Memory Joggers) and, when a statistic or method is described, the chapter summary is a step-by-step listing of the essential procedures. The final chapter is a step-by-step summary of the entire screening and diagnostic processes, from test selection through decision making by the multidisciplinary team. The theoretical underpinnings of the proposed strategies are explained where appropriate. If time permits, you can go back and review the research evidence and theoretical developments.

Perhaps the best initial indication of the usefulness of the contents is your ability to answer the following questions:

1. Are the tests you are using technically adequate?
2. Are the tests you are using the best ones currently available?
3. Are you using grade-equivalent scores (e.g., 5.3) to make decisions about learning-disabled children?
4. Is the screening procedure used in your school technically sound?
5. Are the correct children being labeled learning-disabled?
6. Are the placement decisions appropriate and in the best interests of the children?
7. Does the multidisciplinary team in your school function effectively?

8. Is your diagnosis of individual skill weaknesses accurate?

If you do not know or are not sure of the answers to these questions, you will probably find some of the material in this book useful in your work. In essence, those answers test the veracity of your screening and diagnostic practices; the information given in the succeeding chapters can determine whether the practices are sound and, in fact, whether they really work.

These remarks, it is hoped, have sparked an interest in the topic. Certainly your job responsibilities suggest you have, at least, a vested interest in the assessment process.

ACKNOWLEDGMENTS

IN writing this book, I have benefitted greatly from the advice, criticism, and encouragement of many colleagues and students. Should these paragraphs fail to acknowledge any assistance that I have received, it is not because of a lack of appreciation but through my oversight.

First, I thank the graduate students in my classes over the past five years. The students in the measurement course provided valuable feedback on the clarity, meaning, and feasibility of the contents, which stimulated constant revision and refinement of the chapters. In the dissertation seminars, the doctoral students kept my ideas alive by their puzzled looks and perceptive comments. I am especially grateful to these students, who have always taught me so much when I have listened. I have been rewarded by learning much more from them than I could compress into this small volume.

Second, I am indebted to several colleagues for their conscientious and helpful reviews of portions of earlier drafts of the manuscript. I extend my appreciation to William H. Angoff (Educational Testing Service), Gary L. Brager (Baltimore County School System), Ronald K. Hambleton (University of Massachusetts, Amherst), Samuel A. Livingston (Educational Testing Service), Cecil R. Reynolds (Texas A & M University), and Gilbert B. Schiffman (The Johns Hopkins University). The editorial assistance and suggestions by Robin P. Gallico, Martin S. Gould, and Barbara G. Zirkin, of The Johns Hopkins University, were also extremely useful in the preparation of the final version of the manuscript.

Third, I am particularly grateful to Ann W. Hall for her skillful deciphering of my handwriting and translations into typescript form. For typing the entire manuscript, including 49 tables and 617 references, a noteworthy accomplishment by any standards, she deserves special recognition.

Finally, I express sincere appreciation to my family and close friends, especially to my parents, Anne and Murray, for their continuous encouragement and supportiveness in all of my projects, to my wife, Marion O. Smith-Waison, and my two daughters, Corinne and Marisa Berk-Smith, for their patience and understanding during the strange hours and conditions under which this book was written, and to Frances S. Ellison, for her sense of responsibility and flexibility, which allowed me to concentrate on writing. After all, without them, the meaningfulness of this product would be significantly diminished.

CONTENTS

LIST OF MEMORY JOGGERS

**SCREENING AND DIAGNOSIS
OF CHILDREN WITH
LEARNING DISABILITIES**

Chapter 1

TOWARD A DEFINITION OF LEARNING DISABILITIES

Introduction

PROBABLY the stickiest task that every practitioner and researcher must tackle before identifying a learning-disabled child is to define the construct *learning disabilities*, preferably in operational terms. The considerable amount of confusion and fragmentation in the field of learning disabilities that has occurred over the past 20 years can be traced to this initial step. If the definition of learning disabilities is imprecise or ambiguous, then all succeeding tasks contingent upon the definition, such as screening, diagnosis, and remediation, will be afflicted with the imprecision or ambiguity (cf. Tucker, Stevens, & Ysseldyke, 1983). Therefore, clarification must begin with the definition.

The purpose of this chapter is to survey and analyze the definitions proposed by experts in the field and by legislative mandate in order to provide some insight into the current problems with screening and diagnosis. The presentation is organized according to the following topics: (1) historical developments, (2) common elements in the definitions, (3) criticisms of federal definitions, (4) theoretical versus operational definitions, and (5) definitions used in research and practice. Several conclusions regarding the state of definitions will then be given (see also Berk, 1983).

Historical Developments

Prior to the 1960s, a variety of terms were used to refer to the disorders that were later to fall under the rubric of learning disabilities. These included *minimal brain dysfunction, psychoneurological learning disorder, central processing dysfunction, exogenous,* and *perceptually handicapped.* More specific disorders were given labels, such as *dyslexia* for severe reading disabilities and *aphasia* for delays in learning to talk. The number of these terms increased *ad infinitum* as specialists attempted to describe the conditions they observed.

3

In 1962, Samuel A. Kirk coined the term *learning disabilities* in the first edition of his popular textbook *Educating Exceptional Children*. Shortly thereafter, he introduced the term in a presentation at the 1963 Conference on Exploration into the Problems of the Perceptually Handicapped Child. At this conference Kirk also tried to sort out the multiplicity of terms and labels that had been applied to the children of interest:

> There are two kinds of terms that have been applied to those children, either alone or in combination.
>
> The first group of terms refers to causation or etiology. We try to label the child with a term that has biological significance. These terms are *brain injury, minimal brain damage, cerebral palsy, cerebral dysfunction, organic driven-ness, organic behavior disorders, psychoneurological disorders,* and a host of other terms. All of these terms refer to a disability of the brain in one form or another as an explanation of the deviant behavior of the child.
>
> The second group of terms refers to the behavior manifestations of the child, and include a wide variety of deviant behavior. Terms such as *hyperkinetic behavior, perceptual disorders, conceptual disorders, Strauss syndrome, social dyspraxia, catastrophic behavior, disinhibition, learning disorders,* and the various forms of aphasia, apraxia, agnosia, dyslexia and a host of other terms which describe the specific behavior deficit of the child. (pp. 1 – 2)

These two groups of terms were the precursors of the medical and behavioral categories of definitions, respectively. Kirk then presented the term *learning disabilities*:

> Recently, I have used the term "learning disabilities" to describe a group of chidren who have disorders in development in language, speech, reading, and associated communication skills needed for social inter-action. In this group I do not include children who have sensory handicaps such as blindness or deafness, because we have methods of managing and training the deaf and the blind. I also exclude from this group children who have generalized mental retardation. (p. 3)

The definitions of learning disabilities that were to appear in the literature during the next two decades are listed in Table 1.1. Some of them were formulated by individuals; others were developed by committees associated with various parental, professional, educational, or governmental organizations.

Medical Definitions

The substance and orientation of these definitions reflect the different perspectives and changes in the field that occurred within that period of time. The influences of medicine, psychology, and education were the most profound. For example, several of the earlier definitions stressed *medical-neurological* or biologically based factors by expressing learning disabilities as etiologies, usually related to a particular type of brain dysfunction or disorder of the central nervous system. This focus is illustrated in the definitions of Myklebust and Clements (see also Cruickshank, 1967; Johnson & Myklebust, 1967; Ross, 1976; Wender, 1971). These definitions fostered the notion that the locus of damage or dysfunction was internal to the child.

MEMORY JOGGER

Table 1.1

Chronology of Selected Definitions of Learning
Disabilities over the Past Two Decades

Date	Source	Definition
1962	Samuel A. Kirk	A learning disability refers to a retardation, disorder, or delayed development in one or more of the processes of speech, language, reading, spelling, writing, or arithmetic resulting from a possible cerebral dysfunction and/or emotional or behavioral disturbance and not from mental retardation, sensory deprivation, or cultural or instructional factors. (p. 263)
1963	Helmer R. Myklebust	We use the term "psychoneurological learning disorders" to include deficits in learning, at any age, which are caused by deviations in the central nervous system and which are not due to mental deficiency, sensory impairment, or psychogenicity. The etiology might be disease and accident, or it might be development. (p. 27)
1964 – 65	Barbara Bateman	Manifest an educationally significant discrepancy between their estimated intellectual potential and actual level of performance related to basic disorders in the learning processes, which may or may not be accompanied by demonstrable central nervous system dysfunction, and which are not secondary to generalized mental retardation, educational or cultural deprivation, severe emotional disturbance, or sensory loss. (p. 220)
1966	Task Force I – sponsored by National Society for Crippled Children and Adults and National Institutes of Neurological Diseases and Blindness, National Institutes of Health (Clements, 1966)	The term "minimal brain dysfunction syndrome" refers to children of near average, average, or above average general intelligence with certain learning or behavioral disabilities ranging from mild to severe, which are associated with deviations of function of the central nervous system. These deviations may manifest themselves by various combinations of impairments in perception, conceptualization, language, memory, and control of attention, impulse, or motor function. (p. 9 – 10)
1966	James J. Gallagher	Children with developmental imbalances are those who reveal a developmental disparity in psychological processes related to education of such a degree (often four years or more) as to require the instructional programming of developmental tasks appropriate to the nature and level of the deviant developmental process. (p. 28)
1968 – 69	National Advisory Committee on Handicapped Children; Children with Specific Learn-	Children with special learning disabilities exhibit a disorder in one or more of the basic psychological processes involved in understanding or using spoken or written

Date	Source	Definition
	ing Disabilities Act of 1969 (P.L. 91-230)	languages. These may be manifested in disorders of listening, thinking, talking, reading, writing, spelling or arithmetic. They include conditions which have been referred to as perceptual handicaps, brain injury, minimal brain dysfunction, dyslexia, development aphasia, etc. They do not include learning problems which are due primarily to visual, hearing, or motor handicaps, to mental retardation, emotional disturbance, or to environmental disadvantage. (p. 4)
1969	James C. Chalfant & Margaret A. Scheffelin	Characteristics which are often mentioned include disorders in one or more of the processes of thinking, conceptualization, learning, memory, speech, language, attention, perception, emotional behavior, neuromuscular or motor coordination, reading, writing, arithmetic, discrepancies between intellectual achievement potential and achievement level, and developmental disparity in the psychological processes related to education. (p. 1)
1975	Part A of the Education of the Handicapped Act (P.L. 91-230), as amended by the Education for All Handicapped Children Act of 1975 (P.L. 94-142), which is Part B	Children with specific learning disabilities are defined as those children who have a disorder in one or more of the basic psychological processes involved in understanding or in using language, spoken or written, which disorder may manifest itself in imperfect ability to listen, think, speak, read, write, spell, or do mathematical calculations. Such disorders include such conditions as perceptual handicaps, brain injury, minimal brain dysfunction, dyslexia, and developmental aphasia. Such term does not include children who have learning problems which are primarily the result of visual, hearing, or motor handicaps, of mental retardation, of emotional disturbance, or of environmental, cultural, or economic disadvantage. (Sec. 602)
1979	Samuel A. Kirk & James J. Gallagher	A specific learning disability is a psychological or neurological impediment to spoken or written language or perceptual, cognitive, or motor behavior. The impediment (1) is manifested by discrepancies among specific behaviors and achievements or between evidenced ability and academic achievement, (2) is of such nature and extent that the child does not learn by the instructional methods and materials appropriate for the majority of children and requires specialized procedures for development, and (3) is not primarily due to severe mental retardation, sensory handicaps, emotional problems, or lack of opportunity to learn. (p. 285)
1981	National Joint Committee for Learning Disabilities — composed of representatives from American Speech-Language-Hearing Association, Associa-	Learning disabilities is a generic term that refers to a heterogeneous group of disorders manifested by significant difficulties in the acquisition and use of listening, speaking, reading, writing, reasoning or mathematical abilities. These disorders are intrinsic to the individual and presumed to be due to cen-

Date	Source	Definition
	tion for Children and Adults with Learning Disabilities, Council for Learning Disabilities, Division for Children with Communication Disorders, International Reading Association, and The Orton Dyslexia Society (see Hammill, Leigh, McNutt, & Larsen, 1981)	tral nervous system dysfunction. Even though a learning disability may occur concomitantly with other handicapping conditions (e.g., sensory impairment, mental retardation, social and emotional disturbance) or environmental influences (e.g., cultural differences, insufficient/inappropriate instruction, psychogenic factors), it is not the direct result of those conditions or influences. (p. 5)

Confronted with this charge of detecting brain dysfunction, the educational diagnostician conveyed dissatisfaction and frustration. First, the medical vocabulary was foreign. Second, and more important, however, the required assessment procedures, instruments, and competencies were just not within the purview of educators, especially learning disability specialists, and medical evidence was essential in order to link learning disabilities to minimal brain damage. Bryan and Bryan (1978) explained the problem:

> The stronger the direct evidence for brain damage, such as seizures and paralysis, the less likely the diagnostic conclusion is to be "minimal" damage. The less direct the medical evidence, the more the reliance upon social and academic performance, and the more likely the diagnosis of "minimal brain dysfunction." By definition, the linkage of brain damage with learning disabilities through direct evidence becomes an impossibility. (p. 29)

Finally, even if the difficulties of locating dysfunctions in the brain were overcome and specific damage was identified, instructional programming to ameliorate or eliminate the damage would be pointless. There is little meaningful activity via prescriptions in which the educator could engage that would make any corrective difference.

Behavioral Definitions

As a result of the discontent over definitions with etiologic implications, a major shift in emphasis could be anticipated. The definitions that followed relied heavily upon educational and psychological (or psychoeducational) factors. These *behavioral* definitions concentrated on behavioral characteristics such as the inability to read, listen, think, speak, write, spell, or perform arithmetic calculations, irrespective of etiology. These elements are evident to varying degrees in all of the other definitions in Table 1.1. The attempt to blend diverse psychoeducational variables into a single framework was most clearly documented in the 1968 National Advisory Committee on Handicapped Children definition, which was included in Public Law 91-230, Children with Specific Learning Disabilities Act of 1969, the Elementary and Secondary Amendments of 1969. This legislation was extended in 1974 as part of Public Law 93-380, the Education of the Handicapped Amendments, and again in 1975 when the definition was changed only slightly for inclusion in Public Law 94-142, the Education for all Handicapped Children Act of 1975. These federal definitions underscored the domain of *language-related problems* as the distinguishable category of disorders that constitutes special (or specific) learning disabilities.

The other definitions proposed by the authorities listed in Table 1.1 represented particular educational, psychological, or psychoeducational positions. For example, Kirk (1962) emphasized specific learning problems, Bateman (1965) stressed the discrepancy between achievement and potential, Gallagher (1966) focused on the irregular development of mental abilities, and Chalfant and Scheffelin (1969) related psychological processes to academic disorders.

Common Elements in the Definitions

An analysis of all of these definitions and others that have accumulated reveal several common elements or components that circumscribe the limits of what are called learning disabilities (see Chalfant & King, 1976; Gearheart, 1981; Myers & Hammill, 1976; Wallace & McLoughlin, 1979). Johnson and Morasky (1980) have extracted five functional characteristics that are explicitly or implicitly contained in most definitions:

1. Some principle of discrepancy or disparity between a child's actual performance and predicted potential or capacity;
2. General role of the central nervous system, although few contemporary definitions focus on the necessity for demonstrating neurological pathology or dysfunction for inclusion in a learning disability category;
3. Primary physiological problems are excluded;
4. Some special problem areas are excluded, such as cultural disadvantage, mental retardation, and emotional disturbance; and
5. The relevance of the problem to the learning process in terms of educational growth, development, and performance. (pp. 5 – 6)

Perhaps the simplest observation that can be made about the definitions is that they delineate what learning disabilities are as well as what they are not; that is, there are elements of inclusion and elements of exclusion in each definition.

Elements of Inclusion

There are four elements of inclusion in most definitions: (1) normal intelligence, (2) ability-achievement discrepancy, (3) academic disorder, and (4) psychological process disorder.

NORMAL INTELLIGENCE. The first distinguishing characteristic pertains to level of intelligence. The child with a learning disability should possess normal intelligence and can possess even gifted intelligence on verbal or nonverbal measures. Although this notion that a learning disability is not attributable to a child's lack of intelligence or mental subnormality is generally accepted in the profession, there is no explicit statement about intelligence level in any of the definitions in Table 1.1. The intelligence element is inferred from that part of the "exclusion clause" indicating that a learning disorder is not primarily attributable to mental retardation. Given the criteria traditionally employed to identify the mentally retarded, the definitions of learning disability automatically exclude children who are below a certain level of intelligence. This approach to designating the intelligence element leads to the conclusion that the specification of intelligence level in all of the definitions is vague, indirect, and indefinite.

ABILITY—ACHIEVEMENT DISCREPANCY (underachievement). While a child with a learning disability should have normal mental ability, he or she should also exhibit an achievement deficit relative to that ability in at least one academic subject area. In other words, in spite of average or above average potential, severe learning problems must be clearly evidenced. This difference between measured ability and measured achievement has been expressed as a "discrepancy," "disparity," "imbalance," "deficit," "gap," or "intraindividual difference" in the various definitions. It is noteworthy that a statement of discrepancy or underachievement does not appear in either the National Advisory Committee on Handicapped Children (1968) definition or the P.L. 94-142 (1975) definition. In 1977, however, the *Procedures for Evaluating Specific Learning Disabilities*, published in the *Federal Register* (U.S.O.E., 1977), did stipulate:

[A] child has a specific learning disability if:

(1) The child does not achieve commensurate with his or her age and ability levels in one or more of the areas listed [below]. . .when provided with learning experiences appropriate to the child's age and ability levels; and

(2) The [multidisciplinary] team finds that a child has a severe discrepancy between achievement and intellectual ability in one or more of the following areas:
   (i)   Oral expression;
   (ii) Listening comprehension;
   (iii) Written expression;
   (iv) Basic reading skill;
   (v)   Reading comprehension;
   (vi) Mathematics calculation; or
   (vii) Mathematics reasoning. (p. 65083)

The omission of a "severe discrepancy between achievement and intellectual ability" in the original definition has turned out to be a major oversight, inasmuch as the discrepancy element has emerged as the primary focus of the criteria for identifying learning-disabled children.

Despite the emphasis given to the ability-achievement discrepancy and the proliferation of methods to define "discrepancy" operationally (see Chapter 6), none of the definitions provides any guidelines or standards for determining what is a significant or severe discrepancy. Although this ambiguity in the federal specifications is not especially surprising in view of the earlier congressional definitions, it is nevertheless troublesome from the standpoint that the responsibility is then thrust on local and state agencies. As Ysseldyke and Algozzine (1982) metaphorically and so accurately observed, "Local or state education agencies must flesh out the skeletal structure offered by the federal agency" (p. 44).

ACADEMIC DISORDER. The areas of academic disorder or ability-achievement discrepancy usually stated in the definitions are reading, writing, spelling, and arithmetic. Listening, speaking, and thinking are also listed in the federal definitions. These areas were partitioned further in the *Procedures* (U.S.O.E., 1977) quoted previously. It is interesting to note that the words "may be" are used in these definitions. This suggests the possibility that an individual's process disorder need not be manifested in an academic deficit in order to satisfy the legal requirements for a specific learning disability.

PSYCHOLOGICAL PROCESS DISORDER. Underlying the ability-achievement discrepancy is a disorder in basic psychological or learning processes such as memory, perception, closure, modality, and sequencing. Impairment in one or more of these processes may take the following forms: (a) loss of the process, (b) inhibition of the development of the process, or (c) interference with the function of the process (Myers & Hammill, 1976). Children frequently exhibit problems with varying degrees of severity in several processes. The processes related to understanding and using spoken and written language are usually stated in the definitions of learning disabilities. The authors of most of the definitions in Table 1.1 view these processing abilities as the precipitating or causative factors involved in the discrepancy. Interestingly, although process disorders appear in the 1968 and 1975 federal definitions, they are not mentioned as part of the identification criteria in the *Procedures for Evaluating Specific Learning Disabilities* (U.S.O.E., 1977).

Associated with the definitions are certain models of psychological processes. Two models that have received a considerable amount of attention in the field are Chalfant and Scheffelin's (1969) information-processing model and Kirk and Kirk's (1971) psycholinguistic model. Wallace and McLoughlin (1979) have summarized the salient features of these models:

1. The learner must be able to receive, integrate, and do something with information which he [or she] takes in.
2. All modalities (vision, hearing, touch, etc.) must be considered important factors in learning, either on an individual basis or combined.
3. Psychological processes overlap, are ongoing, and are not unitary functions.
4. The effort is made to distinguish between processing information in a meaningful or nonmeaningful way, in a symbolic or nonsymbolic way, and in a verbal or nonverbal way.

5. These descriptions generally include an explanation of their effects on academic learning. (pp. 30 – 31)

The last feature is particulary significant in that the linkage between the processes and academic disorders has been extremely difficult to establish. The processes are typically "test-identified" (Mann, 1971). In fact, the perceptually oriented tests, such as the Illinois Test of Psycholinguistic Abilities and Developmental Test of Visual Perception, that accompanied the learning disability movement tended to interpret the intent of the process component in the various definitions. The use of these tests implies that a process disorder is manifested in a language disorder. Unfortunately, the tests designed to measure auditory, visual, sensory integration, and haptic process disorders have less than desirable technical characteristics (see Coles, 1968; Salvia & Ysseldyke, 1981).

Elements of Exclusion

Elements of exclusion delineate the characteristics of children that exclude them from being identified as learning disabled. These elements relate to the problems of mental subnormality, visual or hearing impairment (sensory deficit), motor deficit, severe cultural neglect, and/or severe emotional disturbance. All of the behavioral definitions in Table 1.1, except those by Gallagher (1966) and Chalfant and Scheffelin (1969), can be considered "definitions by exclusion." They designate what a learning-disabled child is not. The exclusion clause specifies, in essence, that if a child is not deaf, blind, emotionally disturbed, mentally retarded, or disadvantaged, yet exhibits learning problems, he or she must have a learning disability. These elements were reinforced in relation to an ability-achievement discrepancy in the 1977 criteria outlined in the *Federal Register* (U.S.O.E., 1977):

(b) The [multidisciplinary] team may not identify a child as having a specific learning disability if the severe discrepancy between ability and achievement is primarily the result of:

(1) A visual, hearing, or motor handicap;
(2) Mental retardation;
(3) Emotional disturbance; or
(4) Environmental, cultural or economic disadvantage. (p. 65083)

It is often stated or implied in the definitions that these other handicapping conditions must be *primary* problems or causal agents. For example, suppose a mentally retarded child satisfied all but one of the inclusion criteria in the definition of a specific learning disability (i.e., normal intelligence). That child would be classified and placed according to the primary condition; he or she would be ineligible for learning disability programs and services because the learning disability detected may be a secondary condition caused by the retardation. Although this primacy qualification was not intended to preclude or otherwise discourage the teacher of the mentally retarded from treating the child for the learning disorder as well as the other problems, the net effect of the exclusionary statement has been to deny many mentally retarded children the benefits of learning disability programming. This dilemma is also generalizable to children with the other "primary" handicaps.

Certainly the authors of the definitions did not anticipate that the exclusion clause would automatically exclude special types of handicapped children with learning disabilities from receiving appropriate remedial services. Nonetheless, this inadvertent denial of services to children who are entitled to them has been one consequence of the clause. Perhaps some of the ensuing problems and controversy over the exclusion clause would not have arisen had the elements of inclusion in the definitions been more clearly described (cf. Hammill, 1974).

If each definition was stripped of its exclusion clause, what remains is essentially a statement that *a learning disability is an inability to learn* in a specific cognitive area. This connotes a strong sense of circularity within the definition, leaving the core of the problem undefined and unspecified. More will be said about this ambiguity in the next section.

Criticisms of Federal Definitions

The foregoing analysis of the major elements of the definitions in Table 1.1 has exposed a few of the weaknesses, problems, disadvantages, and points of controversy which demand attention. The negative appraisal suggested by these observations is consistent with the conclusions reached by many of the experts in the field (Bryan, 1974; Bryan & Bryan, 1978; Bryant, 1972; Gearheart, 1981; Hallahan & Cruickshank, 1973; Lerner, 1981; Mercer, 1979; Myers & Hammill, 1976; Wallace & McLoughlin, 1979). Although most of the comments address the general definitional issue of devising unambiguous and noncontradictory criteria that would be accepted by the professionals, there have been specific attacks on the two key federal definitions: the 1968 P.L. 91-230 definition and the 1975 P.L. 94-142 definition. As mentioned previously, the 1975 version was just a slight rewording of the earlier definition, with no substantive changes. Each sentence in these definitions has been scrutinized, and criticisms have been directed from different perspectives (Cruickshank, 1977; Hammill, 1974; Hammill et al., 1981; Kirk, 1974; Myers & Hammill, 1976; National Joint Committee for Learning Disabilities, 1981; Wiederholt, 1974).

Functions

Before examining these criticisms, however, it is essential to consider the purposes and functions of the definitions. Certainly if a definition is criticized for not being operational when, in fact, it was never conceived with that intent in mind, such a criticism would be invalid. Initially, the federal definitions provided *theoretical* statements for understanding and delimiting the conditions called specific learning disabilities. They were not intended to be *operational* definitions that guide the selection of children for particular research studies or the diagnosis and treatment of children in a school or clinical setting. In addition, these definitions were designed to primarily serve administrative and financial functions. They furnish a foundation for developing screening and identification procedures that can be used as the bases for making classifications, for estimating incidence (or prevalence) rates, and for distributing funds. The decision about the amount of funding that each state agency is to receive for educational programs for learning-disabled children and for professional training depends almost entirely on how the federal definition is interpreted (see Bersoff & Veltman, 1979, pp. 16 – 19).

Criticisms

Given these functions, the federal definitions are admittedly ambiguous. But this ambiguity is also attributable to the nature of the construct *learning disabilities* and the target population. The domain encompassing learning disabilities is both broad in scope and complex in substance. Historically, it evolved out of numerous and diverse categories of handicapping conditions. Consequently, the children falling within the limits of this domain represent a wide variety of learning handicaps, and they fail to learn for a variety of reasons (Keogh, 1983).

Another persistent criticism related to these definitions is the inability to *obtain professional consensus*. Although the 1968 definition was perhaps more acceptable to researchers and practitioners than most others, there is still considerable disagreement and dissatisfaction with the 1975 version. To a large extent, this lack of consensus can be explicated in terms of the historical developments in the field, specifically the nature of the professional population. As discussed earlier, the roots of the learning disability movement were planted in medicine, education, and psychology. Although much of the progress that has occurred represents to varying degrees the confluence of theoretical and philosophical approaches in these disciplines, the original diversity in the professional population has remained and has even increased as a result of the specializations that have emanated from the movement itself, specialties like learning disability specialist, reading specialist, diagnostic-prescriptive teacher, educational diagnostician, and speech/language/audiology specialist, for example. Consequently, the variability and quantity of professional viewpoints on "what is a specific learning disability" would be more conducive to disagreement than agreement.

The disagreements with the definitions have often focused on particular words, phrases, and clauses (Hammill et al., 1981). In fact, much of the controversy that has developed over some of the terminology stems from this inherent diversity of professional viewpoints. The specific criticisms are described as follows:

1. *"Children" is unnecessarily restrictive.* The use of the term *children* in the definitions implies, contrary to fact, that learning disabilities do not afflict adults and that the law applies only to children. There has been a recent trend toward programming for adults with learning disabilities. Other developments in the field include the name changing of professional associations (e.g., Association for Children and Adults with Learning Disabilities, previously adults were omitted from the title) and the founding of new organizations for that segment of the population (e.g., LAUNCH, an acronym for Leadership, Action, Unity, Nurturing, Citizenship, and Harmony). These developments furnish sufficient evidence to warrant the inclusion of adults in the definitions. Obviously, adults are part of the population of learning-disabled persons, although they are not included in the coverage of the Education for All Handicapped *Children* Act of 1975.

2. *"Basic psychological processes" cannot be identified or clearly defined.* At present, it is doubtful whether the authorities on learning disabilities can identify what these processes are or whether they can define them precisely. As noted previously, these processes have assumed meaning by way of the tests that were developed to measure them. These test-identified processes, especially in the perceptual/language area, have proven to be one baneful result of the learning disability movement; not only do the tests provide the illusion of defining the basic processes, but their supporting literature belies their poor psychometric foundation.

What happened in this instance is that the original intent of the phrase was lost and replaced with a few theories of psychological processes and accompanying tests. The phrase was supposed to focus on the intrinsic causes of learning disabilities, as opposed to extrinsic or environmental causes, and to direct attention away from the medical-neurological orientation so predominant in the early years. Since the 1968 definition, however, the phrase has engendered confusion and debate instead of clarifying this important causal distinction.

3. *"In understanding or in using language, spoken or written" is redundant.* Understanding and using spoken language are synonymous with "listen" and "speak," and understanding and using written language are synonymous with "read," "write," and "spell."

4. *"Spell" is redundant.* Spelling is subsumed under written language, as stated in the preceding criticism. It also does not appear in the seven areas designated in the *Procedures for Evaluating Specific Learning Disabilites* (U.S.O.E., 1977). Sentence one of the definition needs to be rewritten in order to eliminate these redundancies.

5. *"Conditions" cannot be clearly defined.* Although the list of conditions, including perceptual handicaps, brain injury, minimal brain dysfunction, dyslexia, and developmental aphasia, was specified for the purpose of clarifying "disorders," it has just added confusion and misinterpretation. The professional polemics over the definitions of these conditions have not yet abated. Therefore, they only invite further controversy.

6. *"Does not include. . .which are primarily the result of" makes assumptions that are not supported in practice.* This expression assumes that diagnosticians can competently distinguish between primary and secondary handicapping conditions. It is often very difficult to discern whether an emotionally disturbed child developed an achievement deficit as a result of the emotional problem or whether a learning-disabled child acquired emotional problems due to poor achievement performance. In fact, it is almost impossible to differentiate between handicaps such as learning disability, emotional disturbance, and mental retardation where the conditions exist in a mild to moderate degree. For nonachievers with borderline intelligence and disruptive classroom behavior, the differences between these discrete categories can be negligible (Hallahan & Kauffman, 1977). In other words, for the vast majority of learning disability referrals, not only is it difficult to determine which condition is primary, but in many instances the conditions themselves are not readily discernible.

Another problem with the exclusion clause is "the widespread misconception that learning disabilities can occur neither in conjunction with other handicapping conditions nor in the presence of environmental, cultural, or economic disadvantage" (Hammill et al., 1981, p. 338). This interpretation is incorrect. The definition states only that learning disabilities are not *"primarily the result of visual, hearing, or motor handicaps, of mental retardation, of emotional disturbance, or environmental, cultural, or economic disadvantage"* [italics added]. The primacy qualification implies that these other conditions or situations can be secondary or tertiary problems, as manifested in multiply handicapped learning-disabled children.

Response to the Criticisms

As these criticisms of the federal definitions have mounted since the 1970s, so have the suggestions for changes. However, the bulk of these suggestions have been isolated and expert specific (e.g., Myers & Hammill, 1976). Not until February, 1980, was there any initiative to recommend changes on a systematic basis. The National Joint Committee for Learning Disabilities (NJCLD) was formed with this charge in mind. It was composed of representatives from six professional organizations concerned with the definition of learning disabilities (see Table 1.1). The work of the committee culminated in a critique of the P.L. 94-142 definition and a proposal of a new definition. This was presented in a position paper at the final meeting in January, 1981. The new definition is presented in Table 1.1.

The NJCLD Committee was convinced that its definition was a substantial improvement over extant definitions, particularly the P.L. 94-142 definition. Although the definition does address most of the aforementioned criticisms, it, too, uses expressions that are either not clearly defined or difficult to verify in practice:

1. *"significant difficulties,"* which is analogous to "severe discrepancy" in the *Procedures for Evaluating Specific Learning Disabilities* (U.S.O.E., 1977).
2. *"due to central nervous system dysfunction,"* which is imbued with the same difficulties of establishing causality as "basic psychological processes."
3. *"it is not the direct result of those conditions or influences,"* which is analogous to the exclusion clause and primacy qualification in the P.L. 94-142 definition.

Although the definition has certain advantages over its predecessors by omission of some of the ambiguous, redundant, and misleading terminology, the three expressions of commission noted here tend to vitiate these advantages. This is unfortunate because the changes do seem to advance the field toward a "better definition" (McLoughlin & Netick, 1983). It is possible that the gains resulting from the NJCLD's efforts may eventually be masked by the criticisms and controversy that have plagued previous efforts. As a theoretical definition of learning disabilities, it can always be criticized as ambiguous. What this new definition contributes beyond the federal definitions and whether it is accepted by the profession, however, will only be answered in time.

Theoretical Versus Operational Definitions

In the foregoing discussion of federal definitions, a distinction was made between theoretical and operational definitions. This distinction is crucial inasmuch as professionals have typically expected more of definitions than it was ever possible for them to deliver. Very often, theoretical definitions, such as those in Table 1.1, have been criticized for not furnishing operational guidelines for research and practice. A *theoretical*, or constitutive, definition of learning disabilities defines the construct "learning disabilities" using other constructs indicated by the elements of inclusion and exclusion (see Margenau, 1950, p. 236). In order to be scientifically useful, the construct must possess constitutive meaning, that is, it must be capable of being used in theory. (For a further discussion of this issue, see Torgerson, 1958, pp. 4 – 5.)

By contrast, an *operational*, or epistemic, definition defines the construct at the level of observation by providing explicit instructions, guidelines, or criteria. From a research perspective, Kerlinger (1973) offered the following description:

An *operational definition* assigns meaning to a construct or a variable by specifying the activities or "operations" necessary to measure it. Alternatively, an operational definition is a specification of the activities of the researcher in measuring a variable or in manipulating it. An operational definition is a sort of manual of instructions to the investigator. It says, in effect, "Do such-and-such in so-and-so a manner." In short, it defines or gives meaning to a variable by spelling out what the investigator must do to measure it. (p. 31)

Typically, the theoretical definitions of learning disabilities have been *operationalized* with specific identification criteria, such as "two or more years below grade level," rather than with a statement of operational definition per se. Thurlow and Ysseldyke (1979) have commented that despite the fact that there has been no operational definition of learning disabilities, and the fact that criteria used in identifying children as learning disabled have been both highly variant and nebulous, educators *have* for some time been making decisions about children" (p. 16).

Considering the functions of these two types of definition, the theoretical definition must be developed first. Once the conceptualization of learning disabilities is understood and the admissible conditions delimited in that definition, then restrictive operational definitions for specific research and practical purposes can be generated. The operational definitions, however, should reflect the theoretical underpinnings of the construct. These underpinnings have been expressed usually as elements of inclusion and exclusion (see Chalfant, & King, 1976).

The notion of definition development advanced here suggests that one theoretical definition should be adopted and there may be any number of attendant operational definitions that may be designed to serve different purposes (cf. Senf, 1977). Such diversity is evidenced as learning disabilities has been operationally defined in research studies and practical applications.

Definitions Used in Research and Practice

Several surveys of the definitions and criteria used to identify learning disabled children for research purposes and for special services eligibility have been reported. They revealed how the theoretical definitions are interpreted (or misinterpreted) and what elements in those definitions are deemed most important and meaningful.

Research

In any study of learning-disabled children, the target population must be defined and the sample selected. In essence, the criteria for selecting the sample, in essence, constitute the operational definition of learning disabilities accepted by the researcher. They are most often derived from state definitions and less often from federal definitions, either the 1968 P.L. 91-230 definition or

1975 P.L. 94-142 definition (Kavale & Nye, 1981). As such, the selection or identification criteria can be categorized according to the four elements of inclusion (normal intelligence, ability-achievement discrepancy, academic disorder, psychological process disorder) and also to the elements of exclusion described previously.

Table 1.2

Definition Criteria Used in Research Studies of Learning-
Disabled Subjects Compiled in Three Independent Surveys

Element	Harber (1981)	Olson and Mealor (1981)	Kavale and Nye (1981)
Normal intelligence	53%	42%	26%
Ability-achievement discrepancy	68%ᵃ	51%	69%ᵃ
Academic disorder	27%	87%ᵃ	24%
Psychological process disorder	5%	35%	57%
Exclusion clause	42%	72%	73%
No. of studies specifying criteria	62	71	304
Journals reviewed	*Journal of Learning Disabilities*	*Journal of Learning Disabilities*	*Journal of Learning Disabilities*
	Learning Disability Quarterly	*Learning Disability Quarterly*	*Learning Disability Quarterly*
		Journal of School Psychology	*Journal of School Psychology*
		Psychology in the Schools	*Psychology in the Schools*
			Exceptional Children
			Journal of Special Education
			Journal of Educational Psychology
			Child Development
			Journal of Experimental Child Psychology
			Educational Research Quarterly
Years reviewed	1978–80	1975–80	1968–80
		(except *LDQ*)	(except *LDQ* and *ERQ*)

ᵃMost prominent element of inclusion

Three independent analyses of the criteria employed in research articles between 1968 and 1980 were published in 1981 (Harber, 1981; Kavale & Nye, 1981; Olson & Mealor, 1981). While the two major learning disability journals were of primary interest in all three analyses, eight other educational and psychological journals that publish studies using learning-disabled subjects were also surveyed by Kavale and Nye (1981). The percentages of studies specifying each type of criterion expressed as elements of inclusion and exclusion are presented in Table 1.2. (*Note*: These percentages are based on only the studies reviewed that did specify identification criteria.)

There are obviously marked discrepancies in the findings of the three analyses. These may be attributable to one or more of the factors listed at the bottom of the table: number of studies, journals reviewed, and years reviewed. Although Harber's results should be embedded in the results of the other two analyses and Olson and Mealor's results should be reflected in Kavale and Nye's results, few consistencies emerge.

These consistencies are stated and explained as follows:

1. An ability-achievement discrepancy is the most prominent or a prominent element of inclusion in a majority of the studies reviewed. This element is consistent with earlier results reported by Torgesen and Dice (1980). The consistency of this evidence across all of the analyses indicates the emphasis attached to a discrepancy score in identifying learning-disabled children.

2. A statement about normal or above-normal intelligence as a criterion for being learning disabled appears to have received increased attention in recent years. In the studies published since 1978 (which specified criteria), more than half reported an intelligence criterion. This is surprising in view of its omission as an element of inclusion in all of the definitions; it is either implied or a part of the exclusion clause.

3. The linkage of the ability-achievement discrepancy with a psychological process disorder has diminished with the recency of the studies reviewed. In Harber's analysis of studies between 1978 and 1980, 5%, or three studies, mentioned impairment in one or more of the basic learning processes; one study included the presence of both hard and soft neurological signs. The analyses of studies for 1975 to 1980 and 1968 to 1980 reported 35% and 57%, respectively. This trend may be indicative of the impact of the 1977 *Procedures* that do not acknowledge "process disorders" as part of the identification criteria and of the difficulties encountered in measuring these processes reliably and validly (Salvia & Ysseldyke, 1981; Thurlow & Ysseldyke, 1979).

4. Areas of academic disorder were identified in a large percentage of the studies analyzed by Olson and Mealor, but the percentage was extremely low in both the Harber and the Kavale and Nye analyses. There is no

readily apparent explanation for this inconsistency. Interestingly, the listing of the seven areas of possible "severe discrepancy" in the 1977 *Procedures* has had little influence on the researchers' specification of those areas.

5. An exclusion clause was designated in a significant number of the studies in the three analyses. It was the most prominent feature in the Kavale and Nye review. The categories of exclusion frequently included emotional disturbance, sensory handicaps, mental retardation, and cultural disadvantage. These represent the major categories in the federal definitions and in the 1977 *Procedures*.

The foregoing observations suggest that in much of the research conducted with learning-disabled subjects, the term "learning disabled" tends to be defined by an ability-achievement discrepancy score rarely linked to a process disorder. The discrepancy score is considered in conjunction with not being emotionally disturbed, deaf, blind, mentally retarded, or culturally disadvantaged. It was evident in all of the analyses that these criteria vary markedly from study to study. In addition, 40% of the original pool of studies reviewed between 1975 and 1980 did not specify any criteria for identification. Clearly, the state of operational definitions in research on learning disabilities is an "impediment to the orderly accumulation of knowledge" (Senf, 1977, p. 8).

Practice

In order to gain some insight into the ways that practitioners define learning disabilities and whether the federal definitions are being adopted, several investigators undertook surveys during the 1970s. Some of these surveys were relatively limited in scope, examining the practices in individual states such as Colorado (Vaughan & Hodges, 1973), while others sought to determine what

Table 1.3

Definitions of Learning Disabilities Adopted by State
Departments of Education Based on Two Independent Surveys

Definition Adopted	Gillespie, Miller, and Fielder (1975) (n = 50)	Mercer, Forgnone, and Wolking (1976) (n = 50)
1968 P.L. 91-230 definition	16%	26%
Modified 1968 P.L. 91-230	38%	36%
Other definition	38%	32%
No definition	8%	6%

*Includes follow-up data on 8 states compiled by Mercer (1979) not included in originally published results.

definitions were being used by the 50 state departments of education. Two surveys conducted by Gillespie, Miller, and Fielder (1975) and Mercer, Forgnone, and Wolking (1976) are particularly informative. Their results are summarized in Table 1.3. It appears from the table that among the 50 states, few accepted the 1968 federal definition of learning disabilities.

In a more recent study by Thurlow and Ysseldyke (1979), 44 Child Service Demonstration Centers in 26 states were surveyed regarding their use of the 1968 definition, the 1975 P.L. 94-142 definition, the 1977 *Procedures,* some other definition or no definition at all. These centers were established to develop and to refine exemplary instructional programs capable of serving as models of what services ought to be. Of the 38 centers responding to the definition question, the following results were recorded: (1) 1968 definition — 24%, (2) 1975 definition — 5%, (3) 1977 *Procedures* — 68%, and (4) other — 8%. Obviously these centers found the P.L. 94-142 definition less attractive than the P.L 91-230 definition, but the 1977 criteria for identification specifying an ability-achievement discrepancy in one or more of seven academic areas were adopted by more than two-thirds of the centers (cf. Mann et al., 1983). The ability-achievement discrepancy was also the major operational criterion employed by the researchers, as shown in Table 1.2.

Other definitional information compiled by Mercer et al. (1976) can be related to the findings in Table 1.2. Based on 42 states responding in the survey, the elements of inclusion and exclusion were analyzed. The percentages of state definitions addressing these elements were reported as follows: (1) normal intelligence — 26%, (2) ability-achievement discrepancy — 29%, (3) academic disorder — 74%, (4) psychological process disorder — 86%, and (5) exclusion clause — 62%. These statistics denote a strong emphasis on process and/or language disorders. In fact, process disorders is the core of the state definitions of learning disabilities. Furthermore, the areas of academic disorder (i.e., reading, writing, spelling, arithmetic) and the various exclusionary categories were also prominent. These elements are directly associated with either the 1968 P.L. 91-230 definition or variations of that definition. These types of definitions were adopted by over half of the states.

The different emphases in Table 1.2 and 1.3 seem to be a function of the theoretical-versus-operational definition issue. The figures in Table 1.2 reflect the researchers' attempts to operationally define learning disabilities; the figures in Table 1.3 are derived from constitutive definitions. The researchers focused on the ability-achievement discrepancy and the exclusionary categories, whereas the state departments of education attached the greatest weight in defining learning disability to the process disorders, the academic disorders, and the exclusionary categories.

These emphases in the state definitions are reflected in a heavy reliance on test scores for identification or placement decisions. A multidisciplinary team composed of a variety of professionals makes the final decision. Indeed, recent studies of the team decision-making process indicate that available psychometric information such as ability-achievement discrepancy scores has little influence on the actual decisions (Ysseldyke, Algozzine, Rickey, & Graden, 1982; Ysseldyke, Algozzine, & Thurlow, 1980). The eligibility decisions tended to be made in spite of data, either supportive or not supportive of the decision (for details see Chapter 8).

The foregoing analysis of state definitions of learning disabilities reveals the generic nature of the term (Lloyd, Hallahan, & Kauffman, 1980). There is substantial evidence that the definitions remain nonoperational and highly variable. The summary by Gillespie et al. (1975) reflects these characteristics:

> A child displaying specific behavioral characteristics could be eligible for learning disabilities programs in some states, but not in others. Moreover, in all but two states, the child must fit the description of learning disabilities used by the state if he or she is to receive special services provided by state monies. (p. 62)
>
> State legislation suffers from a professional failure to define and make explicit the behavioral characteristics of the learning disabled child. As a result, no complete operational definition exists. Even when agreement does occur in legislation, definitions tend not to be behavioral in nature and are, therefore, of little use for making relevant educational decisions. (p. 67)

Conclusions

This critical review of definitions of learning disabilities and the efforts to circumscribe the specific characteristics of those disabilities suggests that definite progress has occurred in four areas: (1) sorting out the key issues and points of controversy, (2) isolating the characteristics of learning-disabled children from other handicapping conditions, (3) eliminating some of the ambiguous, redundant, and misleading terminology, and (4) establishing rules and regulations for identifying these children. However, despite all of these developments, the most recent P.L. 94-142 federal definition and the 1981 NJCLD definition emphasize the role of psychological processes and the central nervous system, respectively. These constructs are extremely difficult to define and to measure; usually they are test named and test identified.

Confronted with an array of global concepts in these definitions, researchers and practitioners have tended to devise expeditiously their own operational criteria for identification. The ability-achievement discrepancy has emerged as the primary element in this process, which is reflective of the 1977 *Procedures* (see Weener & Senf, 1982). Consequently, learning disabilities has become a category of *underachievement* (Algozzine & Sutherland, 1977; Ysseldyke & Algozzine, 1979), and the research evidence that is accumulating substantiates this position (Kirk & Elkins, 1975; Warner, Schumaker, Alley, & Deshler, 1980; Ysseldyke, Algozzine, Shinn, & McGue, 1982).

What is especially troublesome in this progression of theoretical and operational definitions is that there is no empirical foundation at any level; clinical intuition and expediency form the underlying rationale. For example, although there has been a considerable amount of attention devoted to ability-achievement discrepancies with more than a dozen different procedures recommended to date, there is virtually no evidence to indicate whether any particular procedure is better than any other in identifying children with learning disabilities. In fact, if a local educational agency (LEA) employs the "two or more years below grade level" criterion, an ability-achievement discrepancy (or expectancy) formula, and clinical judgment as part of a multidisciplinary team assessment, it is not known at present whether any one or a combination of those procedures can correctly differentiate learning-disabled children from all other children (cf. Ysseldyke & Algozzine, 1983).

Ceteris paribus, it is imperative that classroom teachers, learning disability specialists, educational administrators, and school psychologists perform a scrupulous reexamination of their definitions of learning disability and the methods that are being used to screen and diagnose learning-disabled children. The use of tests that are purported to measure psychological processes is inappropriate in view of the current state of assessment devices. In addition, the most popular ability and achievement tests require scrutiny from a technical perspective. Guidelines for conducting these reviews are presented in the next chapter.

Summary

This chapter surveyed the key definitions of learning disabilities proposed by the experts in the field and by legislative mandate over the past two decades. The historical developments that contributed to the emergence of medical and behavioral definitions were examined. An analysis of the elements of inclusion and exclusion common to most definitions was then presented. The former included normal intelligence, ability-achievement discrepancy, academic disorder, and psychological process disorder; the latter dealt with the problems of mental subnormality, visual or hearing impairment, motor deficit, severe cultural neglect, and severe emotional disturbance. Particular attention was also devoted to the 1968 and 1975 federal definitions, the specific criticisms of those definitions, and the National Joint Committee for Learning Disabilities 1981 response to the criticisms. Finally, a comparison between theoretical and operational definitions was drawn in terms of the criteria used to identify learning-disabled children for research purposes and for special services eligibility. It was concluded that the ability-achievement discrepancy has emerged as the primary element in most definitions, and as a consequence, learning disabilities has become a category of underachievement.

References

Algozzine, B., & Sutherland, J. Nonpsychoeducational foundations of learning disabilites. *Journal of Special Education,* 1977, *11,* 91 – 98.

Bateman, B. Learning disabilities — yesterday, today, and tomorrow. *Exceptional Children,* 1964, *31,* 167 – 177.

Bateman, B. An educator's view of a diagnostic approach to learning disorders. In J. Hellmuth (Ed.), *Learning disorders* (Vol. I). Seattle: Special Child Publications, 1965. Pp. 219 – 236.

Berk, R.A. Toward a definition of learning disabilities: Progress or regress? *Education & Treatment of Children,* 1983, *6,* in press.

Bersoff, D.N., & Veltman, E.S. Public Law 94 – 142: Legal implications for the education of handicapped children. *Journal of Research and Development in Education,* 1979, *12,* 10 – 22.

Bryan, T.H. Learning disabilities: A new stereotype. *Journal of Learning Disabilities,* 1974, *7,* 304 – 309.

Bryan, T.H., & Bryan, J.H. *Understanding learning disabilities* (2nd ed.). Sherman Oaks, CA: Alfred, 1978.

Bryant, N.D. Subject variables: Definition, incidence, characteristics, and correlates. In N.D. Bryant & C.E. Kass, *Final report: LTI in learning disabilities* (Vol. I, U.S.O.E. Grant No. OEG-0-71-4425-604, Project No. 127145). Tucson: University of Arizona, 1972. Pp. 5 – 158.

Chalfant, J.C., & King, F.S. An approach to operationalizing the definition of learning disabilities. *Journal of Learning Disabilities,* 1976, *9,* 228 – 243.

Chalfant, J.C., & Scheffelin, M.A. *Central processing dysfunctions in children: A review of research* (NINDS Monograph No. 9). Bethesda, MD: U.S. Department of Health, Education, and Welfare, 1969.

Clements, S.D. *Minimal brain dysfunction in children: Terminology and identification* (NINBB Monograph No. 3, Public Health Service Bulletin, No. 1415). Washington, DC: U.S. Department of Health, Education, and Welfare, 1966.

Coles, G.S. The learning-disabilities test battery: Empirical and social issues. *Harvard Educational Review,* 1968, *48,* 313 – 340.

Cruickshank, W.M. *The brain-injured child in home, school and community.* Syracuse, NY: Syracuse University Press, 1967.

Cruickshank, W.M. Myths and realities in learning disabilities. *Journal of Learning Disabilities,* 1977, *10,* 51 – 58.

Gallagher, J.J. Children with developmental imbalances: A psychoeducational definition. In W. M. Cruickshank (Ed.), *The teacher of brain-injured children: A discussion of the bases of competency.* Syracuse, NY: Syracuse University Press, 1966. Pp. 21 – 34.

Gearheart, B.R. *Learning disabilities: Educational strategies.* St. Louis: Mosby, 1981.

Gillespie, P.H., Miller, T.L., & Fielder, V.D. Legislative definitions of learning disabilities: Roadblocks to effective service. *Journal of Learning Disabilities,* 1975, *8,* 660 – 666.

Hallahan, D.P., & Cruickshank, W.M. *Psychoeducational foundations of learning disabilities.* Englewood Cliffs, NJ: Prentice-Hall, 1973.

Hallahan, D.P., & Kauffman, J.M. Labels, categories, behaviors: ED, LD, and EMR reconsidered. *Journal of Special Education,* 1977, *11,* 139 – 149.

Hammill, D.D. Learning disabilities: A problem in definition. *Division for Children with Learning Disabilities Newsletter,* 1974, *4,* 28 – 31.

Hammill, D.D., Leigh, J.E., McNutt, G., & Larsen, S.C. A new definition of learning disabilities. *Learning Disability Quarterly,* 1981, *4,* 336 – 342.

Harber, J.R. Learning disability research: How far have we progressed? *Learning Disability Quarterly,* 1981, *4,* 372 – 381.

Johnson, D.J., & Myklebust, H.R. *Learning disabilities: Educational principles and practices.* New York: Grune & Stratton, 1967.

Johnson, S.W., & Morasky, R.L. *Learning disabilities* (2nd ed.). Boston: Allyn & Bacon, 1980.

Kavale, K., & Nye, C. Identification criteria for learning disabilities: A survey of the research literature. *Learning Disability Quarterly,* 1981, *4,* 383 – 388.

Keogh, B.K. Classification, compliance, and confusion. *Journal of Learning Disabilities,* 1983, *16,* 25.

Kerlinger, F.N. *Foundations of behavioral research* (2nd ed.). New York: Holt, Rinehart and Winston, 1973.

Kirk, S.A. *Educating exceptional children.* Boston: Houghton Mifflin, 1962.

Kirk, S.A. Behavioral diagnosis and remediation of learning disabilities. In *Proceedings of the Conference on Exploration into the Problems of the Perceptually Handicapped Child.* Evanston, IL: Fund for Perceptually Handicapped Children, 1963. Pp. 1 – 4.

Kirk, S.A. *Introduction to state of the art: Where are we in learning disabilities?* Los Angeles: Association for Children with Learning Disabilities and California Association for Neurologically Handicapped Children Publications, 1974.

Kirk, S.A., & Elkins, J. Characteristics of children enrolled in the child services demonstration centers. *Journal of Learning Disabilities,* 1975, *8,* 630 – 637.

Kirk, S.A., & Gallagher, J.J. *Educating exceptional children* (3rd ed.). Boston: Houghton Mifflin, 1979.

Kirk, S.A., & Kirk, W.D. *Psycholinguistic learning disabilities: Diagnosis and remediation.* Chicago: University of Illinois Press, 1971.

Lerner, J.W. *Learning disabilities: Theories, diagnosis, and teaching strategies* (3rd ed.). Boston: Houghton Mifflin, 1981.

Lloyd, J., Hallahan, D.P., & Kauffman, J.M. Learning disabilities: A review of selected topics. In L. Mann & D.A. Sabatino (Eds.), *The fourth review of special education.* New York: Grune & Stratton, 1980. Pp. 35 – 60.

Mann, L. Psychometric phrenology and the new faculty psychology: The case against ability assessment and training. *Journal of Special Education,* 1971, *5,* 3 – 14.

Mann, L., Davis, C.H., Boyer, C.W., Jr., Metz, C.M., & Wolford, B. LD or not LD, That was the question: A retrospective analysis of child service demonstration centers' compliance with the federal definition of learning disabilities. *Journal of Learning Disabilities,* 1983, *16,* 14 – 17.

Margenau, H. *The nature of physical reality.* New York: McGraw-Hill, 1950.

McLoughlin, J.A., & Netreick, A. Defining learning disabilities: A new and cooperative direction. *Journal of Learning Disabilities,* 1983, *16,* 21 – 23.

Margenau, H. *The nature of physical reality.* New York: McGraw-Hill, 1950.

Mercer, C.D. *Children and adolescents with learning disabilities.* Columbus, OH: Merrill, 1979.

Mercer, C.D., Forgnone, D., & Wolking, W.D. Definitions of learning disabilities used in the United States. *Journal of Learning Disabilities,* 1976, *9,* 47 – 57.

Myers, P., & Hammill, D. *Methods for learning disorders.* New York: Wiley, 1976.

Myklebust, H.R. Psychoneurological learning disorders in children. In S.A. Kirk & W. Becker (Eds.). *Conference on Children with Minimal Brain Impairment.* Urbana: University of Illinois, 1963.

National Advisory Committee on Handicapped Children. *Special education for handicapped children* (First Annual Report). Washington, DC: U.S. Department of Health, Education, and Welfare, January 31, 1968.

National Joint Committee for Learning Disabilities. *Learning disabilities: Issues on definition.* Unpublished position paper, January 30, 1981. (Available from Drake Duane, NJCLD Chairperson, c/o The Orton Dyslexia Society, 8415 Bellona Lane, Towson, MD 21204)

Olson, J.L., & Mealor, D.J. Learning disabilities identification: Do researchers have the answer? *Learning Disabilities Quarterly*, 1981, *4*, 389 – 392.

Public Law 94-142. Education for All Handicapped Children Act, S.6, 94th Congress [Sec 613 (a) (4)] 1st session, June 1975. Report No. 94-168.

Ross, A.O. *Psychological aspects of learning disabilities and reading disorders*. New York: McGraw-Hill, 1976.

Salvia, J., & Ysseldyke, J.E. *Assessment in special and remedial education* (2nd ed.). Boston: Houghton Mifflin, 1981.

Senf, G.M. A perspective on the definition of LD. *Journal of Learning Disabilities*, 1977, *10*, 537 – 539.

Thurlow, M.L., & Ysseldyke, J.E. Current assessment and decision-making practices in model LD programs. *Learning Disability Quarterly*, 1979, *2*, 15 – 24.

Torgerson, W.S. *Theory and methods of scaling*. New York: Wiley, 1958.

Torgesen, J.K., & Dice, C. Characteristics of research on learning disabilities. *Journal of Learning Disabilities*, 1980, *13*, 531 – 535.

Tucker, J., Stevens, L.J., & Ysseldyke, J.E. Learning disabilities: The experts speak out. *Journal of Learning Disabilities*, 1983, *16*, 6 – 14.

U.S. Office of Education. Assistance to states for education for handicapped children: Procedures for evaluating specific learning disabilities. *Federal Register*, 1977, *42*(250), 62082 – 62085.

Vaughn, R.W., & Hodges, L. A statistical survey into a definition of learning disabilities: A search for acceptance. *Journal of Learning Disabilities*, 1973, *6*, 658 – 664.

Wallace, G., & McLoughlin, J.A. *Learning disabilities: Concepts and characteristics* (2nd ed.). Columbus, OH: Merrill, 1979.

Warner, M.M., Schumaker, J.B., Alley, G.R., & Deshler, D.D. Learning disabled adolescents in the public schools: Are they different from other low achievers? *Exceptional Education Quarterly*, 1980, *1*, 27 – 36.

Weener, P.D., & Senf, G.M. Learning disabilities. In H.E. Mitzel, J.H. Best, & W. Rabinowitz (Eds.), *Encyclopedia of educational research* (5th ed.). New York: Free Press, 1982. Pp. 1059 – 1068.

Wender, P. *Minimal brain dysfunction in children*. New York: Wiley-Interscience, 1971.

Wiederholt, J.L. Historical perspectives on the education of the learning disabled. In L. Mann & D.A. Sabatino (Eds.), *The second review of special education*. Philadelphia: Journal of Special Education Press, 1974. Pp. 103 – 152.

Ysseldyke, J.E., & Algozzine, B. Perspectives on assessment of learning disabled students. *Learning Disability Quarterly*, 1979, *2*, 3 – 13.

Ysseldyke, J.E., & Algozzine, B. *Critical issues in special and remedial education*. Boston: Houghton Mifflin, 1982.

Ysseldyke, J.E., & Algozzine, B. LD or not LD: That's not the question! *Journal of Learning Disabilities*, 1983, *16*, 29 – 31.

Ysseldyke, J.E., Algozzine, B., Richey, L., & Graden, J. Declaring students eligible for learning disability services: Why bother with the data? *Learning Disability Quarterly*, 1982, *5*, 37 – 44.

Ysseldyke, J.E., Algozzine, B., Shinn, M.R., & McGue, M. Similarities and differences between low achievers and students classified learning disabled. *Journal of Special Education*, 1982, *16*, 73 – 85.

Ysseldyke, J.E., Algozzine, B., & Thurlow, M.L. (Eds.). *Placement team decision-making: A naturalistic investigation* (Research Report No. 41). Minneapolis: University of Minnesota Institute for Research on Learning Disabilities, 1980.

Chapter 2

SELECTING AN APPROPRIATE BATTERY OF TESTS

Introduction

THE first step in preparing for screening and diagnosis is to select an appropriate battery of tests that will yield the data needed for individual decision making. With more than 250 million standardized tests administered to 44 million elementary and secondary students each year, there is a strong dependence on test data for a variety of educational decisions.

For purposes of screening children for learning disabilities, standardized ability and achievement tests need to be chosen in order to determine skill deficits in the seven academic areas specified in the Rules and Regulations for implementing P.L. 94-142 (U.S.O.E., 1977b). Once the area(s) is identified, skill-development strengths and weaknesses must be pinpointed so that instructional prescriptions can be planned and executed. These diagnostic decisions require the use of criterion-referenced tests.

It is especially important that the tests that are selected satisfy the most rigorous standards of technical quality. This is a necessary but not sufficient condition to assure that the decisions for which they are used will be valid and reliable. The other conditions pertain to the correct use of the tests and interpretation of the scores.

This chapter evaluates the technical quality of standardized, norm-referenced tests, criterion-referenced tests, and informal measures to encourage the selection of the best instruments available. The key indices of test quality and the standards for judging whether a test is psychometrically defensible are also described. The presentation is couched within a legal framework set by P.L. 94-142 and the subsequent rules and regulations for its implementation. The chapter is organized according to six topics: (1) legal regulations, (2) criticisms of tests and test users, (3) indices of test quality, (4) technical quality of standardized, norm-referenced tests, (5) technical quality of criterion-referenced tests, and (6) technical quality of informal measures.

Legal Regulations

In a class action suit against the Philadelphia school system, a federal district court ordered the system to develop a procedure that was "reasonably calculated to identify all of its learning-disabled students" (*Frederick L.* v. *Thomas*, 1976). It was indicated, however, that only system-wide screening of the entire student body followed by individual testing of those subsequently found to be possibly learning-disabled would suffice. This interpretation is consistent with the heavy reliance on standardized tests specified in P.L. 94-142 for assessing a severe discrepancy between ability and achievement and for diagnosing the nature of the specific disability (see U.S.O.E., 1977a, p. 42497). Bersoff and Veltman (1979) stress that the law "encourages the use of batteries of tests both in evaluating a child suspected of having a disability and in determining an appropriate educational program" (p. 18).

Given this mandate for using formal instruments in screening and diagnosis, particular attention needs to be directed at the quality of available measurement devices. Certainly a comprehensive assessment of an individual should also include informal measures, developmental and medical histories, cumulative records, and similar relevant sources of data. However, the importance of the decisions makes it imperative that technically defensible instruments constitute the core of the screening procedure. The Rules and Regulations for the implementation of both P.L. 93-112 and P.L. 94-142 require that "state and local educational agencies shall insure at a minimum, that *tests and other evaluation materials have been validated for the specific purpose for which they are used*" [italics added] (U.S.O.E., 1977a, p. 42496).

Criticisms of Tests and Test Users

Standardized tests and testing practices have been the objects of close thorough scrutiny over the past decade. Public and professional criticisms of tests are constantly increasing (Brim, 1965; Cronbach, 1975; Kamin, 1975; Laosa, 1973; Nairn et al., 1980), and the testing of learning-disabled children has not been immune to these criticisms (Adelman, 1978; Coles, 1968; Kirk & Kirk, 1978; Sabatino & Miller, 1980; Salvia & Ysseldyke, 1981; Thurlow & Ysseldyke 1979; Wallace & Larsen, 1978; Ysseldyke, 1979). Regrettably, some of the criticism is legitimate.

Swanson and Watson (1982) have identified seven major criticisms of the construction and use of standardized tests:

1. Many standardized tests are technically inadequate.
2. Many tests are not properly administered and not properly interpreted.
3. Many standardized tests are not useful for instructional purposes.
4. Many standardized tests are used for the wrong purposes.
5. Many standardized tests are racially and ethnically biased.
6. Many standardized tests foster misconceptions about genetic endowment and

learning ability.
7. Some uses of standardized tests and test scores represent an invasion of privacy.
   (pp. 83 – 88)

While an examination of the arguments and evidence related to all of these criticisms is beyond the scope of this chapter, the first five will be addressed in the course of the presentation.

First, the incorrect selection of tests and the misuse and misinterpretation of test scores in screening and diagnosis for learning disabilities are widespread and continue essentially unchecked. For example, some of the most popular tests used for these purposes (e.g., Gates-MacGinitie Reading Tests, Key Math Diagnostic Arithmetic Test, Detroit Tests of Learning Aptitude, Bender Visual Motor Gestalt Test, Frostig Developmental Test of Visual Perception, and Illinois Test of Psycholinguistic Abilities) happen to be among the most technically inadequate tests available (LaGrow & Prochnow-LaGrow, 1982; Shepard & Smith, in press; Thurlow & Ysseldyke, 1979; Ysseldyke, Algozzine, Regan, & Potter, 1980; Ysseldyke, Regan, & Schwartz, 1980). The grade-equivalent, age-equivalent, and IQ scores commonly used to determine the presence of an ability-achievement discrepancy are the statistically weakest and most inaccurate indices of individual performance (see Chapter 3 for explanation).

Second, these testing practices draw attention not only to the poor quality of many of the ability, achievement, and perceptual-motor and language tests, but also raise serious questions about the competence of the professionals who use them. Salvia and Ysseldyke (1981, p. 532) attribute much of the test abuse to the "ignorance and overzealousness" of test users. Concerns about the training of teachers and psychologists involved in psychoeducational assessment have been expressed for some time (Bransford, 1974; Kirp & Kirp, 1976; Mc-Daniels, 1979; Meyers, Sundstrom, & Yoshida, 1974; Ysseldyke, 1978b). However, few studies have actually documented the consequences of incompetent selection, administration, scoring, and interpretation of tests (e.g., Bennett, 1980; Bennett & Shepherd, 1982; Davis & Shepard, in press; Miller & Chansky, 1972; Oakland, Lee, & Axelrad, 1975). A recent review of these studies by Bennett (1981) lead to the following conclusions:

1. Assessment personnel may not fully possess the knowledge and skill necessary for proper selection and interpretation of assessment tools.
2. A lack of assessment knowledge and skill may have negative effects on the placement process (e.g., erroneous placement). (p. 444)

He stresses that "knowledge and skill deficiencies . . . can lead to test misuse and abuse, which in turn can result in the provision of inaccurate data to those who must make decisions about the identification, classification, programming, and placement of exceptional children" (p. 444).

Despite the federal support of teacher training programs and the requirements of P.L. 94-142 in this area (Harvey, 1978), it has been extremely difficult to train teachers in assessment, whether at the preservice, in-service, or continuing education levels. The lists of competencies for learning disability specialists, clinical teachers, and regular teachers involved in mainstreaming that have been proposed, usually by experts, occasionally include assessment skills (Cassidy-Bronson, 1983; Cegelka, 1982; Division for Children with Learning Disabilities, 1978; McNutt & Mandelbaum, 1980) but often do not (Redden & Blackhurst, 1978; Reynolds, 1980). There is considerable disagreement over what are the functions and competencies of these special teachers (Blackhurst & Hofmeister, 1980; Freeman & Becker, 1979; Heller, 1982; Newcomer, 1978, 1982; Shores, Cegelka, & Nelson, 1973; Stedman & Paul, 1981), and there has been virtually no empirical verification that any of the competencies make a difference in the classroom (Schofer & Lilly, 1980). These problems are reflected in the state certification standards for special education personnel (Patton & Braithwaite, 1980; Stinnett, 1974; Woellner, 1979). The variability in course requirements from state to state renders assessment skills as a hit-and-miss competency.

In an attempt to tackle a few of these issues and to improve testing practices related to learning disabilities, the remainder of this chapter and the next will be devoted to clarifying major areas of confusion, recommending tests and testing strategies that are psychometrically defensible, and presenting guidelines for correct score use and interpretation.

Indices of Test Quality

Most of the indices one can use to evaluate the quality of a test relate to either validity or reliability. These terms are defined as follows:

Validity refers to the intent or purposes for which the test is designed and the scores are used.

Reliability refers to the stability or dependability of the test scores or of the decisions based on those scores.

The determination of validity and reliability involves both judgmental and statistical procedures. It should be clear, however, that regardless of the sophistication of the methods used to estimate these properties, the questions about test quality that are being answered are very simple and fundamental, such as:

Validity

1. How accurately does the test sample from the domain of behaviors it was designed to measure? (content validity)
2. How accurately do the behaviors measured by the test match the curriculum of the school district? (curricular validity)
3. How accurately does the test predict future learning problems? (predictive validity)

4. How accurately does the test differentiate between children who have a learning disability and those who do not? (decision or discriminant validity)

Reliability

5. How dependable are the test scores for individual diagnosis of learning disabilities? (equivalent forms or retest reliability)
6. How much confidence can be placed in the learning disability classification decisions made with the test scores? (decision reliability)
7. How well do the items consistently measure the same skill? (internal consistency reliability)
8. How consistently do different observers record the same behaviors? (interobserver reliability)

If some of these questions are pertinent to a particular test application, but they are unanswerable from the information provided in a test manual, should the test be used? In other words, if a test possesses some technical inadequacies and/or there is no higher quality test available, is it better to go ahead and use it rather than use no test at all? Contrary to current testing practices, an inadequate test, a battery of inadequate tests, or any test of indeterminable quality should not be used for an important decision about an individual. Using information from such tests frequently will produce misclassifications and mislabeling of children at the level of mass screening and incorrect diagnoses of specific disorders at the level of individual evaluation.

It is also possible that tests that are technically sound may be applied incorrectly. For example, if a standardized achievement test does not accurately reflect the curricular emphasis in a school district, the decisions based on the resultant scores that focus on the student's achievement or instructional effectiveness in that district's program may be invalid (see question 2 and Chapter 3). The correct application of tests and use of test scores are cited in the U.S.O.E. (1977a) regulations:

    (b) Tests and other evaluation materials [should] . . include those tailored to assess specific areas of educational need and not merely those which are designed to provide a single general intelligence quotient;

    (c) Tests are selected and administered so as best to ensure that . . . the test results accurately reflect the child's aptitude or achievement or whatever other factors the test purports to measure. (p. 42496)

The foregoing comments about test quality suggest that the test selection process should concentrate first on standardized tests that are technically adequate. The aforementioned questions concerning psychometric properties can serve as a guide to whether appropriate validity and reliability evidence exists. More specific benchmarks for judging technical adequacy will be offered shortly.

Technical Quality of Standardized, Norm-referenced Tests

A standardized, norm-referenced test is deliberately constructed to determine an individual's performance in relation to the performance of others (the norm sample) in a broadly defined content area. The norm sample supplies the data for test development, the estimates of validity and reliability, and the scores used for norm-referenced interpretations (see Chapter 3 for details). The term *standardized* refers to the standardized procedures employed in administering and scoring the test. The majority of the standardized, norm-referenced tests presently available are also developed professionally by commercial test publishers. These tests are the ones most frequently used in screening children for learning disabilities.

Standards for Technical Quality

In evaluating the technical quality of norm-referenced tests, the *Standards for Educational and Psychological Tests* (APA/AERA/NCME, 1974) should serve as the guide. It is the "bible" of acceptable measurement practices. These standards were developed by a joint committee of the American Psychological Association, American Educational Research Association, and National Council on Measurement in Education. Although they are currently undergoing revision[1], the 1974 edition still furnishes the most comprehensive set of criteria for judging: (a) the quality of a test manual and test administration directions, (b) the adequacy of norms and validity and reliability evidence, and (c) the appropriateness of scoring procedures and score uses and interpretations. The standards designating the information that should be included in the test manual are directed at test makers, particularly test publishers; the other standards are aimed primarily at test users for the purpose of obviating incorrect test selection, administration, scoring, and interpretation. Had these standards been followed by both test makers and test users, the aforestated criticisms would probably be unjustified.

Since the *Standards* provides the foundation for the review of tests presented in a subsequent section, familiarity with a few of the key standards in each of the categories mentioned previously is essential. A list of these standards follows. For explanations and further information on specific standards, the reader is encouraged to consult the original document.

---

[1]A new edition of the *Standards for Educational and Psychological Tests* titled *Joint Technical Standards for Educational and Psychological Testing* is currently being developed by a joint committee of APA, AERA, and NCME representatives with Melvin R. Novick as chairperson. A draft version of the *Standards* prepared for professional review in February, 1983, suggests it will be far more extensive in breadth and depth of coverage than the 1974 edition and will provide separate sections on test use in special education, ability and achievement testing in elementary or secondary education, and testing adults with handicapping conditions. Expected publication date is 1984.

Test Manual

- When a test is published or otherwise made available for operational use, it should be accompanied by a manual (or other published or readily available information) that makes every reasonable effort to follow the recommendations of these standards, and, in particular, to provide the information required to substantiate any claims that have been made for its use. (p. 9)
- A test manual should describe fully the development of the test: the rationale, specifications followed in writing items or selecting observations, and procedures and results of item analysis or other research. (p. 11)
- The test, the manual, the record forms, and other accompanying material should help users make correct interpretations of the test results and should warn against common misuses. (p. 13)
- The test manual should state explicitly the purposes and applications for which the test is recommended. (p. 14)
- The test manual should describe clearly the psychological, educational, or other reasoning underlying the test and nature of the characteristic it is intended to measure. (p. 15)
- The test manual should identify any special qualifications required to administer the test and interpret it properly. (p. 15)
- Evidence of validity and reliability, along with other relevant research data, should be presented in support of any claims made. (p. 16)

Test Administration

- The directions for administration should be presented in the manual with sufficient clarity and emphasis so that the test user can duplicate, and will be encouraged to duplicate, the administrative conditions under which the norms and the data on reliability and validity were obtained. (p. 18)
- A test user is expected to follow carefully the standardized procedures described in the manual for administering a test. (p. 64)
- The test administrator is responsible for establishing conditions, consistent with the principle of standardization, that enable each examinee to do his [or her] best. (p. 65)
- Test users should seek to avoid bias in test selection, administration, and interpretation; they should try to avoid even the appearance of discriminatory practice. (p. 60)

Norms

- Norms should be published in the test manual at the time of release of the test for operational use. (p. 20)

- Norms presented in the test manual should refer to defined and clearly described populations. These populations should be the groups with whom users of the test will ordinarily wish to compare the persons tested. (p. 20)
- Norms reported in any test manual should be based on well-planned samplings rather than on data collected primarily because it is readily available. Any deviations from the plan should be reported along with descriptions of actions taken or not taken with respect to them. (p. 21)
- In reporting norms, test manuals should use percentiles for one or more appropriate reference groups or standard scores for which the basis is clearly set forth; any exceptional type of score or unit should be explained and justified. Measures of central tendency and variability always should be reported. (p. 22)
- Derived scales used for reporting scores should be carefully described in the test manual to increase the likelihood of accurate interpretation of scores by both the test interpreter and the examinee. (p. 22)
- Where it is expected that a test will be used to assess groups rather than individuals (i.e., for schools or programs), normative data, based on group summary statistics, should be provided (p. 24).

Validity

- A manual or research report should present the evidence of validity for each type of inference for which use of the test is recommended. If validity for some suggested interpretation has not been investigated, that fact should be made clear. (p. 31)
- Statements about validity should refer to the validity of particular interpretations or of particular types of decisions (p. 31)
- Wherever interpretation of subscores, score differences, or profiles is suggested, the evidence justifying such interpretation should be made explicit. (p. 31)
- If the manual suggests that the user consider an individual's responses to specific items as a basis for assessment, it should either present evidence supporting this use or call attention to the absence of such data. The manual should warn the reader that inferences based on responses to single items are subject to extreme error. (p. 31)
- When a test user plans to make a substantial change in test format, instructions, language, or content, he should revalidiate the use of the tests for the changed conditions. (p. 33)

Reliability

- The test manual or research report should present evidence of reliability, including estimates of the standard error of measurement, that permits the reader to judge whether scores are sufficiently dependable for the intended uses of the test. If any of the necessary evidence has not been collected, the absence of such information should be noted. (p. 50)
- Standard errors of measurement and reliability coefficients should be provided for every score, subscore, or combination of scores (such as a sum, difference, or quotient) that is recommended by the test manual (either explicitly or implicitly) for other than merely tentative or pilot use. (p. 50)

- For instruments that yield a profile having a low reliability of differences between scores, the manual should explicitly caution the user against interpretation of such differences, except as a source of tentative information requiring external verification. (pp. 50 – 51)
- The procedures and samples used to determine reliability coefficients or standard errors of measurement should be described sufficiently to permit a user to judge the applicability of the data reported to the individuals or groups with which he [or she] is concerned. (p. 51)

Scoring and Score Interpretation

- The procedures for scoring the test should be presented in the test manual with a maximum of detail and clarity to reduce the likelihood of scoring error. (p. 18)
- A test user is responsible for accuracy in scoring, checking, coding, or recording test results. (p. 66)
- The test user shares with the test developer or distributor a responsibility for maintaining test security. (p. 67)
- A test score should be interpreted as an estimate of performance under a given set of circumstances. It should not be interpreted as some absolute characteristic of the examinee or as something permanent and generalizable to all other circumstances. (p. 68)
- A test user should consider the total context of testing in interpreting an obtained score before making any decisions (including the decision to accept the score). (p. 68)
- Test scores should ordinarily be reported only to people who are qualified to interpret them. If scores are reported, they should be accompanied by explanations sufficient for the recipient to interpret them correctly. (p. 68)
- A system of reporting test results should provide interpretations. (p. 69)
- Test users should avoid the use of terms such as IQ, IQ equivalent, or grade equivalent where other terms provide more meaningful interpretations of a score. (p. 70)
- A test user should examine differences between characteristics of a person tested and those of the population on whom the test was developed or norms developed. His responsibility includes deciding whether the differences are so great that the test should not be used for that person. (p. 71)

In this list of standards, those most germane to the selection of a test relate to the norm sample, validity, and reliability. The specifications in these areas constitute the basis for determining the technical adequacy or inadequacy of any measurement device. Although it is impossible to control the manner in which this information will be used in selecting an appropriate battery, the characteristics of technical adequacy should at least be known.

Norm Sample

The norm sample provides the foundation for the statistical properties of the test and all score interpretations. Its value is contingent on how well it reflects the target population of children for which the test is designed. That is, the key criterion for judging the sample's adequacy is its *representativeness*. The sample must be composed of the same kinds of children in proportion to the total population that the norms supposedly represent. The most important elements of this representativeness are age, grade, sex, race, ethnicity, socioeconomic status, geographic region, and intelligence or ability. Another consideration is the recency of the norms. Interpreting an individual's performance in relation to children who were given the test 10 years ago would not be meaningful; it is unlikely that the sample is sufficiently representative and relevant for inferences about current performance. As the *Standards* indicate, all of this information describing the norm sample should be presented in the test manual for the user's review.

Coupled with representativeness is *sample size*. The sample should contain a large enough number of children to assure that the statistical indices of validity and reliability and normative scores such as percentile ranks and stanines are stable and accurate. With small samples of say, less than 100 children per grade or age level, these indices and norms can fluctuate markedly. A further reason for using an adequate sample size is to permit representativeness to occur. Larger samples of several thousand children can provide a broader spectrum of ability and demographic characteristics than smaller samples of a few hundred.

Both representativeness and sample size are of particular concern when standardized tests are administered to special populations of children with learning disabilities or other handicapping conditions. If one of the stated purposes of a test is to identify learning-disabled children or to differentiate them from non-learning-disabled children, then an appropriate proportion of these children *must* be included in the norm sample. Based on a national estimate of about 3% (U.S.D.E., 1980, p. 166), the attribute *learning disability* should be represented in the sample along with all of the elements mentioned above. Unless this segment of the population is represented, normative interpretations of the scores of learning-disabled children will be very limited. This point is illustrated by Salvia and Ysseldyke (1981) with one of the most popular tests:

> The Illinois Test of Psycholinguistic Abilities is often used to identify children with psycholinguistic dysfunctions that presumably underlie academic difficulties. Yet the norm sample included "only those children demonstrating average intellectual functioning, average school achievement, average characteristics of personal-social adjustment, sensory-motor integrity, and coming from predominantly English-speaking families" (Paraskevopoulos & Kirk, 1969, pp. 51 – 52). How can a test be used to identify children whose academic difficulties are caused by psycholinguistic dysfunction when such children are *excluded* from the normative sample? (p. 121)

Validity

Validity is the most important technical characteristic of a test. It is the *degree to which a test achieves the purposes for which it was designed*. For if a test does not perform its intended functions satisfactorily, why use it? This definition suggests five considerations in determining validity:

1. *It relates to the intent or purposes for which a test is constructed.* There can be several different purposes of a test. An appropriate type of validity evidence would be needed to "validate" the use of the scores for each purpose. As the legal regulations for implementing P.L. 94-142 state, "tests and other evaluation materials. . .[should be] validated for the specific purpose for which they are used" (U.S.O.E., 1977a, p. 42496).

2. *It is inferred from the way in which the test scores are used and interpreted.* Validity focuses on the scores and the specific ways in which they are used and interpreted, not on the test itself. The *Standards for Educational and Psychological Tests* (APA/AERA/NCME, 1974) emphasize that there should be

   evidence of validity for each type of inference for which use of the test is recommended. (p. 31)

   Statements about validity should refer to the validity of particular interpretations or of particular types of decisions. (p. 31)

3. *It is specific to a particular score use.* The results of any validity study are restricted to one or perhaps only a few uses of the test scores. The evidence must be interpreted in relation to the designated use(s). No test is valid for all uses. "If a user wants to use a test in a situation for which the use of the test has not been previously validated, or for which there is no supported claim for validity, he [or she] is responsible for validation. . . He [or she] who makes the claim for validity is responsible for providing the evidence" (APA/AERA/NCME, 1974, p. 33).

4. *It is determined ultimately by judgment.* Inasmuch as validity is inferred, not measured, it is judgmental. The data that are gathered and the statistical procedures that can be employed to obtain validity evidence for a given score use supply the bases for rendering a judgment about the degree of validity attained.

5. *It is expressed by degree.* Although some validity evidence can be expressed as statistical indices (e.g., validity coefficients), validity is an interpretation of those indices in terms of degree; it is not an attribute that can be assessed as all or none. Although *valid* and *invalid* are common summary terms, their underlying meaning is best expressed by degree, usually adequate-marginal-inadequate, or high-moderate-low.

There are three major categories or types of validity: content, criterion related, and construct. A brief description of the question each type answers and the method typically used to arrive at that answer is presented in Table 2.1

CONTENT VALIDITY. Content validity refers to the extent that the items on the test constitute a representative sample of the domain of items the test is intended to measure. The key element is the *adequacy of the sampling*. Suppose a

MEMORY JOGGER

Table 2.1

Characteristics of Three Types of Validity

Type of Validity	Question Posed	Method for Answering
1. Content	How accurately does the test sample from the domain of behaviors it was designed to measure?	Evaluate the extent to which the test items match the content specifications
2. Criterion related		
a. Predictive	How accurately does test performance predict future performance on a criterion measure?	Evaluate the relationship between the test scores and the criterion measure
b. Concurrent	How accurately does test performance estimate current standing on a criterion measure?	Same as above
3. Construct	How accurately can test performance be explained in terms of psychological constructs?	Empirically test hypothesized relationships between the test scores and specified constructs

reading comprehension test was developed to measure literal, interpretative, and applied skills. A total of 100 passages and 500 items constituted the domain. Since it is impractical and unnecessary to use all of these items on the test to measure performance in the domain, only a sample of 10 passages and 50 items were selected. If the 50 items are representative of the 500, then performance on the sample can be generalized to performance on the domain. That is, if a student answered 40 of the 50 items correctly or 80%, it is possible to infer that she could answer approximately 400 items correctly in the domain. A nonrepresentative sample would not permit such inferences about domain performance. If the 50 items dealt almost exclusively with literal skills and only a few items tapped the upper two skill levels, this sample would be judged inadequate and, in fact, biased in favor of lower level comprehension skills.

The foundation for any judgment of content validity is the definition of the content domain. If an explicit definition is provided, including a content outline, instructional and behavioral objectives, and a table of specifications or "test blueprint," the sampling of the items and their distribution across the domain can be planned systematically as the test is structured. In other words, the test maker can build content validity into the test. Once the test is completed, a critical inspection of the items in relation to those specifications can reveal the degree of content validity attained. This review process is usually executed by a panel of judges who possess expertise in the content area being tested.

These steps in determining content validity can also be deduced by following the inference rules for arguments in elementary logic:

Premise 1:   If the outline, objectives, and blueprint
(Definition of   accurately reflect the content domain,
content domain)

                           and

Premise 2:   if each item measures the objective it
(Match between   is intended to measure,
items and objectives

                           then,

Conclusion 1:   the items measure their corresponding
(Content validity   objectives and the content defined by those
for subtests)   objectives.

                           . ˙ . (therefore)

Conclusion 2:   all of the items accurately reflect the
(Content validity   content domain.
for total test)

CRITERION – RELATED VALIDITY. Criterion-related validity refers to the extent to which test performance is related to some criterion measure of performance. As Table 2.1 indicates, there are two kinds of criterion-related validity: predictive and concurrent. This distinction is a function of the time when the criterion data are obtained as the use of the test scores. In the case of predictive validity, those data are gathered at a future point in time; for concurrent validity, the criterion data are collected at the same time as the test data.

The purposes for conducting criterion-related validity studies should be made clear. Evidence of *predictive validity* is applicable when one wishes to determine whether particular test scores are useful in predicting future performance. The accuracy of this prediction can be judged from specific statistical indices such as validity coefficients and standard errors of estimate. (*Note:* The standard error of estimate should not be confused with the standard error of measurement to be discussed shortly in the section on reliability.) These indices measure the degree of relationship between the test scores and the criterion. A perfect relationship is indicated by a validity coefficient of $+1.00$ -1.00. The strength of the relationship decreases as the magnitude of the coefficient approaches 0. For the standard error of estimate, the ideal value is 0, meaning no error of prediction. The worst possible prediction occurs as the standard error approaches the standard deviation of the criterion. If either of these statistics is reported in the technical manual for a standardized test, the corresponding range of values can be used to appraise the degree of predictive validity or accuracy. For example, a coefficient of .64 between a verbal ability test (the predictor) administered in grade 3 and a reading test (the criterion) administered in grade 5 suggests a moderate degree of accuracy. Certainly one cannot infer that poor verbal ability is a "definite" sign of later reading difficulty.

In contrast to this predictive framework, *concurrent validity* is concerned with whether the test scores can be substituted for some less efficient, more expensive method of obtaining the criterion information. For example, suppose the criterion was teacher ratings of reading achievement, derived from the performances of students on many different tests. From the teacher's perspective, this information was diverse and time-consuming to gather. Therefore, it was desirable to locate a single standardized reading test that could serve the same purpose and was easy to administer and score. The reading comprehension subtest of the Iowa Tests of Basic Skills was considered first because it was already being administered to all students as part of the district-wide testing program. However, its concurrent validity with teacher ratings was unknown. The subtest scores were then correlated with the ratings. The resulting validity coefficient was .88. A high degree of concurrent validity was inferred from this estimate, and the reading comprehension subtest was substituted for the criterion ratings as the primary determinant of reading achievement.

In reviewing the evidence of criterion-related validity studies, either predictive or concurrent, the test user must pay special attention to two common troublespots — an inadequate criterion and an inadequate sample. Too often, tests are validated against criterion measures that may have questionable validity and reliability, particularly those pertaining to "success." An operational definition of a criterion that satisfies the standards for technical adequacy can be difficult to achieve. For example, researchers still use grade-point average as the operational definition of school success, yet most are cognizant of its limitations. The seriousness of the criterion definition problem can be succinctly stated: *If the criterion is inadequate, so is the validity study.* The scientific worth of the study can depend on the appropriateness and quality of the criterion chosen. It is the responsibility of the test user to examine closely the description of the criterion and all evidence relevant to judging its technical adequacy that should be reported in the test manual (APA/AERA/NCME, 1974, pp. 33 – 34).

The characteristics of the sample selected for the study should also be scrutinized for representativeness and adequate size. The standards previously discussed in the context of an adequate norm sample are applicable to samples in criterion-related validity studies. Studies based on nonrepresentative samples and/or samples with too few students will frequently yield results that can be misleading. Therefore, both the criterion and the sample must be evaluated to assure that these deficiencies, if they do exist, are taken into consideration in interpreting the statistical indices of a validity study and, finally, in judging the predictive or concurrent validity of the test scores.

CONSTRUCT VALIDITY. Construct validity refers to the extent that test performance can be explained in terms of psychological constructs. A construct is a theoretical idea "constructed" for the purposes of explaining and organizing an existing body of knowledge. Examples are reading comprehension, intelligence, verbal ability, learning disability, and language. When the scores are interpreted on a verbal ability test, for example, the test user is implying that there is a psychological quality (the construct) called verbal ability and its meaning can be inferred to some degree from the performance on the test. The determination of construct validity involves verifying these implications, that is, studying the constructs presumed to account for test performance. Such research is expected to identify all factors that influence the performance and to describe their nature and strength. In essence, one is pursuing an answer to a very fundamental question: What does the test measure?

As these characteristics of construct validation suggest, the evidence necessary to judge construct validity cannot be found in a single study; rather, it is derived from the results of many different studies (Cronbach & Meehl, 1955). Formulating hypotheses about test performance is usually the first step. A variety of empirical investigations are then conducted to confirm these hypotheses. Quite often the results of the statistical analyses performed in the course of test construction and the findings of relevant criterion-related validity studies meaningfully contribute to the evidence of construct validity.

TRINARY CONCEPTUALIZATION OF VALIDITY. The preceding three types of validity and the standards used to judge their adequacy provide the foundation for evaluating the validity evidence of most standardized tests. Guion (1980) described the content, criterion-related, and construct components of validity "as a holy trinity representing three different roads to psychometric salvation" (p. 386). However, this traditional "trinary conceptualization" of validity has limitations. First, the categories overlap, and in some instances it may be difficult to squeeze a particular source of invalidity (e.g., administrator bias) into a single slot. The *Standards* (APA/AERA/NCME, 1974) note that content, criterion related, and construct validities "are interrelated operationally and logically; only rarely is one of them alone important in a particular situation" (p. 26). Obviously it is unnecessary to label the type of validity in order to gather evidence to support a specific test score use. Second, a compartmentalized thinking of validity could foster the notion that there are alternatives and a test user need only pick one of them. This could lead to the incorrect conclusion, for example, that because there is no evidence of predictive validity, the test is invalid for all score uses. Finally, the three categories are inadequate for classifying the diverse forms of invalidity that may be suspected in terms of possible test score interpretations, uses, and inferences.

UNIFIED CONCEPTUALIZATION OF VALIDITY. The recent trend toward a "unified conceptualization" of validity (Cronbach, 1980; Guion, 1977, 1980;

Linn, 1980; Messick, 1979; Tenopyr, 1977) seems to suggest a more useful framework. Such a conceptualization would de-emphasize the types of validity and instead emphasize the data-gathering process and the methods to obtain the kinds of evidence essential to answer the validity question. The test maker would concentrate on the inferences to be made with the scores and the sources that could invalidate those inferences. Subsequently, evidence would be accumulated so that the test user can judge the degree of validity attained.

Proceeding along this line of thought, there are three score uses germane to screening decisions about learning-disabled children that require attention: (1) the use of standardized test scores for individual decisions at the local level, (2) the use of discrepancy scores for classifying children as learning disabled and non-learning disabled, and (3) the use of test scores with sex, racial, and ethnic subgroups of the learning-disabled population. Each of these is an important validity issue that the teacher or clinician must confront and address before screening decisions can be considered defensible.

CURRICULAR VALIDITY. One of the most typical complaints of standardized achievement tests is that they do not measure the *curriculum* in a given school district, i.e., they do not "mirror the curriculum." Standardized tests survey broad domains of content, some of which may be reflected in the local curriculum and some of which may not. In fact, they are expressly designed to minimize local, state, and regional content biases (Green, 1983; Mehrens, 1983). This insensitivity to specific program emphases can raise questions about the validity of the scores. If the achievement test scores do not accurately measure achievement in the program, their validity is weakened. The degree of invalidity is contingent upon the match between what the test measures and what the curriculum covers.

Curricular validity refers to the extent that items on the test measure the content of a local curriculum (cf. McClung, 1979, p. 682). While conceptually similar to content validity (Madaus, 1983; Schmidt et al., 1983) and even viewed as synonymous with content validity (Cureton, 1951; Hopkins & Stanley, 1981; Madaus et al., 1982), curricular validity is operationally very different. In the case of standardized, norm-referenced tests, it does not focus on the content domain the test was designed to measure but deals with a specific domain to which the test is later applied. The relevance of the test in a specific application is being evaluated. Rarely would perfect congruence between the two domains ever occur (see for example, Bower, 1982; Madaus et al., 1982).

Evidence of curricular validity is obtained by determining the degree of incongruence, or mismatch. This is based on a systematic, judgmental review of the test against the curricular objectives or materials by content experts. These experts may be classroom teachers or curriculum specialists; they are the only professionals in a position to judge curricular validity. The review can vary as a function of the following: (a) single grade versus cumulative grade content, (b)

(b) specificity of objectives or content/process matrix, (c) internal versus external determination, and (d) curricular materials versus actual classroom activities (for details, see Schmidt, 1983a, 1983b; Schmidt et al., 1983). What emerges from this process are several estimates of content overlap, including the amount of content in common, the percentage of the local curriculum measured by the test, and the percentage of items on the test not covered by the curriculum. The second estimate in particular can furnish evidence of the curricular validity of the test.

When a standardized test is found to have low curricular validity, alternative testing procedures should be considered. One procedure involves customizing the test by developing supplementary items to fill in the identified measurement gaps. These items would be administered and scored in conjunction with the standardized test. Technical problems arise in evaluating the validity and reliability of the "supplementary test" and in equating its scores to the appropriate national norms. Another procedure is to choose a lower level test that provides a better curriculum match. Administering this below-grade-level test is called out-of-level testing. Its advantages and disadvantages are discussed in Chapter 3.

INSTRUCTIONAL VALIDITY. A concern related to curricular validity is whether standardized achievement tests measure *what is actually taught* in the schools. Very often it is simply assumed or implied that evidence of curricular validity means that the objectives guided the instruction and the curricular materials were used in the classroom. This does not necessarily follow, as several studies have demonstrated (Hardy, 1983; Leinhardt & Seewald, 1981; Leinhardt, Zigmond, & Cooley, 1981; Poynor, 1978; Schmidt et al., 1983). What is measured by the test is not always the same as what is taught, especially with regard to standardized tests. Hence, a distinction has been made between these different domains to which the test items can be referenced (Schmidt et al., 1983). When the domain is the instruction actually delivered, a "measure of whether schools are providing students with instuction in the knowledge and skills measured by the test" (McClung, 1979, p. 683) is called instructional validity.

Instructional validity refers to the extent to which the items on the test measure the content actually taught to the students. Several techniques have been proposed for assessing the overlap between the test and the instruction. Popham (1983) has identified four data-sources for describing whether students have received instruction that would enable them to perform satisfactorily on a test: (1) observations of classroom transactions, (2) analyses of instructional materials, (3) instructor self-reports, and (4) student self-reports. Although he views these sources as methods for determining the adequacy of test preparation (Yalow & Popham, 1983), they can be considered as techniques for gathering evidence of instructional validity. Unfortunately, Popham's (1983) evaluation of those techniques suggests that the process of estimating the percentage of a standardized test that has been covered by teaching is fraught with difficulties. Most of these are methodological problems in executing the data-gathering procedures, so as to provide *adequate* evidence (see Leinhardt, 1983; Schmidt et al., 1983). They stem, in large part, from the variability of instructional content, not only among different classes but within a single classroom. Therefore, despite the importance of instructional validity, further research is required before it can be measured reliably, validly, and practically.

DECISION VALIDITY. The effectiveness of any screening procedure resides in the extent to which it can identify the designated target population. In screening children for learning disabilities, it is necessary to distinguish between those who possess a disability and those who do not. This is, in fact, a classification decision of learning disabled or non – learning disabled. The accuracy of this decision-making process can reveal the value of the screening procedure. Only when the accuracy is known can one determine how many children are correctly and incorrectly identified.

Decision validity refers to the extent to which a test or testing procedure can yield accurate decisions according to a criterion classification. This may be perceived as analogous to concurrent validity. The principal difference lies in what is being studied: the *decisions* reached on the basis of test scores or just the *test scores*. An investigation of decision validity examines the relationship between the decisions made using a specific test or testing procedure and the decisions made using a criterion procedure. Suppose the criterion procedure for screening children involved judgments by classroom teachers, scores from several tests (both formal and informal), and the findings of developmental and medical histories. If ability-achievement discrepancy scores from standardized test batteries could be employed in place of all of this information as the screening procedure, the decision-making process could be easier and more efficient. The decision validity of the discrepancy score procedure can be ascertained by comparing the number of correct decisions resulting from that procedure with the number resulting fom the criterion procedure. That is, how many correct (and incorrect) LD and non-LD classifications were made using the two procedures. This can be answered by a percentage of correct decisions such as 91% or a validity coefficient such as .68. Either index supplies evidence of the effectiveness of the screening procedure (for details, see Chapter 5).

The significance of decision validity evidence to screening for learning disabilities can be demonstrated by pondering the simple questions such evidence would answer:

1. Does the screening procedure work?
2. Is it effective?
3. Are the right children identified?

4. Are there learning-disabled children not receiving special programs to which they are entitled?

If the teacher, learning disability specialist, clinician, or administrator answers "I don't know" or "no" to any one or all of the above questions, how can continued use of the screening procedure be justified. The unmeasurable and potentially harmful effects of this type of practice should not be tolerated.

Obtaining evidence to substantiate important decisions about children is within the grasp of every decision maker. Given the value of this evidence to the screening process, one chapter (5) in this volume has been devoted entirely to this topic. In addition, since the same evidence is just as applicable to diagnostic decisions, another chapter (6) describes the methods for determining the decision validity of a criterion-referenced test used for individual mastery-nonmastery classifications. Both chapters demonstrate the utility of a decision model that has been employed in medicine, psychology, and psychiatry for more than 25 years.

SEX, RACIAL, AND ETHNIC BIAS. Among the criticisms of standardized tests listed at the beginning of this chapter, few have been as vexing and thorny to test makers and test users as the criticisms that pertain to sex, racial, and ethnic bias. A charge of bias can be directed against any available test quite easily. What is not quite so easy is to obtain incontrovertible evidence to substantiate or to refute that charge. The need for dense arguments from logical, theoretical, and empirical perspectives can be best illustrated by the unscientific character of the plaintiffs' and defendants' arguments in the major legal cases on bias to date, for example, the *Larry P.* case (*Larry P., et al.* v. *Wilson Riles, et al.*, 1972, 1979).

For obvious reasons, the term *bias* represents a socially volatile concept. The controversy over bias in testing that has emerged in the past decade has added numerous negative overtones and connotations to its meaning. Possibly the only positive outgrowth of the polemics surrounding bias was its galvanizing effect on the measurement community. In the late 1960s and early 1970s psychometricians hastened to provide definitions of bias in terms of objective criteria, to develop rigorous and precise methods for studying bias, and to conduct empirical investigations of test bias. The subsequent proliferation of methods to detect bias and studies to determine whether or not specific tests are biased has not yet abated.

The research and discourse on bias are organized in terms of validity issues and, in fact, reflect the traditional trinary scheme described previously: content, criterion related, and construct. Bias in the content of the test has been investigated judgmentally and statistically. A *judgmental review* or logical analysis (Shepard, 1982) is intended to detect stereotypic, culture-specific, and offensive language and to assure fair representation in the work roles and life-styles of sex, racial, and ethnic groups (Tittle, 1982). The *statistical analysis* based on an appropriate experimental design (Schmeiser, 1982) is conducted to detect discrepancies in item performance between specific groups (e.g., males and females, blacks and whites, Hispanics and whites). When such discrepancies are found, an *a posteriori (judgmental) analysis* is employed to discern whether true item bias is present and, if it is, to deduce explanations for why it occurred and consider procedures for eliminating it (Scheuneman, 1982).

An item is biased if individuals with the same ability have an unequal probability of answering the item correctly as a function of their group membership. This definition is similar to those proposed by Pine (1977) and Scheuneman (1979). Operationally, bias is inferred from differences in performance between groups. The differences are computed using one or more statistical methods (see reviews by Angoff, 1982, and Ironson, 1982); these methods have been examined in several studies (Burrill, 1982).

Interestingly, item bias has been the predominant form of bias investigation undertaken by publishers of ability and achievement tests. It is also the most important. Initially, the content or behaviors that a test measures are an integral part of all score inferences. Since the item is the most fundamental level of content analysis and the foundation for these inferences, *item bias studies are necessary for all tests.* However, they are not sufficient for all test score inferences and uses. For example, additional studies would be required if the scores are used to make predictions about future performance. Second, charges of bias from numerous sources frequently include a citation of specific items that are claimed to be biased against a minority population. These sources can be public or professional organizations such as Parents in Action on Special Education (PASE), the National Education Association, and the Association of Black Psychologists (Jackson, 1975; Williams, 1970, 1971), or individual citizens and organizations as plaintiffs (e.g., *Armstead, et al.* v. *Starkville Mississippi Municipal Separate School District*, 1972; *Larry P., et al.* v. *Wilson Riles, et al.*, 1972; *PASE, et al.* v. *Joseph P. Hannon, et al.*, 1980). Third, the results of bias studies at the subtest and total test levels do not preclude the presence of bias at the item level. For example, a predictive bias study that finds no sex bias does not rule out the possibility that specific items on the test may be biased against females. Fourth, item bias studies can be incorporated into the early stages of test construction and item analysis to minimize the chances of bias accusations arising later. Finally, the elimination of item bias may decrease the likelihood of test bias, although research evidence is needed to verify this relationship.

The *test bias* literature has focused almost exclusively on intelligence and aptitude tests (Jensen, 1980). The studies have dealt with predictive and construct validity issues. *Predictive bias* may be defined as follows:

Bias exists in regard to predictive validity when there is systematic error in the prediction of the criterion score as a function of group membership.

This definition is a less technical version of the definitions proffered by Cleary

(1968), Cleary, Humphreys, Kendrick, and Wesman (1975), and Reynolds (1982a). A slight restatement of Reynolds' (1982b, p. 194) definition of *construct bias* follows:

> Bias exists in regard to construct validity when a test measures different psychological constructs as a function of group membership or measures the same construct but with differing degrees of accuracy.

The statistical methods used to detect these two types of bias are no less numerous and varied than those employed in item bias studies (see review by Reynolds, 1982a). The indices that result are intended to signal possible bias and indicate, for example, whether a test predicts the criterion with greater accuracy for whites than for blacks or whether the constructs measured by the test are different for these groups.

Where bias is inferred, the test scores for the group in question should be reported by the publisher, especially when the bias is against females or minorities. The nature of the bias should be fully explained. Indeed, all pertinent research evidence should accompany any presentation of scores partitioned by sex, racial, or ethnic subpopulations. As the *Standards for Educational and Psychological Tests* (APA/AERA/NCME, 1974) specify:

> A test user should investigate the possibility of bias in tests or in test items. Wherever possible, there should be an investigation of possible differences in criterion-related validity for ethnic, sex, or other subsamples that can be identified when the test is given. The manual or research report should give the results for each subsample separately or report that no differences were found. (p. 43)

This suggests that test scores may not be validly used without taking account of group differences. In view of the political and social implications of these distinctions, the decision maker should be very cautious in interpreting differential validity evidence.

While the bias literature has concentrated very heavily in the areas of item bias, predictive bias, and construct bias, many other types of bias have been described in relation to minority group populations (Baca & Chinn, 1982; Gonzales, 1982; Oakland, 1980; Oakland & Matuszek, 1977; Reschly, 1979; Samuda, 1975; Sattler, 1982, Chap. 19; Ysseldyke, 1979). Examples are atmosphere bias, linguistic bias, examiner bias, and decision-making bias. They appear to occur at several points in the assessment process: before, during, and after. The descriptions of these various sources of invalidity are usually couched in the context of the litigation involving charges of racial or ethnic bias (see reviews by Bersoff, 1979, 1982, in press; Jensen, 1980, Chap. 2; Oakland & Laosa, 1977; Reschly, 1979) or the P.L. 94-142 mandate for *nondiscriminatory evaluation*. The "Protection in Evaluation Procedures" provisions of the law state:

> [P]rocedures to assure that testing and evaluation materials and procedures utilized for the purposes of evaluation and placement of handicapped children will be se-

lected and administered so as not to be racially or culturally discriminatory. Such materials or procedures shall be provided and administered in the child's native language or mode of communication, unless it clearly is not feasible to do so, and no single procedure shall be the sole criterion for determining an appropriate educational program for a child. (Sec. 612)

As with other parts of P.L. 94-142, this section is also rather ambiguous. Bersoff and Veltman (1979) observed that "nowhere do the regulations define the concept [of nondiscriminatory evaluation] nor indicate what instruments meet the test of nondiscrimination" (p. 18). A follow-up series of reports by the Coordinating Office for Regional Resource Centers (CORRC) explored the meaning of these regulations. Volume II of these reports entitled *With Bias Toward None* (CORRC, 1976) concluded that assessment procedures are likely to be less biased if (1) procedural safeguards are followed and (2) a variety of data are incorporated into classification and placement decisions.

Reliability

Reliability refers to the *degree of consistency between two or more measurements of the same thing.* Where the common thread running through the preceding section on validity is *accuracy,* the counterpart in this section on reliability is *consistency.* The concern is with the consistency of individual scores over repeated measurements using a single test or equivalent tests. This meaning of reliability should be viewed in the context of the following points:

1. *It is a necessary but not sufficient condition for validity.* Consider the archer who shoots his entire quiver of arrows into the upper right quadrant of the target, far from the bull's-eye; he is certainly consistent but very inaccurate. Test scores can be highly consistent but measure the wrong thing or be used inappropriately. That is, evidence of high reliability is no guarantee that an adequate degree of validity is present. (*Note*: Low reliability, however, can restrict the degree of validity that is desired.) For the archer whose arrows repeatedly hit the bull's-eye, both consistency and accuracy are attained. In Gronlund's (1981) words, *"reliability merely provides the consistency that makes validity possible"* (p. 94).

2. *It is inferred from the way that the test scores are used and interpreted.* Reliability focuses on the scores and the specific way that they are used and interpreted, not on the test itself. "The test manual or research report should present evidence of reliability . . . that permits the reader to judge whether scores are sufficiently dependable for the intended uses of the test" (APA/AERA/NCME, 1974, p. 50).

3. *It is specific to a particular type of consistency.* Test scores are not just reliable in general. The evidence of reliability must be interpreted in relation to the type of consistency that is most appropriate. This may be the consistency of student responses over time, over item samples (test forms), and/

or within a single item sample. The consistency among observers or scorers may also be of interest. The designated uses of the scores will dictate which type(s) of consistency is appropriate and, therefore, the analysis that must be conducted.

4. *It is determined ultimately by judgment.* Despite the numerous statistical methods that can be employed to obtain reliability evidence, reliability coefficients and standard errors of measurement furnish the indices for judging the degree of reliability attained.

MEMORY JOGGER

Table 2.2

Characteristics of Five Types of Reliability

Type of Reliability	Question Posed	Method for Answering
1. Stability	How stable are the test scores over time?	*Test-retest*: Administer one test twice to the same group with an intervening period of time between the two administrations
2. Equivalence (parallel forms)	To what extent are the two test forms equivalent?	*Equivalent forms*: Administer two forms of the same test to the same group at the same time
3. Stability and Equivalence	To what extent are the test scores on two equivalent forms stable over time	*Test-retest and equivalent forms*: Administer two forms of the same test to the same group with an intervening period of time between the administration of each form
4. Internal Consistency	To what extent do all of the test items measure the same construct?	*Split-half*: Administer one test to one group; split the test into halves (e.g., even-numbered and odd-numbered items); correlate the scores from the halves; then substitute the correlation in Spearman-Brown formula to obtain estimate for full-length test *Kuder-Richardson*: Administer one test to one group; score the test and apply $K\text{-}R_{20}$ formula
5. Interscorer Consistency or Interobserver Consistency	To what extent do different scorers produce the same results? To what extent do different observers record the same behaviors?	*Interclass correlation*: Obtain two sets of scores/observations from two independent scorers/observers at the same point in time; correlate the scores

5. *It is expressed by degree.* Reliability is primarily statistical in nature. The interpretation of the various indices of reliability is in terms of degree rather than all or none. While *reliable* and *unreliable* are terms often used to characterize tests, their meanings are more accurately expressed as adequate-marginal-inadequate or high-moderate-low.

There are at least five different types of reliability that account for four different sources of error in the test scores. Each may be estimated by using any one of several methods. A brief description of the question each type answers and the method typically used to arrive at that answer is presented in Table 2.2.

The degree of reliability in each case is assessed by means of two indices: (1) a reliability coefficient and (2) a standard error of measurement. These indices are analogous to the validity coefficient and standard error of estimate that were specified previously as the statistical indices of predictive validity. The similarities and differences between these indices are a function of the set(s) of test scores used in the computations. Table 2.3 displays this comparison. Both the validity coefficient and the reliability coefficient are correlations; the standard error of estimate and standard error of measurement are different types of standard error (or standard deviation).

MEMORY JOGGER
Table 2.3
Comparison of Statistical Indices of Validity and Reliability

Characteristic	Correlation Coefficient				Standard Error			
	Index	Meaning	Range of Values	Ideal Value	Index	Meaning	Range of Values	Ideal Value
Validity	Validity coefficient	Degree of relationship between test scores and the criterion	−1.00 to +1.00	−1.00 or +1.00	Standard error of estimate	Amount of error of prediction	0 to standard deviation of criterion	0
Reliability	Reliability coefficient	Degree of relationship between two (or more) measures of the same construct	0 to +1.00*	+1.00	Standard error of measurement	Amount of error of measurement	0 to standard deviation of test scores	0

*Although it is statistically possible for negative coefficients to occur, they would be theoretically meaningless in the interpretation of reliability; a 0 means the scores are all error, and a +1.00 means they are free of error.

Perfectly reliable measurement is indicated by a reliability coefficient of +1.00 and a standard error of measurement of 0. In other words, where the coefficient reflects the degree of *consistency* of scores over repeated testings, the standard error measures the degree of *inconsistency* of an individual's scores over repeated testings. When the ideal value occurs, an individual's obtained score on the test is, in fact, his or her *true score,* unaffected by error. Just how close one comes to this ideal is contingent, in part, on which type of reliability is considered. The types listed in Table 2.2 are examined next.

STABILITY. The stability of test scores is estimated with the test-retest method. A test is administered twice to the same group of students with an intervening period of time between the two administrations. Two sets of scores result, one from the first testing and a second from the retesting. A correlation coefficient is then computed between these scores in order to determine the stability or consistency of the scores over the designated time interval.

One important factor that can influence the magnitude of the stability coefficient is the length of the time interval. It may range from a few minutes to several years. For many standardized ability and achievement tests, the coefficient is estimated over a period of months usually within the same year. The length in all cases should be based on the decisions to be made with the scores. Short intervals of a couple of weeks or less tend to produce somewhat inflated coefficients, inasmuch as many students remember their answers from the first testing and this will raise their scores on the second (see discussion of "testing effect" in Chapters 6 and 7). Long intervals of several months tend to yield lower coefficients due not only to the instability of the scores but also to changes in the characteristics of the students that cannot be controlled.

The norm-referenced tests that are selected for screening purposes should possess stability coefficients in the .80s and .90s, preferably above .90. In the elementary grades these coefficients should be inspected closely. They tend to be high when the interval is less than a year and relatively lower across years. This seems to occur for both ability and achievement test scores.

EQUIVALENCE. Equivalence (or parallel forms) reliability is estimated using two separate but equivalent, parallel, or alternate forms of a test. The forms are constructed systematically from the same content specifications so that, at least from an initial judgmental perspective, they both appear to measure the same material. This can be accomplished by drawing two samples of items from the domain of items developed from the specifications or by building the two forms item by item according to content and difficulty level. The former method is preferable since a reliability coefficient derived from the latter does not take into account item sampling error.

Despite the apparent similarities of the two forms, equivalence can only be verified statistically. The test forms are administered to the same group of students in close succession with no intervening time. Frequently the items from the two forms are included in one test, where form A items may be even numbered and form B items odd numbered. This procedure is intended to minimize the effects of certain factors that could lower the degree of equivalence. For example, fatigue at the end of the test should theoretically influence performance equally on items from both forms when the items alternate (A, B, A, B, etc.); if form A items were administered first and form B items administered second, only form B would be affected.

The two administrations produce two sets of scores, one from each form. These scores can then be correlated to determine the degree to which the items on each form measure the same construct. While a correlation coefficient, of say .80, provides one answer to the question, a more revealing statistic is the square of the correlation, multiplied by 100, or $r^2 \times 100$, where r represents the correlation coefficient. The resulting percentage, in this example 64% ($.80^2 \times 100$), indicates how much is in common between the two forms. That is, 64% of what is being measured by form A is also being measured by form B. This percentage, known as the amount of explained variance, can be computed and interpreted for any correlation. However, it is especially useful in interpreting an equivalence coefficient. A relatively high correlation can be misleading in this context. The coefficient of .80 means that only 64% is in common between the forms and, in fact, more than a third ($1 - .64 \times 100 = 36\%$), known as unexplained variance, is not accounted for. These figures suggest that a coefficient of .90 or above is required to demonstrate equivalence adequately.

In addition to the correlation coefficient, other statistics need to be reported in order to assess equivalence. These are the average score (mean), the spread of scores (variance or standard deviation), and the item analysis results (difficulty and discrimination) for each test form. Such information should be presented in the test manual so the test user can fully inspect all evidence pertinent to the consistency of test scores over different item samples.

STABILITY AND EQUIVALENCE. One of the most rigorous approaches to reliability is to combine the stability and equivalence procedures. Two equivalent test forms are administered to the same students with a time interval between the administrations. The correlation between the test scores obtained under these conditions reflects their stability over time, their equivalence over item samples, and the changes in the characteristics of the students when the time period is lengthy. Since the combination of these sources of error or variation is greater than any single component tapped by the preceding estimates of reliability, this estimate will be the lowest, particularly if the period elapsing between the test administrations is several months or longer. Of course, all of the types of reliability evidence and guidelines for its interpretation mentioned in the previous sections apply to this stability-equivalence estimate.

INTERNAL CONSISTENCY. Unlike the three categories of reliability discussed up to this point that require two test administrations with the same test or equivalent forms to one group of students, the estimates of internal consistency are based on one test administered to one group only one time. There are two major strategies test publishers use to determine internal consistency: (1) the split-half method using the Spearman-Brown prophecy formula and (2) the Kuder-Richardson formula 20. Each is described briefly here.

The *split-half method* is essentially an approximation of the equivalent forms method. Instead of using two separate forms, a single test is split into halves that resemble a form A and a form B. While it is desirable to divide the test to obtain the most equivalent halves, usually the even-numbered items comprise one form and the odd-numbered items comprise the other. The scores that result on each half can then be correlated as before. Since this correlation is estimated from parts of the same test, it indicates the degree of consistency between scores that are internal to the test. If we started with a 50-item test and correlated the two 25-item halves, the coefficient would measure the relationship between two equivalent forms, 25 items in length. One final step is needed to estimate the reliability for the original 50-item test. Substituting the split-half coefficient into the Spearman-Brown formula will furnish an estimate for the full-length test.

This reliability coefficient measures the adequacy of item sampling from the same content domain. It reveals nothing about the stability of the scores. Inasmuch as split-half estimates tend to be higher than any other estimate of reliability, the test user should avoid overzealous interpretations of those coefficients. They should not even be reported for speeded tests, because the estimates are so highly inflated. More will be said about this limitation shortly.

An alternative approach to internal consistency is the use of the *Kuder-Richardson formulas*. One of these formulas, often called the $K\text{-}R_{20}$, is computed from the scores on each item and the total test scores. It is not necessary to split the test in any special way. Yet, the $K\text{-}R_{20}$ yields a coefficient that is equal to the average of all possible split-half coefficients for the group tested. It obviates the bias that can creep into the estimate based on only one particular split.

A generalized version of the $K\text{-}R_{20}$ formula applicable to most any item scoring format is *coefficient alpha* (Cronbach, 1951). It can be used to estimate internal consistency reliability for tests that have dichotomously scored items (correct-incorrect; 1-0) and also tests or scales that employ multipoint scoring systems (e.g., agree-uncertain-disagree; 2-1-0). Since alpha is occasionally reported in test manuals, users should know that for norm-referenced tests containing only dichotomously scored items, the reliability coefficient computed using the $K\text{-}R_{20}$ or alpha formula is identical.

Another popular formula is the $K\text{-}R_{21}$, which is a modified version of the $K\text{-}R_{20}$. While it is simpler to compute, it is also an underestimate of the $K\text{-}R_{20}$. The modification is based on the assumption that all of the items on the test have the same difficulty level (percentage correct). To the extent that this assumption is not upheld for the group of students tested, the coefficient will be an underestimate of internal consistency. When the assumption is upheld, the $K\text{-}R_{21}$ coefficient will equal the $K\text{-}R_{20}$ coefficient. The computational simplicity of the $K\text{-}R_{21}$ is a noteworthy advantage of the coefficient for teachers who wish to estimate reliability for their own tests. Since test publishers conduct reliability studies by computer, the $K\text{-}R_{21}$, $K\text{-}R_{20}$, or alpha coefficient may be reported in test manuals.

The interpretation of the Kuder-Richardson estimates of internal consistency is similar to that of the split-half estimates. Both approaches indicate the degree to which the items in a test are *homogeneous* — measure the same construct. If one major skill area is being tested, individual students should perform consistently well on the easy items and consistently poorly on the difficult items on the test. Consistent performance furnishes empirical verification that the content specifications define a single ability or skill.

To the extent that performance is inconsistent, such that some students answer one series of questions correctly and another series incorrectly or answer easy items incorrectly and difficult items correctly, it is possible that the test is measuring two or more different skills. When this occurs, particular clusters of items or subtests related to specific skills may emerge, with consistent peformance on the items within each subtest, e.g., vocabulary, reading comprehension. The internal consistency coefficient for each subtest should reveal the degree of homogeneity attained in relation to the a priori specifications. In standardized test batteries consisting of numerous subtests, a coefficient of .90 or above supplies ample evidence of subtest homogeneity and an adequate criterion for reliable, individual screening decisions.

Given this interpretation and the typical characteristics of standardized tests, one caveat must be stated. The preceding estimates of internal consistency are not appropriate for speeded tests, where time limits are imposed so that essentially all students are not able to consider all of the items. Under timed conditions, the resulting test scores will produce spuriously inflated reliability coefficients. Since most standardized ability and achievement test manuals designate time limits for completion of each section of the test, caution must be observed in interpreting any estimate of internal consistency. Where speededness is a significant problem in this context, the other types of reliability coefficients may be more meaningful and accurate.

In addition to this consideration, it is important to note that none of the foregoing estimates of internal consistency reliability should be accepted in lieu of an estimate of stability, equivalence, or the combination of the two. Each estimate quantifies a different type of consistency. If a stability coefficient is essential in order to select a particular screening test or to interpret the scores correctly, it must be reported. If two or more test forms at the same level are available from the publisher, evidence of equivalence must be demonstrated, not assumed. An internal consistency coefficient cannot provide either of these types of information. Consequently, it should not be substituted for coefficients that may be more appropriate in a specific test application.

INTERSCORER CONSISTENCY. The standardized tests currently accessible to teachers usually employ an objective item format, such as multiple choice. This characteristic facilitates either manual or computer scoring that cannot be influenced by individual judgment; that is, the scoring is totally objective, not subjective. In certain academic subjects, such as writing and speaking, and in areas where skills must be observed directly, objectivity in scoring is problematic. The individuals who score an essay test or record target behaviors may allow their own judgments, biases, and/or opinions to contaminate the results. This is possible whenever writing samples or essays are required or behavioral checklists or rating scales are used.

The problem is that if scores vary markedly from one scorer to another, how can one discern the true score? This fluctuation or inconsistency between scorers, judges, observers, or raters must be minimized in order to provide useful data. The most effective strategies for achieving interscorer consistency are to delineate very specific, operational criteria for scoring (or recording) and then to train the persons involved so that their tasks can be executed as objectively as possible.

One method to measure the degree of objectivity attained and, in essence, the effectiveness of those strategies is to estimate interscorer consistency. Over the past 30 years more than 20 different statistical indices have been recommended (see review by Berk, 1979). Among the various indices, the correlation coefficient used to express the previous types of reliability can also be applied here. Two sets of scores/ratings by two independent scorers/observers are obtained on one group of students at the same point in time. The results are then correlated to estimate the scoring consistency. In this case, the index, referred to as an *interclass correlation*, assesses the amount of error in the scores due to the person(s) who did the scoring. No other source of error is considered.

The criterion for an adequate level of interscorer consistency may vary as a function of the content or behaviors being measured, the particular scoring procedures followed, and the index used. Very often, as scorers/observers are being trained, several reliability checks are conducted so that by the completion of training (and sometimes retraining), a near perfect level of consistency is attained. When coefficients are finally estimated, they usually fall in the .90s. For large-scale writing assessments and perceptual/psychomotor instruments, interclass correlations in that vicinity are required to assure dependable individual decisions.

FACTORS AFFECTING RELIABILITY. In previous sections several factors were discussed that affect the magnitude of particular reliability coefficients. For example, the *time interval* between test and retest administrations influences the estimate of stability; a short interval produces a higher coefficient and a lengthy interval can result in a relatively lower coefficient. In estimating internal consistency, it was stressed that a *speeded test* can spuriously inflate the coefficient. These factors and others must be considered in interpreting the reliability evidence reported in standardized test manuals so that the evaluation of technical quality for the purpose of selecting an appropriate test is accurate.

Three additional factors that must be addressed in interpreting the reliability indices of standardized tests are test length, the spread of scores, and test difficulty. First, in general, *the longer the test, the higher the reliability coefficient.* This is frequently explained in terms of the adequacy of item sampling. Test users should be especially wary of short subtests in standardized test batteries; their reliabilities are typically too low to justify the use of their scores for individual decision making.

Second, *the greater the spread of scores, the higher will be the reliability coefficient.* When the scores are distributed over a wide range, the position of each score relative to everyone else's score is less likely to change over repeated testings. This improves the consistency of the scores. A factor that increases the spread will also increase reliability. For example, coefficients estimated with heterogeneous samples of students will be higher than those based on homogeneous samples. A sample containing a wide range of ability will yield higher indices than a restricted sample of, say, learning-disabled students only. This will also occur when coefficients are computed from the scores of students in several grade levels as compared to any single grade level. Such coefficients can be very misleading. In selecting standardized tests, only the estimates reported on a sample similar to the group for which the test is being chosen should be scrutinized.

Third, *a moderately easy test will yield a higher reliability coefficient than a test that is extremely easy or extremely difficult.* This occurs because test items in the moderately easy range, where from 40% to 70% of the students answer each item correctly, increase the spread of test scores. A test that contains either a large number of very easy items or very hard items will produce little variability in the total scores. Therefore, as indicated previously, a factor that affects the score range will affect reliability. By inspection of the item difficulty levels reported in a standardized test manual, the user should then be able to explain, in part, the reason for a particularly high or particularly low estimate of reliability.

The relationship between test difficulty and the ability of the students to be tested also affects the reliability of the scores. The scores around the midpoint of a distribution for a grade level test or multi – grade level test (e.g., primary, intermediate) are the most reliable. Scores at the extremes also tend to be reliable but least discriminating. Again, by reviewing the item difficulty levels, one should attempt to identify the test level that best matches a learning-disabled child's functional level. Alternatively, if the child has scored on previous on-grade-level tests near the bottom of the score distribution, it would be more appropriate to select a lower grade level test. This procedure, known as out-of-level testing, may be the only recourse a teacher has in order to assure meaningful test results for many learning-disabled children (for further details, see Chapter 3).

Liberalized Conceptualization of Reliability. Similar to the trend toward a unified conceptualization of validity, during the past decade there has been gradual movement toward a liberalized conceptualization of reliability. The basic approach that uses a statistical method called analysis of variance originated over 45 years ago (Burt, 1936; Hoyt, 1941). The subsequent contributions of Ebel (1951), Haggard (1958), and Medley and Mitzel (1963) were the precursors of this conceptualization of reliability known as *generalizability theory* (Cronbach, Rajaratnam, & Gleser, 1963). The various extensions of these earlier works culminated in a monograph by Cronbach, Gleser, Nanda, and Rajaratnam (1972), which stands as the most authoritative and comprehensive treatment of the topic.

Generalizability theory borrows its statistical models and research designs from traditional analysis of variance procedures (Lindquist, 1953; Winer, 1971). Instead of concentrating on the aforementioned types of reliability, the theory deals with the isolation and mensuration of all possible sources of error that could affect the scores as well as the measurement process. In other words, where classical reliability theory is restricted to estimating a single source of error at a time, generalizability theory can differentiate among multiple sources of error. The statistical indices used to assess the magnitude of these errors are generalizability coefficients and variance components. The former "reliability-like" coefficients provide estimates of the extent to which the observed scores are confounded with the identified sources of error and, consequently, indicate the degree to which a sample of observations can be generalized to a specified universe of observations. The estimated variance components quantify the amount of variation attributable to the sources of error controlled in the study. The *Standards* (APA/AERA/NCME, 1974), in fact, emphasize that "the estimation of clearly labeled components of score variance is the most informative outcome of a reliability study, both for the test developer wishing to improve the reliability of his [or her] instrument and for the user desiring to interpret test scores with maximum understanding" (p. 49). It is expected that this emphasis will continue in the new edition of the *Standards,* now in draft form.

The characteristics of generalizability theory have been documented in several articles and monographs (Berk, 1979; Brennan, 1983; Cronbach et al., 1972; Shavelson & Webb, 1981). In contrast to extant methods for estimating reliability, one of its most prominent features is it *flexibility.* Generalizability theory permits the comprehensive analysis of different test structures corresponding to different test score uses. The theory makes it possible to estimate variance components so that they reflect the particular facets of interest in a given situation. Studies can be designed to accommodate different numbers of students, items, subtests, test forms, observers/judges, behaviors, intervals, observation periods, settings, and occasions. Clearly, test users should anticipate reports of generalizability coefficients and variance components in the technical manuals of standardized tests.

Evaluation of Technical Quality

Critical reviews of standardized, norm-referenced tests can facilitate the selection of the highest quality instruments. When they are written by testing experts and based on the *Standards for Educational and Psychological Tests*, the information can be valuable in steering test users toward the adequate tests and away from the inadequate tests. There are several resources that publish such reviews: (1) *The Eighth Mental Measurements Yearbook*[2] (Buros, 1978); (2) textbooks of Salvia and Ysseldyke (1981) and Sattler (1982); (3) journals including *Journal of Educational Measurement, Measurement and Evaluation in Guidance, Journal of Counseling Psychology, Journal of Special Education, Journal of School Psychology,*

MEMORY JOGGER

Table 2.4

Ratings of the Technical Adequacy of Selected Intelligence and Ability Tests[*]

Intelligence/Ability Test	Norms	Validity	Reliability
Cognitive Abilities Test	+	+	+
Culture Fair Intelligence Tests	−	+	+
Detroit Tests of Learning Aptitude	−	−	−
Full-Range Picture Vocabulary Test	−	−	−
Goodenough-Harris Drawing Test	−	−	−
Henmon-Nelson Tests of Mental Ability	−	−	−
Kuhlmann-Anderson Intelligence Tests	+	+	+
McCarthy Scales of Children's Abilities	+	+	+
Otis-Lennon School Ability Test	+	+	+
Peabody Picture Vocabulary Test	−	+	+
Primary Mental Abilities Test	−	+	−
Quick Test	−	−	+
Short Form Test of Academic Aptitude	+	+	+
Slosson Intelligence Test	−	−	−
Stanford-Binet Intelligence Scale	+	−	−
Wechsler Intelligence Scale for Children-Revised (WISC-R)	+	+	+
Woodcock-Johnson Psychoeducational Battery	+	+	+

+   indicates technically adequate

−   indicates technically inadequate (either psychometric characteristic is inadequate or no data are reported in the manual)

[*]*Sources*: Salvia & Ysseldyke (1981), Thurlow & Ysseldyke (1979), and Ysseldyke et al. (1980a)

---

[2]The ninth edition of the *MMY* under the editorship of James V. Mitchell, Jr., and Joseph C. Witt is now in press. It should be available from the Buros Institute of Mental Measurements in 1984.

Table 2.5

Ratings of the Technical Adequacy of Selected Achievement Tests[*]

Achievement Test	Norms	Validity	Reliability
Brigance Inventory of Basic Skills	−	−	−
California Achievement Tests	+	+	+
Diagnostic Reading Scales (Spache)	−	−	−
Durrell Analysis of Reading Difficulty	−	−	−
Gates-MacGinitie Reading Tests	−	−	+
Gates-McKillop Reading Diagnostic Tests	−	−	−
Gilmore Oral Reading Test	−	−	−
Gray Oral Reading Test	−	−	−
Iowa Tests of Basic Skills	+	+	+
Key Math Diagnostic Arithmetic Test	−	−	−
Metropolitan Achievement Tests	+	+	+
Peabody Individual Achievement Tests	+	+	+
Silent Reading Diagnostic Tests	−	+	+
SRA Achievement Series	+	−	−
Stanford Achievement Test	+	+	+
Stanford Diagnostic Mathematics Test	+	+	+
Stanford Diagnostic Reading Test	+	+	+
Wide Range Achievement Test	−	−	−
Woodcock Reading Mastery Tests	+	+	+

+ indicates technically adequate

− indicates technically inadequate (either psychometric characteristic is inadequate or no data are reported in the manual)

[*]Sources: Salvia & Ysseldyke (1981), Thurlow & Ysseldyke (1979), and Ysseldyke et al. (1980a)

Table 2.6

Ratings of the Technical Adequacy of Selected Perceptual-Motor and Language Tests[*]

Perceptual-Motor/Language Test	Norms	Validity	Reliability
Bender Visual Motor Gestalt Test	−	−	−
Carrow Elicited Language Inventory	−	−	−
Developmental Test of Visual-Motor Integration (Beery)	−	−	−
Developmental Test of Visual Perception (Frostig)	−	−	−
Illinois Test of Psycholinguistic Abilities	−	−	−
Memory for Designs Test	−	−	+
Motor-Free Visual Perception Test	−	−	−
Northwestern Syntax Screening Test	−	−	−
Purdue Perceptual-Motor Survey	−	−	−
Utah Test of Language Development	−	−	−
Wepman Auditory Discrimination Test	−	−	−

+ indicates technically adequate

− indicates technically inadequate (either psychometric characteristic is inadequate or no data are reported in the manual)

[*]Sources: Salvia & Ysseldyke (1981), Thurlow & Ysseldyke (1979), and Ysseldyke et al. (1980a)

Psychology in the Schools, Journal of Learning Disabilities, and *ETS News on Tests.* In addition, there are particular articles and monographs that have critiqued the tests most widely used with special populations (Arter & Jenkins, 1979; Coles, 1968; Farr & Anastasiow, 1969; Larsen, Rogers, & Sowell, 1976; Shepard et al., 1981; Thurlow & Ysseldyke, 1979; Ysseldyke et al., 1980a).

Beyond these evaluations of tests, there are books and pamphlets that describe the characteristics of the tests in catalogue form, including (1) *Tests in Print III* (Mitchell, 1983); (2) *Tests and Measurements in Child Development* (Johnson, 1976); (3) ETS Test Collection Bibliographies; (4) measurement textbooks (e.g. Anastasi, 1982; Gronlund, 1981; Mehrens & Lehmann, 1980; Sattler, 1982); (5) textbooks and handbooks on the assessment of exceptional children (e.g., Backer, 1977; Compton, 1980; Gearheart & Willenberg, 1980; McLoughlin & Lewis, 1981; Salvia & Ysseldyke, 1981; Swanson & Watson, 1982; Wallace & Larsen, 1978; Zigmond, Vallecorsa, & Silverman, 1983).

Confronted with this array of materials on tests and the sheer volume of standardized tests currently available, teachers and specialists might find the task of test selection more complicated and time-consuming than initially anticipated. Therefore, it seems appropriate to present here a brief review of the tests useful for individual screening decisions. It should be regarded as a preliminary analysis and starting point for further evaluation of the tests in terms of specific applications with learning-disabled children.

NORMS, VALIDITY, AND RELIABILITY. Among the critical reviews cited at the beginning of this section, those conducted by Ysseldyke and his colleagues (Salvia & Ysseldyke, 1981; Thurlow & Ysseldyke, 1979; Ysseldyke et al., 1980a) appear to be quite comprehensive and meaningful to decisions about learning-disabled children. The *Standards* were employed as the criteria for technical adequacy in three categories: norms, validity, and reliability. This was qualified further by stating that if the test manual did not include the essential information, the test was judged technically inadequate (Ysseldyke, 1978a). In other words, no analysis of reliability and validity studies outside of that reported in the manual was considered. The findings of their reviews[3] have been compiled and assembled into three tables (Tables 2.4, 2.5, and 2.6) for convenience: one for intelligence and ability tests, one for achievement tests, and one for perceptual-motor and language tests. Each standardized test was rated as either technically adequate (" + ") or technically inadequate ("−"), by category.

---

[3]Inasmuch as three different sources with different authors were used to arrive at these ratings, inconsistencies among the ratings of a single test did occur. Discrepancies were also observed between the tabular ratings and the descriptive appraisal of several tests in Salvia and Ysseldyke (1981). In all of these cases, the final rating was based on the conclusions reached in the descriptive appraisal.

In Table 2.4, 7 of the 17 *intelligence and ability tests* were rated technically adequate in all three categories.[*] These tests are the Cognitive Abilities Test, Kuhlmann-Anderson Intelligence Tests, McCarthy Scales of Children's Abilities, Otis-Lennon School Ability Test, Short Form Test of Academic Aptitude, WISC-R, and Woodcock-Johnson Psychoeducational Battery. Among the 19 *achievement tests* listed in table 2.5, 8 met the criteria: California Achievement Tests, Iowa Tests of Basic Skills, Metropolitan Achievement Tests, Peabody Individual Achievement Tests, Stanford Achievement Test, Stanford Diagnostic Mathematics and Reading Tests, and Woodcock Reading Mastery Tests. Finally, the lowest ratings were assigned to the *perceptual-motor and language tests*, with no test worthy of recommendation. This state of test inadequacy in the area associated with processing disorders lends credence to the notion that the measurement technology lags far behind the search for underlying ability deficits in learning-disabled children. Under no condition could the use of any test named in Table 2.6 be justified.

BIAS. Since so much attention in the learning disabilities literature has been devoted to the topic of nondiscriminatory assessment and bias, a survey of standardized, norm-referenced tests from the perspective of sex, racial, and/or ethnic bias seems apropos. A review of the judgmental and statistical methods employed to "debias" the most popular ability and achievement tests was written recently by representatives of six major test publishers—CTB/McGraw-Hill, The Riverside Publishing Company, The Psychological Corporation, Science Research Associates, The American College Testing Program, and Educational Testing Service. The bias analyses conducted to date are summarized in the *Handbook of Methods for Detecting Test Bias* (Berk, 1982). Table 2.7 was developed to provide an indication of which types of analysis have been completed for 16 standardized tests.

This table and the chapter from which the information was derived (Green et al., 1982) reveal that with the exception of 4 tests (CIRCUS, Sequential

---

[*]At the time this chapter was being written, a new measure of intelligence and achievement for children 2¹/₂ to 12¹/₂ years of age was published, the Kaufman Assessment Battery for Children (K-ABC). Developed by Kaufman and Kaufman (1982), it is described as the first major individually administered intelligence test to separate problem-solving abilities from acquired knowledge. It contains 16 subtests and yields scores in 4 global areas: Sequential Processing, Simultaneous Processing, Mental Processing Composite (Sequential plus Simultaneous), and Achievement. Although the recency of the battery has not permitted any extensive reviews of its technical adequacy to be conducted, a cursory examination indicates the following: (1) exceptional children were systematically included in the norm sample in representative proportions, (2) there is substantial evidence of criterion-related and construct validity, (3) both judgmental review and statistical item bias studies were completed to minimize sex and racial bias, and (4) split-half reliability coefficients for the global scales are adequate for elementary age children. In addition, the mental processing and achievement scales were normed on the same samples, an important condition for discrepancy score analysis (see Chapter 4). Certainly these positive signs suggest that the K-ABC deserves serious attention by school psychologists and learning disability specialists, and further psychometric scrutiny.

MEMORY JOGGER

Table 2.7

Bias Analyses Conducted for Selected Ability and Achievement Tests[a]

Ability/Achievement Test	*Judgmental Review*	*Statistical Analyses*
California Achievement Tests	+	+
CIRCUS	+	−
Cognitive Abilities Test	+	+
Comprehensive Tests of Basic Skills	+	+
Iowa Tests of Basic Skills	+	+
Metropolitan Achievement Tests	+	+
Metropolitan Readiness Tests	+	+
Otis-Lennon School Ability Test	+	+
Sequential Tests of Educational Progress	+	−
Short Form Test of Academic Aptitude	+	−
SRA Achievement Series	+	+
SRA Educational Ability Series	+	+
Stanford Achievement Test	+	−
Test of Cognitive Skills	+	+
Tests of Achievement and Proficiency	+	+
Wechsler Scales	+	+

+ indicates systematic analysis of the test for sex, racial, and/or ethnic bias has been completed

− indicates no analysis for bias is reported by the test publisher

[a]*Source*: Green et al. (1982)

Tests of Educational Progress, Short Form Test of Academic Aptitude, and Stanford Achievement Test), there have been extensive judgmental reviews and statistical studies of bias in most of the current ability and achievement test batteries. The statistical analyses have focused primarily on item bias; predictive and construct bias studies have been conducted for only the WISC-R. These ratings in Table 2.7 should not be misconstrued to mean these tests are unbiased. The determination of bias is a function of both the quality of the studies and the interpretation of the findings. Certainly the test user is in a better position to reach that decision objectively than either the publishers or researchers (see Madaus et al., 1982). However, the commitments and activities of test publishers to eliminate bias in the instruments they develop are significant; bias research is not in the abysmal state that some professionals have suggested Duffey, Salvia, Tucker, & Ysseldyke, 1981; Ysseldyke, 1979; Ysseldyke & Algozzine, 1982).[5]

---

[5]Their appraisal is typically confined to bias in selection models (Jensen, 1980, pp. 391 – 420; Petersen

→

RECOMMENDATIONS. If Tables 2.4 through 2.7 along with other available test reviews are examined carefully from the standpoint of selecting ability and achievement test batteries that are technically adequate and have been investigated for bias, the best combinations of tests produced by the same publisher seem to be the following:

1. Otis-Lennon School Ability Test (OLSAT) and Metropolitan Achievement Tests (MAT, 1978 edition) or Stanford Achievement Test (SAT, 7th edition) published by The Psychological Corporation
2. Cognitive Abilities Test (CogAT) and Iowa Tests of Basic Skills (ITBS) published by The Riverside Publishing Co.
3. Test of Cognitive Skills (TCS) and Comprehensive Tests of Basic Skills (CTBS, Form U) published by CTB/McGraw-Hill
4. Short Form Test of Academic Aptitude (SFTAA) and California Achievement Tests (CAT-70) published by CTB/McGraw-Hill

The OLSAT-MAT combination is preferred because both batteries satisfy the technical adequacy and bias specifications and were also normed on the same standardization sample. Conormed tests are advantageous in computing ability-achievement discrepancy scores (see Chapter 4). The OLSAT succeeds the Otis-Lennon Mental Maturity Test (OLMMT). It yields a single School Ability Index as opposed to separate subtest scores on different categories of ability. The SAT may also be used with the OLSAT (Form S), although it lacks statistical item bias evidence.

The CogAT-ITBS is another comprehensive battery combination. Unlike the OLSAT, the CogAT provides battery scores for Verbal, Nonverbal, and Quantitative abilities. The CogAT and ITBS are technically adequate in all respects, having been thoroughly investigated for bias, and are conormed.

The TCS-CTBS combination, in general, resembles the preceding battery combinations. The TCS, which is the successor to the highly rated Short Form Test of Academic Aptitude (SFTAA), produces four subtest scores for Sequences, Analogies, Memory, and Verbal Reasoning, plus the Cognitive Skills Index for the total test. Although neither the TCS nor the CTBS appears in Tables 2.4 and 2.5, respectively, which are major omissions in the reviews, the technical adequacy and evidence on bias for the two tests are similar to that found for the other batteries. In addition, they are conormed. Alternatively, the SFTAA—CAT can also be used, although they are earlier CTB/McGraw-Hill ability-achievement test batteries. They are as technically defensible as the most recent batteries with the exception that there are no statistical item bias

---

& Novick, 1976). Such bias is not a characteristic of a test or its component items. The problem of selection relates to how a test (biased or unbiased) is used to select persons from a given pool of applicants. The most important types of bias that require attention in the context of "nonbiased assessment" are not addressed. They are item bias, predictive bias, and construct bias, which could invalidate the inferences and decisions to be made with the test scores (Berk, 1982).

studies on the SFTAA. The SFTAA and CAT-70 were also conormed.

The foregoing ratings of 47 standardized tests and these ability-achievement test combinations especially should serve as a stimulus for further evaluation and study of their utility in specific screening applications. Three factors in particular merit special attention: (1) the curricular validity of the achievement tests in relation to programs at the local level, (2) the effectiveness of the tests via screening procedures for identifying children with learning disabilities (see Chapter 5), and (3) the fair use of the tests with sex, racial, and ethnic subgroups of the learning-disabled population. These issues must be addressed by test users before the selection of any ability and achievement tests can be judged psychometrically defensible. The choice among the four top-rated battery combinations may, in fact, be determined easily after a curricular validity analysis of the MAT, SAT, ITBS, CTBS, and CAT has been completed. Furthermore, many other tests not listed in the tables should be considered in order to measure the seven areas of possible performance deficit specified in the *Procedures for Evaluating Specific Learning Disabilities* (U.S.O.E., 1977b, p. 65083). The other reviews cited previously can help guide the selection of instruments in the different content areas.

Technical Quality of Criterion-referenced Tests

Many of the indices of technical quality that distinguish a well-constructed criterion-referenced test from a poorly constructed one can be lumped into the same categories of validity and reliability defined previously for standardized, norm-referenced tests. However, there are marked differences in the statistics used. Inasmuch as each type of test is designed systematically to yield scores for *particular* uses, the selection and estimation of the technical characteristics are governed primarily by the intended interpretation(s) of the test scores and the subsequent decisions based on them. Ergo, the technical aspects of the development process must be addressed in order to assure meaningful results.

The characteristics of standardized, norm-referenced tests and criterion-referenced tests differ as a function of their respective purposes and the decisions for which the scores are used. These purposes and decisions are presented in Table 2.8. The technical characteristics of the tests are outlined in Table 2.9. The special emphases assigned to certain procedures in the development of each test reflect the aforestated purposes. For example, interpretation of performance on a criterion-referenced test in terms of a well-defined content area requires rigorous domain specifications based on objectives and an item review (item-objective congruence). Since the scores on the test are used to classify students as masters and nonmasters of an objective in order to expedite individualized instruction, empirical item analysis procedures are recommended to determine whether the items are instructionally sensitive or discriminate between mastery and nonmastery group performance (Berk, 1980c).

Methods for setting the mastery standard, the estimation of classification errors (decision validity), and the estimation of decision consistency are also very important elements in the development of the criterion-referenced test. A further description of these characteristics will be given in the next section and in Chapters 6 and 7.

Standards for Technical Quality

In evaluating the technical quality of criterion-referenced tests, there is no single set of standards or guidelines one can follow analogous to the *Standards for Educational and Psychological Tests* (APA/AERA/NCME, 1974) used for norm-referenced tests. While it is possible to search through the *Standards* and glean some standards relevant to criterion-referenced tests, the product of this effort will be far from adequate. A recent draft of the next edition of the *Standards* that will be published in 1984 suggests that much more attention will be devoted to standards for criterion-referenced tests. Until that document becomes available, however, test users must rely on the guidelines recommended by a few of the experts in the field (e.g., Swezey & Pearlstein, 1975; Walker, 1977).

Perhaps the most up-to-date and comprehensive collection of standards for selecting and evaluating criterion-referenced tests is the list of questions compiled by Hambleton (1982), which is the extension of an earlier work by Hambleton and Eignor (1978). There are a total of 38 questions written for test users that address the key considerations in judging technical quality: (1) the objectives, (2) the items, (3) test administration, (4) the mastery standard, (5) validity, (6) reliability, and (7) scoring and score interpretation. A sample of

MEMORY JOGGER

Table 2.8

Purposes of Norm-referenced and Criterion-referenced Tests and the
Decisions for Which the Scores Are Used

	Norm-referenced Test	*Criterion-referenced Test*
Purpose	To determine a student's relative standing in comparison to all other students in the norm sample in a broadly defined content area	To determine a student's performance level with respect to a well-defined content area and prespecified mastery standard
Decisions	Screen for learning disabilities; identify children who exhibit a severe ability-achievement discrepancy in one or more subject areas	Diagnose specific learning disabilities; pinpoint skill development weaknesses 1. Identify the instructional objectives that have not been mastered 2. Analyze the degree of nonmastery to suggest the specific deficiencies that need remediation

MEMORY JOGGER

Table 2.9

Technical Characteristics of Norm-referenced and Criterion-referenced Tests[a]

Characteristic	Norm-referenced Test	Criterion-referenced Test
Content Domain Specification	Content outline Table of specifications	Instructional and behavioral objectives
Item Construction	Objective Short answer Essay	Objective Short answer Essay Cloze
Test Length	Based on reliability	Based on decision validity and decision reliability
Item Analysis	Difficulty index Discrimination index Choice response analysis to revise faulty items	Item-objective congruence Difficulty indices (mastery and nonmastery groups) Discrimination index (between mastery and nonmastery group performance) Choice response analysis to revise faulty items
Norm Sample	Required	———————————
Mastery Standard	———————————	Required
Validity	Content (Curricular) Criterion related Construct	Content (Curricular) Criterion related (Decision) Construct
Reliability	Stability Equivalence Stability and equivalence Internal consistency Interscorer consistency	Decision consistency (Stability or stability and equivalence)

[a]Adapted from Berk (1984).

the most important questions related to these topics follows. For explanations and further information on specific questions, the reader should consult the appropriate section in Hambleton's (1982, pp. 375 – 378) chapter.

Objectives

- Do the objectives measured in the test provide a comprehensive coverage of the area they purport to measure?

Source note: From "Advances in criterion-referenced testing technology" by Ronald K. Hambleton, in C.R. Reynolds and T.B. Gutkin (Eds.), *The Handbook of School Psychology*, Copyright© 1982, John Wiley & Sons. Reprinted by permission of the author and John Wiley & Sons, Inc.

- Does the set of objectives measured by the test have "curricular relevance"?
- Are the objectives clearly written?
- Is it possible to "tailor" the test to meet local needs by selecting objectives that will be measured?
- Is an acceptable justification provided for including each objective in the test?

Items

- Was the item review process carried out correctly?
- Does the content of the test items match the content defined by the objectives they were written to measure?
- Are the test items technically sound?
- Is the chosen format appropriate for providing valid test score information in relation to the objectives measured by the test?
- Are the test items representative of the item domains they were drawn from?
- Are the test items free of bias and stereotyping?
- Was a suitable sample of examinees used to pilot test the items?
- Were item statistics used correctly in building the test?

Test Administration

- Do the test directions inform examinees about the tests' purposes, time limits, marking answer sheets (or booklets) and scoring? Are sample questions available?
- Are the answer sheets easy for examinees to use?
- Are the test administrators' directions complete?
- Are the responsibilities of the examiner before and after testing described clearly in the administrator's manual?

Mastery Standard

- Is an explanation offered in the technical manual for the selection of a standard-setting method? (Alternatively, is a process described in the technical manual to help users select and apply a standard-setting method?)
- Was the standard-setting method implemented correctly?

Validity

- Is evidence offered for the validity of the mastery classifications?
- Is validity evidence offered for each intended use of the test scores?
- Are the results of validation studies reported in the technical manual?
- Does the technical manual provide a discussion of factors which might influence the validity of test scores and decisions?

Reliability

- Are the samples of examinees included in any reliability studies of a suitable size, and representative of the population(s) in which the test will be used?
- Are the correct kinds of reliability indexes reported?

- Are the appropriate reliability indexes high enough to justify the use of the test for the intended purpose and situation?
- Is a discussion of the factors that influence reliability indices provided in the technical manual?

Scoring and Score Interpretation

- If hand scoring is possible, is it relatively easy to do?
- Are guidelines offered in the technical manual for correctly interpreting test scores?
- Do the score report forms address the specific need of users?
- Are the score report forms convenient and understandable?
- Are convenient score report forms available if individuals choose to score the tests by hand?

In this list of questions, those most critical to the selection of a commercially developed criterion-referenced test relate to the mastery standard, validity, and reliability. Interestingly, however, the bulk of available criterion-referenced tests are built by classroom teachers and district – and state-level evaluators. It seems appropriate, then, to describe these technical characteristics for both test users and test makers. The information in Table 2.9 and the preceding questions may also be viewed either as criteria for selecting a criterion-referenced test or as guidelines for constructing one. Since two subsequent chapters (6 and 7) treat the three characteristics in the context of diagnostic decision making, only a brief examination of alternative statistical methods is given here.

Mastery Standard

The mastery standard is the cutting score used to determine whether a student is a master or nonmaster of a particular instructional objective (for a detailed explanation and examples, see Chapter 6). More than 20 different methods for setting performance standards have been recommended in the measurement literature. Despite several extensive reviews of these methods by Berk (1980b), Hambleton (1980b; Hambleton & Powell, 1983), Livingston and Zieky (1982), Popham (1981, Chap. 16), and Shepard (1980, in press), standard setting is still the stickiest technical topic. One of the simplest frameworks for understanding the various methods is the bilevel classification scheme devised by Berk (1980b). It can be used to sort out all of the approaches that have been proposed. The first level partitions the methods into two major categories based on their assumptions about the acquisition of the underlying trait or ability: state models and continuum models. The second level classifies the methods according to whether they are based purely on judgment or incorporate both judgmental and empirical information: judgmental methods and judgment-empirical methods/models.

STATE MODELS. State models assume that mastery is an all-or-nothing state; the standard is set at 100%. Deviations from this true state are presumed attributable to classification errors, false mastery and/or false nonmastery errors (see Chapter 6). After a consideration of these errors, the standard is adjusted downward to values less than 100%. Glass (1978) referred to these models as "counting backwards from 100%" (p. 244). The various models that fall into the judgmental-empirical category employ decision rules to identify the mastery standard that minimizes the consequences of classification errors.

Considering the amount of research that has accumulated on standard setting, the state models have received relatively little attention. The lack of attention might be due to the statistical complexity of the models (see Macready & Dayton, 1980), and to a few limitations that render them less compatible with current practices in criterion-referenced testing than the continuum models (Berk, 1980b).

CONTINUUM MODELS. Continuum models assume that mastery is a continuously distributed ability that can be viewed as an interval on a continuum, i.e., an area at the upper end of the continuum circumscribes the boundaries for mastery. This assumption appears to fit the design and intent of most criterion-referenced tests. It is therefore not surprising that much of the research on standard setting has concentrated on these models.

The *judgmental methods* are based on judgments of the probability that masters would select particular distractors (incorrect choices) in a multiple-choice item (Nedelsky, 1954) or the probability that they would answer the item correctly (Angoff, 1971; Ebel, 1979; Jaeger, 1978). The subjectivity of these item content decisions used to arrive at an overall mastery standard has been expressed succinctly as: Judges have the sense that they are "pulling the probabilities from thin air" (Shepard, 1980, p. 453). This problem is reflected in the inconsistency of judgments within a single method and also across methods.

The *judgmental-empirical methods* are based on some type of judgment and actual or simulated data, judgmental data, and/or distribution assumptions (Berk, 1980b). The role of judgment in these methods should not be underestimated. That is, the judgmental component usually supplies the foundation for much of the statistical estimation of probabilities of correct classification decisions and false mastery/false nonmastery decision errors (for a further explanation, see Chapter 6).

The judgmental-empirical methods differ according to other characteristics as well, including their overall purpose, statistical sophistication, and practicability. Perhaps the most important initial distinction pertains to their purpose. Only the criterion groups (Berk, 1976) and contrasting groups (Livingston & Zieky, 1982) approaches are intended to *select* a mastery standard. All of the remaining methods presume that a standard already exists. Subsequently, this standard is translated into a cutting score for the test (e.g., 4 out of 5 items correct), and decision error rates based on various assumptions are estimated. In some cases, those rates can be used to adjust the cutting score.

The decision-theoretic approaches, which are the most theoretically and statistically complex continuum methods, are actually not techniques for setting standards or optimizing mastery decisions; they *are* techniques for minimizing the consequences of measurement and sampling errors once the true cutting score has already been chosen (van der Linden, 1980).

RECOMMENDATIONS. This review suggests preference should be given to the judgmental-empirical methods based on the continuum model. The criterion groups and contrasting-groups approaches especially appear to fit the requirements of decisions made by classroom teachers and learning disability specialists. A detailed explication of those approaches is presented in Chapter 6. That presentation is oriented toward teachers who construct their own diagnostic tests. For test users who are interested in selecting a commercially developed or customized criterion-referenced test, it is important that the procedures for setting mastery standards are described fully in the manual so their statistical soundness and appropriateness can be evaluated. Too often, a cutting score, such as 3 out of 3 items answered correctly, which indicates mastery, is designated in the manual or on a computer printout with no accompanying explanation.

For individual diagnostic decisions, it is also recommended that a mastery standard be chosen for each item cluster or subtest keyed to an instructional objective. There is nothing implicit in any of the methods that dictates that the standard has to be identical for all subtests. There is no basis for the customary use of one "blanket mastery standard" such as 80% for all objectives. There are three reasons for this position. First, objectives vary in level of complexity and, therefore, applying the same standard to different objectives will be insensitive to that variability. Second, the difficulty and discrimination indices of items measuring one objective may be quite different from the indices of items measuring other objectives; consequently, it is unrealistic to expect a high proportion of students will attain the same standard for each objective. Third, since the instruction associated with different objectives is rarely given the same time allotment and emphasis, performance on some objectives might be noticeably better than the performance on others. Again, this is inconsistent with setting the same standard for all objectives.

Validity

From Table 2.9 it is apparent that all of the types of validity described for standardized tests are also applicable to criterion-referenced tests. However, inasmuch as validity relates to the purposes for which a test is constructed and is specific to a particular score use, the emphases are quite different. The few relatively recent discussions of validity for criterion-referenced tests by Hambleton (1980b, in press), Linn (1979b, 1980), and Millman (1979) stress content, criterion related, and decision validity.

CONTENT VALIDITY. One theme permeating much of the research on criterion-referenced measurement is that content validity via explicit content domain specifications is essential to assure clarity and meaning in test score interpretation. Numerous strategies that extend or replace existing objectives-based specifications have been proposed (see Chapter 3). For commercially developed tests, these specifications must be reported in the manual in order to judge the content representativeness as well as the *curricular* and *instructional validity* of the items.

When a test is customized, such that teachers select objectives from a catalogue and items previously matched to those objectives are generated to compose the test, this review process is especially important. Three characteristics must be evaluated: (1) the match between the objectives and the curriculum, (2) the match between the items and the objectives (item-objective congruence), and (3) the representativeness of the items. Several procedures for assessing the last two involving rating scales and matching tasks have been suggested by Berk (1980c) and Hambleton (1980b). Methods for determining curricular and instructional validity were mentioned in the validity section on standardized tests. (*Note*: Curricular validity is not a special concern in teacher-made criterion-referenced tests since the tests are usually built from curricular specifications; similarly, instructional validity is reflected in the instructional materials actually used in the classroom.)

Another related issue in this content review is *bias*. Although most attention has been directed at "debiasing" standardized intelligence, ability, and achievement tests, due in part to litigation, the P.L. 94-142 mandate for nondiscriminatory evaluation would also apply to criterion-referenced tests. Clearly, they are "testing . . . materials . . . utilized for the purposes of evaluation and placement of handicapped children" (Sec. 612). A convenient review form prepared by Hambleton (1980a), shown in Table 2.10, can be used by teachers to detect stereotypic, culture-specific, and offensive language in the tests they construct and in those developed commercially. In addition, statistical item and test bias studies of criterion-referenced tests should be conducted by publishers with the rigor and commitment accorded such studies of norm-referenced tests. Only when the results of these studies are reported in the test manuals can the users determine whether the tests are "racially or culturally discriminatory."

CRITERION–RELATED VALIDITY. Despite the importance attached to the preceding procedures for establishing content validity and curricular and instructional validity, they are necessary but not sufficient to support the diverse interpretations and uses of criterion-referenced tests (cf. Linn, 1980). Other kinds of evidence are needed. For example, mastery decision making provides a specific focus for investigations of criterion-related validity. As noted in the previous description of this topic, the most complex and problematic aspect of

Table 2.10

Item Review Form to Detect Bias·

Reviewer: _____ Date: _____ Objective: _____

This review form has been designed to assist in the identification of test items which may reflect sex, cultural, racial, regional and/or ethnic content bias and stereotyping. Place your name, the date, and the objective number at the top of the review form.

In the spaces at the right under the heading "Test Item Number" provide the numbers of the test items you will review. When the number of test items for review exceeds ten, use a second review form.

Next, read each test item and answer the six questions below. Use "✔" for YES, "X" for NO, "?" for UNSURE, and "NA" for NOT APPLICABLE. When your rating is negative ("X" or "?"), indicate what you think is the problem in the test item and suggest a revision on your copy of the test item.

When you have completed your review task, staple the test items to your review form(s) and return.

	Test Item Number									
1. Is the item free of *offensive* sex, cultural, racial, regional and/or ethnic content?										
2. Is the item free of sex, cultural, racial, and/or ethnic stereotyping?										
3. Is the item free of language which could be offensive to a segment of the examinee population?										
4. Is the item free from descriptions which could be offensive to a segment of the examinee population?										
5. Will the activities described in the item be equally familiar (or equally unfamiliar) to all examinees?										
6. Will the words in the item have a common meaning for all examinees?										

·*Source:* Revised version of Hambleton (1980a) review form by Ronald K. Hambleton, May 1981. Reprinted by permission of the author.

this line of inquiry pertains to the definition of the success or, in this case, the mastery criterion. An operational definition must be specified and criterion successful (masters) and unsuccessful (nonmasters) students have to be identified (for details, see Chapter 6). The criterion-related validity studies may be predictive or concurrent depending upon how success is defined, e.g., success in the next unit of instruction or course, success in the current program. Publishers are urged to obtain this type of validity evidence so that the specific uses of the scores by teachers are appropriate and defensible.

DECISION VALIDITY. The previous section on decision validity stressed the significance of knowing the extent to which a test can yield accurate decisions. When mastery-nonmastery classification decisions constitute the framework for diagnosing skill-development strengths and weaknesses, the ultimate value or usefulness of the criterion-referenced test is contingent on the nature of the decision validity evidence. If the probabilities of correct and incorrect (false mastery and false nonmastery) classifications for a given subtest are judged acceptable, then that subtest is effective; if the probabilities are unacceptable, then the subtest is ineffective and virtually useless in accomplishing what it was designed to do. Such evidence is also crucial in attempting to justify the selection of the mastery standard. Furthermore, when decision validity evidence is not available, it seems pointless even to compute a reliability index (see Chapter 7). The step-by-step procedures for gathering, interpreting, and reporting this evidence are outlined in Chapter 6. The procedures are presented in conjunction with the criterion-groups approach to setting mastery standards.

Reliability

Similar to the topic of standard setting, the literature is replete with studies and reviews of criterion-referenced test reliability. More than a dozen indices have been proposed, and critical reviews of those indices have been completed by Berk (1980a, in press), Hambleton, Swaminathan, Algina, Coulson (1978), Linn (1979a), Millman (1979), and Traub and Rowley (1980).

DECISION CONSISTENCY. One strategy that reflects the purpose, decisions, and characteristics of the criterion-referenced test defined in Table 2.9 is to determine the consistency of mastery-nonmastery classification decisions. Two possible indices of decision consistency are p, percentage of students consistently classified as masters and nonmasters across repeated measures with one test form or equivalent test forms, and x, percentage of students consistency classified beyond that expected by chance. The research comparing various one – and two-administration estimates of these indices reveals that the Hambleton and Novick (1973) method for estimating p (described in detail in Chapter 7) and the Huynh (1976) method for estimating p and x may be especially useful (Berk, 1980a; Subkoviak, 1980). When distinctions among degrees of mastery and nonmastery along the score continuum are desirable, not just the qualitative mastery-nonmastery classification assumed by the p and x indices, the Livingston (1972) $k^2 (X, T_x)$ index derived from classical test theory should be considered.

Whatever approach to reliability is chosen, the method of estimation, rationale for selection, and the resulting indices should be reported in the criterion-referenced test manual. For teacher-made tests used for diagnostic decisions, the easily calculable and interpretable p index based the test-retest method is recommended. Either a stability or stability-equivalence estimate can be obtained. Chapter 7 is devoted entirely to the p index.

Evaluation of Technical Quality

As indicated previously, the bulk of available criterion-referenced tests are built at the classroom, district, and state levels. Relatively few criterion-referenced tests have been prepared by commercial test publishers. Those that have been published, sometimes called criterion-referenced testing systems or diagnostic-prescriptive instructional packages, unfortunately were developed prior to the emergence of an adequate testing technology. Consequently, their overall quality is less than desirable.

MASTERY STANDARD, VALIDITY, AND RELIABILITY. Several critical reviews of criterion-referenced tests have appeared in *The Eighth Mental Measurements Yearbook* (Buros, 1978) and many more will be seen in the soon-to-be-published ninth edition of the *MMY* (Mitchell & Witt, in press). However, the most comprehensive appraisal of the major tests that has been completed to date is the review by Hambleton and Eignor (1978). They developed numerous guidelines for evaluating the quality of criterion-referenced tests and their accompanying manuals, most of which were listed in a preceding section. Nine of these guidelines pertain to the technical characteristics of the mastery standard, validity, and reliability. [*Note*: In Hambleton's (1982) revision of these guidelines, 10 relate to these characteristics.] Hambleton and Eignor's ratings of the acceptability of eight popular test packages published between 1974 and 1977 are summarized in Table 2.11 according to those three characteristics. Their original rating scheme has been adapted so that the symbols resemble the rating format used for the standardized tests. Each criterion-referenced test was rated as either technically acceptable (" + "), technically acceptable with reservations ("✓"), or technically unacceptable (" − "), by category.

The generally poor quality of these tests (as shown in Table 2.11) illustrates the gap between theory and practice in the decade of the 70s and is clearly communicated in Hambleton and Eignor's (1978) comments on the primary technical problems with the various tests:

[1] Test score reliability was not handled very well in most of the manuals. Either (a) inappropriate information relative to the stated uses of the test scores was offered, or (b) no information was offered.

[2] Cut-off scores are typically offered, but there is no rationale offered for setting cut-off scores. Procedures used for setting cut-off scores are not explained, nor is any evidence offered for the "validity" of cut-off scores (for example, do those examinees classified as "masters" typically perform better than "nonmasters" on some appropriately chosen external criterion measure?).

[3] Factors affecting the validity of scores are not offered in any of the manuals.

[4] Only a few of the manuals introduced the notion of "error" in test scores. It is extremely important for users to have some indication of the "stability" of their objective scores and/or "consistency of mastery/non-mastery decision." (p. 325)

RECOMMENDATIONS. These conclusions about the most popular tests barely capture the concerns that a teacher might have in selecting a particular test.

MEMORY JOGGER

Table 2.11

Ratings of the Technical Acceptability of Selected Criterion-referenced Tests[a]

Test	Mastery Standard	Validity	Reliability
Diagnosis: An Instructional Aid — Mathematics and Reading	–	–	–
Diagnostic Mathematics Inventory	–	+	–
Fountain Valley Support System in Mathematics	–	–	–
Individual Pupil Monitoring System — Mathematics	–	–	–
Mastery: An Evaluation Tool — Mathematics	✔	✔	–
Mastery: An Evaluation Tool — SOBAR Reading	✔	✔	–
Prescriptive Reading Inventory	✔	+	–
Skills Monitoring System — Reading	✔	+	✔

+ indicates technically acceptable

✔ indicates technically acceptable, with reservations

– indicates technically unacceptable (either data offered were unsuitable or improperly used or no data were offered)

[a]*Source*: Adapted from the ratings by Hambleton and Eignor (1978)

The time-consuming task of assessing curricular validity still rests with the classroom teacher. Evidence that available tests are unbiased with regard to sex, racial, and ethnic subgroups of the learning-disabled population does not exist; in fact, the investigation of bias in criterion-referenced tests by publishers has hardly begun.

Given these significant technical inadequacies, none of the aforementioned tests are worthy of recommendation for use in the diagnosis of specific learning disabilities at the classroom level. Unless the inadequacies have been corrected in test editions subsequent to the 1978 ratings, the individual mastery-nonmastery decisions made with the scores from those tests would be psychometrically indefensible. At present, teachers are advised to construct their own criterion-referenced tests based on the criteria defined in the preceding sections and in Chapters 6 and 7.

Technical Quality of Informal Measures

In the introduction to this chapter, norm-referenced tests and criterion-referenced tests were labeled as formal instruments or measures. P.L. 94-142 emphasizes the use of such tests for screening and diagnosis because their technical quality is known, and consequently, many of them are psychometrically defensible. In contrast, informal measures are widely used by learning disability specialists, reading specialists, and classroom teachers for diagnosis of learning problems, yet their quality is unknown, and they are defensible only in terms of curricular validity, i.e., high degree of congruence with the instructional program.

Informal measures can exist in a variety of forms. They may consist of the following classroom materials:

1. tests and quizzes
2. behavior checklists and inventories
3. rating scales
4. seat-work exercises
5. orally administered exercises
6. informal teaching lessons
7. individually administered written assignments

These measures typically focus on specific skills as opposed to surveying broad domains of content (Wallace & Kauffman, 1973).

Among the different subject areas, the one that has received a preponderance of attention is *reading*. There are numerous books and pamphlets that contain informal reading inventories, or IRIs (e.g., Burns & Roe, 1980; The Reading Clinic, 1964), and provide collections of sources and guidelines for constructing do-it-yourself measures (e.g., Johns, Garton, Schoenfedler, & Skriba, 1977; Johnson & Kress, 1965; Mann & Suiter, 1974). In regard to their technical quality, Pikulski (1974) argues that

> classroom use of informal reading inventories that are based on materials that are being considered for instruction probably does not need to be subjected to most traditional evaluation procedures by which reliability and validity are judged. There *is* a strong case for "face validity." (p. 143)

This author concurs with that position based on the practical constraints and the types of decisions that are made within the classroom. The trouble is that their use has been extended to school and district level decisions, including screening and diagnosis. This practice is an entirely inappropriate and an invalid use of the test scores.

This strong emphasis on reading and reading difficulties has also fostered the notion the "reading disability is learning disability." Inasmuch as basic reading skill and reading comprehension constitute only two of the seven potential discrepancy achievement areas defined in the *Procedures for Evaluating Specific Learning Disabilities* (U.S.O.E., 1977b), this notion is imperceptive and inaccurate. As Coles (1968) pointed out:

> An individual might be learning disabled and still have adequate reading skills; his [or her] problems can be in other areas such as speaking and writing. Despite this, the overwhelming number of children identified as learning disabled in either

schools or clinics are poor readers; they may or may not have other language difficulties. (p. 316)

Heretofore, speaking, listening, writing, and perceptual motor assessment especially have been given less attention. This is evidenced by the relative spar-
sity and poor quality of informal, as well as formal, measures in these areas (see
Brown, Backlund, Gerry, & Jandt, 1979; Hammill & Bartel, 1978; Mead, in
press; Quellmalz, in press; Salvia & Ysseldyke, 1981).

Many of the informal measures referred to previously have often been considered as one type of criterion-referenced test. Actually they are objectives-
referenced tests without technical support. Their value as tools in the
teaching-learning process resides principally in detecting individual strengths
and weaknesses on a day-to-day basis, which permits the teacher to monitor
each student's progress in the instructional program (Beldin, 1970). The resulting information can assist the teacher in formulating and reformulating remedial programs to meet each student's needs.

As far as formal screening and diagnosis of children with learning disabilities are concerned, these informal measures should play a supplementary and
comparatively minor role. This is due in large part to their unknown technical
properties and suspected unreliability (Fuchs, Fuchs, & Deno, 1981) as well as
invalidity (Powell, 1971). The scoring and interpretation of the scores from
most informal measures, particularly the direct observational checklists and
rating scales, are highly subjective and, therefore, lack replicability from one
teacher to another. Consequently, individual diagnostic decisions derived from
their data base would be confounded with the idiosyncratic interpretations of
the scores by different teachers.

Therefore, it is recommended that once the primary information has been
extracted from the selected formal instruments, the informal measures should
serve to fill in the assessment gaps where formal devices are either inadequate
or unavailable and to furnish *suggestive* information about individual skill
strengths and weaknesses. The informal measures should not be used either to
confirm or to disconfirm the evidence obtained from the formal devices (cf.
Bennett, 1982). These functions appear to be consistent with the Rules and
Regulations for compliance with P.L. 94-142 (U.S.O.E., 1977b).

Summary

This chapter presented standards and specific guidelines for selecting
standardized, norm-referenced ability and achievement tests for large-scale
screening. In the evaluation of these tests, particular emphasis was given to the
technical characteristics of norms, validity, and reliability. Brief definitions of
the characteristics were provided along with criteria for judging their adequacy.
A step-by-step procedure for selecting a battery of standardized tests is listed:

1. Evaluate the quality of the standardized tests currently being used for screening and/or as part of the district-wide testing program
   a. Use Tables 2.4 through 2.7 as a starting point
   b. Determine the curricular validity of the achievement tests
   c. Analyze available evidence related to sex, racial, and ethnic bias for both the ability and achievement tests
   d. Estimate the level of the tests appropriate for the learning-disabled children in the district
   e. Identify the areas of possible achievement deficit among the seven areas listed in the *Procedures for Evaluating Specific Learning Disabilities* (U.S.O.E., 1977b) that are not measured by the testing program
2. Consider adding or substituting technically adequate ability and achievement tests where they are needed to fill in gaps in the coverage
3. From steps 1 and 2, pair the ability and achievement tests that are either conormed or have comparable norms
   a. Match the verbal ability test with the verbally based achievement subtests (e.g., vocabulary, reading comprehension, capitalization, punctuation, usage, spelling)
   b. Match the quantitative ability test with the mathematics achievement subtests (e.g., concepts, problems, computations)
   c. Alternatively, the nonverbal ability test can be used in conjunction with the reading, language, and mathematics achievement subtests; however, this approach is not as sound as a and b on either conceptual or statistical grounds (for an explanation, see Chapter 8)

A similar framework was also provided for selecting commercially developed criterion-referenced tests to pinpoint skill weaknesses in the subject areas identified by the screening procedure. The evaluation of these tests according to guidelines for setting the mastery standard and estimating validity and reliability produced rather negative findings. Consequently, the test user may be required to assume the role of test maker in order to obtain usable diagnostic tests. A step-by-step procedure for selecting and constructing criterion-referenced tests is summarized as follows:

1. Evaluate the quality of accessible criterion-referenced tests developed by commercial publishers
   a. Use Table 2.11 as a starting point
   b. Determine the curricular validity of the tests
   c. Conduct a judgmental review of the items for possible bias using the form in Table 2.10
2. Construct criterion-referenced tests in the specific content areas where they are needed
   a. Use the guidelines presented in Table 2.9 and the resources cited in

the text to initiate the process

b. Use the procedures in Chapters 6 and 7 to set the mastery standard and estimate decision validity and reliability

The final section in the chapter was devoted to a discussion of informal measures. It was emphasized that due to their unknown technical characteristics, except curricular validity, and suspected unreliability, they should be used principally to detect individual skill strengths and weaknesses on a day-to-day basis. In regard to screening and diagnosis, the informal measures should not be used either to confirm or to disconfirm the evidence gathered from the formal assessment devices.

References

Adelman, H.S. Diagnostic classification of learning problems: Some data. *American Journal of Orthopsychiatry,* 1978, *48*, 717 – 726.

Anastasi, A. *Psychological testing* (5th ed.). New York: Macmillan, 1982.

Angoff, W.H. Scales, norms, and equivalent scores. In R.L. Thorndike (Ed.), *Educational measurement* (2nd ed.). Washington, DC: American Council on Education, 1971. Pp. 508 – 600.

Angoff, W.H. Use of difficulty and discrimination indices for detecting item bias. In R.A. Berk (Ed.), *Handbook of methods for detecting test bias.* Baltimore, MD: Johns Hopkins University Press, 1982. Pp. 96 – 116.

APA/AERA/NCME Joint Committee. *Standards for educational and psychological tests* (rev. ed.) Washington, DC: American Psychological Association, 1974.

Armstead et al. v. *Starkville Mississippi Municipal Separate School District,* No. EC 70-51-5 (N.D. Miss., 1972).

Arter, J.A., & Jenkins, J.R. Differential diagnosis — prescriptive teaching: A critical appraisal. *Review of Educational Research,* 1979, *49*, 517 – 555.

Baca, L., & Chinn, P.C. Coming to grips with cultural diversity. *Exceptional Education Quarterly,* 1982, *2*, 33 – 45.

Backer, T.E. *A directory of information on tests* (TM Report 62). Princeton, NJ: ERIC Clearinghouse on Tests, Measurement, and Evaluation, Educational Testing Service, 1977.

Beldin, H.O. Informal reading testing: Historical review and review of the research. In W.K. Durr (Ed.) *Reading difficulties: Diagnosis, correction, and remediation.* Newark, DE: International Reading Association, 1970. Pp. 67 – 84.

Bennett, R.E. Methods for evaluating the performance of school psychologists. *School Psychology Monograph,* 1980, *4*, 45 – 59.

Bennett, R.E. Professional competence and the assessment of exceptional children. *Journal of Special Education,* 1981, *15*, 437 – 446.

Bennett, R.E. Cautions on the use of informal measures in the educational assessment of exceptional children. *Journal of Learning Disabilities,* 1982, *15*, 337 – 339.

Bennett, R.E., & Shepherd, M.J. Basic measurement proficiency of learning disability specialists. *Learning Disability Quarterly,* 1982, *5*, 177 – 184.

Berk, R.A. Determination of optimal cutting scores in criterion-referenced measurement. *Journal of Experimental Education,* 1976, *45*, 4 – 9.

Berk, R.A. Generalizability of behavioral observations: A clarification of interobserver agreement and interobserver reliability. *American Journal of Mental Deficiency,* 1979, *83*, 460 – 472.

Berk, R.A. A consumers' guide to criterion-referenced test reliability. *Journal of Educational*

Measurement, 1980, *17*, 323 – 349; Errata, 1981, *18*, 131.(a)

Berk, R.A. A framework for methodological advances in criterion-referenced testing. *Applied Psychological Measurement*, 1980, *4*, 563 – 573.(b)

Berk, R.A. Item analysis. In R.A. Berk (Ed.), *Criterion-referenced measurement: The state of the art*. Baltimore, MD: Johns Hopkins University Press, 1980. Pp. 49 – 79.(c)

Berk, R.A. (Ed.). *Handbook of methods for detecting test bias*. Baltimore, MD: Johns Hopkins University Press, 1982.

Berk, R.A. Criterion-referenced tests. In T. Husén & T.N. Postlethwaite (Eds.), *International encyclopedia of education: Research and studies*. Oxford, England: Pergamon Press, 1984.

Berk, R.A. Selecting an index of reliability. In R.A., Berk (Ed.), *A guide to criterion-referenced test construction*. Baltimore, MD: Johns Hopkins University Press, in press.

Bersoff, D.N. Regarding psychologists testily: Legal regulation of psychological assessment in the public schools. *Maryland Law Review*, 1979, *39*, 27 – 120.

Bersoff, D.N. The legal regulation of school psychology. In C.R. Reynolds & T.B. Gutkin (Eds.), *The handbook of school psychology*. New York: Wiley, 1982. Pp. 1043 – 1074.

Bersoff, D.N. *Larry P. and PASE*: Judicial report cards on the validity of individual intelligence tests. In T.R. Kratochwill (Ed.), *Advances in school psychology* (Vol. 2). Hillsdale, NJ: Erlbaum, in press.

Bersoff, D.N., & Veltman, E.S. Public Law 94-142: Legal implications for the education of handicapped children. *Journal of Research and Development in Education*, 1979, *12*, 10 – 22.

Blackhurst, A.E., & Hofmeister, A.M. Technology in special education. In L. Mann & D.A. Sabatino (Eds.), *The fourth review of special education*. New York: Grune & Stratton, 1980. Pp. 119 – 228.

Bower, R. *Matching standardized achievement test items to local curriculum objectives*. Symposium paper presented at the annual meeting of the National Council on Measurement in Education, New York, March 1982.

Bransford, L. Social issues in special education: Stop gap measures may be a form of cultural genocide. *Phi Delta Kappan*, 1974, *55*, 530 – 532.

Brennan, R.L. *Elements of generalizability theory*. Iowa City, IA: American College Testing Program, 1983.

Brim, O.G., Jr. American attitudes towards intelligence tests. *American Psychologist*, 1965, *20*, 125 – 130.

Brown, K.L., Backlund, P., Gurry, J., & Jandt, F. *Assessment of basic speaking and listening skills: State of the art and recommendations for instrument development* (Vols. 1 and 2). Boston: Bureau of Research and Assessment, Massachusetts Department of Education, 1979.

Burns, P.C., & Roe, B.D. *Informal reading assessment*. Chicago: Rand McNally, 1980.

Burrill, L.E. Comparative studies of item bias methods. In R.A. Berk (Ed.), *Handbook of methods for detecting test bias*. Baltimore, MD: Johns Hopkins University Press, 1982. Pp. 161 – 179.

Buros, O.K. (Ed.) *The eighth mental measurements yearbook*. Highland Park, NJ: Gryphon Press, 1978.

Burt, C. The analysis of examination marks. In P. Hartog & E.C. Rhodes (Eds.), *The marks of examiners*. London: Macmillan, 1936.

Cassidy-Bronson, S.A. *The verification of competencies important for special educators and the development of a classroom observation checklist based on the competencies*. Unpublished doctoral dissertation, The Johns Hopkins University, 1983.

Cegelka, W.J. The competencies needed by persons responsible for classifying children with learning disabilities. *Journal of Special Education*, 1982, *16*, 65 – 71.

Cleary, T.A., Test bias: Prediction of grades of Negro and white students in integrated colleges. *Journal of Educational Measurement*, 1968, *5*, 115 – 124.

Cleary, T.A., Humphreys, L.G., Kendrick, S.A., & Wesman, A. Educational uses of tests with disadvantaged students. *American Psychologist,* 1975, *30,*15 – 41.

Coles, G.S. The learning-disabilities test battery: Empirical and social issues. *Harvard Educational Review,* 1968, *48,* 313 – 340.

Compton, C. *A guide to 65 tests for special education.* Belmont, CA: Fearon Education, 1980.

CORRC (Coordinating Office on Regional Resource Centers). *With bias toward none.* Lexington: University of Kentucky, 1976.

Cronbach, L.J. Coefficient alpha and the internal structure of tests. *Psychometrika,* 1951, *16,* 292 – 334.

Cronbach, L.J Five decades of public controversy over mental testing. *American Psychologist,* 1975, *30,* 1 – 14.

Cronbach, L.J. Validity on parole: How can we go straight? In W.B. Schrader (Ed.), *New directions for testing and measurement* (No. 5)—*Measuring achievement: Progress over a decade.* San Francisco: Jossey-Bass, 1980. Pp. 99 – 108.

Cronbach, L.J., Gleser, G.C., Nanda, H., & Rajaratnam, N. *The dependability of behavioral measurements: Theory of generalizability for scores and profiles.* New York: Wiley, 1972.

Cronbach, L.J., & Meehl, P.E. Construct validity in psychological tests. *Psychological Bulletin,* 1955, *52,* 281 – 302.

Cronbach, L.J., Rajaratnam, N., & Gleser, G.C. Theory of generalizability: A liberalization of reliability theory. *British Journal of Statistical Psychology,* 1963, *16,* 137 – 163.

Cureton, E.E. Validity. In E.F. Lindquist (Ed.), *Educational measurement.* Washington, DC: American Council on Education, 1951. Pp. 621 – 694.

Davis, W.A., & Shepard, L.A. The use of tests and clinical-judgment by specialists in the diagnosis of learning disabilities. *Learning Disabilities Quarterly,* in press.

Division for Children with Learning Disabilities. *Competencies for teachers of learning disabled children and youth.* Reston, VA: Author, 1978.

Duffey, J.B., Salvia, J., Tucker, J., & Ysseldyke, J.E. Nonbiased assessment: A need for operationalism. *Exceptional Children,* 1981, *47,* 427 – 434.

Ebel, R.L. Estimation of the reliability of ratings. *Psychometrika,* 1951, *16,* 407 – 424.

Ebel, R.L. *Essentials of educational measurement.* Englewood Cliffs, NJ: Prentice-Hall, 1979.

Farr, R., & Anastasiow, N. *Tests of reading readiness and achievement: A review and evaluation.* Newark, DE: International Reading Association, 1969.

Frederick, L. v. *Thomas,* 419 960 (E.D. Pa. 1976), *aff'd,* 557 F.2d 373 (3d Cir. 1977).

Freeman, M., & Becker, R. Competencies for professionals in learning disabilities: An analysis of teacher perceptions. *Learning Disability Quarterly,* 1979, *2,* 70 – 79.

Fuchs, L., Fuchs, D., & Deno, S. *Reliability and validity of curriculum-based informal reading inventories* (Research Report No. 59). Minneapolis: University of Minnesota Institute for Research on Learning Disabilities, October 1981.

Gearheart, B.R., & Willenberg, E.P. *Application of pupil assessment information.* Denver, CO: Love, 1980.

Glass, G.V. Standards and criteria. *Journal of Educational Measurement,* 1978, *15,* 237 – 261.

Gonzales, E. Issues in the assessment of minorities. In H.L. Swanson & B.L. Watson, *Educational and psychological assessment of exceptional children: Theories, strategies, and applications.* St. Louis: Mosby, 1982. Pp. 375 – 389.

Green, D.R. *Content validity of standardized achievement tests and test curriculum overlap.* Symposium paper presented at the annual meeting of the National Council on Measurement in Education, Montreal, April 1983.

Green, D.R., Coffman, W.E., Lenke, J.M., Raju, N.S., Handrick, F.A., Loyd, B.H., Carlton, S.T., & Marco, G.L. Methods used by test publishers to "debias" standardized tests. In R.A. Berk (Ed.), *Handbook of methods for detecting test bias.* Baltimore, MD: Johns

Hopkins University Press, 1982. Pp. 228 – 313.

Gronlund, N.E. *Measurement and evaluation in teaching* (4th ed.). New York: Macmillan, 1981.

Guion, R.M. Content validity — The source of my discontent. *Applied Psychological Measurement,* 1977, *1,* 1 – 10.

Guion, R.M. On trinitarian doctrines of validity. *Professional Psychology,* 1980, *11,* 385 – 398.

Haggard, E.A. *Intraclass correlation and the analysis of variance.* New York: Dryden Press, 1958.

Hambleton, R.K. *Review methods for criterion-referenced test items.* Paper presented at the annual meeting of the American Educational Research Association, Boston, April 1980.(a)

Hambleton, R.K. Test score validity and standard-setting methods. In R.A. Berk (Ed.), *Criterion-referenced measurement: The state of the art.* Baltimore, MD: Johns Hopkins University Press, 1980. Pp. 80 – 123.(b)

Hambleton, R.K. Advances in criterion-referenced testing technology. In C.R. Reynolds & T.B. Gutkin (Eds.), *The handbook of school psychology.* New York: Wiley, 1982. Pp. 351 – 379.

Hambleton, R.K. Validating the test scores. In R.A. Berk (Ed.), *A guide to criterion-referenced test construction.* Baltimore, MD: Johns Hopkins University Press, in press.

Hambleton, R.K., & Eignor, D.R. Guidelines for evaluating criterion-referenced tests and test manuals. *Journal of Educational Measurement,* 1978, *15,* 321 – 327.

Hambleton, R.K., & Novick, M.R. Toward an integration of theory and method for criterion-referenced tests. *Journal of Educational Measurement,* 1973, *10,* 159 – 170.

Hambleton, R.K., & Powell, S. A framework for viewing the process of standard setting. *Evaluation and the Health Professions,* 1983, *6,* 3-24.

Hambleton, R.K., Swaminathan, H., Algina, J., & Coulson, D.B. Criterion-referenced testing and measurement: A review of technical issues and developments. *Review of Educational Research,* 1978, *48,* 1 – 47.

Hammill, D.D., & Bartel, N.R. *Teaching children with learning and behavior problems* (2nd ed.). Boston: Allyn & Bacon, 1978.

Hardy, R. *Measuring instructional validity: A report of an instructional validity study for the Alabama High School Graduation Examination.* Paper presented at the annual meeting of the American Educational Research Association, Montreal, April 1983.

Harvey, J. Regional collaboration. In J. Smith (Ed.), *Personnel preparation and Public Law 94-142: The map, the mission and the mandate* (2nd ed.). Boothwyn, PA: Educational Resources Center, 1978.

Heller, H.W. Professional standards for preparing special educators: Status and prospects. *Exceptional Education Quarterly,* 1982, *2,* 77 – 86.

Hopkins, K.D., & Stanley, J.C. *Educational and psychological measurement and evaluation* (6th ed.). Englewood Cliffs, NJ: Prentice-Hall, 1981.

Hoyt, C.J. Test reliability estimated by analysis of variance. *Psychometrika,* 1941, *6,* 153 – 160.

Huynh, H. On the reliability of decisions in domain-referenced testing. *Journal of Educational Measurement,* 1976, *13,* 253 – 264.

Ironson, G.H. Use of chi-square and latent trait approaches for detecting item bias. In R.A. Berk (Ed.), *Handbook of methods for detecting test bias.* Baltimore, MD: Johns Hopkins University Press, 1982. Pp. 117 – 160.

Jackson, C.D. On the report of the Ad Hoc Committee on Educational Uses of Tests with Disadvantaged Students: Another psychological view from the Association of Black Psychologists. *American Psychologist,* 1975, *30,* 86 – 90.

Jaeger, R.M. *A proposal for setting a standard on the North Carolina High School Competency Test.* Paper presented atthe annual meeting of the North Carolina Association for Research in Education, Chapel Hill, 1978.

Jensen, A.R. *Bias in mental testing.* New York: Free Press, 1980.

Johns, J.L., Garton, S., Schoenfelder, P., & Skriba, P. *Assessing reading behavior: Informal reading inventories.* Newark, DE: International Reading Association, 1977.

Johnson, M.S., & Kress, R.A. *Informal reading inventories.* Newark, DE: International Reading Association, 1965.

Johnson, O.G. *Tests and measurements in child development: Handbook II* (Vol. 1). San Francisco: Jossey-Bass, 1976.

Kamin, L.J. Social and legal consequences of IQ tests as classification instruments: Some warnings from our past. *Journal of School Psychology,* 1975, *13,*317 – 323.

Kaufman, A.S., & Kaufman, N.L. *The Kaufman Assessment Battery for Children.* Circle Pines, MN: American Guidance Service, 1982.

Kirk, S.A., & Kirk, W.D. Uses and abuses of the ITPA. *Journal of Speech and Hearing Disorders,* 1978, *43,* 58 – 75.

Kirp, D., & Kirp, L. The legalization of the school psychologists' world. *Journal of School Psychology,* 1976, *14,* 83 – 89.

LaGrow, S.J., & Prochnow-LaGrow, J.E. Technical adequacy of the most popular tests selected by responding school psychologists in Illinois. *Psychology in the Schools,* 1982, *19,* 186 – 189.

Laosa, L.M. Reform in educational and psychological assessment: Cultural and linguistic issues. *Journal of the Association of Mexican American Educators,* 1973, *1,* 19 – 24.

Larry P., et al. v. *Wilson Riles, Superintendent of Public Instruction for the State of California, et al.,* 343 F. Supp. 1306, (N.D. Cal., 1972); *aff'd* 502 F. 2d 963 (9th Cir., 1974).

Larry P., et al. v. *Wilson Riles, Superintendent of Public Instruction for the State of California, et al.,* No. C-71-2270 (N.D. Cal., Oct. 11, 1979).

Larsen, S.C., Rogers, D., & Sowell, V. The use of selected perceptual tests in differentiating between normal and learning disabled children. *Journal of Learning Disabilities,* 1976, *9,* 32 – 37.

Leinhardt, G. Overlap: Testing whether it is taught. In G.F. Madaus, (Ed.), *The courts, validity, and minimum competency testing.* Boston: Kluwer-Nijhoff, 1983. Pp. 153 – 170.

Leinhardt, G., & Seewald, A.M. Overlap: What's tested, what's taught? *Journal of Educational Measurement,* 1981, *18,* 85 – 96.

Leinhardt, G., Zigmond, N., & Cooley, W.W. Reading instruction and its effects. *American Educational Research Journal,* 1981, *18,* 343 – 361.

Lindquist, E.F. *Design and analysis of experiments in psychology and education.* Boston: Houghton Mifflin, 1953.

Linn, R.L. Issues of reliability in measurement for competency-based programs. In M.A. Bunda & J.R. Sanders (Eds.), *Practices and problems in competency-based measurement.* Washington, DC.: National Council on Measurement in Education, 1979. Pp. 90 – 107.(a)

Linn, R.L. Issues of validity in measurement for competency-based programs. In M.A. Bunda & J.R. Sanders (Eds.), *Practices and problems in competency-based education.* Washington, DC: National Council on Measurement in Education, 1979. Pp. 108 – 123.(b)

Linn, R.L. Issues of validity for criterion-referenced measures. *Applied Psychological Measurement,* 1980, *4,* 547 – 561.

Livingston, S.A. Criterion-referenced applications of classical test theory. *Journal of Educational Measurement,* 1972, *9,* 13 – 26.

Livingston, S.A., & Zieky, M.J. *Passing scores: A manual for setting standards of performance on educational and occupational tests.* Princeton, NJ: Educational Testing Services, 1982.

Macready, G.B., & Dayton, C.M. The nature and use of state mastery models. *Applied Psychological Measurement,* 1980, *4,* 493 – 516.

Madaus, G.F. Minimum competency testing for certification: The evolution and evaluation of test validity. In G.F. Madaus (Ed.), *The courts, validity, and minimum competency testing.* Boston: Kluwer-Nijhoff, 1983. Pp. 21 – 61.

Madaus, G.F., Airasian, P.W., Hambleton, R.K., Consalvo, R.W., & Orlandi, L.R. Development and application of criteria for screening commercial, standardized tests. *Educational Evaluation and Policy Analysis,* 1982, *4*, 401 – 415.

Mann, P., & Suiter, P. *Handbook in diagnostic teaching.* Boston: Allyn & Bacon, 1974.

McClung, M.S. Competency testing programs: Legal and educational issues. *Fordham Law Review,* 1979, *47*, 651 – 712.

McDaniels, G. Assessing handicapped students: Beyond identification. In W.B. Schrader (Ed.), *New directions for testing and measurement* (No. 1) — *Measurement and educational policy: Proceedings of the 1978 ETS Invitational Conference.* San Francisco: Jossey-Bass, 1979. Pp. 3 – 7.

McLoughlin, J.A., & Lewis, R.B. *Assessing special students: Strategies and procedures.* Columbus, OH: Merrill, 1981.

McNutt, G., & Mandelbaum, L.H. General assessment competencies for special education teachers. *Exceptional Education Quarterly,* 1980, *1*, 21 – 29.

Mead, N.A. Listening and speaking skills. In R.A. Berk (Ed.), *Performance assessment: Methods and applications.* Baltimore, MD: Johns Hopkins University Press, in press.

Medley, D.M., & Mitzel, H.E. Measuring classroom behavior by systematic observation. In N.L. Gage (Ed.), *Handbook of research on teaching.* Chicago: Rand McNally, 1963. Pp. 247 – 328.

Mehrens, W.A. *Inferences to which domain and why and implications of any mismatch.* Symposium paper presented at the annual meeting of the National Council on Measurement in Education, Montreal, April 1983.

Mehrens, W.A., & Lehmann, I.J. *Standardized tests in education* (3rd ed.). New York: Holt, Rinehart and Winston, 1980.

Messick, S. *Test validity and the ethics of assessment.* Paper presented at the annual meeting of the American Psychological Association, New York, September 1979.

Meyers, C.E., Sundstrom, P., & Yoshida, R.K. The school psychologist and assessment in special education. *School Psychology Monograph,* 1974, *2*, 1 – 57.

Miller, C., & Chansky, N. Psychologists' scoring of WISC protocols. *Psychology in the Schools,* 1972, *9*, 144 – 152.

Millman, J. Reliability and validity of criterion-referenced test scores. In R.E. Traub (Ed.), *New directions for testing and measurement* (No. 4) — *Methodological developments.* San Francisco: Jossey-Bass, 1979. Pp. 75 – 92.

Mitchell, J.V., Jr. (Ed.). *Tests in print III.* Lincoln, NE: Buros Institute of Mental Measurements, 1983.

Mitchell, J.V., Jr., & Witt, J.C. (Eds.). *The ninth mental measurements yearbook.* Lincoln, NE: Buros Institute of Mental Measurements, in press.

Nairn, A., & Associates. *The reign of ETS: The corporation that makes up minds.* Washington, DC: Author, 1980.

Nedelsky, L. Absolute grading standards for objective tests. *Educational and Psychological Measurement,* 1954, *14*, 3 – 19.

Newcomer, P.L. Competencies for professionals in learning disabilities. *Learning Disability Quarterly,* 1978, *1*, 69 – 77.

Newcomer, P.L. Competencies for professionals in learning disabilities. *Learning Disability Quarterly,* 1982, *5*, 241 – 252.

Oakland, T.D. Nonbiased assessment of minority group children. *Exceptional Education Quarterly,* 1980, *1*, 31 – 46.

Oakland, T.D., & Laosa, L.M. Professional, legislative, and judicial influences on psychoeducational assessment practices in schools. In T.D. Oakland (Ed.), *Psychological and educational assessment of minority children.* New York: Brunner/Mazel, 1977. Pp. 21 – 51.

Oakland, T.D., Lee, S., & Axelrad, K. Examiner differences on actual WISC protocols. *Journal of School Psychology,* 1975, *13,* 227 – 233.

Oakland, T.D., & Matuszek, P. Using tests in nondiscriminatory assessment. In T.D. Oakland (Ed.), *Psychological and educational assessment of minority children.* New York: Brunner/Mazel, 1977. Pp. 52 – 69.

Paraskevopoulos, J.N., & Kirk, S.A. *The development and psychometric characteristics of the revised Illinois Test of Psycholinguistic Abilities.* Urbana: University of Illinois Press, 1969.

Parents in Action on Special Education (PASE), et al. v. *Joseph P. Hannon, General Superintendent of Schools in Chicago, et al.,* No. 74 C 3586 (N.D. Ill., July 7, 1980).

Patton, J.M., & Braithwaite, R.L. PL 94-142 and the changing status of teacher certification/recertification: A survey of state education agencies. *Teacher Education and Special Education,* 1980, *3,* 43 – 47.

Petersen, N.S., & Novick, M.R. An evaluation of some models for culturefair selection. *Journal of Educational Measurement,* 1976, *13,* 3 – 29.

Pikulski, J. A critical review: Informal reading inventories. *Reading Teacher,* 1974, *28,* 141 – 151.

Pine, S.M. Applications of item characteristic curve theory to the problem of test bias. In D.J. Weiss (Ed.), *Applications of computerized adaptive testing* (RR 77-1). Minneapolis: Department of Psychology, Psychometric Methods Program, University of Minnesota, March 1977. Pp. 37 – 43.

Popham, W.J. *Modern educational measurement.* Englewood Cliffs, NJ: Prentice-Hall, 1981.

Popham, W.J. *Issues in determining adequacy-of-preparation.* Symposium paper presented at the annual meeting of the American Educational Research Association, Montreal, April 1983.

Powell, W. Validity of the IRI reading levels. *Elementary English,* 1971, *48,* 637 – 642.

Poynor, L. *Instructional dimensions study: Data management procedures as exemplified by curriculum analysis.* Paper presented at the annual meeting of the American Educational Research Association, Toronto, April 1978.

Public Law 93-112. Rehabilitation Act of 1973, Section 102a, July 26, 1973.

Public Law 94-142. Education for All Handicapped Children Act, S.6, 94th Congress [Sec 613(a) (4)] 1st session, June 1975. Report No. 94-168.

Quellmalz, E.S. Writing skills. In R.A. Berk (Ed.), *Performance assessment: Methods and applications.* Baltimore, MD: Johns Hopkins University Press, in press.

The Reading Clinic. *Informal reading inventory.* Philadelphia: Psychology of Reading Department, Temple University, 1964.

Redden, M.R., & Blackhurst, A.E. Mainstreaming competency specifications for elementary teachers. *Exceptional Children,* 1978, *45,* 615 – 617.

Reschly, D.J. Nonbiased assessment. In G.D. Phye & D.J. Reschly (Eds.), *School psychology: Perspectives and issues.* New York: Academic Press, 1979. Pp. 215 – 253.

Reynolds, C.R. Methods for detecting construct and predictive bias. In R.A. Berk (Ed.), *Handbook of methods for detecting test bias.* Baltimore, MD: Johns Hopkins University Press, 1982. Pp. 199 – 227.(a)

Reynolds, C.R. The problem of bias in psychological assessment. In C.R. Reynolds, & T.B. Gutkin (Eds.), *The handbook of school psychology.* New York: Wiley, 1982. Pp. 178 – 208.(b)

Reynolds, M.C. (Ed.). *A common body of practice for teachers: The challenge of Public Law 94-142 to teacher education.* Washington, D.C.: American Association of Colleges of Teacher Education, 1980.

Sabatino, D.A., & Miller, T.L. The dilemma of diagnosis in learning disabilities: Problems and potential directions. *Psychology in the Schools,* 1980, *17,* 76 – 86.

Salvia, J., & Ysseldyke, J.E. *Assessment in special and remedial education* (2nd ed.). Boston: Houghton Mifflin, 1981.

Samuda, R.S. *Psychological testing of American minorities: Issues and consequences.* New York: Harper & Row, 1975.

Sattler, J.M. *Assessment of children's intelligence and special abilities* (2nd ed.). Boston: Allyn & Bacon, 1982.

Scheuneman, J.D. A new method of assessing bias in test items. *Journal of Educational Measurement*, 1979, *16*, 143 – 152.

Scheuneman, J.D. A posteriori analyses of biased items. In R.A. Berk (Ed.), *Handbook of methods for detecting test bias.* Baltimore, MD: Johns Hopkins University Press, 1982. Pp. 180 – 198.

Schmeiser, C.B. Use of experimental design in statistical item bias studies. In R.A. Berk (Ed.), *Handbook of methods for detecting test bias.*, Baltimore, MD: Johns Hopkins University Press, 1982. Pp. 64 – 95.

Schmidt, W.H. Content biases in achievement tests. *Journal of Educational Measurement*, 1983, *20*, 165-178.(a)

Schmidt, W.H. *Methods of examining mismatch.* Symposium paper presented at the annual meeting of the National Council on Measurement in Education, Montreal, April 1983.(b)

Schmidt, W.H., Porter, A.C., Schwille, J.R., Floden, R.E., & Freeman, D.J. Validity as a variable: Can the same certification test be valid for all students? In G.F. Madaus (Ed.), *The courts, validity, and minimum competency testing.* Boston: Kluwer-Nijhoff, 1983. Pp. 133 – 151.

Schofer, R.C., & Lilly, M.S. Personnel preparation in special education. In L. Mann & D.A. Sabatino (Eds.), *The fourth review of special education.* New York: Grune & Stratton, 1980. Pp. 367 – 390.

Shavelson, R., & Webb, N. Generalizability theory: 1973 – 1980. *British Journal of Mathematical and Statistical Psychology*, 1981, *34*, 133 – 166.

Shepard, L.A. Standard setting issues and methods. *Applied Psychological Measurement*, 1980, *4*, 447 – 467.

Shepard, L.A. Definitions of bias. In R.A. Berk (Ed.), *Handbook of methods for detecting test bias.* Baltimore, MD: Johns Hopkins University Press, 1982. Pp. 9 – 30.

Shepard, L.A. Setting performance standards. In R.A. Berk (Ed.), *A guide to criterion-referenced test construction.* Baltimore, MD: Johns Hopkins University Press, in press.

Shepard, L.A., & Smith, M.L. An evaluation of the identification of children with learning disabilities in Colorado. *Learning Disability Quarterly*, in press.

Shepard, L.A., Smith, M.L., Davis, A., Glass, G.V., Riley, A., & Vojir, C. *Evaluation of the identification of perceptual-communicative disorders in Colorado* (Final Report). Boulder: Laboratory of Educational Research, University of Colorado, February 20, 1981.

Shores, R., Cegelka, P. & Nelson, C.M. A review of research on teacher competencies. *Exceptional Children*, 1973, *40*, 192 – 197.

Stedman, D.J., & Paul, J.L. (Eds.) *New directions for exceptional children* (No. 8) — *Professional preparation for teachers of exceptional children.* San Francisco: Jossey-Bass, 1981.

Stinnett, T.M. *A manual on standards affecting school personnel in the United States.* Washington, DC: National Education Association, 1974.

Subkoviak, M.J. Decision-consistency approaches. In R.A. Berk (Ed.), *Criterion-referenced measurement: The state of the art.* Baltimore, MD: Johns Hopkins University Press, 1980. Pp. 129 – 185.

Swanson, H.L., & Watson, B.L. *Educational and psychological assessment of exceptional children: Theories, strategies, and applications.* St. Louis: Mosby, 1982.

Swezey, R.W., & Pearlstein, R.B. *Guidebook for developing criterion-referenced tests.* Arlington, VA: U.S. Army Research Institute for the Behavioral and Social Sciences, August 1975.

Tenopyr, M.L. Content-construct confusion. *Personal Psychology*, 1977, *30*, 47 – 54.

Thurlow, M.L., & Ysseldyke, J.E. Current assessment and decision-making practices in model LD programs. *Learning Disability Quarterly,* 1979, *2,* 15 – 24.

Tittle, C.K. Use of judgmental methods in item bias studies. In R.A. Berk (Ed.), *Handbook of methods for detecting test bias.* Baltimore, MD: Johns Hopkins University Press, 1982. Pp. 31 – 63.

Traub, R.E., & Rowley, G.L. Reliability of test scores and decisions. *Applied Psychological Measurement,* 1980, *4,* 517 – 545.

U.S. Department of Education. *To assure the free appropriate public education of all handicapped children* (Second Annual Report to Congress on Implementation of Public Law 94-142: The Education for All Handicapped Children Act). Washington, DC: Author, 1980.

U.S. Office of Education. Education of handicapped children: Implementation of Part B of the Education of the Handicapped Act. *Federal Register,* 1977, *42*(163), 42474 – 42518.(a)

U.S. Office of Education. Assistance to states for education for handicapped children: Procedures for evaluating specific learning disabilities. *Federal Register,* 1977, *42*(250), 62082 – 62085.(b)

van der Linden, W.J. Decision models for use with criterion-referenced tests. *Applied Psychological Measurement,* 1980, *4,* 469 – 492.

Walker, C.B. *Standards for evaluating criterion-referenced tests.* Los Angeles: Center for the Study of Evaluation, University of California, 1977.

Wallace, G., & Kauffman, J.M *Teaching children with learning problems.* Columbus, OH: Merrill, 1973.

Wallace, G., & Larsen, S.C. *Educational assessment of learning problems: Testing for teaching.* Boston: Allyn & Bacon, 1978.

Williams, R.L. Danger: Testing and dehumanizing Black children. *Clinical Child Psychology Newsletter,* 1970, *9,* 5 – 6.

Williams, R.L. Abuses and misuses in testing black children. *Counseling Psychologist,* 1971, *2,* 62 – 77.

Winer, B.J. *Statistical principles in experimental design* (2nd ed.). New York: McGraw-Hill, 1971.

Woellner, E.H. *Requirements for certification, 1979 – 1980.* Chicago: University of Chicago Press, 1979.

Yalow, E.S., & Popham, W.J. Content validity at the crossroads. *Educational Researcher,* 1983, *12,* in press.

Ysseldyke, J.E. Implementing the "Protection in evaluation procedures" provisions of P.L. 94-142. In *Developing criteria for the evaluation of the protection in evaluation procedures provision of Public Law 94-142.* Washington, DC: Bureau of Education for the Handicapped, U.S. Office of Education, 1978.(a)

Ysseldyke, J.E. Who's calling the plays in school psychology? *Psychology in the Schools,* 1978, *15,* 373 – 378.(b)

Ysseldyke, J.E. Issues in psychoeducational assessment. In G.D. Phye & D.J. Reschly (Eds.), *School psychology: Perspectives and issues.* New York: Academic Press, 1979. Pp. 87 – 121.

Ysseldyke, J.E., & Algozzine, B. *Critical issues in special and remedial education.* Boston: Houghton Mifflin, 1982.

Ysseldyke, J.E., Algozzine, B., Regan, R.R., & Potter, M. Technical adequacy of tests used by professionals in simulated decision making. *Psychology in the Schools,* 1980, *17,* 202 – 209.(a)

Ysseldyke, J.E., Regan, R.R., & Schwartz, S.Z. *The use of technically adequate tests in psychoeducational decision making* (Research Report No. 28). Minneapolis: University of Minnesota Institute for Research on Learning Disabilities, April 1980.(b)

Zigmond, N., Vallecorsa, A., & Silverman, R. *Assessment for instructional planning in special education.* Englewood Cliffs, NJ: Prentice-Hall, 1983.

Chapter 3

USING AND INTERPRETING
THE TEST SCORES

Introduction

ONCE the battery of tests has been selected, the administration schedule
must be planned. Certain factors should be considered at this planning
stage to assure that the individual scores that result are valid and reliable indi-
cators of test performance (achievement or ability). A few key questions need
to be answered prior to administration:

1. Should all students at a given grade level be administered the same level
   test or should students receive functional level tests instead?
2. What type of scores are required to make the necessary screening or
   diagnostic decisions?
3. How will the scores be used for individual decision making?

These questions pertain to the way that test scores are used and interpreted. As
emphasized in the preceding chapter, any issue related to score use becomes a
validity issue. If the scores are used for purposes for which they were never intended or they are misinterpreted, those uses and interpretations are invalid.

The goal of this chapter is to describe the various types of scores available to
classroom teachers, learning disability specialists, and clinicians so that only
the scores appropriate for screening and diagnostic decisions are chosen, and
then interpreted correctly. Given the array of the types of scores from standardized tests that one must confront—percentile ranks, stanines, scaled scores,
grade equivalents, etc., the selection process is not simple. Guidelines for facili-
tating the process are proffered in two major sections: (1) score referencing and
(2) types of test scores. In addition, the topic of out-of-level or functional testing of learning-disabled children is discussed at length. The advantages and
disadvantages are outlined, and the effect of that mode of test administration
on scoring is examined.

Score Referencing

Suppose a test of functional reading was administered to a fifth-grade class. If each item correct counts one point and there are 40 items, then a student's *raw score* is simply the number of points earned. For example, one student might score 32 out of the total number of 40. How would this raw score be interpreted? Certainly it furnishes an index or numerical summary of an individual's performance, but without further information, it says virtually nothing in regard to level of performance. Even if the raw score were expressed as a *percentage correct*, where a score of 32/40 means 80% of the items were answered correctly, no additional information is still provided. The raw score or percentage correct on the reading test, as well as on any other test, has no intrinsic meaning by itself. Its meaning and interpretability are a function of the content or behaviors being measured and the ways the score is used. A score can be referenced to these elements to produce different meanings. There are four types of score referencing: content (or domain) referencing, norm referencing, criterion referencing, and ipsative referencing.

Content-referenced Interpretations

The first step in the development of a test is the specification of what the test is to measure. If one cannot clearly define what a test measures, then the resulting scores are virtually meaningless. From the standpoint of score interpretation, a score *must* be referenced to the *content domain* prior to any other type of referencing. In the preceding example, a teacher might say that the student's score on the test tells that she acquired 80% of the functional reading skills in the areas of survival signs, directional vocabulary, map symbols, and simple forms.

The rigor and precision with which the domain is defined can enhance or diminish the content-referenced interpretation. The interpretation may be vague or explicit. One popular misconception is that the scores on most standardized tests do possess specific content meaning. Few available tests, in fact, exhibit any direct, substantial link with an explicitly defined body of content. The tests frequently survey broad domains of content such as reading, mathematics, language, and social studies. Rarely do these tests reflect even the curricular emphases in a single school district (Jenkins & Pany, 1978a).

Since the 1970s, the leading proponents of criterion-referenced tests have argued that the traditional approach to defining a content domain, which includes a content outline, a list of objectives, and a table of specifications or similar "blueprint," tends to produce an *ambiguous* domain definition. The arguments focus on the subjectivity involved in composing those specifications. That is, the selection of content topics and objectives is quite arbitrary, typically representing only one test maker's conceptualization of the domain. Such specifications would be open to different interpretations by different test

makers. Coupled with this criticism is the charge that traditional item construction procedures are also ambiguous inasmuch as they can result in a set of
items that manifest the biases and idiosyncrasies of each test maker. Consequently, different test makers would probably develop different items from the
same specifications.

In order to overcome these deficiences of the traditional approach, several
new strategies have been devised: (1) amplified objectives, (2) IOX test specifications, (3) mapping sentences, (4) item transformations, (5) item forms, and
(6) algorithms (for details, see Millman, 1980; Popham, 1980; Roid, in press;
Roid & Haladyna, 1982). These strategies strive to provide an *unambiguous* definition of a domain and implicitly or explicitly constitute sets of rules for
generating the items, such that any two test makers would construct identical
items from the same specifications. However, the extent to which the strategies
can actually supply an unambiguous link between a behavioral domain and the
corresponding test items varies markedly from one strategy to the other (Berk,
1980a). Nonetheless, since they do improve score interpretations, tests built according to those strategies are often referred to as *domain referenced* (Berk, 1980b;
Popham, 1978).

From these developments in the measurement community, it is clear that
meaningful test scores do not occur automatically or haphazardly. The relationship between the scores and the content domain must be planned deliberately and systematically to assure meaningful results. Standardized tests are
extremely limited in this regard. The content-referenced interpretations of particular subtest scores are usually restricted to the name of the subtest, such as
reading comprehension or mathematics computations. For screening decisions
this is adequate; for diagnostic-prescriptive decisions, this information is
worthless. Criterion-referenced tests, in contrast, are designed expressly to furnish very specific content – or domain-referenced score interpretations (Nitko,
1980a). The scores are usually linked to behaviorally stated objectives, so a
teacher can pinpoint a student's strengths and weaknesses and then act accord-
ingly to tailor the instruction to his or her needs.

Norm-referenced Interpretations

A test score can be given additional meaning as it is referenced to the performance of a group of students, often called a *norm sample* (see Chapter 2). For
norm-referenced interpretations, simply ranking the raw scores on a test from
highest to lowest can reveal the position of each individual's score in relation to
others in the norm group. By observing, for example, that a student's score falls
in the top 10% or bottom 50%, a teacher can make a normative interpretation
of individual performance. That score ranking or position makes it possible to
infer high, average, or low performance. If the highest score on the 40-item
reading test was 21, that score is still high *relative* to the performance of other

students in the class. The *absolute* meaning of the extent of that student's knowledge never enters into the normative interpretation.

Another common approach to norm-referenced interpretations at the classroom level is to reference a student's raw score to a *normative score* such as the average (mean) score, which is computed from the performance data of all students in the class. This operation facilitates inferences such as above-average or below-average achievement. For example, in the case of the functional reading test, if the mean score in the class is 35, an individual score of 32 can then be referenced to that point in order to make the interpretation: Lolita performed slightly below average on that test.

Referencing becomes more sophisticated in the context of standardized tests. The raw scores of students in a national standardization sample are transformed into different types of scores that indicate an individual's *relative standing* or position in comparison to all other students in the norm sample. These scores, known as *derived scores*, may be of several types, including grade and age equivalents, percentile ranks, and standard scores. They will be described in the next section. Depending upon the norm sample to which the scores are referenced, it may be possible to compare an individual's performance to the performance of children in a particular class, school, district, state, or the entire nation.

Criterion-referenced Interpretations

An alternative interpretation is to reference the test score to a standard or *criterion level of performance* in the domain. This type of referencing is one distinguishing characteristic of a criterion-referenced test (another is the explicit definition of the content domain, as discussed previously). In the reading test example, if a cutting score of, say, 7 out of 10 items or 70%, were set as the standard for mastery of the map symbols objective, an individual raw score of 9 on that collection of items can then be referenced to the standard to make the inference: Boomy has mastered the map symbols objective. In other words, a child's performance is interpreted in terms of what he or she can and cannot do irrespective of the performance of other students. No transformation of scores is required. Methods for determining performance standards for diagnostic tests are reviewed in Chapter 6.

Ipsative Interpretations[1]

Unlike the preceding types of score interpretation, which reference an individual's score to a content domain, norm sample, and performance standard, there is a fourth type of interpretation that is particularly relevant to the

---

[1]The relationship between ipsative score interpretations and the analysis of discrepancy scores and profiles discussed in this section was brought to my attention by William H. Angoff (personal communication, 1983). His perceptive thoughts on the topic are most appreciated.

screening and diagnosis of children with learning disabilities: *ipsative* or *intraindividual* interpretation (Angoff, 1971). Instead of comparing a single test score to a normative score (interindividual) or a cutting score, an ipsative interpretation involves a comparison of two or more scores obtained by the same individual. In screening, the discrepancy between an ability test score and an achievement test score for one child is an ipsative comparison. For example, if Julia's verbal ability score of 40 was compared to her punctuation test score of 23, a discrepancy score of 17 is produced. This discrepancy, which may denote a learning disability in punctuation skills, represents an ipsative interpretation of Julia's two scores. Since the scores used to compute the discrepancy are usually derived scores from norm-referenced tests, the interpretation of the discrepancy is both normative as well as ipsative (see Chapter 4).

From a diagnostic perspective, the analysis of an individual's profile of strengths and weaknesses is also ipsative. The different scores on a profile chart require the interpretation of intraindividual comparisons. When the strengths and weaknesses are inferred from normative data, as in a WISC-R subtest profile (for details, see Chapter 4), the evaluation of performance is also normative. If, however, those inferences are based on mastery standards, the evaluation is criterion referenced (see next section).

These examples indicate that *the decisions concerning the status of learning-disabled children are typically reached via ipsative score interpretations*. Depending upon the nature of the test scores contributing to these interpretations, they may also be norm referenced or criterion referenced.

Types of Test Scores

The use of scores for individual decision making, either screening or diagnosis, imposes special qualifications on the score scale or metric. If one expects to compute score differences as in an ability-achievement discrepancy, the chosen metric must possess the appropriate statistical properties. These properties are not the same in all metrics. Therefore, it is essential that the test user be cognizant of the advantages and disadvantages of each type of score so that the appropriate metric is chosen in a particular application. Of special interest in this presentation is the metric that best fits the concept of an ability-achievement discrepancy.

There are numerous types of norm-referenced test scores that are derived from the basic raw score. Salvia and Ysseldyke (1981) classify these derived scores into two categories: developmental scores and scores of relative standing. *Developmental scores* reflect individual developmental levels expressed in terms of grade placement or age. Examples include grade-equivalents, age equivalents, and intelligence quotients. *Scores of relative standing* designate individual positions/ranks within a particular norm group. Percentile ranks and the various standard scores such as *z*-scores, *T*-scores, deviation IQs, stanines, and normal curve equivalents fall into this category.

In this section, each one of these norm-referenced test scores is defined and then evaluated according to its usefulness for screening learning-disabled children. In addition, criterion-referenced test scores are discussed from the perspective of diagnostic decision making.

Grade Equivalents

A grade-equivalent score is the grade for which a given test performance is average. It is not designed to tell what grade level of work a student can perform. As Gronlund (1981) emphasized, "It represents the typical performance of average pupils in average schools and should not be considered a standard of excellence to be achieved by others" (p. 373).

The score itself is expressed in two numbers: year and month. For example, a score of 6.3 means sixth grade third month, where the range is from 6.0 to 6.9. The scale is partitioned into tenths rather than twelfths as in the calender year. This is based on the assumption of no change in performance over the summer months.

In screening for learning disabilities, this metric is often employed to determine whether a student with "normal" intelligence has an achievement level that is two or more years below his or her grade placement. For example, if a fifth grader (e.g., 5.5 or fifth grade fifth month) scores at a third-grade level on a reading comprehension subtest (e.g., 3.1), he or she is exhibiting a deficit of more than two years below grade level (e.g., 2.4). Where this approach is not used, an ability-achievement discrepancy criterion may be set. The ability component is usually expressed in terms of a mental age or age-equivalent score (e.g., 5-2) or an IQ (e.g., 125); the achievement component is simply the grade-equivalent score on an achievement test as defined previously (for details, see Chapter 4).

The value of the various discrepancy procedures rests initially on the appropriateness of grade-equivalent scores for those specific uses. Evaluated in this context, grade-equivalent scores are completely inappropriate. The reasons for this conclusion are explained next.

Grade-equivalent scores have been the object of considerable criticism for over 30 years (see Angoff, 1971; Berk, 1981; Cole, 1982; Flanagan, 1951; Hills, 1983; Horst, 1976; Horst, Tallmadge, & Wood 1974; Linn, 1981; Linn & Slinde, 1977; Reynolds, 1981; Williams, 1980). As the widespread application of the scores to learning disability identification suggests, and as Linn (1981) has observed, "despite the criticisms the popularity of these scores has continued almost unabated" (p. 92). The underlying question that needs to be answered is: *What is wrong with using grade-equivalent scores to screen learning-disabled children?*

The deficiences of grade-equivalent scores are acknowledged in a variety of sources, from test manuals to measurement textbooks. Even professional associations have expressed opposition to their continued use. For example, at the 1981 Delegates Assembly meeting of the International Reading Association, it was resolved that "the president or executive director of the Association write to test publishers urging them to eliminate grade equivalents from their tests."

Before examining the specific problems it seems apropos to present a few statements about grade equivalents from standardized achievement test manuals:

> First. . . they do not indicate how well a given student or class *should* read. . . Secondly, the units of the grade scale are not equal to one another. A difference of one grade level between scores near the lower end of the scale is a larger difference than one grade level near the upper end of the scale. For this reason, it is not technically correct to add grade scores to obtain averages or subtract them to obtain gain scores or other difference scores. Also, grade scores are not very useful for assessing a student's position relative to others in his [or her] grade as he [or she] moves through the grades. (*Teacher's Manual, Gates-MacGinitie Reading Tests,* Survey, D, 1965, pp. 5 – 6; Gates & MacGinitie, 1965)

> Identical grade-equivalents earned on different tests do not necessarily represent equally good performance. For comparing pupil's present status in a group from test to test, the grade-equivalent scores may be misleading, particularly if the pupil's performance is well above or *well below average* [italics added] . . . they should not be used to determine a pupil's standing in his [or her] grade or his [or her] relative performance on different tests. (*Teacher's Guide, Iowa Tests of Basic Skills,* Forms 7/8, 1978, p. 23; Hieronymus, Lindquist, & Hoover, 1978)

These statements are exemplary of those made by many test publishers.

DEFICIENCIES. Grade-equivalent scores have nine serious deficiencies:

1. *Grade equivalents invite seemingly simple but misleading interpretations* (Linn, 1981, p. 92). For example, a grade-equivalent score of 3.2 attained by a sixth-grade student on a reading test does not mean that he or she possesses third-grade reading skills. In fact, there are no data on how third graders would have performed on the intermediate level test. The 3.2 score is intended to indicate that the student can read sixth-grade materials as well as the average third grader. However, this inference is even questionable, insofar as 3.2 is based on statistical projection. Of course, the same confusion occurs in attempting to interpret scores above grade level.

2. *Grade equivalents assume that the rate of learning is constant throughout the school year and that either no growth occurs during the summer or that growth does occur equivalent to one month of growth during the school year* (Flanagan, 1951). There is substantial evidence to the contrary (see Beggs & Hieronymus, 1968); learning rates are irregular, and there is often an achievement loss over the summer months due to forgetting.

3. *Grade equivalents yield different growth rates at different score levels* (Cole, 1982). A low scoring student can have a normal expected growth in one year of .7 grade units, whereas for an average student it can be 1.0 units, and for

a high scoring student it can exceed 1.0 units. This lack of equivalence across score levels can be traced to the fact that grade equivalents do not approximate equal intervals.

4. *Grade equivalents are derived primarily from interpolation and extrapolation rather than from real data* (Angoff, 1971). The normative data for most tests are usually collected at one point in the year. How then are grade equivalents obtained for every month? They are extrapolated at the upper and lower ends of the growth curve. This estimation produces scores that are systematically too low in the fall and too high in the spring. Therefore, there would be a high probability of overidentifying learning-disabled children (increased false positives) if screening is conducted in the fall or of underidentifying them (increased false negatives) if screening is conducted in the spring. Furthermore, in discussing this problem in the context of program evaluation, Horst et. al. (1974) emphasized that these "curve-fitting procedures used to generate such scores introduce errors large enough to invalidate any evaluation" (p. 10).

5. *Grade equivalents are virtually meaningless in the upper grade levels for subjects that are not taught at those levels.* Due to the relative stability of the average reading level in the population after junior high school and to the extrapolation of grade equivalents at the upper grade levels from the earlier grades, the growth curve between age and achievement flattens out in the upper grades (Angoff, 1971; Reynolds, 1981). This means that grade equivalents at these grade levels become meaningless with large fluctuations resulting from a raw score difference of only two or three points on a 100-item test.

6. *Grade equivalents do not represent an equal-interval scale.* This means that the score units are not equal on different parts of the scale. One year's growth from 2.0 to 3.0 might represent greater achievement than the growth from 4.0 to 5.0. The expression "performs at grade level" or "two years below grade level" acquires different meanings depending upon which part of the grade scale the student is measured. This problem of unequal score units precludes the use of arithmetic operations such as addition, subtraction, multiplication, and division. Certainly the computation of statistics as simple as a group average score and standard deviation are completely inappropriate. Therefore, just subtracting grade equivalents to determine a discrepancy between ability and achievement violates a fundamental property of the grade scale. If a discrepancy were calculated, it would be impossible to interpret correctly.

7. *Grade equivalents exaggerate the significance of small differences in performances* (Angoff, 1971). A student who performs only slightly below the median or 50th percentile for his or her grade level may appear to be as much as one or two years below grade level on the grade equivalent scale, the typi-

cal criterion for screening learning-disabled children. Consequently, this distortion of a student's actual achievement level can result in overidentification (increased false positives).

8. *Grade equivalents are affected by changes in educational customs regarding promotion from grade to grade* (Gulliksen, 1950). Grade equivalents that are determined under one system of promotion, such as on the basis of achievement, cannot be compared with grade equivalents established under a different system of promotion, such as the present custom of promoting students on the basis of age. Angoff (1971) also noted that the grade-equivalent scale is necessarily dependent on the way in which a subject-matter area is emphasized in the curriculum throughout the grades and from one school and community to another.

9. *Grade equivalents vary markedly from publisher to publisher, from test to test, from subtest to subtest within the same test battery, from grade to grade, and from percentile to percentile.* Williams (1980) has assembled 22 tables and 12 figures using data from a dozen standardized tests to illustrate these different types of variability. This phenomenon greatly complicates any type of comparison. For example, it is virtually impossible to interpret an individual's relative strength in two subject areas (e.g., reading and mathematics) based on the grade-equivalent scores from two tests. The reason is that the grade units stretch and contract at different points of the scale for different subjects. Two scores with identical relative standing (percentile rank) from two different tests within a grade level can produce different grade equivalents (Cole, 1982, p. 3). Given the consistency with which these inconsistencies in the scale occur, it is statistically possible to increase or to decrease the incidence of learning disabilities at the local and state levels by selecting a standardized test based on its grade-equivalent distributions (Williams, 1980, p. 7). The implications of this for federal funding to state educational agencies can be rather disconcerting.

As if these deficiences of grade-equivalent test scores are not serious enought, the use of grade equivalents to grade basal reading series and other curricular materials exacerbates the problem even more. The incongruence between the scores and the materials is worse than that among the scores from subtest to subtest at a single grade level (cf. Jenkins & Pany, 1978a, 1978b). Yet, the placement of learning-disabled children into remedial programs commonly involves both types of grade equivalents.

The foregoing evidence on how grade equivalents can distort a student's actual achievement level and their inappropriateness for analyzing ability-achievement discrepancies indicate only one conclusion about the usefulness of grade scores: *There is no technically sound reason to justify their use in the screening and diagnosis of children with learning disabilities.* The popularity of grade equivalents among learning disability specialists and clinicians belies their inadequacies and the erroneous decisions they cause. As demonstrated in this section, "their simplicity is far more apparent than real" (Angoff, 1971, p. 525); however, the serious consequences of their continued use will be far more real than apparent.

Age Equivalents

An age-equivalent score is the age at which a given test performance is average. For example, a raw score of 36 on an ability test, which corresponds to an age equivalent of 11-6, means that the students in the norm sample who are eleven and one-half years old earned an average score of 36 on that test. This interpretation bears a close resemblance to the interpretation of grade equivalents. It is, in fact, almost identical because age equivalents are essentially grade equivalents when the norm group is composed of only students in a grade that is appropriate for their chronological age (Mehrens & Lehmann, 1978).

The differences between the two metrics are threefold: (1) age equivalents are scaled in terms of age level rather than grade level, (2) the scale is partitioned into twelfths instead of tenths, so the age equivalent of 11-6 cited previously would have a possible age range of 11-0 to 11-11, and (3) age scores are expressed with a hyphen between the year and month as opposed to a decimal point. These distinctions are obviously matters of form, not substance.

Unfortunately, it is the common characteristics of age equivalents and grade equivalents that are problematic. Since both scales are developed using the same procedures, all of the major statistical and educational deficiences of grade equivalents are equally applicable to age equivalents.

Given that age equivalents are most often reported for mental ability tests (*mental age*) and reading tests (*reading age*), the aforementioned deficiencies would appear to render these uses invalid. This verdict is especially troublesome when one considers that mental age is a component of many reading expectancy formulas. These formulas usually yield the ability score from which an ability-achievement discrepancy is computed (for details, see Chapter 4). Ergo, age equivalents are as useless for measuring ability level as grade equivalents are for measuring achievement level; certainly the combination is entirely inappropriate for measuring a discrepancy.

Intelligence Quotients

An intelligence quotient (IQ) is a ratio of an individual's mental age (MA) to chronological age (CA), multiplied by 100, or

$$IQ = \frac{MA}{CA} \times 100. \tag{3.1}$$

It permits an inference about a person's relative intelligence level. For example, if Ziggy performed at a mental age of 11-6, but he was only 10 years old, his IQ would be 115, which is above average.

The fact that mental age is the primary ingredient in the formula automatically raises serious questions about its statistical soundness. The age-equivalent score, which is, at best, on an ordinal scale, is treated as though it were on a ratio scale. In addition, among the deficiences of age scores, the variability of the scores within different chronological age groups is particularly bothersome (Salvia & Ysseldyke, 1981). The standard deviations of the IQs are not constant across age levels, with the result that any single quotient can mean different things at different ages. Another issue concerns the maximum value that can be set for chronological age (the denominator). There does not seem to be a satisfactory answer to the question: When does a person stop growing intellectually?

The significance of these problems in screening for learning disabilities becomes evident when one attempts to use specific reading expectancy formulas to estimate an ability score or more sophisticated discrepancy procedures such as regression analysis (see Chapter 4). Those formulas that do not contain a mental age component by itself include mental age as an implicit component of the IQ score. Therefore, the quotient is used with some frequency in this context of screening.

Because of the technical inadequacies of the IQ ratio, it has been replaced in recent years with a *deviation IQ*. It is a standard score that has been proposed as a remedy for the aforestated headaches associated with the intelligence quotient. Indeed, various forms of the deviation IQ are now being reported for the most popular intelligence tests such as the WISC-R, Otis-Lennon, and Stanford-Binet. A further description of this metric is presented in a subsequent section on standard scores.

Percentile Ranks

A percentile rank indicates the percentage of children in a norm group who score *below*[2] a given raw score point, thereby locating an individual's position or relative standing in the norm group. A student can be assigned a rank between 1 and 99 depending upon the frequency distribution of raw scores in the group. For example, if Buffy had a raw score of 45 on a language test that translated into a percentile of 66, one can say that she obtained a score higher than 66% of the students in the school (the norm group), or 66% of the students earned a raw score lower than 45.

Unlike all of the preceding metrics, the interpretation of percentile ranks is

---

[2]Mehrens and Lehmann (1978, p. 143) have noted that statisticians differ in their definitions of a percentile rank. Sometimes it is the percentage that scored *at or below* a given raw score point. While this discrepancy may be viewed as trivial, the ranks that result will be different and so will the interpretations. Therefore, test users should know precisely which definition is appropriate in order to interpret the scores correctly.

direct and readily understood. The ranks can also be computed easily for virtually any norm sample, local to national, if so desired (for details, see Lyman, 1978). Of course the sample must be identified or defined for the interpretation of an individual rank to have meaning. A student does not simply have a rank; he or she has a rank in a particular group. This norm-referenced interpretation using percentile ranks has proven to be very useful for individual decision making.

Percentile ranks, however, are not without disadvantages. Perhaps the most obvious limitation in relation to screening procedures is that the scale is ordinal rather than interval, and consequently, no arithmetic operations can be performed, especially discrepancy analysis. Furthermore, the inequality of percentile units on different parts of the scale requires that special caution be exercised in interpreting differences in rank. Typically, because most students in a norm group tend to score near the middle of a score distribution, the differences in percentile points in this area are quite small. The converse occurs at the extreme ends of the distribution, where few students have very high or very low scores. These characteristics imply that greater weight should be given to differences in rank at the extremes than near the middle. In fact, Gronlund (1981) recommends that small differences in rank around the midpoint (50th percentile or median) generally can be disregarded.

Standard Scores

Standard scores are transformed raw scores with a predetermined mean and standard deviation. The resulting scale from this *linear transformation* retains the same distribution shape as the original raw-score distribution. In fact, if the raw scores were plotted on one axis and the transformed scores on another, a straight line would connect the plotted points. Some of these characteristics and the computation of three widely used standard score scales—z, T, and deviation IQ—are illustrated in Table 3.1

Table 3.1

Characteristics of z, T, and Deviation IQ Standard Scores

Standard Score	Formula	Computation[a]	Mean	SD
z	$\dfrac{x - \bar{X}}{SD_.}$	$\dfrac{42 - 35}{5} = 1.4$	0	1
T	$50 + 10(z)$	$50 + 10(1.4) = 64$	50	10
Deviation IQ	$100 + 15(z)$	$100 + 15(1.4) = 121$	100	15[b]

[a]Computation of each standard score is for the raw score of 42 (X) on a 50-item test with a mean ($\bar{X}$) of 35 and a standard deviation ($SD_.$) of 5.
[b]A standard deviation of 16 is also used.

Z-SCORES. The z-score is the simplest and basic standard score from which the others are derived. It always has a mean of 0 and a standard deviation of 1. An individual z-score is expressed in terms of the number of *standard deviation units* a raw score is above or below the mean, e.g., + 1.4. In other words, since a raw-score mean and standard deviation can be calculated for any norm sample distribution, only two additional steps are needed to convert the raw scores into standard deviation units: subtract the raw score from the mean score and divide that quantity by the standard deviation (see formula in Table 3.1). Inasmuch as the formula yields both positive and negative values plus decimals, some test users prefer to use other standard scores.

T-SCORES. The *T*-score is a standard score with a mean of 50 and a standard deviation of 10. As shown in Table 3.1 it can be computed by multiplying the z-score by 10 and adding 50 to the product. This transformation will eliminate the negative values and decimals of the z-score.

DEVIATION IQs. The deviation IQ is a standard score with a mean of 100 and a standard deviation of 15 (WISC-R) or 16 (Otis-Lennon; Stanford-Binet). As noted previously, this score was devised to overcome the weaknesses of the IQ ratio. It does so by providing an interval scale that is calculated separately for each age group within the norm sample. The transformation is executed with a formula analogous to the one used for *T*-scores, except that the mean and standard deviation are different (see Table 3.1). Although *T*-scores could certainly be used with intelligence tests, a mean and standard deviation that more closely reflects the score distribution of the IQ ratio are selected instead in order to retain the IQ concept. Since the standard deviations of deviation IQ scales often differ from one intelligence test to another (e.g., 12, 15, 16, 20), test users should not compare two or more individual IQs unless they are produced from the same test (see Chapter 8 for tables that demonstrate this point).

STANINES. A stanine is a normalized standard score with a mean of 5 and a standard deviation of about 2. The scale range is from 1 to 9. Its name is derived from the fact that it divides the raw score distribution into nine parts, or *standard nines*. Each stanine encompasses a band of raw scores one-half standard deviation unit wide. This results in a 9-point scale with equal units.

Stanines can be computed quite easily by first ranking the raw scores from highest to lowest and then assigning designated percentages of raw scores to stanine score bands as follows (see also Durost, 1961; Lyman, 1978):

Stanine	Percentage of Raw Scores
9	4%
8	7%
7	12%

6	17%
5	20%
4	17%
3	12%
2	7%
1	4%

As these percentages suggest, the stanines correspond to a symmetrical distribution. It is, in fact, a normal curve with the tails lopped off. Because the raw scores are forced into this shape regardless of the shape of the original distribution, albeit *normalized*, stanines are called *normalized standard scores*. (This is distinguished from the preceding three types of linear standard score.) More will be said about normalized scores in the next section. Compared with the other standard score scales, however, the stanine scale is limited and does not permit the fine discrimination among performance levels that is often required for individual decision making.

NORMAL CURVE EQUIVALENTS. A normal curve equivalent is a normalized standard score with a mean of 50 and a standard deviation of 21.06. The scale values range from 1 to 99. The scores resemble percentile ranks but are assumed to have equal intervals. Although the normal curve equivalent was introduced as a metric for the Title I Evaluation and Reporting System (Tallmadge & Wood, 1976), it may have some utility for individual normative decisions.

EVALUATION. Several advantages of standard scores should now be evident from an examination of Table 3.1 and the preceding descriptions:

1. They are easy to compute, to use, and to interpret.
2. They constitute an equal-interval scale, which allows a variety of arithmetic and statistical operations to be performed on the data.
3. They provide an accurate representation of an individual's achievement/ability/intelligence level on a norm-referenced test. All score transformations are derived from the raw scores; no interpolation or extrapolation of scores in the distribution is needed.
4. They facilitate test to test, subtest to subtest, grade to grade, and age to age score comparisons by supplying the test user with a *mechanism for translating the raw scores of tests with different content, means, and standard deviations into the same language* — a *common metric*.

This last advantage is especially important in the analysis of ability-achievement discrepancies. A common metric for both ability and achievement test scores is a necessary but not sufficient condition for determining a severe discrepancy; several other test characteristics must also be present (see Chapter 4).

In addition, the interchangeability of the different scores with percentiles under certain conditions eliminates virtually all computations. Conversion tables are readily available for most tests (see, for example, Lyman, 1978, and Reynolds, 1981), so that a practitioner can pick the z-score or T-score for each test and then simply subtract the two scores to obtain a discrepancy score (for details, see Chapter 8). Alternatively, statistical computer programs that calculate these various scores can be easily acquired for most computers currently being used in school districts and state educational agencies.

Comparison of Norm-referenced Test Scores

The interrelationships among the four types of standard score and percen-

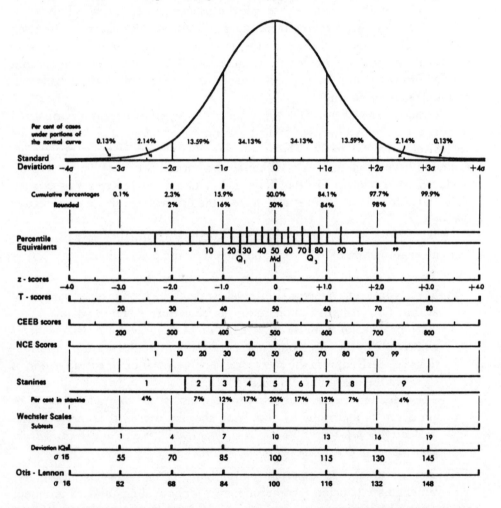

Figure 3.1. (MEMORY JOGGER) Comparison of percentile ranks and selected standard scores based on the normal curve. From H. G. Seashore, *Methods of Expressing Test Scores* (Test Service Notebook 148), September 1980. Courtesy of Psychological Corporation, New York, New York.

tile ranks are depicted in Figure 3.1. The normal or bell-shaped curve provides the reference point for drawing conclusions about the possible relationships. This means that either the original raw score distribution must be *normal* or it must be *normalized* for the relationships to be true.

NORMALIZED SCORES. Regardless of the shape of a raw score distribution, it is possible to normalize the scores so that the shape of the transformed score distribution will be normal. In essence, the raw scores are forced to fit the normal curve as closely as possible. The normalization process involves only one intermediary step added to the previous *linear* transformation. The raw scores must first be converted to percentile ranks and then the ranks are converted to z-scores. These are normalized z-scores as opposed to linear z-scores. (Remember that in the linear transformation the original shape of the raw-score distribution remains unchanged.) Normalized T-scores and deviation IQs can be computed from the formulas in Table 3.1 based on the *normalized* z-scores.

Although it is rarely necessary actually to perform any of these computations, the concept of normalized scores must be fully understood so that Figure 3.1 is interpreted correctly. For the vast majority of standardized tests that would most likely be used in screening for learning disabilities, test publishers furnish normalized scores. The distribution of scores for the norm sample usually approaches normality in any case. If a particular standard score is not reported, it can easily be obtained from conversion tables. In fact, once percentile ranks have been computed for achievement or ability test raw scores, normalized z – and T-scores can be found in these tables (see Chapter 8).

INTERRELATIONSHIPS AMONG SCORES. As Figure 3.1 clearly illustrates, the test user can move from one scoring system to another depending on the scoring needs of a specific decision application. A raw score that is one standard deviation above the mean, for example, is equivalent to a percentile rank of 84, a z-score of + 1.0, a T-score of 60, a national curve equivalent (NCE) of 72, a stanine of 7, and deviation IQs of 115 (Wechsler Scales) and 116 (Otis-Lennon). The most striking similarity among the scores is the midpoint, where a raw score mean is equal to a z-score of 0, a T-score, percentile rank, and NCE of 50, a stanine of 5, and a deviation IQ of 100. These metrics are essentially different names for the same level of performance. Each metric just expresses the quantity in a different form. The interrelationships among the different metrics can be extremely useful in relating achievement and ability test batteries to arrive at an estimate of discrepancy.

OTHER NORMATIVE SCORES. The different developmental scores and scores of relative standing described thus far are the types of scores encountered most frequently on standardized tests and/or that appear to be relevant to the assessment of learning-disabled children. There are many other scoring systems in use. Some of these are included in Figure 3.1. However, for a further discussion of this topic and scores such as the *C*-scaled score and sten score plus test-specific scores developed for specific aptitude and intelligence tests, the reader is referred to Lyman's (1978) review.

Criterion-referenced Test Scores

Dissimilar to all of the preceding derived scores, the scores from criterion-referenced tests require no transformations or conversion tables. A simple *raw score* and *percentage correct* supply the necessary metrics from which inferences about mastery and nonmastery can be made. At present, there is ample evidence of their utility in many types of decision applications, from individual diagnosis to high school graduation or professional certification to program evaluation (see Fremer, 1978; Gifford & Hambleton, 1979; Mills & Hambleton, 1980). This presentation, however, will be restricted to the diagnostic use of the scores for pinpointing a learning-disabled child's skill-development weaknesses. The manner in which the scores are reported as well as how they are interpreted can greatly influence their value for guiding remedial prescriptions.

DOMAIN–REFERENCED INTERPRETATIONS. Despite the more than 50 descriptions and definitions of a criterion-referenced test that have appeared in the literature over the past two decades (Gray, 1978; Nitko, 1980b, in press), there is general agreement that the test is intended *"to ascertain an individual's status with respect to a well-defined behavioral domain"* (Popham, 1978, p. 93). The importance of obtaining rigorous and precise domain specifications to maximize the interpretability of an individual's score was emphasized previously. Once the domain is delimited and clearly specified and a sample of test items is generated from these specifications, statements about how much a student knows or his or her level of skill in a given content domain can be made. For example, on the instructional objective "Alphabetize groups of words," a student might answer three out of eight items correctly. This raw score of 3 on the item sample can be expressed as a percentage correct of 38% in the item domain (all possible items that could be written for the objective). In other words, based on a sample of eight items keyed to the instructional objective, a teacher can infer that Evita knows very little about alphabetizing words by first and second letter. Just what alphabetizing skills are most troublesome would require a more detailed analysis of *which* 5 items on the subtest were answered incorrectly. This type of analysis will be illustrated shortly.

Domain-referenced interpretations such as the preceding are most meaningful with objectives that are measured with discrete pieces of information or learning tasks. This does not imply that the interpretations are limited to low-level cognitive skills and ultraspecific objectives, only that the description of an individual's performance is perhaps the simplest in relation to these skills. Where more complex objectives are assessed, the domain-referenced interpretation may require additional qualifications to clarify the meaning. For example, a 38% level of performance linked to the objective "Write a coherent paragraph" would necessitate some explanation about the nature of the paragraph and the criteria for judging coherency. In all cases, it is the domain specification that can facilitate or impede this interpretation. A precise interpretation of performance is made possible only by a precise definition of the content domain.

MASTERY INTERPRETATIONS. Beyond the domain-referenced interpretations of an individual's score, one can reference the score to a mastery standard. Although this referencing is not essential, it can greatly enhance the value of the score for various types of decision making (Berk, 1984). It is, in fact, considerably more difficult and actually less efficient instructionally to use only a domain-referenced interpretation for diagnostic decisions.

The mastery standard that is set for each objective permits two levels of diagnosis: instructional objective and behavioral objective. First, one can identify which instructional objectives or major skill categories in a subject area have not been mastered. Second, for those objectives not mastered, the degree of nonmastery and the items missed can be analyzed in terms of the explicit subskills or behavioral objectives. This information is especially useful in suggesting the specific deficiencies that need remediation. Thereby, a profile of strengths and weaknesses is produced that can guide ipsative interpretations of performance and individualized instructional prescriptions.

The score information requirements for these two levels of diagnosis are delineated as follows: number of items measuring each objective, number of items answered correctly, percentage correct, mastery standard, items answered incorrectly. These data should be reported in a clear and understandable format so that a teacher can quickly and easily appraise each child's performance.

Depending on the school or clinical setting where the diagnosis is to occur, two types of reports may be required — individual and group. The *individual report* of test results would be appropriate where the test is administered to one student at a time as he or she is referred for diagnosis. A sample report format is shown in Table 3.2. This report displays at a glance all of the essential data for diagnostic decisions. However, it must be used in conjunction with the domain specifications in order to interpret the scores. The report readily provides answers to several important questions:

1. *Which objectives were not mastered?*
   3 and 5
2. *What is the degree of nonmastery in each case?*
   For objective 3, Cookie scored far below the mastery standard.
   For objective 5, Cookie scored just one point below the cutoff.
3. *What specific skill weaknesses contributed to this poor performance?*
   For objective 3, most of the items missed related to the following behav-

ioral objectives:

Identify one and two syllable written words.

Divide words into syllables using the dictionary.

For objective 5, the items missed were concentrated in the following two behavioral objectives:

Identify words that have been made from the root word.

Identify word meanings of pictures representing the words.

Notice that question 3 can be answered only by analyzing the items answered incorrectly in relation to the behavioral objectives from which the items were constructed.

Since the number of items keyed to each behavioral objective is rather low, usually less than 5, the data base for decisions concerning "which specific skill weakness" may be very unreliable. Missing one or two items, in particular, should be interpreted merely as *suggestive evidence* as opposed to conclusive evidence of a possible skill deficiency. If other corroborative data are available, such as the results of quizzes, practice exercises, and the like, more confidence can be placed in the diagnosis.

Table 3.2

Sample Student Report of Criterion-referenced Test Results

Test Date: 11/3/82

Name: Cookie Silver

School: John F. Kennedy Elementary School

Teacher: Carol Devos

Grade: 2

Test: Introductory Dictionary Skills

Objective	Number of Items	Correct No.	%	Mastery No.	%	Items Answered Incorrectly
1. Alphabetize groups of words	8	6	75	6	75	7, 8
2. Locate entry words in the dictionary	14	12	86	11	79	18, 20
3. Syllabicate words	17	8	47	14	82	25, 28, 29, 30, 31, 36, 37, 38, 39
4. Use guide words	7	5	71	5	71	43, 44
5. Recognize word meanings	6	4	67	5	83	50, 52

Objectives Matered = 1, 2, 4

A second type of report is the *group report*. This report can display the subtest and item results for any group of students and instructional objective; that

Table 3.3

Sample Classroom Summary Report by Objective

Test Date: 11/3/82

School: John F. Kennedy Elementary School

Teacher: Carol Devos

Grade: 2

Number of Students: 24

Test: Introductory Dictionary Skills

Objective 5: Recognize word meanings

	Correct				Items Answered Incorrectly			
Student	No.	%	47	48	49	50	51	52
Abrams, Marion	6	100						
Mills, James	6	100						
Prince, Barbara	6	100						
Boyd, Anne	5	83		X				
Fisher, Corinne	5	83		X				
Ford, Maurice	5	83						X
Simmons, Marisa	5	83		X				
Wagner, Scott	5	83		X				

ALL STUDENTS ABOVE HAVE MASTERED THE OBJECTIVE*

Armstrong, Tyrone	4	67		X			X	
Silver, Cookie	4	67				X		X
Thyde, Francis	4	67	X	X				
Barnes, Vanessa	3	50	X	X		X		
Bray, Timothy	3	50		X		X		X
Cohen, Martin	3	50	X	X		X		
Kramer, Patricia	3	50	X	X				X
London, Bradley	3	50		X	X			X
Meyer, Evita	3	50	X	X				X
Whitney, Monica	3	50	X	X			X	
Peck, Gertrude	2	33	X			X	X	X
Rowe, Julia	2	33	X	X		X	X	
Oden, Joshua	1	17	X	X	X	X	X	
Ranson, Stephen	1	17	X	X		X	X	X
Storm, Andrew	1	17	X		X	X	X	X
Wright, Philip	1	17	X	X	X	X	X	

---

*Mastery standard = 5 or 83%

is, it summarizes the performance of a class on a single objective. A sample format is presented in Table 3.3. The information in this report can guide the teacher in grouping students with similar skill weaknesses, objective by objective. A group profile of items missed can also identify instructional problem areas that may affect masters as well as nonmasters. For example, item 48 was

Table 3.4

Sample Classroom Summary Report of Number of Objectives Mastered

Test Date: 11/3/82

School: John F. Kennedy Elementary School

Teacher: Carol Devos

Grade: 2

Number of Students: 24

Test: Introductory Dictionary Skills

Student	Objectives Mastered No.	Objectives Mastered %	1	2	3	4	5
Fisher, Corinne	5	100					
Simmons, Marisa	5	100					
Abrams, Marion	4	80					
Boyd, Anne	4	80					
London, Bradley	4	80					X
Whitney, Monica	4	80					X
Barnes, Vanessa	3	60			X		X
Bray, Timothy	3	60			X		X
Cohen, Martin	3	60		X			X
Ford, Maurice	3	60	X	X			
Kramer, Patricia	3	60				X	X
Meyer, Evita	3	60			X		X
Mills, James	3	60		X	X		
Prince, Barbara	3	60			X	X	
Armstrong, Tyrone	2	40	X		X		X
Peck, Gertrude	2	40	X			X	X
Rowe, Julia	2	40			X	X	X
Silver, Cookie	2	40		X	X		X
Storm, Andrew	2	40	X			X	X
Thyde, Francis	2	40			X	X	X
Wagner, Scott	2	40		X	X	X	
Oden, Joshua	1	20	X	X	X		X
Ranson, Stephen	1	20		X	X	X	X
Wright, Philip	1	20	X	X	X		X

very difficult for both categories of students. This item measured the behavioral objective "Identify the most common meaning of words from among multiple meanings in the dictionary." Perhaps not enough instruction was given on this objective or the instruction that did occur was ineffective.

Certainly there are many formats one could use to report the foregoing individual and group test scores. Commercial test publishers and local school districts often provide a variety of computerized test reports for use by teachers, parents, and principals (see Fremer, 1978). The score and identification information vary from one report to another as a function of who will be using the results and the decisions to be made. The data at one level of decision making are simply aggregated to furnish a summary at the next higher level. As the two sample formats illustrated, the group report is just a summary of several individual reports.

Another type of group report and example of data aggregation provides a summary of the performance of students for the collection of objectives measured by the total test. One sample format with this information is shown in Table 3.4. It answers two questions about each student's achievement:

1. How many objectives were mastered?
2. Which objectives were not mastered?

Note that the second question could be answered by the preceding group format in Table 3.3. The unique contribution of this report then resides in the data needed to answer the first question. These data are obtained by tallying the mastery results by objective from a set of individual reports and assembling the final figures as a group summary.

Although less diagnostic information is presented in this report compared with the report in Table 3.3, it can be extremely useful in assessing overall performance at the completion of an instructional unit. If necessary, letter grades can also be assigned according to how much skill a student exhibits at the end of the marking period (see Gronlund, 1974; Millman, 1970). The grades can represent the *number of objectives mastered*. For example, where there are five instructional objectives, a grading scheme such as the following may be employed:

Grade	Number of Objectives Mastered
A	5
B	4
C	2 or 3
D	1
E	0

This scheme is arbitrary, although the letter grade scale and the number of objectives in this instance does not permit very much latitude for being arbitrary.

Conclusions

The foregoing examination of various types of developmental scores and scores of relative standing that are used for norm-referenced interpretations indicates that only standard scores such as z-scores and T-scores possess the technical properties and practical advantages essential for the analysis of ability-achievement discrepancies. Under no condition should grade equivalents, age equivalents, or intelligence quotients be used for this purpose. These conclusions are obviously contrary to most extant practices.

For diagnostic decisions about a specific learning disability, raw scores and percentages correct on a criterion-referenced test supply the basic information from which mastery and nonmastery inferences can be drawn. Both domain-referenced and mastery interpretations of individual performance seem to provide the most meaningful framework for determining which objectives were not mastered, the degree of nonmastery, and the specific skill weaknesses contributing to nonmastery.

These descriptions of norm-referenced and criterion-referenced test scores serve to emphasize the very important distinction between a *norm* and a *standard*, respectively. A norm reflects the typical performance of some group, not a level of performance one strives to achieve. In contrast, a standard is a goal to be attained that is not set according to the performance of the group tested. A norm indicates what is; a standard indicates what ought to be.

Out-of-level Test Administration and Scoring

The discussion of norm-referenced test scores up to this point has presumed that a standardized test is administered to learning-disabled children on *grade level*, that is, the test intended for the grade in which they are enrolled; for example, fifth graders are given a fifth-grade or intermediate level test, the level recommended by the publisher. The alternative to on-level testing is *out-of-level* testing, where the test is administered at a child's functional, or skill, level. For example, if a fifth grader scores below the chance score on a fifth-grade test, a fourth-grade or lower level test would be more appropriate, a level where the child is more likely to function intellectually (functional level). Out-of-level testing is a common practice with low-achieving students in general and learning-disabled children in particular, especially those participating in Title I programs (Long, 1979; Long, Schaffran, & Kellogg, 1977; Powers & Gallas, 1978; Roberts, 1976; Slaughter & Gallas, 1978; Wilson & Donlon, 1980).

Most standardized, norm-referenced achievement and ability tests are expressly designed to measure performance at one grade level or at multiple levels (usually two or three grades), and their respective norm samples and technical properties relate to that (those) particular level(s). Unfortunately, the technical characteristics are optimal for only those children who score in the middle range on the test. In other words, the most valid and reliable measurement of fifth graders is obtained for students who score around the midscore on a fifth-grade test. For students who score extremely high, near the test ceiling, or extremely low, near the test floor, the measurement can be both invalid and unreliable (Horst, Tallmadge, & Wood, 1974). Certainly the *floor effect* is more troublesome in testing learning-disabled children. One tactic used to avoid this effect is out-of-level testing (see review by Arter, 1982).

Major Reasons for Testing Out of Level

Among the different reasons for considering out-of-level testing, three concerns seem to be articulated most often: (1) the test is too hard, (2) the students score below the chance level, and (3) the test content and the curriculum do not match.

TEST IS TOO HARD. When students are overwhelmed by the difficulty of a test, they may respond by giving up, running from the room, and/or crying (Yoshida, 1976). Such behaviors are indicative of frustration and low or no motivation. Students in this situation also tend to guess on most of the items. All of these responses have a negative effect on the resulting test scores, to the extent that the scores are usually invalid. In order to lessen frustration, increase motivation, and reduce guessing, an easier test is administered, which is typically one or two grade placement levels below the "hard test." This test appears to yield more positive reactions and, consequently, more valid scores (Haynes & Cole, 1982).

STUDENTS SCORE BELOW CHANCE LEVEL. The most frequent reason given for deciding to test out of level is that the student(s) scored below the expected chance score. When students answer so few items correctly, it is almost impossible to differentiate among their levels of achievement or ability; scores at the end of test scale supply virtually no information for norm-referenced interpretations (cf. Cole & Nitko, 1981). The range of reliable scores is between the chance or floor level (lower limit) and the ceiling level (upper limit), generally from 30% to 75% of the items correct (Ayrer & McNamara, 1973; Roberts, 1976). Therefore, it is desirable to obtain scores *in range*, and the majority of studies on this topic focus on the proportion of scores lying within these limits (Cleland & Idstein, 1980; Crowder & Gallas, 1978; Long, Schaffran, & Kellogg, 1977). The scores from on-level tests, which are difficult for learning-disabled children, frequently fall outside of this range, below the lower limit.

On the surface, the problem seems easily identifiable via an individual's test score. Its solution also seems apparent — administer a lower level test. However, the research on chance scores does not support the notion that they are automatically invalid. In fact, as Arter (1982) points out, there is mounting evidence to the contrary (Jones, Barnette, & Callahan, 1983; Stewart, 1980; Wilson & Donlon, 1980).

The fundamental question is: What does a chance score mean? Fry (1971) defined it as the

> score on a standardized reading test that can be obtained by a well-trained Orang-outang under these special conditions. A slightly hungry Orangoutang is placed in a small cage that has an oblong window and four buttons. The Orangoutang has been trained that every time the reading teacher places a neatly typed multiple choice item from a reading test in the oblong window, all that he (the Orangoutang) has to do to get a bit of banana is to press a button, any of the buttons, which incidentally, are labeled A, B, C, and D.
>
>   . . . On the average, the Orangoutang will get 25 percent or one out of every four reading test items correct by chance if he marks every item. (p. 360)

His (Fry) "Orangoutang score" is computed as the total number of items divided by the number of choices per item on a multiple-choice test. With four-choice items, the mean chance score is 25% of the total; with five-choice items, 20%.

Embedded within this definition is the assumption of random guessing. This assumption is fallacious based on how students actually answer test questions. Although guessing increases as test scores decrease, Arter (1982) concluded that recent studies suggest "students, even low achieving students, do not invariably display true random behavior on tests" (p. 9). There are numerous factors that could produce a chance-level score (see MacRae & Green, 1971; Stewart, 1980), the least prominent of which is pure random responses.

Contrary to popular belief, then, an individual chance score should not necessarily be judged as invalid due to random guessing. It should be viewed more perceptively as a signal of possible invalidity. Inquiring into the causes(s) for poor performance might very well reveal the score to be valid. Moreover, the chance-level scoring of several students in a class should not serve as the sole criterion for determining whether to test out of level. Again, the underlying causes of those performances should be examined. The findings of this examination should dictate the appropriate action; in some cases, the action might be to administer a lower level test.

TEST CONTENT AND CURRICULUM MISMATCH. Another reason for testing out of level is to obtain a close match between what is tested and what is to be taught. Different levels of achievement tests cover different content with different skill emphases (Raffeld, 1980). The test content may or may not be congruent with a particular curriculum and the actual instruction that has occurred (see Chapter 2). Methods for analyzing the degree of incongruence or mismatch have been reported in several major studies (Armbruster, Stevens, & Rosenshine, 1977; Floden, Porter, Schmidt, & Freeman, 1980; Freeman et al., 1980; Jenkins & Pany, 1978a; Porter, Schmidt, Floden, & Freeman, 1978; Tenenbaum & Miller, 1977).

Suppose a particular investigation found that the coverage and emphases in the reading comprehension subtest of an on-level test did not reflect the local curriculum. Depending on the percentage of mismatch, for example 40%, the scores on the test could be invalid measures of achievement *in the program*. Essentially, the students would be tested on only 60% of the material that is part of the program.

This ever-present source of invalidity demonstrates the importance of carefully and systematically inspecting the test's content in relation to the curriculum. If a lower level test provides a better match than the on-level test, it should be considered for administration. The final decision, however, should not rest on the results of the content analysis alone. Additional justification for out-of-level testing should be sought in terms of one or both of the preceding reasons. Furthermore, these pluses should be weighed against the disadvantages of testing out of level.

Disadvantages

While the aforementioned reasons for choosing out-of-level testing can be perceived as its primary advantages, there are also several disadvantages and troublespots associated with implementing this testing strategy.

NEED TO DETERMINE FUNCTIONAL LEVEL. If a teacher is contemplating out-of-level testing, he or she must decide how to determine the appropriate test levels to be administered. A student's functional level is usually estimated by one or more of the following methods: (1) previous standardized test performance, (2) performance on "locator tests" that are available from test publishers, (3) teacher ratings of performance. Teacher judgment often incorporates the data from previous tests or locator tests (Fuentes & Jeffress, 1978; Haenn & Proctor, 1978; Slaughter & Gallas, 1978). Currently, however, there is insufficient evidence to support the use of locator tests by themselves (Haynes & Cole, 1982).

INCONVENIENT ADMINISTRATION SCHEDULE. There are a variety of practical problems typically encountered in planning and executing an on-level standardized testing program. These problems are compounded when multiple levels of a test battery must be administered within a class or any other group setting (Gabriel, Arter, & Demaline, 1980). The majority of the students may be administered the on-level test, but some of the remaining students may receive the next lower level test, and others an even lower level test. The logistics for scheduling these administrations will certainly vary with the out-of-level testing needs in each application. Test users should not underestimate the complexity of this scheduling. (*Note*: Individualized testing is not affected by these scheduling problems.)

REQUIRES SCALED SCORES AND TRANSFORMATION TO DERIVED SCORES. Once a test is administered out of level, the norm sample and the derived scores based on that sample are invalid for the students tested. In other words, if a fifth-grade student is tested with a third-grade test, the norm-referenced interpretation of his or her performance in terms of third-grade norms is incorrect. The percentile rank or standard score of the fifth grader should be derived from fifth-grade norms.

How then can the raw scores of students tested out of level be expressed on a normative score scale that permits valid inferences about their performance? The procedure for equating the scores on different tests, such as a fifth-grade reading comprehension with third-grade reading comprehension, is known as vertical equating. This equating is also essential for the analysis of group data in program evaluation at a single grade level, where different out-of-level as well as on-level tests are given.

Vertical equating is the process of equating tests that differ in difficulty so that they are roughly "exchangeable," i.e., converting to a common scale the scores on forms of a test designed for populations at different grade levels (Slinde & Linn, 1977, p. 23). (This type of equating contrasts with horizontal equating, which involves equating test forms that are developed to measure the same content at the same grade level for the same population.) However, as Linn (1981) pointed out, "tests that are designed to measure achievement at different grade levels differ not only in the difficulty but [also] in the content specifications for the items" (p. 101). These characteristics complicate the task. In general, as the disparity between actual grade level of the student (e.g., fifth grader) and nominal grade level of the test (e.g., third-grade test) increases, test equating becomes more difficult. Equating tests at adjacent grade levels has been accomplished satisfactorily (see, for example, Slinde & Linn, 1979); equating tests that differ more drastically in difficulty, say two or three grade levels apart, is troublesome.

There are four models test publishers use to equate various tests: linear, equipercentile, one-parameter logistic (Rasch), and three-parameter logistic. The first two models are traditional; the other two logistic or latent trait models constitute a relatively recent innovation in the field (Marco, 1981). The linear and equipercentile models have been used for three decades and are, by far, the most popular (Angoff, 1971; Flanagan, 1951). The empirical research over the past five years that has compared the precision of these models with the logistic models suggests that some methods are better under some circumstances and other methods are better under other circumstances (see Arter, 1982; Butera & Raffeld, 1979; Holland & Rubin, 1982; Jaeger, 1981; Kolen, 1981; Kolen & Whitney, 1982; Linn, 1981).

The net effect of all of this research on test score equating is that it is now possible to translate the raw scores on different levels of a test into one scale. The names that have been assigned to this type of scale vary from publisher to publisher. The scores are often called *scaled scores,* expanded standard scores, growth scores, or achievement development scores. It is usually assumed that these scores constitute an equal-interval scale. Furthermore, scaled scores can be referenced to any set of normative data, thereby permitting, for example, the conversion of third-grade test scores of fifth graders to fifth-grade percentiles or standard scores.

Although there are systematic equating errors associated with these scaled scores, they are typically smaller than the measurement errors associated with floor effects (Horst et al., 1974, p. 16). Therefore, it is advisable to consider scaled scores for tests administered out of level and then to transform these scores into the appropriate standard scores for norm-referenced interpretations. In particular, when standardized achievement tests are administered out of level for screening purposes, the use of scaled scores or transformed scaled scores is clearly preferable to the simplest, direct, but incorrect use of out-of-level derived scores.

Conclusions

This presentation on out-of-level testing has concentrated on the fundamental issues pertinent to obtaining valid and reliable test scores for learning-disabled children. While the practical and statistical disadvantages of executing such a testing program can be problematic, one also needs to consider the consequences of not testing out of level.

A comparison of out-of-level testing with on-level testing is outlined in Table 3.5. The sharp differences between the two strategies according to six factors discussed in this section lead to two conclusions: (1) if an on-level standardized test is very difficult and the scores that result are below the chance level, it is likely that those scores will not be sufficiently discriminating for screening decisions, and (2) if the list of advantages of on-level testing were balanced against the disadvantages of out-of-level testing in this context, those advantages become almost irrelevant. In other words, *out-of-level testing may be the only strategy for assuring in-range scores that are sufficiently discriminating for many learning-disabled children.* It should be evident from Table 3.5 that this is the primary advantage of out-of-level testing; it is also probably the only one that really matters. A recent study by Haynes and Cole (1982) confirms this position.

Since standardized test batteries that are most useful for screening are administered in either small or large group settings, procedures for overcoming the practical disadvantages of out-of-level testing are needed. Some suggestions for tackling the administration and scoring problems are proffered as follows:

1. Use past standardized test performance as a guide for determining current functional level for the same test series.
2. Group students who will be taking the same level test, where possible.
3. Use multilevel tests that encompass several grades, such as primary or intermediate, rather than single grade level tests if the functional levels of the children are diverse; this practice can reduce the number of different test levels that must be administered.

MEMORY JOGGER

Table 3.5

Comparison of Out-of-level and On-level Testing Strategies

Factor	Out of Level	On Level
Difficulty of test	Moderately difficult test can decrease guessing, minimize frustration, and increase motivation	Very difficult test can increase guessing, create frustration, and decrease motivation
Chance level scores	Can produce a large proportion of scores in-range that do discriminate among achievement levels	Can produce scores below the expected chance score that do not discriminate among achievement levels
Level of test	Need to determine appropriate functional level test by previous test performance, locator tests, and/or teacher ratings	Grade placement determines on-level test
Test administration	Inconvenient to administer different level tests to different students within a classroom setting	Convenient to test all students with the same test at the same time
Type of score	Requires use of scaled scores based on vertical equating procedures, which are "more or less accurate"	No need for scaled scores
Score transformation	Need to transform scaled scores into on-level derived scores for norm-referenced interpretations	No transformation is necessary; derived scores are obtained directly from student performance

4. Request scaled scores from the test publisher for all test levels when the answer sheets are processed.
5. Request conversion tables or the appropriate technical manual for transforming the scaled scores to the desired derived scores, especially percentile ranks, for on-level score interpretations.

Summary

This chapter reviewed the numerous types of norm-referenced and criterion-referenced test scores that teachers can use for screening and diagnostic decisions. Among the various developmental scores (grade equivalents, age equivalents, intelligence quotients) and scores of relative standing (percentile ranks, standard scores), only standard scores such as z-scores and T-scores possess the technical properties and practical advantages essential for the analysis of ability-achievement discrepancies. Nine arguments were given for not using developmental scores for this purpose. When diagnostic decisions are made from the results of a criterion-referenced test, raw scores and percentage correct scores should supply the information necessary for domain-referenced and mastery interpretations of individual performance. This seems to provide the most meaningful framework for determining which objectives were not mastered, what the degree of nonmastery is, and what specific skill weaknesses contribute to nonmastery. Finally, the critical issues related to out-of-level versus on-level testing were discussed. It was concluded that out-of-level testing may be the only strategy for assuring in-range standardized test scores that are sufficiently discriminating for many learning-disabled children. A few suggestions were offered for dealing with the administration and scoring problems associated with such a testing program.

References

Angoff, W.H. Scales, norms, and equivalent scores. In R.L. Thorndike (Ed.), *Educational measurement* (2nd ed.). Washington, DC: American Council on Education, 1971. Pp. 508 – 600.

Armbruster, B.B., Stevens, R.O., & Rosenshine, B. *Analyzing content coverage and emphasis: A study of three curricula and two tests* (Technical Report No. 26). Urbana-Champaign: Center for the Study of Reading, University of Illinois, 1977.

Arter, J.A. *Out-of-level versus in-level testing: When should we recommend each?* Paper presented at the annual meeting of the American Educational Research Association, New York, March 1982.

Ayrer, J.E., & McNamara, T.C. Survey testing on an out-of-level basis. *Journal of Educational Measurement*, 1973, *10*, 79 – 84.

Beggs, D.L., & Hieronymus, A.N. Uniformity of growth in the basic skills through the school year and during the summer. *Journal of Educational Measurement*, 1968, *5*, 91 – 97.

Berk, R.A. A comparison of six content domain specification strategies for criterion-referenced tests. *Educational Technology*, 1980, *20*, 49 – 52.(a)

Berk, R.A. Introduction. In R.A. Berk (Ed.), *Criterion-referenced measurement: The state of the art.* Baltimore, MD: Johns Hopkins University Press, 1980. Pp. 3 – 9.(b)

Berk, R.A. What's wrong with using grade-equivalent scores to identify LD children? *Academic Therapy*, 1981, *17*, 133 – 140.

Berk, R.A. Criterion-referenced tests. In T. Husén & T.N. Postlethwaite (Eds.), *International encyclopedia of education: Research and studies.* Oxford, England: Pergamon Press, 1984.

Butera, B.J., & Raffeld, P.C. *Investigation of vertical scaling for out-of-level testing.* Paper presented at the annual meeting of the American Educational Research Association, San Francisco, April 1979.

Cleland, W.E., & Idstein, P.M. *In-level versus out-of-level testing of sixth grade special education students.* Paper presented at the annual meeting of the National Council of Measurement in Education, Boston, April 1980.

Cole, N.S. *Grade equivalent scores: To GE or not to GE.* Division D vice-presidential address presented at the annual meeting of the American Educational Research Association, New York, March 1982.

Cole, N.S. *Grade equivalent scores: To GE or not to GE.* Division D vice-presidential address presented at the annual meeting of the American Educational Research Association, New York, March 1982.

Cole, N.S., & Nitko, A.J. Measuring program effects. In R.A. Berk (Ed.) *Educational evaluation methodology: The state of the art.* Baltimore, MD: Johns Hopkins University Press, 1981. Pp. 32 – 63.

Crowder, C.R., & Gallas, E.J. *Relation of out-of-level testing to ceiling and floor effects on third and fifth grade students.* Paper presented at the annual meeting of the American Educational Research Association, Toronto, March 1978.

Durost, W.N. *The characteristics, use, and computation of stanines.* New York: Harcourt Brace Jovanovich, 1961.

Flanagan, J.C. Units, scores, and norms. In E.F. Lindquist (Ed.), *Educational measurement.* Washington, DC: American Council on Education, 1951. Pp. 695 – 763.

Floden, R.E., Porter, A.C., Schmidt, W.H., & Freeman, D.J. Don't they all measure the same thing? Consequences of standardized test selection. In E.L. Baker & E.S. Quellmalz (Eds.), *Educational testing and evaluation: Design, analysis, and policy.* Beverly Hills, CA: Sage, 1980. Pp. 109 – 120.

Freeman, D.J., Kuhs, T.M., Porter, A.C., Knappen, L.B., Floden, R.E., Schmidt, W.H., & Schwille, J.R. *The fourth grade mathematics curriculum as inferred from textbooks and tests.* Paper presented at the annual meeting of the American Educational Research Association, Boston, April 1980.

Fremer, J.J., Jr. *Using and interpreting the results of criterion-referenced tests: Promise, progress, and unresolved problems.* Invited paper presented at the first Johns Hopkins University National Symposium on Educational Research, Washington, DC, October 1978.

Fry, E. The orangoutang score. *Reading Teacher,* 1971, *24,* 361 – 362.

Fuentes, E.J., & Jeffress, E.L. *The use of teacher estimates of chidren's achievement in selecting appropriate test levels vs. blanket out-of-level testing: The problem of an efficient method of matching the student's functional level with the proper test level.* Paper presented at the annual meeting of the American Educational Research Association, Toronto, April 1978.

Gabriel, R.M., Arter, J.A., & Demaline, R.E. *Functional level testing: Selecting the right test evel* (Workshop Package, Title I Technical Assistance Centers). Portland, OR: Northwest Regional Educational Laboratory, 1980.

Gates, A.I., & MacGinitie, W.H. *Gates-MacGinitie Reading Tests, Teacher's manual* (Survey D). New York: Teachers College Press, 1965.

Gifford, J.A., & Hambleton, R.K. *Construction and use of criterion-referenced tests in program evaluation studies* (Report No. 102). Amherst: Laboratory of Psychometric and Evaluative Research, School of Education, University of Massachusetts, March 1979.

Gray, W.M. A comparison of Piagetian theory and criterion-referenced measurement. *Review of Educational Research,* 1978, *48,* 223 – 249.

Gronlund, N.E. *Improving marking and reporting in classroom instruction.* New York: Macmillan, 1974.

Gronlund, N.E. *Measurement and evaluation in teaching* (4th ed.). New York: Macmillan, 1981.

Gulliksen, H. *Theory of mental tests.* New York: Wiley, 1950.

Haenn, J.F., & Proctor, D.C. *A practitioner's guide to out-of-level testing.* Paper presented at the annual meeting of the American Educational Research Association, Toronto, April 1978.

Haynes, L.T., & Cole, N.S. *Testing some assumptions about on-level versus out-of-level achievement testing.* Paper presented at the annual meeting of the National Council on Measurement in Education, New York, March 1982.

Hieronymus, A.N., Lindquist, E.F., & Hoover, H.D. *Iowa Tests of Basic Skills, Teacher's guide* (Forms 7/8). Boston: Houghton Mifflin, 1978.

Hills, J.R. Interpreting grade-equivalent scores. *Educational measurement: Issues and practice*, 1983, *2*, 15, 21.

Holland, P.W., & Rubin, D.B. (Eds.). *Test equating.* New York: Academic Press, 1982.

Horst, D.P. *What's bad about grade-equivalent scores, ESEA Title I evaluation and reporting system* (Technical Report No. 1). Mountain View, CA: RMC Research Corporation, 1976.

Horst, D.P., Tallmadge, G.K., & Wood, C.T. *Measuring achievement gains in educational projects* (RMC Report UR-243). Los Altos, CA: RMC Research Corporation, October 1974.

Jaeger, R.M. Some exploratory indices for selection of a test equating method. *Journal of Educational Measurement*, 1981, *18*, 23 – 38.

Jenkins, J.R., & Pany, D. Curriculum biases in reading achievement tests. *Journal of Reading Behavior*, 1978, *10*, 345 – 357.(a)

Jenkins, J.P., & Pany, D. Standardized achievement tests: How useful for special education. *Exceptional Children*, 1978, *44*, 448 – 453.(b)

Jones, E.D., Barnette, J.J., & Callahan, C.M. *Out-of-level testing for special education students with mild learning handicaps.* Paper presented at the annual meeting of the American Educational Research Association, Montreal, April 1983.

Kolen, M.J. Comparison of traditional and item response theory methods for equating tests. *Journal of Educational Measurement*, 1981, *18*, 1 – 11.

Kolen, M.J., & Whitney, D.R. Comparison of four procedures for equating the Tests of General Educational Development. *Journal of Educational Measurement*, 1982, *19*, 279 – 293.

Linn, R.L. Measuring pretest-posttest performance changes. In R.A. Berk (Ed.), *Educational evaluation methodology: The state of the art.* Baltimore, MD: Johns Hopkins University Press, 1981. Pp. 84 – 109.

Linn, R.L., & Slinde, J.A. The determination of the significance of change between pre and posttesting periods. *Review of Educational Research*, 1977, *47*, 121 – 150.

Long, J.V. *Out-of-level survey testing in Title I – Further empirical examination.* Paper presented at the American Educational Research Association, San Francisco, April 1979.

Long, J.V., Schaffran, J.A., & Kellogg, T.M. Effects of out-of-level survey testing on reading achievement scores of Title I, ESEA students. *Journal of Educational Measurement*, 1977, *14*,203 – 213.

Lyman, H.B. *Test scores and what they mean* (3rd ed.). Englewood Cliffs, NJ: Prentice-Hall, 1978.

MacRae, D.J., & Green, D.R. Comment by (on Fry's "Orangoutang score"). *Reading Teacher*, 1971, *24*, 364.

Marco, G.L. Equating tests in an era of test disclosure. In B.F. Green (Ed.), *New directions for testing and measurement* (No. 11) – *Issues in testing: Coaching, disclosure, and ethnic bias.* San Francisco: Jossey-Bass, 1981. Pp. 105 – 122.

Mehrens, W.A., & Lehmann, I.J. *Measurement and evaluation in education and psychology* (2nd ed.). New York: Holt, Rinehart and Winston, 1978.

Millman, J. Reporting student progress: A case for a criterion-referenced marking system. *Phi Delta Kappan*, 1970, *52*, 226 – 230.

Millman, J. Computer-based item generation. In R.A. Berk (Ed.), *Criterion-referenced measurement: The state of the art.* Baltimore, MD: Johns Hopkins University Press, 1980. Pp. 32 – 43.

Mills, C.N., & Hambleton, R.K. *Guidelines for reporting criterion-referenced test score information.* Paper presented at the annual meeting of the American Educational Research Association, Boston, April 1980.

Nitko, A.J. Criterion-referencing schemes. In S.T. Mayo (Ed.), *New directions for testing and measurement* (No. 6) – *Interpreting test performance.* San Francisco: Jossey-Bass, 1980. Pp. 35 – 71.(a)

Nitko, A.J. Distinguishing the many varieties of criterion-referenced tests. *Review of Educational Research*, 1980, *50*, 461 – 485.(b)

Nitko, A.J. Defining "criterion-referenced test." In R.A. Berk (Ed.), *A guide to criterion-referenced test construction*. Baltimore, MD: Johns Hopkins University Press, in press.

Popham, W.J. *Criterion-referenced measurement*. Englewood Cliffs, NJ: Prentice-Hall, 1978.

Popham, W.J. Domain specification strategies. In R.A. Berk (Ed.), *Criterion-referenced measurement: The state of the art*. Baltimore, MD: Johns Hopkins University Press, 1980. Pp. 15 – 31.

Popham, W.J. *Modern educational measurement*. Englewood Cliffs, NJ: Prentice-Hall, 1981.

Porter, A.C., Schmidt, W.H., Floden, R.E., & Freeman, D.J. Practical significance in program evaluation. *American Educational Research Journal*, 1978, *15*, 529 – 539.

Powers, S., & Gallas, E.J. *Implications of out-of-level testing for ESEA Title I students*. Paper presented at the annual meeting of the American Educational Research Association, Toronto, March 1978.

Raffeld, P.C. *Functional level testing and the content shift*. Paper presented at the annual meeting of the American Educational Research Association, San Francisco, April 1979.

Reynolds, C.R. The fallacy of "two-years below grade level for age" as a diagnostic criterion for reading disorders. *Journal of School Psychology*, 1981, *19*, 350 – 358.

Roberts, O.H. *Out-of-level testing: ESEA Title I evaluation and reporting system* (Technical Paper No. 6). Mountain View, CA: RMC Research Corporation, 1976.

Roid, G.H. Generating the test items. In R.A. Berk (Ed.), *A guide to criterion-referenced test construction*. Baltimore, MD: Johns Hopkins University Press, in press.

Roid, G.H., & Haladyna, T.M. *A technology for test-item writing*. New York: Academic Press, 1982.

Salvia, J., & Ysseldyke, J.E. *Assessment in special and remedial education* (2nd ed.). Boston: Houghton Mifflin, 1981.

Slaughter, H.B., & Gallas, E.J. *Will out-of-level norm-referenced testing improve the selection of program participants and the diagnosis of reading comprehension in ESEA Title I programs?* Paper presented at the annual meeting of the American Educational Research Association, Toronto, April 1978.

Slinde, J.A., & Linn, R.L. Vertically equated tests: Fact or phantom? *Journal of Educational Measurement*, 1977, *14*, 23 – 32.

Slinde, J.A., & Linn, R.L. A note on vertical equating via the Rasch model for groups of quite different ability and tests of quite different difficulty. *Journal of educational Measurement*, 1979, *16*, 159 – 165.

Stewart, B.L. Discussion: Assessing the reliability and validity of chance level scores. In G. Echternacht (Ed.), *New directions for testing and measurement* (No. 8) — *Measurement aspects of Title I evaluation*. San Francisco: Jossey-Bass, 1980. Pp. 55 – 58.

Tallmadge, G.K., & Wood, C.T. *User's guide: ESEA Title I evaluation and reporting system*. Mountain View, CA: RMC Research Corporation, 1976.

Tenebaum, A.B., & Miller, C.A. *The use of congruence between the items in a norm-referenced test and the content in a compensatory education curricula in the evaluation of achievement gains*. Paper presented at the annual meeting of the American Educational Research Association, New York, April 1977.

Williams, T.B. *The distributions of NCE, percentile, and grade equivalent scores among twelve nationally standardized tests*. Paper presented at the annual meeting of the American Educational Research Association, Boston, April 1980.

Wilson, K.M., & Donlon, T.F. Toward functional criteria for functionallevel testing in Title I evaluation. In G. Echternacht (Ed.), *New directions for testing and measurement* (No. 8) — *Measurement aspects of Title I evaluation*. San Francisco: Jossey-Bass, 1980. Pp. 51 – 54.

Yoshida, R.K. Out-of-level testing of special education students with a standardized achievement battery. *Journal of Educational Measurement*, 1976, *13*, 215 – 221.

Chapter 4

EVALUATION OF
CURRENT SCREENING PROCEDURES

Introduction

THE *Procedures for Evaluating Specific Learning Disabilities* U.S.O.E. 1977), which was issued subsequent to Public Law 94-142, stipulated that a "child had a specific learning disability if. . . [he or she] has a severe discrepancy between achievement and intellectual ability in one or more of the following areas: (i) oral expression; (ii) listening comprehension; (iii) written expression; (iv) basic reading skill; (v) reading comprehension; (vi) mathematics calculation; or (vii) mathematics reasoning" (p. 65083). Ergo, the most common strategy for screening children with learning disabilities has been to search for a discrepancy between ability and achievement. This discrepancy concept, which is an ipsative interpretation of individual performance, has emerged as the predominant element in defining learning disabilities in both research and practice (see Chapter 1).

The criterion for underachievement has been operationally defined in a variety of ways. For example, in a review of definitions adopted by researchers in learning disability studies between 1978 and 1980, Harber (1981) found the following types of discrepancy:

Significant discrepancy between potential and achievement (amount of discrepancy not specified)
Significant discrepancy (achievement less than 50% of potential)
Significant discrepancy (achievement less than 70% of potential)
Significant discrepancy (achievement less than 90% of potential)
Significant discrepancy (achievement less than 95% of potential)
One or more years below expectancy
Two or more years below expectancy
Below average performance

This variability among discrepancy procedures is attributable, in large part, to the failure of the federal *Procedures* to specify operational criteria for not only what is *severe*, but just what constitutes a *discrepancy*. As a result, each researcher and practitioner charged with the task of identifying learning disabled children was forced to devise his or her own means for determining eligibility. At present, there are more than a dozen different procedures being used to assess the magnitude or statistical significance of discrepancy scores. Most of them can be categorized as follows: (a) number of years below grade level, (b) ability-achievement discrepancy score, (c) WISC – R Verbal-Performance discrepancy score, and (d) WISC – R profile analysis.

The purpose of this chapter is to evaluate the various procedures in terms of their conceptual and statistical soundness and in relation to the aforestated legal regulations. This evaluation should reveal the key methodological issues involved and the most promising approaches to resolving those issues.

Criteria for Evaluating Discrepancy Procedures

There have been several critical reviews of reading expectancy formulas and other methods for identifying specific disabilities in reading, language, and mathematics (see Berk, 1982a, 1983a; Cone & Wilson, 1981b; Hanna, Dyck, & Holen, 1979; McLeod, 1979; O'Donnell, 1980; Shepard, 1980; Warner, 1981). One point of consensus seems to have emerged: multiple sources of error are encountered in quantifying a discrepancy between ability and achievement. The reliability and validity of the discrepancy estimate are contingent on how effectively these sources are accounted for.

The different sources of error can be divided into two categories: (1) those that pertain to the particular ability and achievement tests chosen for a given application and (2) those that relate to the expectancy or discrepancy estimation procedures. These sources of error expressed as evaluative criteria can be used to judge the quality of the discrepancy procedures.

Ability and Achievement Tests

There are four criteria associated with the characteristics of the tests selected for the analysis and the normative scores they yield:

1. *The score metric should constitute an equal interval scale.* As emphasized in the preceding chapter, metrics such as grade-equivalent scores, age-equivalent scores, and intelligence quotients are completely inappropriate and psychometrically inadequate because they are not interval scales and they possess several serious deficiencies. Percentile ranks are also inappropriate inasmuch as they comprise an ordinal scale. In order to perform the most basic arithmetic calculations, i.e., computing differences and quotients, equal units of measurement are essential. The interval scales often recommended for use in discrepancy analysis are z-scores and T-scores. Deviation IQs and certain scaled scores, however, may also be employed.

2. *Both ability and achievement test scores should be transformed into the same score*

metric. Unless two scores are expressed on the same scale, their sum, difference, product, or quotient is meaningless and uninterpretable. Viewed in conjunction with the preceding criterion, it is essential that the scores on both tests be converted to the same standard score metric.

3. *The tests should satisfy standard criteria for technical adequacy.* Only those ability and achievement tests that have been normed properly and provide sufficient evidence of reliability and validity should be chosen for individual discrepancy decisions (see Chapter 2).

4. *Both ability and achievement tests should be normed on the same national standardization sample.* Unless there is comparability of the norm groups, the discrepancies that occur may be attributable to norming artifacts. The consequences of employing noncomparable norms are indeterminable. There is no way to assess the direction of the sampling errors and their effect on the discrepancy scores. The requirement of comparability, however, would restrict the analysis to ability-achievement batteries such as the Cognitive Abilities Test and Iowa Tests of Basic Skills, Otis-Lennon School Ability Test and Metropolitan Achievement Tests, and Test of Cognitive Skills and Comprehensive Tests of Basic Skills (for the further details, see Chapter 2). Clinicians will probably resist using such test pairs inasmuch as they often prefer the individually-administered intelligence tests to those group-administered ability tests. Since the WISC-R and Stanford-Binet are not conormed with major achievement test batteries, the selection of an appropriate achievement test is problematic. Hanna et al. (1979) have argued persuasively that it would be acceptable to use special combinations of tests and to assume comparability of normative data under the condition that a careful inspection of each test's standardization sample indicates that assumption is justified. It is hoped that this can minimize the probable distortions of ability-achievement score comparisons that are due to sampling errors.

Expectancy or Discrepancy Procedure

There are also several criteria that pertain to the reliability and validity of the discrepancy procedure. These are described as follows:

A discrepancy procedure should take into account

1. *the means and standard deviations of the ability and achievement test score distributions.* This is a necessary but not sufficient condition to estimate the true discrepancy score;

2. *the correlation between the ability and achievement test scores.* If two tests are correlated, the discrepancy score may be less reliable than either the ability or achievement test score; the lower the intercorrelation, the greater the chance of obtaining a highly reliable discrepancy score, assuming each test is highly reliable. Considering the moderate correlations that have

been found for various ability and achievement tests and their reliability coefficients, it is likely that the discrepancy scores will be less reliable than the individual scores from which they were computed (cf. Page, 1980; Salvia & Clark, 1973);

3. *regression toward the mean.* One assumption underlying the discrepancy procedure is that, on the average, a non-learning-disabled child can score at the same level on both an ability and achievement test. This is possible only if the two tests were perfectly correlated ($r = 1.00$). Since in reality the correlation is typically between .50 and .75, depending upon the particular pair of tests, all achievement test scores above and below the mean, especially those at the extremes, tend to move or *regress* toward the mean score. As Shepard (1980) pointed out, "It can be shown both mathematically and theoretically that bright (high-IQ) children have above-average achievement, but their relative position. . . tends not to be as high as it is in the IQ distribution. Conversely, children with low IQs will, on the average, have relatively higher achievement status than IQ status, although they will still tend to be below the mean" (p. 83). In other words, students with high ability scores will generally obtain lower achievement scores, and students with low ability scores may be expected to produce higher achievement scores (see also Cone & Wilson, 1981b). This effect on achievement scores can result in the overidentification of high ability children and underidentification of low ability children;

4. *the unreliability of the ability and achievement test scores.* There is measurement error in all test scores, but there is more error associated with some tests than with others (see Salvia & Ysseldyke, 1981). If the reliability coefficient for each test is not considered in the discrepancy procedure, the discrepancy score can be very misleading. Not only can unreliable tests create discrepancies when there are none, and vice versa, but they can change the direction of the discrepancy. For example, a child identified as learning disabled based on the discrepancy between two unreliable tests may, in fact, be an overachiever;

5. *the unreliability of the ability-achievement difference scores.* Regardless of the magnitude of a discrepancy score — small, medium, or large — the standard error of the difference between an ability and achievement score of one student must be determined in order to claim that the discrepancy is not a chance occurence. This refers to the reliability (statistical significance) of a discrepancy score;

6. *empirical information in determining the criterion for a "severe discrepancy."* A cutoff discrepancy score needs to be set in order to define operationally who has a *severe* discrepancy (Algozzine, Ysseldyke, & Shinn, in press). Once the score is found to be reliable, its effectiveness for screening learning-disabled children can only be established empirically via a decision validity study (see Chapter 5).

Number of Years Below Grade Level

The simplest and most popular, albeit the least defensible, procedure for screening learning-disabled children entails the use of a standardized achievement test, usually a subtest in reading or mathematics, to indicate whether a student with "normal" intelligence has an achievement level that is two or more years below his or her grade placement. This procedure can be expressed as follows:

If GP − AGE > 2, a learning disability is suspected.
where:
    GP = Grade Placement
    AGE = Actual Grade Equivalent Score

For example, if a fifth grader (e.g., GP = 5.5 or fifth grade fifth month) scores at a third-grade level on reading comprehension subtest (e.g., AGE = 3.1), he or she has a deficit of more than two years below grade level (e.g., 2.4). That student would often be labeled as learning disabled, and a diagnostic test battery would be administered to pinpoint the specific weaknesses in reading comprehension.

This practice is rather common in local educational agencies (LEAs) throughout the country (e.g., Kentucky, Hawaii, New Jersey, Utah, Wisconsin). Also much of the recent research on learning disabilities employs the number of years below grade level criterion (e.g., Chapman & Boersma, 1979; Gottesman, 1979; Maloy & Sattler, 1979; Smith & Rogers, 1978; Wallbrown, Vance, & Prichard, 1979). Harber (1981) indicated that 31% of the investigations between 1978 and 1980 adopted this operational definition. In fact, even in the field of neuropsychology, a "commonly used criterion for establishing learning disability is that the child is at least two years behind in a particular subject, such as reading or arithmetic, but not in others. . . achieving normal or near normal performance in some subjects but retarded performance in others" (Kolb & Whishaw, 1980, p. 465).

Johnson and Morasky (1980) evaluated this procedure and others in terms of a larger identification problem:

> Naive approaches to measuring the deficit intensity or the cutoff point at which slowness or lag becomes a problem deficit have discussed such simplistic criteria as grade level, or several grade-months, behind a child's peers. This method of measurement has proven grossly unsatisfactory. Certainly the uneven and erratic nature of the behavior of a learning disabled child in itself precludes the use of this simple measure. Deficits are apt to appear unevenly in separate aspects of behavior as well as appearing to be greater or lesser in a single area at different times. (p. 23)

The major problem with the procedure is its reliance on grade-equivalent scores. The inaccuracy of individual grade equivalents as indices of norm-referenced test achievement and the inaccuracy and inappropriateness of grade-equivalent score discrepancies render their application in this context as indefensible (see Chapter 3). Their use in defining number of years below grade level can result in the systematic overidentification of slow learners and underidentification of gifted learners with real learning problems in particular subjects (Shepard, 1980). In regard to the arbitrarily set cutoff of two years below grade level, Shepard (1980) notes that "because the standard deviation in grade-equivalent units increases with grade level, more and more children will be identified as grade level increases without any real change in learning ability" (p. 81). If there were no alternative procedure available, certainly a graduated cutoff scale would be more reasonable (see Cone & Wilson, 1981b; Shepard et al., 1981). An example is the following:

Grades	Cutoff
1 – 3	1 year or more
4 – 6	1.5 years or more
7 – 9	2.0 years or more
10 – 12	3.0 years or more

Fortunately there are alternatives, and they are examined next.

Ability-Achievement Discrepancy Score

Several procedures have been proposed for determining a discrepancy between ability and achievement. The ingredients that make up a formula for computing the discrepancy vary considerably from one procedure to another. A formula typically consists of a special combination of two or more of the following ingredients:

$$
\begin{aligned}
\text{MA} &= \text{Mental Age (age-equivalent score)} \\
\text{CA} &= \text{Chronological Age} \\
\text{IQ} &= \text{Intelligence Quotient} \\
\text{AB} &= \text{Intelligence or Ability (standard score)} \\
\text{GP} &= \text{Grade Placement} \\
\text{YS} &= \text{Years in School (GP} - 1.0) \\
\text{AA} &= \text{Arithmetic Achievement (grade-equivalent score)} \\
\text{AGE} &= \text{Actual Grade Equivalent Score} \\
\text{EGE} &= \text{Expected Grade Equivalent Score} \\
\text{AL} &= \text{Actual Level of Achievement (standard score)} \\
\text{EL} &= \text{Expected Level of Achievement (standard score)}
\end{aligned}
$$

The *ability or expectancy component* usually contains mental age (MA), an intelligence quotient (IQ), or an intelligence or ability score in standard form (AB). Chronological age (CA) is also incorporated into a few of the formulas; sometimes grade placement (GP) and arithmetic achievement (AA) are included in this component. The *achievement component* is simply a score on an achievement test, typically a grade-equivalent score (AGE), rarely a raw score or standard score (AL). Not only are there serious problems with a few of these ingredients, particularly MA and AGE, but the manner in which they are used to arrive at the discrepancy score is also troublesome.

Ability Component

Ability is measured either by an IQ or AB score or by an expectancy formula that includes IQ or MA. These are the alternative definitions of ability employed in the 12 procedures cited most frequently in the literature on learning disabilities. The salient characteristics of those procedures are described in Table. 4.1. The procedures are ranked in order of increasing computational complexity.

MEMORY JOGGER

Table 4.1

Salient Characteristics of Twelve Procedures for
Computing an Ability-achievement Discrepancy Score

(Listed in order of increasing computational complexity)

Source	Ability Component (Expectancy formula)	Variables Considered	Achievement Component	Discrepancy	Criterion for LD
Harris (1961, pp. 128 – 130)	$MA - 5.0$	MA	AGE	EGE – AGE	NS*
Harris (1971, pp. 229 – 300)	$\dfrac{2MA + CA}{3} - 5.2$	MA,CA	AGE	EGE – AGE	NS*
Young (1976)	$\dfrac{IQ}{100} \times GP$	IQ,GP	AGE	EGE – AGE	NS*
Bond and Tinker (1967, p. 91 – 95)	or $(\dfrac{IQ}{100} \times YS) + 1.0$	IQ,YS	AGE	EGE – AGE	NS*
B E H (1976)	$CA (\dfrac{IQ}{100} + .17) - 2.5$	IQ,CA	AGE	EGE – AGE	50 % below EGE

Horn (Torgerson & Adams, 1954, pp. 84 – 85)	$\dfrac{MA + CA}{2} - 5.0$ (where CA = 6.0 to 8.5) $\dfrac{3MA + 2CA}{5} - 5.0$ (where CA = 8.6 to 9.9) $\dfrac{2MA + CA}{3} - 5.0$ (where CA = 10.0 to 12.0 $\dfrac{3MA + CA}{4} - 5.0$ (where CA = 12.0 or above)	MA,CA	AGE	EGE − AGE	NS*
Monroe (1932, pp. 1 – 17)	$\dfrac{MA + CA + AA}{3} - 5.0$	MA,CA,AA	AGE	$\dfrac{AGE}{EGE} \times 100$	Less than 80
Myklebust (1968)	$\dfrac{MA + CA + GP}{3}$	MA,CA,GP	AGE	$\dfrac{AGE}{EGE} \times 100$	Less than 90
Erickson (1975)	AB (z-score)	AB	AL (z-score)	AB − AL	10 % with largest negative discrepancies
Hanna et al. (1981)	AB (T-score)	AB	AL (T-score)	AB − AL	Greater than 8 points (true difference)
Shepard (1980)	AB (z-score)	AB	AL (z-score)	AL − EL (residual from regression of IQ on AL)	10 % with greatest deviation at each grade level
McLeod (1979)	IQ	IQ	AGE	AGE −EGE (residual)	Varies with tests selected and their technical properties (true residual)

*Not specified. However, various criteria have been applied such as .5, as well as a sliding criterion ranging from .3 for 1st grade to 1.5 for 8th grade (Wilson, 1967).

In addition to those procedures, there is another approach that has received relatively little attention. It involves the substitution of a measure of listening comprehension in lieu of IQ to determine expected reading level (see Durrell & Hayes, 1969; Durrell & Sullivan, 1945; Strang, 1964, pp. 224–226). One procedure even uses listening comprehension plus MA, CA, and AA (Cleland, 1964). However, the controversy over discrepancy procedures that has occurred, especially in the past five years, has focused primarily on the eight expectancy formulas in Table 4.1 (Burg, Kaufman, Korngold, Kovner, 1978; Cone & Wilson, 1981b; Dunlap, Russell, & Ingram, 1979; Hoffman, 1980; McLeod, 1979; Shepard, 1980; Simmons & Shapiro, 1968).

EXPECTANCY FORMULAS. The most popular formula, surprisingly, is not the one that is the easiest to calculate and to interpret. It is the *Harris* (1961) formula. The 5.0 that appears in this formula and also in the Horn (Torgerson & Adams, 1954) and Monroe (1932) formulas represents the six years of nonformal reading instruction that a child receives prior to entering first grade, with one year subtracted because a child's reading grade-equivalent score as a nonreader is 1.0, not 0. The Harris formula seems to be the best predictor of observed reading level for students with IQs between 90 and 129 according to a study by Dore-Boyce, Misner, and McGuire (1975). Unfortunately, it also overidentifies high IQ children and underidentifies low IQ children due to regression toward the mean effect (Rodenborn, 1974; Shepard, 1980; Simmons & Shapiro, 1968).

Another widely used formula is the one devised by *Bond and Tinker* (1967). Their expectancy formula is based on IQ and years in school (YS) instead of just MA. The 1.0 in the formula accounts for the nonreader grade-equivalent score as noted previously. This element renders the formula insensitive to the differential effects of high and low intelligence on prereading skills during the first six years of life. That is, all children are assumed to be equally prepared for beginning reading instruction at 1.0. As Dore-Boyce et al. (1975) pointed out, "placement of the constant (one year's credit) appears to violate Bond and Tinker's major premise that children learn at unequal rates as indicated by the use of IQ as a 'rate of learning' measure" (p. 9). (Young [1976] has suggested a simpler version of their formula that eliminates the + 1.0 by using grade placement [GP] instead of YS.) In contrast to the Harris (1961) formula, the Bond and Tinker formula was found to be the poorest predictor of observed reading level (Dore-Boyce et al., 1975), and it overidentifies low IQ children and underidentifies high IQ children (Rodenborn, 1974; Simmons & Shapiro, 1968). Interestingly, Fields (1979) found that 75% of the children identified as reading disabled based on the Bond and Tinker approach also met the cutoffs on a graduated scale for number of years below grade level.

The other formulas in Table 4.1 constitute variations or extensions of these two preceding formulas. For example, chronological age (CA) and/or grade

MEMORY JOGGER

Table 4.2

Evaluation of Ability-achievement Discrepancy Score Procedures

Criterion	Procedure					
	Expected-actual GE Score Difference	Ratio of Actual to Expected GE Scores	z-score Difference	True Difference Score	Residual Score	True Residual Score
Ability/Achievement Tests^a						
Standard score metric	−	−	+	+	+	−
Same score metric	−	−	+	+	+	−
Comparability of norm groups	−	−	−	+	+	−
Discrepancy Procedure						
Means/Std. devs. of tests	−	−	+	+	+	+
Correlation between tests	−	−	−	+	+	+
Regression toward the mean	−	−	−	−	+	+
Measurement error in test scores	−	−	−	+	−	+
Measurement error in difference scores	−	−	−	+	−	+
Criterion for "severe discrepancy"	−	−	−	−	−	−

^aThe criterion specifying the technical adequacy of the tests used in a discrepancy procedure has been omitted from this list because it must be evaluated independent of the procedure in each application.

placement (GP) are added to MA or IQ in the Harris (1971), Bureau of Education for the Handicapped (BEH, 1976; see also Algozzine, Forgnone, Mercer,
& Trifiletti, 1979; Danielson & Bauer, 1978), Horn (Torgerson & Adams,
1954), Monroe (1932), and Myklebust (1968) formulas.' The weights assigned
to MA and CA in Horn's formulas are intended to adjust for the differences in
predicting observed reading grade from expected reading grade at different age
levels based on a regression analysis (Horn, 1941).

IQ OR STANDARD SCORE. The four nonformula definitions of ability at the
bottom of Table 4.1 include McLeod's (1979) use of an intelligence quotient
and three procedures that transform the intelligence or ability test score into a
z-score (Erickson, 1975; Shepard, 1980) or T-score (Hanna et al., 1981). The
standard score transformation for the ability component (as well as the achievement component) is essential to satisfy the score metric criteria discussed previously.

EVALUATION. Regrettably, most of the procedures in Table 4.1 possess one
or more problems related to the ability component. As suggested previously,
these problems pertain to the score metric. First, IQ scores are mistakenly
treated as a ratio scale (applicable to Bond & Tinker, 1967, and BEH, 1976,
only). Second, MA or age-equivalent scores from the intelligence test furnish
inaccurate measures of development level (applicable to Harris, 1961, 1970;
Horn [Torgerson & Adams, 1954]; McLeod, 1979; Monroe, 1932; and Myklebust, 1968). These IQ and MA scores provide the foundation for the eight expectancy formulas and McLeod's (1979) true residual score procedure. In
addition, the requirements of same standard score metric and comparability of
norm groups from which the scores are derived are considered only by Erickson (1979), Hanna et al. (1981), and Shepard (1980). The top portion of Table
4.2 summarizes these pluses and minuses.

Achievement Component

The achievement component consists of a single achievement test score.
Again it is the type of score that is used that weakens this component. Nine of
the procedures in Table 4.1 express individual achievement in grade-
equivalent score units (AGE). This practice alone can invalidate the procedures. As with the ability component, the Erickson (1975), Hanna et al.
(1981), and Shepard (1980) methods avoid this score metric problem by using
standard scores (AL).

Discrepancy Score

The 12 procedures in Table 4.1 produce a discrepancy score or index that
measures the *magnitude* of the difference between ability and achievement performance levels. These procedures actually reduce to six different ipsative
strategies for operationally defining the discrepancy: (1) expected to actual

grade-equivalent score difference, (2) ratio of actual to expected grade-equivalent scores, (3) ability-achievement z-score difference, (4) true difference score, (5) residual score, and (6) true residual score. An evaluation of these alternatives according to the aforestated criteria is presented in Table 4.2.

EXPECTED TO ACTUAL GRADE-EQUIVALENT SCORE DIFFERENCE. The most common strategy for quantifying a discrepancy between ability and achievement is to compute the difference between expected (EGE) and actual (AGE) grade-equivalent scores (BEH, 1975; Bond & Tinker, 1976; Harris, 1961, 1971; Horn [Torgerson & Adams, 1954]; Young, 1976). As indicated in the table, this strategy fails to meet any of the criteria. All of the sources of error contribute to the discrepancy score. The formulas are structured such that the magnitude of the errors and their impact on the discrepancy cannot even be estimated.

RATIO OF ACTUAL TO EXPECTED GRADE-EQUIVALENT SCORES. A variation of the preceding strategy is to express the actual and expected levels of performance as a ratio (Monroe, 1932; Myklebust, 1968). This application of grade-equivalent scores is incorrect; they cannot be calculated as though they were on ratio scales when they are not even on interval scales. Furthermore, the index that results is afflicted with all of the possible sources of error previously identified.

ABILITY-ACHIEVEMENT Z-SCORE DIFFERENCE. This method developed by Erickson (1975) involves the transformation of individual raw scores on the ability and achievement tests into z-scores, and then the subtraction of the two z-scores. Earlier Winkley (1962) demonstrated the same concept with stanines, using an arbitrary criterion of a two-stanine difference. Although the standard score transformation overcomes the score metric deficiencies of the preceding strategies and accounts for differences across grade levels by using the standard deviation for each grade, it still does not address the other major sources of error listed in Table 4.2.

TRUE DIFFERENCE SCORE. The estimation of a true or reliable difference score between ability and achievement can be viewed as an extension of the Erickson (1975) method, where the resultant standard score is tested only for statistical significance. This is an important extension inasmuch as only one of the other strategies provides a mechanism for determining whether a discrepancy is due to chance or errors of measurement. Interestingly, the procedure for assessing the reliability of a discrepancy between two scores of one student is not new (Payne & Jones, 1957). Its application to the problem of learning-disability identification, however, is quite recent (Elliott, 1981; Hanna et al., 1981; Page, 1980; Reynolds, 1981a; Salvia & Ysseldyke, 1981; Shepard et al., 1981). Although the manual computation of the formulas is more complicated and time consuming compared to the foregoing procedures, the dividends to accrue from the analysis can be justified. There are also some general guidelines and tables one can use to avoid most of these computations (see Chapter 8 for details).

Whether one chooses *z*-scores (Elliott, 1981; Reynolds, 1981a) or *T*-scores (Hanna et al., 1981) for the transformation, the inference that can be drawn from the results is noteworthy. Suppose a discrepancy score was found to be statistically significant. One can then say that it is *real,* since such a discrepancy would have occurred by chance only 5 times (or less) in a 100. This is one possible definition of a severe ability-achievement discrepancy, where the criterion for a *severe discrepancy* is the *magnitude of the discrepancy needed to reach statistical significance.* The risk of overinterpreting this finding and committing a Type I (alpha) error is minimized by the level of confidence that is set (see Feldt, 1967). Therefore, the probability of mislabeling a normal child as learning disabled (false positive) is quite small if the interpretation of the discrepancy is valid. On the other hand, if the discrepancy score is not significant, it is highly improbable that a severe discrepancy between ability and achievement does exist.

Certainly this strategy possesses several advantages over the alternatives shown in Table 4.2. It also has two disadvantages: potential regression toward the mean effect and no validity data to support the criterion for "severe discrepancy." Clearly, the most direct means to account for regression effect is to use a linear regression analysis. With regard to validity, a separate validity study would be required to verify the effectiveness of the criterion for screening purposes. The procedures used to determine the reliability of an ability-achievement discrepancy score do not supply any data on whether such a discrepancy characterizes only learning-disabled children or whether a proportion of the normal population would exhibit the same discrepancy. These data can be obtained by conducting a decision validity study (see Chapter 5). They would furnish estimates of classification accuracy based on a particular discrepancy score. Both reliability and validity evidence are necessary in order to say, for example, that a severe ability-achievement discrepancy is present and 94% of the children who have that discrepancy also happen to have a learning disability.

RESIDUAL SCORE. One strategy that has received a great deal of attention in recent years is the regression model. Its proponents argue that regression toward the mean effect is the most important consideration in estimating an ability-achievement discrepancy (Burns, 1982; Cone & Wilson, 1981b; McLeod, 1979; Shepard, 1980). The underlying rationale is summarized by Thorndike (1963):

> It is necessary to define "underachievement" as discrepancy of actual achievement from the *predicted* value, predicted on the basis of a regression equation between aptitude and achievement. A failure to recognize this regression effect has rendered questionable, if not meaningless, much of the research on "underachievement." (p. 13)

In regression analysis a difference between expected (or predicted) achievement and actual achievement is called a *residual*. This is the individual discrepancy derived from the regression of ability on achievement.

Similar to the preceding strategy, this regression approach to quantifying a discrepancy is not a new development in the field. It was first applied to the identification of underachieving readers (Woodbury, 1963). Later the model was employed to define the "severe discrepancy" concept (Cone & Wilson, 1980, 1981a; Shepard, 1980; Wilson, 1975).

The advantages of using the residual score as the discrepancy are evident in Table 4.2. Moreover, Shepard (1980) has cited some other pluses worth mentioning:

1. Expected performance is predicted from aptitude scores, so that children from the full ability continuum will be identified. Therefore, LD children are clearly distinguished from slow learners.
2. Grade level is used in the equation, so that apparent discrepancies will not be created by differences in opportunity to learn.
3. By measuring discrepancies in standard errors and taking the 10% with the greatest deviation at each grade level, the percent identified will automatically be the same at each grade level and will not be influenced by scaling artifacts.
4. The multiple regression technique takes variables into account according to their actual relationship to achievement (based on data) rather than concocting a formula (like Bond and Tinker's) that is only accurate at the mean.
5. Finally, as implemented using . . . co-normed tests, errors due to differences in standardization populations are precluded. (p. 84)

Despite all of these reasons for choosing the regression approach, there are several serious deficiencies that tend to offset the advantages. First, there are practical problems in obtaining samples of students that are both large enough to yield stable estimates of regression coefficients and representative of the population to which the equation will be applied. Then there is the ever-present limitation of generalizability of results to other populations. These difficulties alone prompted Cone and Wilson (1981b) to conclude that "the regression method does not appear to hold much promise for individual assessment techniques" (p. 368). Second, the overall effectiveness of the method is questionable. As Shepard (1980) indicates, "it is likely that the. . . [method] falsely labels more normal children as LD than it correctly identifies children who really have a disorder" (p. 88). This bias in favor of false positive classification errors is exactly opposite that typically desired of a screening procedure. It is the false positive errors that need to be minimized or eliminated (see Chapter 5). Third, two important sources of measurement error are neglected: the unreliability of the test scores and the unreliability of the difference (residual) scores. The consequences of these errors have been delineated previously. Fourth, its computational complexity compared to the alternative methods is sure to be a deterrent to widespread use. Although this problem in itself is not insurmountable, given the recent surge of minicomputers and accompanying statistical packages, it can be an obstacle when viewed in conjunction with the practical problems related to sampling.

In addition to these specific deficiencies, one fundamental issue must be resolved: *Is regression analysis an appropriate strategy for identifying children with learning disabilities?* Consider the meaning of a discrepancy between predicted and actual achievement scores. As noted previously, that discrepancy is a residual from the regression analysis of group data. In other words, it is, in fact, *error* of prediction due to the imperfect correlation between ability and achievement. Any single discrepancy score that results from the analysis can then be viewed as a statistical artifact of the correlation between a particular pair of tests and of the particular sample from which it was computed.

Even more troublesome than this interpretation of a discrepancy is simply the use of a regression equation for identification purposes. The remarks of Hanna et al. (1979) on the appropriateness of the method are worth pondering:

> This is an appropriate technique by which to *estimate* (or predict) the scores of one test from the scores of another test. But in considering specific learning disabilities, both scores are known; it is necessary only to *compare* them. Regression equations and standard errors of *estimate* are suitable for the prediction of unknowns. Comparisons of comparable scores and standard errors of *measurement* of differences are appropriate in the profile analysis of presently available knowns. (p. 34)

TRUE RESIDUAL SCORE. Perhaps the most obvious approach to overcome the weaknesses of the preceding two strategies, while capitalizing on their strengths, is to use both strategies in combination. This would entail the following three steps:

1. Compute the regression equation to predict achievement level (EL) from ability level (AB)
2. Compute the discrepancy (residual) between actual (AL) and predicted (EL) achievement for each individual
3. If EL > AL, test the statistical significance of this difference to determine whether it is due to errors of measurement

McLeod (1979) has argued that this true residual score method "is mathematically, psychometrically, and psychologically respectable" (p. 49); yet he illustrates the different steps with intelligence quotients (IQ) and grade-equivalent scores (AGE − EGE). The use of these score metrics coupled with the failure to acknowledge the importance of comparable norm groups render McLeod's application of the method unacceptable.

The net value of the true residual score approach seems to reside in the number of key criteria it satisfactorily addresses. As shown in Table 4.2, that number is impressive. The pluses, however, must be weighed against the aforementioned sampling problems and the inappropriateness of regression analysis, as discussed previously. Furthermore, decision validity evidence would still be required to test the effectiveness of any reliable discrepancy criterion empirically.

Conclusions

One theme that has permeated this evaluation of ability-achievement discrepancy procedures is that important decisions about children must be based on reliable and valid information. To the extent that a given procedure may be neither reliable nor valid, it would be judged useless on the grounds that many of the screening decisions based on such a procedure would be incorrect and the consequences could be damaging to the children. Unfortunately, the eight expectancy formula procedures listed in Table 4.1 fit this description. Clearly, none of those procedures should be employed to screen children for learning disabilities. This conclusion is consistent with the comments reported in the *Procedures for Evaluating Specific Learning Disabilities* (U.S.O.E., 1977), which dealt principally with the BEH (1976) formula:

> *Comment.* Many commenters objected to the formula. . . . Their concerns fell primarily into four areas:
>
> (1) The inappropriateness of attempting to reduce the behavior of children to numbers.:
> (2) The psychometric and statistical inadequacy of the procedure;
> (3) The fear that use of the formula might easily lend itself to inappropriate use to the detriment of handicapped children;
> (4) The inappropriateness of using a single formula for children of all ages, particularly pre-school children.
>
> *Response.* Given the type and number of technical limitations, it has been determined that the formula should not be included in the final regulations.
>
> *Comment.* A few commenters recommended alternative formulae for use in determining the existence of severe discrepancy.
>
> *Response.* None of these formulae were adopted. Each was found to have the same types of technical limitations as the formula in the proposed rules. (p. 65084)

Among the remaining four procedures, the *true difference score method* appears to have the greatest potential. Once a decision validity study is conducted to determine the classification effectiveness of a reliable discrepancy, the only deficiency unaccounted for is regression toward the mean. Indeed, it is possible to adjust the criterion for a severe discrepancy so as to minimize the regression effect bias that often results in the overidentification of high ability students and underidentification of low ability students (see Chapter 8 for details). This hypothesis, however, awaits rigorous empirical verification.

In spite of the fallibility of the method, it comes closest to the previous theme *and* the federal regulations (U.S.O.E., 1977) for identification of learning-disabled children. The notion of a *reliable and valid discrepancy score* via the true difference score method seems to be a meaningful and statistically defensible definition of "severe discrepancy." Inasmuch as research evidence on the method is sparse, its utility must be appraised by local and state educational agencies that use it for screening.

WISC-R Verbal-Performance Discrepancy Score

Another index that has been used by many reading specialists and clinical and school psychologists in screening children for learning disabilities is the discrepancy score between Verbal and Performance IQ on the Wechsler Intelligence Scale for Children-Revised (WISC — R, Wechsler, 1974). Although a few studies have been conducted to explore the utility of the Slosson Intelligence Test (Swanson & Jacobson, 1970), McCarthy Scales of Children's Abilities (DeBoer, Kaufman, & McCarthy, 1974; Goh & Simons, 1980; Goh & Youngquist, 1979; Kaufman & Kaufman, 1974), and the Lorge-Thorndike Intelligence Test (Baker & Kauffman, 1978) for the purpose of screening, the WISC-R has emerged as the preferred instrument for evaluating children with learning disabilities. Therefore, this section will be devoted to an examination of the V-P IQ discrepancy procedure based on the WISC-R.

It seems appropriate that the key criteria employed to evaluate the effectiveness of ability-achievement discrepancy procedures in the previous section be applied here to evaluate this discrepancy procedure. Consequently, the presentation will be organized according to reliability and validity issues (Berk, 1982b). Since a considerable amount of attention and also confusion has been associated with abnormal discrepancy scores, the technical issues germane to that topic will also be examined.

Reliable Discrepancy Score

As defined earlier, a reliable discrepancy is one so large that it is unlikely to have occurred solely by chance or errors of measurement. The reliability or standard error of measurement of the discrepancy scores between the WISC-R Verbal and Performance Scales has been computed by Wechsler (1974, p. 24). He reported the magnitude of the discrepancies required to reach statistical significance as 12 points ($p < .05$) and 15 points ($p < .01$). Discrepancies that equal or exceed these values regardless of direction (V < P or V > P) can be considered reliable.

Abnormal Discrepancy Score

An abnormal discrepancy is one so large that it was obtained by a relatively small percentage of the children in the standardization sample. This issue deals with what Kaufman (1976b) called the normative approach to discrepancy score interpretation; that is, what is the frequency with which discrepancies of various magnitudes occur within the normal population. The incidence of the different discrepancy scores in the norm sample can serve as a base rate for determining an abnormal discrepancy. Kaufman (1976b) reported incidence rates for the WISC-R standardization sample ($n = 2200$). These rates (percentages of cases) for several reliable V-P discrepancies are listed in Table

4.3. They happen to be identical to the rates found by Seashore (1951) for the 1949 WISC standardization sample (n = 2200).

Table 4.3

Percentages of Cases in the WISC-R Norm Sample that Exhibit
Reliable Verbal-Performancy Discrepancy Scores (Kaufman, 1976b)

Verbal-Performance Discrepancy Score*	Percentage in Norm Sample
12 or more	34%
15 or more	24%
20 or more	12%
25 or more	4%

*This is an absolute score that ignores the direction of the discrepancy. It was found, however, that the percentage of Verbal > Performance and Performance > Verbal discrepancies were about equal at these magnitudes (see Kaufman, 1976b).

In an attempt to refine the measurement of an abnormal discrepancy, Silverstein (1973, 1981) and Piotrowski (1978) recommended a formula developed by Payne and Jones (1957) for computing the abnormality of a V-P difference. Abnormal discrepancies were found to be about twice the size of reliable discrepancies at the same confidence levels (see Kaufman, 1982). For example, Silverstein (1981) obtained abnormal discrepancies of 24 points (p = .05) and 32 points (p = .01). Piotrowski (1978) noted that "in regard to the identification of children who are expected to show a wide variability between their 'peaks' and 'valleys' (e.g., learning disabled), differences more in line with the magnitude of the abnormality of the difference or greater might be expected" (p. 570). This observation should be regarded as a hypothesis rather than as a conclusion. One difficulty with Piotrowski's approach, as noted by Reynolds (1979), is that the estimation of discrepancies at the ends of the distribution is very imprecise, which is unfortunately the area where precision is of greater necessity.

Based on the WISC-R standardization data then, if a clinician used a discrepancy of 12 points or more as a cutoff for identifying children with learning disabilities, two out of three children *might* be classified correctly. As the cutoff is set at the more extreme points in the discrepancy score distribution, say, 24 or more, the higher will be the probability of accurately identifying *an* abnormality. However, the diagnostic problem that remains unresolved is *which* abnormality. Kaufman (1979) pointed out that a "half-dozen children may have identical V-P discrepancies of 15 points in the same direction, and yet each may have an entirely different reason for manifesting this discrepancy in his or her ability spectrum" (p. 25). Therefore, an abnormal discrepancy indicates only that a child's performance is abnormal according to the performance of the normal sample; it furnishes no information on etiology. Whether a reliable and/or abnormal discrepancy of a given magnitude is a characteristic of a learning-disabled child is another issue, one that pertains to validity. As Kaufman (1981) has concluded, "research remains to be conducted to show that an abnormal V-P discrepancy. . . is highly predictive of learning disability" (p. 524).

Valid Discrepancy Score

Perhaps the most vital question from the perspective of screening is: Does a reliable V-P discrepancy score of 12 or above differentiate accurately between children who have learning disabilities and those who do not? Studies designed to answer this question are, in essence, testing the decision validity of a reliable discrepancy. The clinician's decision should be substantiated by reliability and validity evidence related to the specific disorder. If the discrepancy is also deemed abnormal, that is interesting to know, although it does not supply information crucial to the decision.

Turning to the validity investigations involving learning-disabled children, one discovers contradictory findings. For just about every study that demonstrated that learning-disabled children exhibit significant Performance > Verbal discrepancy scores on the WISC or WISC-R (Anderson, Kaufman, & Kaufman, 1976; Huelsman, 1970; Lyle & Goyen, 1969; Moore & Wielan, 1981; Naglieri, 1979; Rourke, Young, & Flewelling, 1971; Schiff, Kaufman, & Kaufman, 1981; Smith, Coleman, Dokecki, & Davis, 1977; Vellutino, 1977; Zingale & Smith, 1978), there is another study that reported that such discrepancies do not appear to be substantially different from those found in the normal population (Bloom & Raskin, 1980; Gutkin, 1979a; Rice, 1970; Stevenson, 1979; Strichart & Love, 1979; Thompson, 1980; Vance, Gaynor, & Coleman, 1976; Weiner & Kaufman, 1979). These results strongly imply that reliable V-P discrepancies are not likely to be very useful for differentiating learning-disabled children from normal children or from other exceptional children, including emotionally disturbed and mentally retarded (cf. Kaufman, 1981, p. 523).

Conclusions

From the standpoint of screening and differential diagnosis, the information of greatest value seems to be the magnitude of the Verbal-Performance discrepancy that is both reliable and valid for learning-disabled children. Psychometric evidence on the former is available (12 points or more in either direction); research evidence on the latter is contradictory. It is certainly not uncommon to observe a reliable discrepancy in a normal child. At present, therefore, *a V-P discrepancy score should not be used as a primary screening index.* In fact, it should be weighted cautiously even to confirm or disconfirm other evidence.

Viewed in this clinical context, the abnormality of the discrepancy furnishes little more than a label. An abnormal discrepancy is reliable based on the WISC-R data but is not necessarily valid for children with learning disabilities. More importantly, knowledge of a discrepancy so large as to be called abnormal appears to have no direct bearing on the clinical decision.

WISC-R Profile Analysis

If the preceding discrepancy analysis is employed, the next step is usually an analysis of WISC-R subtest profiles in order to discover some *pattern* of intellectual abilities that can distinguish reading – and learning-disabled children from other children (Belmont & Birch, 1966; Griffiths, 1977; Guyer & Friedman, 1975; Huelsman, 1970; Nolan & Driscoll, 1978; Richmand & Lindgren, 1980; Vance, Wallbrown, & Blaha, 1978). A discernable pattern can furnish the teacher or clinician with clues as to the specific nature of the suspected learning disorder(s). The use of this score information, however, is often restricted to differential diagnosis as opposed to screening. Since a subtest profile is usually analyzed in conjunction with a V-P discrepancy score to arrive at a clinical decision, the information it provides can be pivotal to the subsequent treatment. The research findings and methodological issues pertinent to the effective interpretation of WISC-R profiles are discussed in this section (see also Berk, 1983b).

Research Evidence

The research that has been conducted to ascertain whether there is a profile of WISC-R (or WISC) subtest scores unique to children with learning disabilities has dealt principally with Bannatyne's (1974) recategorization. Several studies have found that reading – and learning-disabled children, especially those with genetic dyslexia, tend to score high on the Spatial subtests (Picture Completion, Block Design, Object Assembly), lower on the Conceptual subtests (Comprehension, Vocabulary, Similarities), and even lower on the Sequencing subtests (Arithmetic, Digit Span, Coding) (see Clarizio & Bernard, 1981; Henry & Wittman, 1981; Keogh & Hall, 1974; Keogh, Wetter, McGinty, & Donlon, 1973; Lutey, 1977; McManis, Figley, Richert, & Fabre, 1978; Robeck, 1971; Rugel, 1974; Smith, 1978; Smith et al., 1977; Zingale & Smith, 1978). Although this Spatial > Conceptual > Sequential LD group profile appears to differ from the profiles of normal, mentally retarded, and emotionally impaired children in many of these studies, the degree to which these differences occur is often insufficient to justify the use of the profile as a primary diagnostic tool. A few recent investigations have, in fact, questioned the validity of the Spatial > Conceptual > Sequential pattern for the diagnosis of individual cases (Groff & Hubble, 1981; Gutkin, 1979a; Moore & Wielan, 1981; Schiff et al., 1981; Thompson, 1981; Vance & Singer, 1979). Explanations for these results seem to reside in the methodological underpinnings of profile interpretation.

Methodological Problems

Applying the research evidence of an LD group profile derived from Bannatyne category scores is problematic (Gutkin, 1979b; Kender, 1972; Ryckman, 1981). While the *group* characteristics are typically indicative of a specific trend, such a trend may or may not be consistent with the *individual* profile of a learning-disabled child. As Thompson (1981) emphasized,

> for the Bannatyne pattern to be of diagnostic utility to the practitioner, not only must it be characteristic of and frequently demonstrated by children with LD, it should not be characteristic of nor frequently demonstrated by children who are not learning disabled. That is, it must be able to differentiate the child with learning disabilities from a child with other developmental and/or behavioral problems. (p. 44)

Kaufman (1981, p. 522) has pointed out that empirical verification for this condition has been found, where, despite *mean group differences* between the categories, the proportion of *individuals within a group* displaying the characteristic profile has been very low (e.g., Clarizio & Bernard, 1981; Gutkin, 1979a; Thompson, 1981). Statistically, this can be explained in terms of the aggregation of data at different levels. That is, where one level of data is aggregated to a higher level such as individual to group, the properties at either level are not necessarily generalizable to the other. In this case, the evidence amassed on the Spatial > Conceptual > Sequential LD group profile does not generalize to the individual profile.

In addition, the interpretation of a WISC-R profile is fraught with methodological difficulties. There are three sources of measurement error that complicate the interpretation: (1) the unreliability of a few of the subtests (Bryan & Bryan, 1978), (2) the unreliability of difference scores between subtests (Conger & Conger, 1975; Hirshoren & Kavale, 1976; Piotrowski & Grubb, 1976; Salvia & Ysseldyke, 1981), and (3) the unreliability of difference scores between the Bannatyne categories (Gutkin, 1979a). Certainly perceptive profile analysis can compensate for some of these weaknesses. The ipsative evaluation of individual subtest and Bannatyne category scores (see Gutkin, 1979a; Reynolds, 1981b), for example, can enhance the clinician's ability to make accurate and reliable interpretations. Unfortunately, however, the simplistic analysis of profiles described in several textbooks on learning disabilities and diagnostic-prescriptive teaching fosters misleading and imperceptive interpretations that focus more on error than on real discrepancies (cf. Salvia & Ysseldyke, 1981, p. 499).

Conclusions

Despite the amount of evidence that has accumulated on the validity of WISC-R profile analysis for the differential diagnosis of learning-disabled children, the generalizability of that information to the individual child does not seem appropriate. There is a growing body of research that fails to support the use of Bannatyne's three-category model, the Spatial > Conceptual > Sequential pattern in particular, for diagnostic purposes. Given this trend, Kaufman (1981) recommends pursuing the four-category model that includes Acquired Knowledge (Information, Arithmetic, Vocabulary). He argued that the "typical" LD profile of low scores on the ACID subtests (*A*rithmetic, *C*oding, *I*nformation, *D*igit Span) is more congruent with the interpretation of this model than with either the three-category model or Wechsler's two-category (Verbal-Performance) system. However, further research is needed to determine the utility of the ACID categorization scheme, especially in view of the findings that group analyses of LD profiles are not necessarily reflective of individual LD profiles. In addition, although there is often more scatter among learning-disabled children than among the standardization sample, some of these children have exceedingly flat profiles. All of these results greatly complicate the interpretation of an individual profile.

When these problems are viewed in conjunction with the various sources of measurement error related to the subtest scores, difference scores between subtests, and difference scores between Bannatyne categories, there is only one logical conclusion: *WISC-R profiles should not be used to diagnose specific learning disabilities* (cf. Dudley-Marling, Kaufman, & Tarver, 1981; Kaufman, 1981). The evidence strongly suggests that the children labeled learning disabled are very heterogeneous (Ryckman, 1981), and it is unlikely to expect one characteristic to be typical of all or even most of them (Clarizio & Bernard, 1981).

Perhaps the contribution of this WISC-R data to the prevention and remediation of learning problems (see Reynolds & Clark, 1983) may prove more valuable. Certainly, the usefulness of the WISC-R profile in that application warrants exploration. Moreover, the Bannatyne categories can still provide a convenient framework for understanding a learning-disabled child's assets and deficits (Kaufman, 1981), even though more research is required to clarify the theoretical and clinical meaning of those inferences.

Summary

A summary of the foregoing evaluation of discrepancy score procedures is presented in Table 4.4. The criteria in this table that are used to judge the effectiveness of a given procedure were derived principally from the criteria listed in Table 4.2. They are indicated as column headings. Among the four categories of procedures employed currently for the screening or differential diagnosis of learning-disabled children, not one satisfies both the statistical and legal criteria. In fact, none of the procedures even meets all of the required psychometric specifications of an appropriate score metric, reliability, and validity. Their methodological deficiencies explicated in each section of this chapter and/or unavailability of conclusive validity evidence render all but one of the procedures worthless for screening purposes. It seems that only the true difference score method merits further attention. This method's usefulness for large scale screening of learning-disabled children, however, cannot be legitimately appraised at this time. Data must be gathered by local and state educational agencies to determine its validity for individual decision making. Nonetheless, the notion of a reliable and valid ability-achievement discrepancy score appears to be the most meaningful and statistically defensible operational definition of "severe discrepancy."

MEMORY JOGGER

Table 4.4

Effectiveness of Four Types of Discrepancy Score Procedures

Category of Procedures	Appropriate Score Metric	Reliable Discrepancy Score	Valid Discrepancy Score	Consistent with U.S.O.E. (1977) Guidelines	Usefulness for Screening	Usefulness for Diagnosis
Number of Years Below Grade Level	No	No	Evidence sparse	Yes	No	No
Ability-Achievement Discrepancy Score (Table 4.2)	Yes[a]	Yes[b]	Evidence sparse	Yes	Yes[c]	No
WISC-R Verbal-Performance Discrepancy Score	Yes	Yes	Evidence contradictory	No	No	No
WISC-R Profile Analysis	Yes	Yes	Evidence contradictory	No	No	No

[a]Only z-score difference, true difference score, and residual score methods.

[b]Only true difference score and true residual score methods.

[c]Only true difference score method should be considered, pending satisfactory decision validity evidence.

References

Algozzine, B., Forgnone, C., Mercer, C.D., & Trifiletti, J. Toward defining discrepancies for specific learning disabilities: An analysis and alternatives. *Learning Disability Quarterly*, 1979, *2*, 25 – 31.

Algozzine, B., Ysseldyke, J.E., & Shinn, M.R. Identifying children with learning disabilities: When is a discrepancy severe? *Journal of School Psychology*, in press.

Anderson, M., Kaufman, A.S., & Kaufman, N.L. Use of the WISC-R with a learning disabled population: Some diagnostic implications. *Psychology in the Schools*, 1976, *13*, 381 – 386.

Baker, A.M., & Kauffman, J.M. Screening LD children with the Lorge-Thorndike. *Academic Therapy*, 1978, *13*, 549 – 552.

Bannatyne, A. Diagnosis: A note on recategorization of the WISC scaled scores. *Journal of Learning Disabilities*, 1974, *7*, 272 – 274.

Belmont, L., & Birch, H.G. The intellectual profile of retarded readers. *Perceptual and Motor Skills*, 1966, *22*, 787 – 816.

Berk, R.A. Effectiveness of discrepancy score methods for screening children with learning disabilities. *Learning Disabilities: An Interdisciplinary Journal*, 1982, *1*, 11 – 24. (a)

Berk, R.A. Verbal-performance IQ discrepancy score: A comment on reliability, abnormality, and validity. *Journal of Clinical Psychology*, 1982, *38*, 638 – 641. (b)

Berk, R.A. An evaluation of procedures for computing an ability-achievement discrepancy score. *Journal of Learning Disabilities*, 1983, in press. (a)

Berk, R.A. The value of WISC-R profile analysis for the differential diagnosis of learning disabled children. *Journal of Clinical Psychology*, 1983, *39*, 133 – 136. (b)

Bloom, A.S., & Raskin, L.M. WISC-R verbal-performance IQ discrepancies: A comparison of learning disabled children to the normative sample. *Journal of Clinical Psychology*, 1980, *36*, 322 – 323.

Bond, G.L., & Tinker, M.A. *Reading difficulties: Their diagnosis and correction* (2nd ed.). New York: Appleton-Century-Crofts, 1967.

Bryan, T.H., & Bryan, J.H. *Understanding learning disabilities*. Sherman Oaks, CA: Alfred, 1978.

Bureau of Education for the Handicapped. *Federal Register*, 1976, *41*(230), 52407.

Burg, L.A., Kaufman, M., Korngold, B., & Kovner, A. *The complete reading supervisor*. Columbus, OH: Merrill, 1978.

Burns, E. Linear regression and simplified reading expectancy formulas. *Reading Research Quarterly*, 1982, *17*, 446 – 453.

Chapman, J.W., & Boersma, F.J. Learning disabilities, locus of control, and other attitudes. *Journal of Educational Psychology*, 1979, *71*, 250 – 258.

Clarizio, H., & Bernard, R. Recategorized WISC-R scores of learning disabled children and differential diagnoses. *Psychology in the Schools*, 1981, *18*, 5 – 12.

Cleland, D.L. Clinical materials for appraising disabilities in reading. *Reading Teacher*, 1964, *7*, 428 – 434.

Cone, T.E., & Wilson, L.R. *Critical issues in operationalizing identification criteria for learning disabilities*. Paper presented at the annual meeting of the National Association of School Psychologists, Washington, DC, April 1980.

Cone, T.E., & Wilson, L.R. *The Iowa learning disabilities evaluation project*. Paper presented at the annual meeting of the National Association of School Psychologists, Houston, April 1981. (a)

Cone, T.E., & Wilson, L.R. Quantifying a severe discrepancy: A critical analysis. *Learning Disability Quarterly*, 1981, *4*, 359 – 371. (b)

Conger, A.J., & Conger, J.C. Reliable dimensions for WISC profiles. *Educational and Psychological Measurement*, 1975, *35*, 847 – 863.

Danielson, L.C., & Bauer, J.N. A formula-based classification of learning disabled chidren: An examination of the issues. *Journal of Learning Disabilities*, 1978, *11*, 163 – 176.

DeBoer, D.L., Kaufman, A.S., & McCarthy, D. *The use of the McCarthy Scales in identification, assessment, and deficit remediation of preschool and primary age children.* Symposium presented at the annual meeting of the Council for Exceptional Children, New York, April 1974.

Dore-Boyce, K., Misner, M., & McGuire, D. Comparing reading expectancy formulas. *Reading Teacher*, 1975, *29*, 8 – 14.

Dudley-Marling, C.C., Kaufman, N.J., & Tarver, S.G. WISC and WISC-R profiles of learning disabled children: A review. *Learning Disability Quarterly*, 1981, *4*, 307 – 319.

Dunlap, W.P., Russell, S.N., & Ingram, C. Determining learning disabilities in mathematics. *Academic Therapy*, 1979, *15*, 81 – 85.

Durrell, D.D., & Hayes, M.T. *Listening-reading series: Manual for listening and reading tests.* New York: Harcourt, Brace & World, 1969.

Durrell, D.D., & Sullivan, H.B. *Durrell-Sullivan Reading Capacity and Achievement Tests: Manual for primary and intermediate tests.* New York: Harcourt, Brace & World, 1945.

Elliott, M. Quantitative evaluation procedures for learning disabilities. *Journal of Learning Disabilities*, 1981, *14*, 84 – 87.

Erickson, M.T. The z-score discrepancy method for identifying reading-disabled children. *Journal of Learning Disabilities*, 1975, *8*, 308 – 312.

Feldt, L.A. Reliability of differences between scores. *American Educational Research Journal*, 1967, *4*, 139 – 145.

Fields, N.A. *A comparison of techniques for the identification of children with reading disabilities.* Unpublished doctoral dissertation, University of North Carolina at Chapel Hill, 1979.

Goh, D.S., & Simons, M.R. Comparison of learning disabled and general education children on the McCarthy Scales of Children's Abilities. *Psychology in the Schools*, 1980, *17*, 429 – 436.

Goh, D.S., & Youngquist, J. Comparison of the McCarthy Scales of Children's Abilities and the WISC-R for learning disabled children. *Journal of Learning Disabilities*, 1979, *12*, 344 – 348.

Gottesman, R.C. Follow-up of learning disabled children. *Learning Disability Quarterly*, 1979, *2*, 60 – 69.

Griffiths, A.N. The WISC as a diagnostic-remedial tool for dyslexia. *Academic Therapy*, 1977, *12*, 401 – 409.

Groff, M.G., & Hubble, L.M. Recategorized WISC-R scores of juvenile delinquents. *Journal of Learning Disabilities*, 1981, *14*, 515 – 516.

Gutkin, T.B. Bannatyne patterns of Caucasian and Mexican-American learning disabled children. *Psychology in the Schools*, 1979, *16*, 178 – 183. (a)

Gutkin, T.B. WISC-R scatter indices: Useful information for differential diagnosis? *Journal of School Psychology*, 1979, *17*, 368 – 371. (b)

Guyer, B.L., & Friedman, M.P. Hemispheric processing and cognitive styles in learning disabled and normal children. *Child Development*, 1975, *46*, 658 – 668.

Hanna, G.S., Dyck, N.J., & Holen, M.C. Objective analysis of achievement-aptitude discrepancies in LD classification. *Learning Disability Quarterly*, 1979, *2*, 32 – 38.

Harber, J.R. Learning disability research: How far have we progressed? *Learning Disability Quarterly*, 1981, *4*, 372 – 381.

Harris, A.J. *How to increase reading ability* (4th ed.). New York: McKay, 1961.

Harris, A.J. *How to increase reading ability* (5th ed.). New York: McKay, 1971.

Henry, S.A., & Wittman, R.D. Diagnostic implications of Bannatyne's recategorized WISC-

R scores for identifying learning disabled children. *Journal of Learning Disabilities*, 1981, *14*, 517 – 520.

Hirshoren, A., & Kavale, K. Profile analysis of the WISC-R: A continuing malpractice. *Exceptional Child*, 1976, *23*, 83 – 87.

Hoffman, J.V. The disabled reader: Forgive us our regressions and lead us not into expectations. *Journal of Learning Disabilities*, 1980, *13* 7 – 11.

Horn, A. *The uneven distribution of the effects of specific factors* (Southern California Education Monographs No. 12). Los Angeles: University of Southern California Press, 1941.

Huelsman, C.B. The WISC subtest syndrome for disabled readers. *Perceptual and Motor Skills*, 1970, *30*, 535 – 550.

Johnson, S.W., & Morasky, R.L. *Learning disabilties* (2nd ed.). Boston: Allyn & Bacon, 1980.

Kaufman, A.S. A new approach to the interpretation of test scatter in the WISC-R. *Journal of Learning Disabilities*, 1976, *9*, 33 – 41. (a)

Kaufman, A.S. Verbal-performance IQ discrepancies on the WISC-R. *Journal of Consulting and Clinical Psychology*, 1976, *44*, 739 – 744. (b)

Kaufman, A.S. *Intelligent testing with the WISC-R*. New York: Wiley-Interscience, 1979.

Kaufman, A.S. The WISC-R and learning disabilities assessment: State of the art. *Journal of Learning Disabilities*, 1981, *14*, 520 – 526.

Kaufman, A.S. The impact of WISC-R research for school psychologists. In C.R. Reynolds & T.B. Gutkin (Eds.), *The handbook of school psychology*. New York: Wiley, 1982. Pp. 156 – 177.

Kaufman, N.L., & Kaufman, A.S. Comparison of normal and minimally brain dysfunctional children on the McCarthy Scales of Children's Abilities. *Journal of Clinical Psychology*, 1974, *30*, 69 – 72.

Kender, J.P. Is there a WISC profile for poor readers? *Journal of Learning Disabilities*, 1972, *5*, 397 – 400.

Keogh, B.K., & Hall, R.J. WISC subtest patterns of educationally handicapped. *Psychology in the Schools*, 1974, *11*, 296 – 300.

Keogh, B.K., Wetter, J., McGinty, A., & Donlon, G. Functional analysis of WISC performance of learning disordered, hyperactive and mentally retarded boys. *Psychology in the Schools*, 1973, *10*, 171 – 181.

Kolb, B., & Whishaw, I.Q. *Fundamentals of human neuropsychology*. San Franciso: Freeman, 1980.

Lutey, C.L. *Individual intelligence testing: A manual and sourcebook* (2nd ed.). Greeley, CO: Carol L. Lutey, 1977.

Lyle, J.G., & Goyen, J. Performance of retarded readers on the WISC and educational tests. *Journal of Abnormal Psychology*, 1969, *74*, 105 – 112.

Maloy, C.F., & Sattler, J.M. Motor and cognitive proficiency of learning disabled and normal children. *Journal of School Psychology*, 1979, *17*, 213 – 218.

McLeod, J. Educational underachievement: Toward a defensible psychometric definition. *Journal of Learning Disabilities*, 1979, *12*, 322 – 330.

McManis, D.L., Figley, C., Richert, M., & Fabre, T. Memory-for-Designs, Bender-Gestalt, Trail Making test, and WISC-R performance of retarded and adequate readers. *Perceptual and Motor Skills*, 1978, *46*, 443 – 450.

Monroe, M. *Children who cannot read: The analysis of reading disabilities and the uses of diagnostic tests in the instruction of retarded readers*. Chicago: University of Chicago Press, 1932.

Moore, D.W., & Wielan, O.P. WISC-R scatter indexes of children referred for reading diagnosis. *Journal of Learning Disabilities*, 1981, *14*, 511 – 514.

Myklebust, H.R. Learning disabilities: Definition and overview. In H.R. Myklebust (Ed.), *Progress in learning disabilities* (Vol. 1). New York: Grune & Stratton, 1968. Pp. 1 – 15.

Naglieri, J.A. *A comparison of McCarthy GCI and WISC-R IQ scores for educable mentally retarded, learning disabled and normal children.* Unpublished doctoral dissertation, University of Georgia. 1979.

Nolan, J.D., & Driscoll, R.L. *Memory deficits in learning disabled chidren.* Paper presented at the annual meeting of the American Psychological Association, Toronto, August 1978.

O'Donnell, L. Intra-individual discrepancy in diagnosing specific learning disabilities. *Learning Disability Quarterly,* 1980, *3,* 10 – 18.

Page, E.B. Tests and decisions for the handicapped: A guide to evaluation under the new laws. *Journal of Special Education,* 1980, *14,* 423 – 483.

Payne, R.W., & Jones, H.G. Statistics for the investigation of individual cases. *Journal of Clinical Psychology,* 1957, *13,* 115 – 121.

Piotrowski, R.J. Abnormality of subtest score differences on the WISC-R. *Journal of Consulting and Clinical Psychology,* 1978, *46,* 569 – 570.

Piotrowski, R.J., and Grubb, R.D. Significant subtest score differences on the WISC-R. *Journal of School Psychology,* 1976, *14,* 202–206.

Reynolds, C.R. Interpreting the index of abnormality when the distribution of score differences is known: Comment on Piotrowski. *Journal of Consulting and Clinical Psychology,* 1979, *47,* 401 – 402.

Reynolds, C.R. The fallacy of "two-years below grade level for age" as a diagnostic criterion for reading disorders. *Journal of School Psychology,* 1981, *19,* 350 – 358. (a)

Reynolds, C.R. A note on determining significant discrepancies among category scores on Bannatyne's regrouping of WISC-R subtests. *Journal of Learning Disabilities,* 1981, *14,* 468 – 469. (b)

Reynolds, C.R., & Clark, J.H. Assessment of cognitive abilities. In K.D. Paget & B.A. Bracken (Eds.), *The psychoeducational assessment of preschool children.* New York: Grune & Stratton, 1983. Pp. 163 – 189.

Rice, D.B. Learning disabilities: An investigation in two parts. *Journal of Learning Disabilities,* 1970, *3,* 149 – 155.

Richman, L.C., & Lindgren, S.D. Patterns of intellectual ability in children with verbal deficits. *Journal of Abnormal Child Psychology,* 1980, *8,* 65 – 81.

Robeck, M.D. Identifying and preventing reading disabilities. In J.A.R. Wilson (Ed.), *Diagnosis of learning difficulties.* New York: McGraw-Hill, 1971.

Rodenborn, L.V. Determining, using expectancy formulas. *Reading Teacher,* 1974, *28,* 286 – 291.

Rourke, B.P., Young, G.C., & Flewelling, R.W. The relationship between WISC verbal performance discrepancies and selected verbal, auditory-perceptual and problem solving abilities in children with learning disabilities. *Journal of Clinical Psychology,* 1971, *27,* 475 – 479.

Rugel, R.P. WISC subtest scores of disabled readers: A review with respect to Bannatyne's recategorization. *Journal of Learning Disabilities,* 1974, *7,* 48 – 55.

Ryckman, D.B. Searching for a WISC-R profile for learning disabled children: An inappropriate task? *Journal of Learning Disabilities,* 1981, *14,* 508 – 511.

Salvia, J., & Clark, J. Use of deficits to identify the learning disabled. *Exceptional Children,* 1973, *39,* 305 – 308.

Salvia, J., & Ysseldyke, J.E. *Assessment in special and remedial education* (2nd ed.). Boston: Houghton Mifflin, 1981.

Schiff, M.M., Kaufman, A.S., & Kaufman, N.L. Scatter analysis of WISC-R profiles for learning disabled children with superior intelligence. *Journal of Learning Disabilities,* 1981, *14,* 400 – 404.

Seashore, H.G. Difference between verbal and performance IQs on the Wechsler Intelligence Scale for Children. *Journal of Consulting Psychology,* 1951, *15,* 62 – 67.

Shepard, L.A. An evaluation of the regression discrepancy method for identifying children with learning disabilities. *Journal of Special Education*, 1980, *14*, 79 – 91.

Shepard, L.A., Smith, M.L., Davis, A., Glass, G.V., Riley, A., & Vojir, C. *Evaluation of the identification of perceptual-communicative disorders in Colorado* (Final Report). Boulder: Laboratory of Educational Research, University of Colorado, February 20, 1981.

Silverstein, A.B. Reliability and abnormality of differences between DTVP subtest scores. *Psychology in the Schools*, 1973, *10*, 204 – 206.

Silverstein, A.B. Reliability and abnormality of test score differences. *Journal of Clinical Psychology*, 1981, *37*, 392 – 394.

Simmons, G.A., & Shapiro, B.J. Reading expectancy formulas: A warning note. *Journal of Reading*, 1968, *2*(8), 625 – 629.

Smith, M.D. Stability of WISC-R subtest profiles for learning disabled children. *Psychology in the Schools*, 1978, *15*, 4 – 7.

Smith, M.D., Coleman, J.M., Dokecki, P.R., & Davis, E.E. Recategorized WISC-R scores of learning disabled children. *Journal of Learning Disabilities*, 1977, *10*, 444 – 449.

Smith, M.D., & Rogers, C.M. Reliability of standardized assessment instruments when used with learning disabled children. *Learning Disability Quarterly*, 1978, *1*, 23 – 31.

Stevenson, L.P. *WISC-R analysis: Implications for diagnosis and educational intervention of LD children.* Paper presented at the annual meeting of the Council for Exceptional Children, Dallas, April 1979.

Strang, R. *Diagnostic teaching of reading.* New York: McGraw-Hill, 1964.

Strichart, S.S., & Love, E. WISC-R performance of children referred to a university center for learning disabilities. *Psychology in the Schools*, 1979, *16*, 183 – 188.

Swanson, M.S., & Jacobson, A.Evaluation of the S.I.T. for screening chidren with learning disabilities. *Journal of Learning Disabilities*, 1970, *3*, 318 – 320.

Thompson, R.J., Jr. The diagnostic utility of WISC-R measures with children referred to a developmental evaluation center. *Journal of Consulting and Clinical Psychology*, 1980, *48*, 440 – 447.

Thompson, R.J., Jr. The diagnostic utility of Bannatyne's recategorized WISC-R scores with children referred to a development evaluation center. *Psychology in the Schools*, 1981, *18*, 43 – 47.

Thorndike, R.L. *The concepts of over- and under-achievement.* New York: Bureau of Publications, Teachers College, Columbia University, 1963.

Torgerson, T.L., & Adams, G.S. *Measurement and evaluation for elementary school teachers.* New York: Holt, Rinehart and Winston, 1954.

U.S. Office of Education. Assistance to states for education for handicapped children: Procedures for evaluating specific learning disabilities. *Federal Register*, 1977, *42*(250), 62082 – 62085.

Vance, H.B., Gaynor, P., & Coleman, M. Analysis of cognitive abilities for learning disabled children. *Psychology in the Schools*, 1976, *13*, 477 – 483.

Vance, H.B., & Singer, M.G. Recategorization of the WISC-R subtest scaled scores for learning disabled children. *Journal of Learning Disabilities*, 1979, *12*, 487 – 491.

Vance, H.B., Wallbrown, F.H., & Blaha, J. Determining WISC-R profiles for reading disabled children. *Journal of Learning Disabilities*, 1978, *11*, 657 – 661.

Vellutino, F.R. Alternative conceptualizations of dyslexia: Evidence in support of a verbal-deficit hypothesis. *Harvard Educational Review*, 1977, *47*, 334 – 354.

Wallbrown, F.H., Vance, H.B., & Prichard, K.K. Discriminating between attitudes expressed by normal and disabled readers. *Psychology in the Schools*, 1979, *16*, 472 – 477.

Warner, M.M. *A comparison of five discrepancy criteria for determing learning disabilities in secondary school populations* (Research Report No. 50). Lawrence: University of Kansas Institute for

Research in Learning Disabilities, June 1981.

Wechsler, D. *Manual for the Wechsler Intelligence Scale for Children-Revised.* New York: Psychological Corporation, 1974.

Weiner, S.G., & Kaufman, A.S. WISC-R vs. WISC for black children suspected of learning or behavior disorders. *Journal of Learning Disabilities,* 1979, *12,* 100 – 105.

Wilson, L.R. Learning disability as related to infrequent punishment and limited participation in delay of reinforcement tasks. *Journal of School Psychology,* 1975, *13,* 255 – 263.

Wilson, R.M. *Diagnostic and remedial reading for classroom and clinic.* Columbus, OH: Merrill, 1967.

Winkley, C.K. Building staff competence in identifying underachievers. In A. Robinson (Ed.), *The underachiever in reading* (Supplementary Educational Monograph No. 92). Chicago: University of Chicago, 1962.

Woodbury, C.A. The identification of underachieving readers. *Reading Teacher,* 1963, *16,* 218 – 223.

Young, B.S. A simple formula for predicting reading potential *Reading Teacher,* 1976, *29,* 659 – 661.

Zingale, S.A., & Smith, M.D. WISC-R patterns for learning disabled children at three SES levels. *Psychology in the Schools,* 1978, *15,* 199 – 204.

Chapter 5

DETERMINING THE DECISION VALIDITY
OF A SCREENING PROCEDURE

Introduction

INASMUCH as the core of the federal guidelines for identification of specific learning disabilities (U.S.O.E., 1977b) and most operational definitions of learning disabilities is an ability-achievement discrepancy, it is crucial to investigate whether the procedures currently being used to measure a *severe* discrepancy are, in fact, effective as they are applied in the screening process. Despite the number and diversity of the procedures described in Chapter 4, there is a dearth of empirical evidence to indicate whether any particular procedure is better than any other. Furthermore, it was emphasized that at present it is not known whether any one of the procedures can correctly sort learning-disabled children from all other children. This deficiency of discrepancy procedures is also generalizable to most all of the individual instruments employed in both screening and diagnosis.

The major objective of this chapter is to proffer a validation model for answering the question: How effective is this screening procedure? The model can also be applied to a single diagnostic test to answer the question: How effective is this test for diagnosing specific learning disabilities? This diagnostic test application will be the topic of Chapter 6. The model can be implemented easily by teachers or specialists at any level of the educational structure and can be adapted to virtually any setting, classroom to clinic. The rationale is explicated next.

Rationale

Suppose the purpose of a procedure is to differentiate children with learning disabilities from all other children. The individual decision that one makes based on that procedure is to *classify* a child as either learning disabled or non-learning disabled. The screening procedure often consists of a battery of tests that yields various ability-achievement discrepancy scores and profiles. This information is then employed as part of a multidisciplinary assessment by a team composed of a classroom teacher, learning disability specialist, school administrator, school psychologist, a physician, or other persons,[1] professional or nonprofessional, as stated in the Rules and Regulations for compliance with P.L. 94-142 (U.S.O.E., 1977b, p. 65083). Ultimately, the value of the procedure hinges on the degree to which it accomplishes its classification function. In other words, it is the *accuracy* or correctness of the classification decision that counts. Therefore, the validity of a procedure that is intended to identify learning-disabled children can be measured by the *number of correct classifications* it produces.

The mechanism for arriving at this statistical index as well as several others is *decision analysis*. The underlying decision theory (Girshick, 1954) has been applied extensively to classification decision making in a variety of related disciplines, especially medicine, psychology, and psychiatry (see Cureton, 1957; Darlington & Stauffer, 1966a, 1966b; Edwards, 1970, Chap. 4; Klein & Cleary, 1967; Lusted, 1968; Meehl & Rosen, 1955; Patton, 1978; Rorer, Hoffman, LaForge, & Hsieh, 1966; Sutcliffe, 1965; Taylor & Russell, 1939; Wiggins, 1973, Chap. 6), but heretofore has received relatively little attention in the field of special education (Harber 1981a, 1981b). Harber (1981b) suggested three reasons for this neglect:

1. Decision analysis may be considered as merely the systematic itemization of what the competent diagnostician does intuitively, and thus not worthy of separate discussion.
2. Special educators may be unfamiliar with the terminology and methods used in the context of decision analysis, and the maxim that it is easier to avoid the unfamiliar than to deal with it may be relevant.
3. The significance of decision analysis to the field of special education may not have been apparent in the past. (pp. 413 – 414)

She emphasized that "it is time to acknowledge and critically evaluate the procedures special educators have applied and do apply, consciously or unconsciously, consistently or [i]nconsistently, to the processes of identification and classification of handicapped students" (p. 414).

In this chapter a decision model is proposed for evaluating the effectiveness of any screening procedure. The following elements are addressed: (1) terminology, (2) selection of criterion groups, (3) correct and incorrect decisions, (4) base rate, (5) incremental validity, (6) sensitivity and specificity, (7) consequences of misclassification, and (8) problems of labeling and low base rate.

---

[1]In a study of 38 model learning disability programs (Child Service Demonstration Centers) in 26 states, Thurlow and Ysseldyke (1979) reported that the placement team typically consisted of between three and 16 different persons, with a classroom teacher, parent, learning disability specialist, school administrator, and special education teacher as the most frequent members. Other persons included on the various teams were a school psychologist, educational diagnos ician, speech/language/audiology specialist, school counselor, child, child psychologist, social worker, physician, paraprofessional aide, juvenile/court officer, neurologist/neuropsychologist, psychiatrist, early childhood specialist, and nurse.

Terminology

The terminology used in this decision model can be defined and illustrated with diagnoses of physical and mental diseases. The *presence* of a characteristic found as a result of a laboratory test or a psychological test has been denoted as a *positive*. For example, if the Wasserman test is positive, the characteristic present is syphilis; if the human chorionic gonadotropin (HCG) test is positive, the presence of that hormone indicates pregnancy. In personality testing, if a person scored 87 on subscale 7 of the Minnesota Multiphasic Personality Inventory (MMPI), the characteristic present is schizophrenia. The *absence* of the characteristic is denoted as a *negative*.

When the presence or absence of the characteristic is verified as correct, the decision is called a *true positive* or a *true negative*. Certainly there are also errors made in medical diagnoses as well as in decisions based on psychological and educational test scores. The two types of error are called *false positive* and *false negative*. If the HCG test mistakenly indicates pregnancy, that is a false positive error; if it mistakenly indicates no pregnancy, that is a false negative error.

Following this established terminology then, the *presence of a learning disability* will be referred to as a *positive*, while the absence, indicating another type of handicapping condition or, more commonly, a normal learning condition, will be called a negative. The correct and incorrect decisions that can result from a screening procedure are depicted in Table 5.1 using the positive-negative classification language.

Table 5.1

Predicted × Actual Classification
Decision Model for a Screening Procedure

		Actual Classification	
		Learning Disability	Normal
Predicted Classification (Screening Procedure)	Learning Disability	True Positive n_1	False Positive n_2
	Normal	False Negative n_3	True Negative n_4

Selection of Criterion Groups

The model is based on the particular samples of *actual* learning-disabled and normal children chosen for study. The method and criteria by which they are selected become the ultimate determinants of decision validity. The samples are typically called *criterion groups*, inasmuch as their selection is guided by specific criteria (criterion variable) that operationally define the handicapping condition. The classification process is a form of the "known-groups" technique employed for many years in the validation of personality tests (Cronbach & Meehl, 1955; Edwards, 1970; Wiggins, 1973). It involves comparing one group of persons known by independent means (criterion variable) to possess more of the designated trait or attribute with a second group known to possess much less. In this application of the technique to the validation of a screening procedure, the trait of interest is the *handicapping condition*. The degree of the condition, which can range from none to severe, and the type of condition, in this case the specific learning disability, constitute the dimensions for differentiating the criterion groups.

The persons involved in the selection of the groups should be qualified for that task. They must have access to the necessary data on each child and be competent to interpret the data. Developing a set of criteria for identifying the children is one step toward assuring a degree of objectivity in selection. The next step is to adhere tenaciously to those criteria and apply them with scrupulous impartiality. If personal biases creep into the selection process, they can only contaminate the results and render an otherwise impeccably executed validity study as invalid. The final judgment that is made which classifies a child as learning disabled or non – learning disabled should be informed, perceptive, and objective.

Learning-Disabled Sample

The first phase in selection involves identifying a "definite" learning-disabled sample that is representative of the target population for which the screening procedure is designed. In a preliminary study, it is advisable to choose the more severe cases as opposed to a mixture of severe, moderate, and borderline cases. If the procedure is highly effective with extreme criterion groups, then it is justified to proceed with more heterogeneous groups for additional analyses. If the screening is ineffective with the extreme groups, then pursuing further a decision validity study of that particular procedure does not seem warranted.

SAMPLING CRITERIA. The criteria for selection should be delineated meticulously. Data from a variety of potentially corroborative sources such as norm-referenced and criterion-referenced tests and developmental and medical histories should be utilized to produce *informed, professional judgments* by teachers and clinicians about each child's condition. Particular attention should be given to the cumulative records of academic performance in the seven areas listed in the Rules and Regulations (U.S.O.E., 1977b). Children who exhibit learning problems over two or more years should be considered as prime candidates for the sample. This type of evidence suggests a more definite LD classification than information gathered for only one year or less.

SAMPLE SIZE. A sample size of not less than 20 and preferably within the range of 50 to 100 should be sought. In general, the larger the sample, the more reliable will be the statistical indices of decision validity described in subsequent sections of this chapter. Method of selection and practical constraints usually govern the final sample size.

SAMPLING METHOD. There are two major strategies one can use to obtain a learning-disabled sample: (1) draw a random sample of children from the total population and then extract the learning-disabled children from that sample or (2) individually pick a certain number of learning-disabled children according to the prespecified criteria. Implementing the first approach would permit a representative sampling of all types of disabilities in proportion to their incidence in the population. These characteristics are highly desirable in determining the effectiveness of a screening procedure. (*Note*: Incidence of learning disabilities will be discussed in the section on base rate.) Unfortunately, the LD selection criteria may need to be applied to all children receiving special services in order to sort out only those with learning disabilities. This task is the primary activity of the second strategy.

The advantages and disadvantages of the two strategies are a function of the following: (a) whether a representative sample or specially composed sample (e.g., severe cases only) of learning-disabled children is required, (b) the type of non-learning-disabled sample needed, and (c) practical constraints related to accessibility of data, availability of staff, and, of course, time and cost. If a representative sample is essential, then there are really no alternatives to the first strategy; if a specially composed sample is important, then either strategy may be used, with the second strategy having several practical advantages over the first.

In particular, the *random sampling* procedure can yield not only a sample of learning-disabled children that is representative of the population but also representative samples of children with other handicapping conditions, as well as those with no handicaps (normals). The advantage of this procedure is the comparability of the designated criterion groups. The diversity of demographic characteristics (e.g., sex, ethnicity, socioeconomic level) in the population is proportionately accounted for in each group. The price one pays for this important advantage, however, is significant. Random sampling in a school district that encompasses a relatively large geographic region can be extremely inconvenient, time-consuming, and costly. For example, if a simple random sample of 400 children at just one grade level was drawn, the 20 learning-disabled children may be distributed across 10 or more different schools. Even if other variations of this sampling strategy were attempted, such as stratified sampling by handicapping condition or cluster sampling by classes or schools, the costs would still be difficult to justify. At present, the disadvantage of low practicability appears to outweigh the advantage of representative groups. The usefulness of this random sampling procedure then diminishes to clinical settings and to school systems with computerized access to the data required by the selection criteria, where factors such as large numbers and proximity are not problematic.

The alternative to random sampling is the *specially composed sampling* strategy. It usually produces a nonrepresentative sample, in that the selection criteria frequency denote only handicapping characteristics. No attention to demographic variables is given. Depending on the purpose and scope of the decision validity study, however, this disadvantage may not be very serious. For preliminary analyses using extreme criterion groups, as mentioned previously, the demographic representativeness of any single sample may be of little concern. What remains troublesome is assuring the comparability of the two samples. The major advantage of the strategy is the relative ease with which the children can be hand picked. From the children receiving special services in a few schools within a limited geographic area, the special learning-disabled sample can be identified by applying the selection criteria. The process is convenient and considerably less time-consuming and costly than the random sampling method. In essence, it is probably fair to conclude that the boon of this strategy is the bane of the random sampling strategy, and vice versa.

Non-Learning-disabled Sample

Selection of the non-learning-disabled sample should be conducted with no less commitment or rigor than that characterizing the selection of the learning-disabled sample. The criterion group chosen for comparison to test the effectiveness of a screening procedure must also be identified with similar definiteness. While the non-learning-disabled sample employed most often consists of normals (e.g., Forness & Esveldt, 1975; Rickey & McKinney, 1978), it is certainly possible to use other handicapped groups such as emotionally disturbed (e.g., Hallahan & Kauffman, 1978) or mentally retarded (e.g., Niesworth & Greer, 1975) or even underachievers (Ysseldyke, Algozzine, Shinn, & McGue, 1982). The choice of the type of sample will depend primarily on the purpose of the decision validity study and the special population(s) with which the screening procedure is to be used.

SAMPLING CRITERIA. Based on the same sources one consults for selecting each learning-disabled child, a set of criteria should be carefully specified defining the non-learning-disabled child. If normals are to constitute the non-LD sample, there should be no present or past evidence of special services or any discernible learning disorder in the available documentation.

SAMPLE SIZE. The sample size should reflect the proportion of the non-learning-disabled condition in the total population. In the case of a normal criterion group, if the incidence of learning disabilities in the population is estimated to be about 5%, then one might presume the remainder of that population with normal intelligence and no apparent learning problems to be 95%. In this example, the total population consists of all children with at least normal intelligence, where those with learning disabilities are a distinguishable subset. Translated into numbers, it would mean that a sample of 400 children would contain a bare minimum number of 20 learning disabled (5%) and a complementary number of 380 normals (95%). Such disproportionate criterion-group sizes are not uncommon, given the most recent incidence figures on learning disabilities. It is even worse for other handicapping conditions, where the prevalence rate is 1% or less. In other words, the sample size for the non-learning-disabled group is predetermined by the size of the learning-disabled group and the base rate (see section on base rate for a further discussion of this issue).

SAMPLING METHOD. The two sampling methods described in regard to the learning-disabled sample are just as appropriate in this context. The only additional point that should be considered in using the specially composed sampling strategy for selecting a group of normals pertains to the comparability of the two groups. Every effort should be made to choose the normals from the same schools from which the learning-disabled children were identified. Furthermore, it would be desirable for the normals to reflect proportionately as many attributes as represented in the learning-disabled sample so that both groups are essentially balanced on all characteristics except handicapping condition. Inasmuch as the pool of normals is usually quite large, matching on group characteristics is not an especially difficult procedure — it is just more inconvenient and time-consuming than not doing so. *The legitimacy of the criterion group comparison resides ultimately in the degree of comparability attained.*

Correct and Incorrect Decisions

Based on the model shown in Table 5.1, it is possible to estimate the probability of each type of correct and incorrect decision. The procedures for computing and interpreting the different probabilities are presented next.

Distributions of Positives and Negatives

The n in each cell of the 2×2 contingency table is simply a count of the number of children in the *actual* learning-disabled sample or normal sample who are *predicted*, for example, to exhibit a particular ability-achievement discrepancy score (the criterion for screening), where:

n_1 = number of children in the learning-disabled sample whose discrepancy score is equal to or greater than the discrepancy score criterion;

n_2 = number of children in the normal sample whose discrepancy score is equal to or greater than the discrepancy score criterion (false positives);

n_3 = number of children in the learning-disabled sample whose discrepancy score is less than the discrepancy score criterion (false negatives);

n_4 = number of children in the normal sample whose discrepancy score is less than the discrepancy score criterion;

N = $n_1 + n_2 + n_3 + n_4$.

Table 5.2

Predicted × Actual Classification Outcomes
for the Screening Procedure in School District A
(N = 400; Base Rate = 5 %)

Actual

		LD	N
Predicted	LD	14 (3.5%)	20 (5%)
	N	6 (1.5%)	360 (90%)

Correct decisions = 93.5%
Incorrect decisions = 6.5%
False negatives = 1.5%
False positives = 5%

EXAMPLE. Suppose a sample of 20 children known to possess learning problems in reading or mathematics was chosen from four elementary schools in school district A. A preponderance of evidence based primarily on teacher judgment and standardized and criterion-referenced test scores gathered over two or more years served as the verification that these children were truly learning disabled. Another sample of 380 children drawn from the same four schools was determined not to possess any identifiable learning problems.

In order to test the effectiveness of one particular screening procedure for picking out the 20 learning-disabled children from the total sample of 400 children, an operational criterion for severe learning disability was specified. Using the Cognitive Abilities Test-Nonverbal score and the Iowa Tests of Basic Skills Reading and Mathematics Concepts subtest scores, a standard score (z-score) discrepancy of .80 or greater between the ability subtest and achievement subtest would provide a reliable index of severe disability. (*Note:* These procedures are described in considerable detail in Chapters 4 and 8.) Once the discrepancy scores for the total sample are computed, one need only count how many learning-disabled and normal children met the criterion (n_1 and n_2, respectively). The results are shown in Table 5.2.

Given these frequency counts in the four cells, the next question is: What cell composition is desirable to indicate the effectiveness of the screening procedure? As suggested previously, cells n_1 and n_4 should contain as many children as possible, and cells n_2 and n_3 should contain few or no children. In other words, *the classification goal is to match the predicted classification yielded by the screening procedure with the actual classification of the selected samples,* LD-LD and N-N. From the data in Table 5.2, there appears to be a relatively good match. However, if the n's were transformed into percentages of N, an evaluation of effectiveness would be visably easier and more meaningful.

Probabilities of Positives and Negatives

Evidence of the effectiveness of a screening procedure can be obtained by expressing the cell frequencies in Table 5.2 as *probabilities* or percentages of the total sample (N). This involves dividing each n by N and multiplying by 100, or

$p(TP) = \dfrac{n_1}{N} \times 100 =$ probability of correctly classifying a learning-disabled child;

$p(FP) = \dfrac{n_2}{N} \times 100 =$ probability of incorrectly classifying a normal child as learning disabled (false positives);

$p(FN) = \dfrac{n_3}{N} \times 100 =$ probability of incorrectly classifying a learning-disabled child as normal (false negatives);

$p(TN) = \dfrac{n_4}{N} \times 100 =$ probability of correctly classifying a normal child.

EXAMPLE. Using the data in Table 5.2, the probabilities are computed as follows:

$$p(TP) = \frac{14}{400} \times 100 = 3.5\%$$

$$p(FP) = \frac{20}{400} \times 100 = 5\%$$

$$p(FN) = \frac{6}{400} \times 100 = 1.5\%$$

$$p(TN) = \frac{360}{400} \times 100 = 90\%$$

INTERPRETATION. These various probabilities have been called indices of discriminative efficiency, discriminant validity, diagnostic accuracy, decision validity, and decision accuracy, depending on the discipline in which they are applied. Hereafter, the term *decision validity* will be employed for the reason that the analyses are testing the validity of using a screening procedure for decision making. If certain probabilities are high, the use of the procedure may be judged valid for a particular decision application; if they are unsatisfactory, the use may be judged invalid. As in the interpretation of other types of validity, the focus is on *how a score or procedure is used*. It is conceivable that the use of a given procedure may be entirely inappropriate in one setting (invalid use) and very appropriate in another (valid use).

Perhaps the best general index of decision validity is the probability of correct decisions, $p(C)$, which is the sum of $p(TP)$ and $p(TN)$, or 93.5% in the preceding example. This quantity measures how well the screening procedure can classify *both* learning-disabled and normal children. It conveys the overall degree of accuracy. The discrepancy score procedure examined previously will sort 93.5% of the children in the population correctly.

Despite its simplicity, $p(C)$ has several limitations: (1) It does not reveal whether the children being classified accurately are the ones with learning disabilities — the target population of the screening procedure. The estimate could be derived only from $p(TN)$. (2) It does not reveal which children and how many in each category are misclassified (one type of misclassification is typically judged more serious than the other). (3) Its magnitude will be governed to a large extent by the incidence (or prevalence) of learning disabilities in the population of interest (an incidence figure such as 7% is determined by the nature of the population; it is not statistically manipulable). The first two problems suggest the need for additional indices that are sensitive to the specific decisions to be made and to the consequences of wrong decisions. The last problem pertains to the base rate of the characteristic. Since the base rate can influence the estimation of all indices of decision validity, it will be discussed next.

Base Rate

Estimates of the incidence of learning disabilities in many school districts have been reported to range from 1% to 30%, and even higher in urban school systems (Kass & Myklebust, 1969; Kirk & Elkins, 1975; Meier, 1971; Myklebust & Boshes, 1969; National Advisory Committee on Dyslexia and Related Reading Disorders, 1969; National Advisory Committee on Handicapped Children, 1968; Silverman & Metz, 1973; Stearns, Norwood, Kaskowitz, & Mitchell, 1977; Wissink, Kass, & Ferrell, 1975). This seems to be due to numerous factors, the most prominent of which is the definition of learning disabilities that is adopted. State-by-state estimates range from .36% to 6.45% for children 3 to 21 years of age (U.S.D.E., 1980, p. 166), as shown in Table 5.3. Nationwide, the total estimate is about 3%, or 1.3 million children (see also Table 5.4).

These estimates are usually rather conservative compared with those at the local level. In a recent study by Ysseldyke, Algozzine, and Richey (1982), it was found that professionals at the school level provide inordinately high estimates of the number of learning-disabled children, especially for the subpopulations of minority children, low socioeconomic status children, and boys. The estimates for high socioeconomic status children and girls were relatively lower but still far above estimates at the state level.

Excluded from these prevalence rates are nine other categories of handicapping condition: speech impaired, mentally retarded, emotionally disturbed, other health impaired, orthopedically impaired, deaf and hard of hearing, visually handicapped, multihandicapped, and deaf and blind. These categories combined account for about 7%, or 2.7 million children, nationwide (see Tables 5.3 and 5.4 for category breakdown).

Despite the number of estimates that have been published since 1968, the accuracy of any single figure is unknown. There are few empirical studies to furnish evidence of prevalence data. Furthermore, in most instances, the numerous problems encountered in obtaining accurate estimates stem from the typically imprecise, nonoperational definitions of learning disabilities (see Chapter 1). The criteria, techniques, and instruments used to identify children with learning disabilities are generated from the definition (Bruininks, Glaman, & Clark, 1971). Certainly the different state-by-state estimates can be explained, in part, by the different definitions employed (see Gillespie, Miller, & Fielder, 1975; Mercer, Forgnone, & Wolking, 1976). Abrams (1980) has summarized a few of the major problems involved:

> All of the problems. . . regarding definitions affect the validity of attempts to count the number of learning disabled children. In addition, etiological classifications are frequently confused with specific symptomatology. . . . Finally, the professional orientation of the researcher may influence the estimate, his [or her] background and viewpoint perhaps tending to influence choice of sample, etiological and symptomatic terminology, definition of the condition studied, and/or conclusion. (pp. 485 – 486)

This state of current practices associated with estimating the base rate unfortunately undermines the confidence one can place in available figures. Wallace and McLoughlin (1979) projected that the "actual number of LD children will probably continue to remain unclear and somewhat confusing until identification procedures are clarified and more objective research is conducted" (p. 12). Although this projection was made several years ago, it still appears to hold true today. Little progress has been evidenced in this area to substantiate the most recent estimates. Therefore, state and local prevalence rates should be regarded as tentative in the conduct of decision validity studies. As the base

MEMORY JOGGER

Table 5.3

Percent[a] of Children Ages 3-21 Years Served Under P.L. 89-313 and P.L. 94-142
By Handicapping Condition[b]

School Year 1979 – 1980

State	Speech Impaired	Learning Disabled	Mentally Retarded	Emotionally Disturbed	Other Health Impaired	Ortho- Pedically Impaired	Deaf and Hard of Hearing	Visually Handi- Capped	Multi- Handi- Capped	Deaf and Blind	Total
Alabama	1.84	2.04	4.57	.46	.07	.05	.15	.07	.17	.01	9.43
Alaska	3.09	6.45	1.02	.38	.07	.18	.23	.05	.08	.01	11.56
Arizona	2.21	4.39	1.35	.86	.12	.17	.18	.06	.14	.00	9.49
Arkansas	2.53	2.92	3.85	.10	.10	.10	.16	.07	.10	.01	9.94
California	2.68	2.91	.98	.70	.88	.38	.18	.07	.00	.01	8.78
Colorado	1.90	3.72	1.24	1.16	.00	.13	.17	.05	.20	.01	8.58
Connecticut	2.50	4.36	1.43	2.02	.16	.09	.21	.11	.01	.00	10.90
Delaware	1.82	6.27	2.53	2.62	.02	.24	.17	.12	.05	.03	13.87
District of Columbia	1.51	1.06	1.23	.42	.17	.22	.05	.05	.16	.04	4.91
Florida	2.73	3.18	1.99	.73	.00	.18	.14	.06	.10	.00	9.10
Georgia	2.20	2.52	2.81	1.30	.14	.05	.19	.07	.17	.00	9.46
Hawaii	.71	4.11	1.26	.22	.00	.10	.19	.03	.11	.01	6.75
Idaho	2.06	3.89	1.49	.27	.28	.24	.24	.12	.31	.01	8.91
Illinois	4.03	3.72	2.60	1.61	.12	.23	.26	.11	.13	.01	12.82
Indiana	4.41	1.60	2.51	.19	.04	.08	.13	.06	.10	.00	9.12
Iowa	2.93	4.37	2.36	.59	.00	.12	.19	.06	.12	.01	10.75
Kansas	3.05	2.96	1.84	.61	.17	.08	.18	.06	.20	.01	9.16
Kentucky	3.39	2.10	3.44	.39	.15	.09	.16	.07	.70	.03	9.91
Louisiana	3.05	3.64	2.56	.64	.18	.09	.21	.07	.15	.00	10.59
Maine	2.45	3.35	2.32	1.62	.14	.15	.20	.06	.38	.00	10.67
Maryland	3.15	5.93	1.53	.46	.24	.14	.24	.09	.28	.00	12.06
Massachusetts	3.90	3.36	2.56	2.36	.54	.03	.62	.11	.03	.03	13.53
Michigan	2.91	2.34	1.68	.97	.00	.22	.17	.06	.00	.00	8.35
Minnesota	2.99	4.52	1.91	.51	.21	.16	.21	.06	.01	.00	10.58
Mississippi	2.92	1.69	3.88	.05	.00	.07	.11	.05	.03	.00	8.80
Missouri	3.82	3.50	2.66	.69	.12	.08	.14	.05	.18	.01	11.24
Montana	2.40	3.26	1.10	.28	.07	.08	.18	.12	.41	.01	7.91
Nebraska	3.67	3.46	2.44	.48	.00	.16	.18	.07	.11	.00	10.58
Nevada	2.09	3.64	.92	.22	.13	.18	.13	.05	.22	.01	7.59
New Hampshire	.95	3.69	1.43	.62	.12	.12	.17	.15	.12	.00	7.38
New Jersey	4.70	3.52	1.46	1.05	.17	.15	.18	.11	.28	.00	11.61
New Mexico	1.49	3.61	1.25	.59	.01	.07	.17	.06	.18	.02	7.43
New York	1.48	1.05	1.63	1.55	1.20	.23	.18	.07	.02	.00	7.41
North Carolina	2.34	2.96	3.78	.32	.08	.10	.20	.07	.13	.00	9.99
North Dakota	2.75	2.94	1.76	.25	.05	.09	.17	.07	.17	.01	8.26
Ohio	3.23	2.87	3.18	.21	.00	.17	.13	.05	.08	.00	9.94
Oklahoma	3.28	4.29	2.36	.10	.06	.06	.14	.06	.11	.01	10.45
Oregon	2.53	4.24	1.28	.48	.14	.27	.36	.13	.02	.00	9.45
Pennsylvania	3.66	2.35	2.50	.63	.01	.11	.24	.12	.03	.00	9.66
Puerto Rico	.14	.36	1.44	.20	.09	.09	.19	.17	.19	.01	2.87
Rhode Island	2.23	5.66	1.29	.71	.12	.12	.17	.04	.07	.01	10.43
South Carolina	3.36	2.60	4.18	.78	.01	.14	.18	.09	.10	.00	11.44
South Dakota	3.65	1.83	.94	.23	.01	.12	.34	.04	.25	.00	7.42
Tennessee	3.67	3.14	2.69	.36	.18	.14	.27	.09	.20	.00	10.74
Texas	2.46	4.31	1.08	.39	.11	.10	.16	.05	.66	.01	9.31
Utah	2.35	3.83	1.00	2.90	.03	.06	.20	.09	.37	.01	10.85
Vermont	3.17	4.49	3.37	.33	.19	.26	.29	.09	.24	.02	12.45
Virginia	3.11	2.70	1.84	.49	.05	.05	.14	.16	.28	.00	8.83
Washington	1.50	2.72	1.45	.71	.16	.13	.17	.05	.17	.01	7.07
West Virginia	2.60	2.36	2.97	.21	.20	.08	.11	.07	.14	.01	8.74
Wisconsin	1.84	2.71	1.75	.87	.07	.11	.15	.05	.10	.01	7.65
Wyoming	2.82	4.91	1.09	.66	.10	.11	.21	.05	.35	.02	10.34
American Samoa	.00	.61	.82	.00	.01	.04	.28	.06	.23	.05	2.09
Guam	1.38	.73	3.34	.10	.00	.00	.35	.10	.46	.03	6.49
Northern Marianas	–	–	–	–	–	–	–	–	–	–	–
Trust Territories	–	–	–	–	–	–	–	–	–	–	–
Virgin Islands	1.12	.58	2.89	.17	.00	.05	.22	.05	.06	.06	5.20
Bur. of Indian Affairs	–	–	–	–	–	–	–	–	–	–	–
U.S. and Territories	2.81	3.03	2.09	.78	.25	.16	.20	.08	.15	.01	9.54

[a]Number of Children Ages 3 – 21 Years Served as a Percent of Estimated Fall, 1979 Enrollment (Ages 5 – 17)
[b]*Source*: U.S. Department of Education (1980, p. 166).

Table 5.4

Number of Children Ages 3-21 Years Served Under P.I 89-313 and P.L. 94-142
By Handicapping Condition[*]

School Year 1979-1980

State	Speech Impaired	Learning Disabled	Mentally Retarded	Emotionally Disturbed	Other Health Impaired	Ortho-Pedically Impaired	Deaf and Hard of Hearing	Visually Handi-Capped	Multi Handi-Capped	Deaf and Blind	Total
Alabama	14,106	15,670	35,127	3,503	516	408	1,157	521	1,307	63	72,378
Alaska	2,739	5,716	906	333	59	156	205	48	68	12	10,242
Arizona	11,275	22,372	6,879	4,359	609	856	898	331	708	16	48,303
Arkansas	11,475	13,250	17,433	475	450	442	718	317	438	29	45,027
California	108,284	117,974	39,810	28,525	35,453	15,194	7,172	2,854	0	267	355,533
Colorado	10,478	20,501	6,808	6,405	0	702	913	285	1,103	33	47,228
Connecticut	14,342	25,019	8,212	11,585	944	537	1,233	642	36	1	62,551
Delaware	1,898	6,528	2,629	2,726	16	252	182	124	48	31	14,434
District of Columbia	1,602	1,128	1,309	450	180	234	50	55	168	41	5,217
Florida	41,072	47,829	29,973	10,931	0	2,735	2,060	853	1,492	18	136,963
Georgia	23,729	27,098	30,274	13,960	1,483	560	2,092	804	1,809	38	101,847
Hawaii	1,202	6,938	2,120	371	4	165	322	52	184	24	11,382
Idaho	4,176	7,891	3,021	538	575	483	483	250	629	20	18,066
Illinois	78,684	72,697	50,770	31,540	2,408	4,402	5,177	2,147	2,450	188	250,463
Indiana	47,783	17,373	27,165	2,053	400	863	1,429	601	1,123	28	98,818
Iowa	16,044	23,961	12,955	3,243	3	673	1,063	321	667	39	58,969
Kansas	12,886	12,528	7,780	2,590	703	339	765	251	852	39	38,733
Kentucky	22,958	4,205	23,321	2,623	1,013	629	1,059	447	649	183	67,087
Louisiana	24,640	29,416	20,713	5,201	1,483	734	1,681	551	1,183	38	85,640
Maine	5,575	7,640	5,293	3,681	,310	346	459	135	860	8	24,307
Maryland	24,488	46,118	11,870	3,616	1,838	1,102	1,868	673	2,152	38	93,763
Massachusetts	40,908	35,246	26,822	24,787	5,640	285	6,487	1,128	283	283	141,869
Michigan	54,127	43,472	31,188	18,063	0	4,128	3,205	1,149	53	0	155,385
Minnesota	23,248	35,201	14,894	3,945	1,661	1,246	1,615	474	42	20	82,346
Mississippi	14,064	8,136	18,720	255	18	322	543	228	130	14	42,430
Missouri	33,337	30,592	23,192	6,000	1,056	717	1,195	430	1,564	51	98,134
Montana	3,879	5,266	1,780	459	111	129	290	190	660	17	12,781
Nebraska	10,548	9,952	7,015	1,386	0	461	511	187	326	0	30,386
Nevada	3,086	5,380	1,365	320	194	266	194	74	319	9	11,207
New Hampshire	1,626	6,320	2,453	1,058	198	206	293	257	213	3	12,627
New Jersey	60,544	45,335	18,849	13,493	2,177	1,882	2,259	1,428	3,551	60	149,578
New Mexico	4,103	9,956	3,439	1,623	17	182	470	156	487	46	20,479
New York	43,751	30,975	47,960	45,692	35,407	6,920	5,208	2,081	542	51	218,587
North Carolina	26,946	34,017	43,507	3,692	900	1,146	2,246	845	1,542	53	114,894
North Dakota	3,258	3,474	2,083	291	60	104	206	87	198	15	9,776
Ohio	65,439	58,214	64,422	4,277	0	3,543	2,676	1,023	1,662	96	201,352
Oklahoma	19,109	25,035	13,781	558	352	365	796	323	643	35	60,997
Oregon	11,819	19,801	5,991	2,265	639	1,243	1,688	599	85	15	44,145
Pennsylvania	72,127	46,307	49,276	12,494	289	2,096	4,804	2,318	525	8	190,244
Puerto Rico	989	2,670	10,539	1,459	663	662	1,372	1,217	1,377	87	21,035
Rhode Island	3,437	8,728	1,989	1,092	187	184	258	61	115	20	16,071
South Carolina	21,021	16,240	26,090	4,882	72	847	1,098	576	622	18	71,466
South Dakota	4,847	2,437	1,245	309	19	163	445	55	327	3	9,850
Tennessee	31,824	27,221	23,302	3,084	1,532	1,170	2,358	796	1,706	9	93,004
Texas	70,555	123,751	31,033	11,084	3,102	2,736	4,578	1,465	19,067	241	267,612
Utah	7,834	12,760	3,327	9,650	108	211	680	303	1,231	23	36,127
Vermont	3,168	4,481	3,363	328	185	264	293	85	241	16	12,424
Virginia	32,101	27,842	18,950	5,025	530	513	1,495	1,642	2,908	45	91,051
Washington	11,495	20,782	11,063	5,466	1,199	1,018	1,302	418	1,265	41	54,049
West Virginia	10,089	9,174	11,552	828	767	321	410	256	545	22	33,964
Wisconsin	15,780	23,283	15,004	7,475	572	915	1,264	414	855	49	65,611
Wyoming	2,697	4,689	1,044	630	100	109	203	46	334	21	9,873
American Samoa	0	49	65	0	1	3	22	5	18	4	167
Guam	382	200	921	27	0	1	97	27	127	8	1,790
Northern Marianas	0	22	9	0	0	0	15	2	9	1	58
Trust Territories	225	92	19	33	57	26	1,140	18	109	23	1,742
Virgin Islands	285	146	732	43	0	13	57	12	15	15	1,318
Bur. of Indian Affairs	883	2,281	821	286	30	39	114	42	343	0	4,839
U.S. and Territories	1,188,967	1,281,379	882,173	331,067	106,292	66,248	82,873	32,679	61,965	2,576	4,036,219

[*]Source: U.S. Department of Education (1980, p. 161).

rate is reflected in the sample sizes of the criterion groups chosen for a particular study, caution must be exercised in interpreting the statistical indices derived from that rate. It can have a considerable effect upon the number of correct decisions that result from using the screening procedure and, consequently, upon the value of the procedure itself (Dawes, 1962; Flom, 1970; Meehl & Rosen, 1955).

Example

Suppose a random sample of 400 children was selected from the elementary school population in school district A. If the base rate of learning disabilities for that population was estimated to be about 5%, one would expect to find close to 20 learning-disabled children and 380 non-learning-disabled children in the total sample, within certain sampling error limits. Exampli gratia, that assumption seems reasonable, since almost all of the physically and mentally handicapping conditions mentioned previously are frequently diagnosed much earlier developmentally than learning disabilities, the 380 non-learning-disabled sample will most likely consist of normals. This extremely low base rate suggests that if *no procedure* were used and all 400 children were presumed to be normal, the probability of correct decisions would be 95% (380/400), and the 5% remaining would be false negative errors. This could be interpreted from the perspective that an empirical justification for using the discrepancy score procedure in district A would then require accuracy in excess of 95%, clearly a nontrivial achievement.

The classification results of the procedure illustrate this point (see Table 5.2). Despite the constraints of the low base rate, the procedure yielded 93.5% correct decisions. Inasmuch as this figure is 1.5% less than using no procedure, employing the discrepancy score procedure for the purpose of screening learning-disabled children in school district A may be viewed as questionable. Even the 3.5% disparity in the false negative error rate (5% − 1.5%) is negligible under these circumstances because that advantage can be offset easily by the cost and time disadvantages of large-scale testing. Based on the $p(C)$ index of decision validity alone, the use of the procedure in this district can be claimed to be invalid; it would be slightly better to do nothing.

Given these consequences of the low base rate, can the procedure be validly used with other populations? Yes, if the base rate is appreciably higher and the increment in decision accuracy is practically significant. Alternative populations where the procedure could prove its worth may include the following: (a) subpopulations within district A such as a particular cluster of schools with a higher incidence of learning disabilities than the district as a whole, (b) special schools and clinics established expressly for the screening, diagnosis, and remediation of learning disabilities, or (c) another school district with a higher base rate.

Incremental Validity

As an example of this secondary application, suppose the same discrepancy score procedure were used with a different sample of 400 children, this time drawn from school district B, where the base rate of the characteristic is 20%. The classification outcomes are displayed in Table 5.5. Notice that although slightly fewer correct decisions are produced with this sample compared to the district A sample, the 91% accuracy that would result from using the procedure exceeds the 80% accuracy that could be expected without using it. This 11% difference is referred to as the *incremental validity* of the procedure (Sechrest, 1963). It quantifies the amount of information that the procedure provides compared with that obtainable from another source.

Table 5.5

Predicted × Actual Classification Outcomes
for the Screening Procedure in School District B

(N = 400; Base Rate = 20%)

Actual

	LD	N
Predicted LD	68 (17%)	24 (6%)
Predicted N	12 (3%)	296 (74%)

Correct decisions = 91%
Incorrect decisions = 9%
False negatives = 3%
False positives = 6%

Incremental validity (*IV*) is expressed as the difference between probabilities of correct decisions associated with one procedure, $p(C)$, and an alternative, $p_A(C)$, which may be another procedure or no procedure, or

$$IV = p(C) - p_A(C).$$

As in this example where the alternative is no procedure, p_A (C) is set equal to 100 − base rate. The index is then computed as

$$IV = 91 - 80 = 11\%$$

Perhaps even more important than this 11% figure in the district B example is the relatively large difference in the false negative error rates. The 20% of the children in the district who are truly learning disabled would be unidentified and untreated if no procedure were used. The discrepancy procedure would reduce this statistic by 17%. Obviously, in this application, there is substantial validity evidence to warrant the use of the procedure to screen learning-disabled children in district B.

These preceding examples of how different base rates can affect the usefulness of a screening procedure demonstrate the principle: *the incremental validity of a procedure decreases as the base rate decreases from 50% toward zero.* If very low base rates of learning disabilities are suspected, as is usually the case, the p(C) index of decision validity for any screening procedure would most likely be less than p(C), which results from a no-screening procedure, where everyone in the sample is presumed to exhibit normal learning characteristics. This would produce negative values for the *IV* index, as in the example of school district A, where:

$$IV = 93.5 - 95 = -1.5\%$$

The problem of evaluating the effectiveness of a screening procedure in the context of a low base rate is generalizable to all handicapping conditions. This phenomenon diminishes the usefulness of p(C) and forces one to explore other indices that are independent of the base rate and the comparison sample. Some of these indices are described next.

Sensitivity and Specificity

In view of the aforementioned limitations of p(C) and the classification probability estimates derived from the base rate, alternative indices generated independent of the base rate should be considered. Such indices are estimated *absolutely* in terms of a given sample, as opposed to *relatively* in terms of the base rate. Their value in determining the usefulness of early identification instruments has already been addressed (see Gallagher & Bradley, 1972; Mercer, 1975; Satz & Fletcher, 1979).

Using the cell frequencies in Table 5.2, two absolute indices are *sensitivity*, expressed as

$$p(SENS) = \frac{n_1}{n_1 + n_2} \times 100 =$$ probability of correctly identifying a learning-disabled child in a sample of actual learning-disabled children,

and *specificity,* expressed as

$$p(\text{SPEC}) = \frac{n_4}{n_2 + n_4} \times 100 = \text{probability of correctly identifying a normal child in a sample of actual normals.}$$

Example

Again, based on the data in Table 5.2, these probabilities are computed as follows:

$$p(\text{SENS}) = \frac{14}{14 + 6} \times 100 = 70\%$$

$$p(\text{SPEC}) = \frac{360}{20 + 360} \times 100 = 95\%$$

Interpretation

As defined previously, the purpose of a screening procedure is to differentiate between learning-disabled and non-learning-disabled children. However, the procedure is actually performing two functions: (1) identifying the children with learning disabilities and (2) simultaneously excluding those without. The degree to which these are accomplished can be measured by $p(\text{SENS})$ and $p(\text{SPEC})$, respectively.

SENSITIVITY. The $p(\text{SENS})$ index quantifies the *sensitivity* of the procedure for the actual positive cases. In other words, how well does the procedure identify learning-disabled children? For the ability-achievement discrepancy score procedure used in school district A, the sensitivity was 70%, which is not an impressive level of effectiveness. This index is much more revealing than the $p(\text{TP})$ estimate of 3.5% derived from the base rate. Clearly, if the $p(\text{SENS})$ index is not high, none of the other indices, absolute or relative, are very meaningful. When $p(\text{SENS})$ is high, at least the procedure has demonstrated effectiveness with the target population. Its discriminative power would then have to be assessed separately using $p(\text{SPEC})$ and/or the base rate probabilities.

SPECIFICITY. Once $p(\text{SENS})$ is judged satisfactory, it is desirable to determine the specificity of the procedure for the actual negative cases. That is, how well does the procedure exclude non-learning-disabled children? Computing $p(\text{SPEC})$ in the preceding example yields a specificity index of 95%. Obviously the discrepancy-score procedure is for more effective at excluding normals than detecting learning-disabled children.

In addition to interpreting these indices of decision validity and those examined in the previous sections that concentrate on the correct decisions, true positives, and true negatives, the error rates must be weighted and incorporated into any evaluation of procedure effectiveness. The issues germane to the topic of misclassifications, false positives, and false negatives are discussed in the next section.

Consequences of Misclassification

Embedded unobtrusively throughout this presentation is the seriousness of decision errors. The value of this chapter, in fact, hinges on the answer to the question: *What are the consequences of making a wrong decision?* If the consequences are trivial, one need not be overly concerned with the validity of using a screening procedure. However, this position does not seem to reflect the sentiment expressed by specialists in the field. To the contrary, the consequences of not identifying a child with learning disabilities or, for that matter, with any other handicapping condition are deemed quite serious.

False Negative Errors (Type I Error)

At present, few practitioners would dispute the importance of correctly identifying learning-disabled children, diagnosing the nature of their specific disability, and then prescribing appropriate instructional plans that are tailored to meet their special needs. If any of these children go unidentified by kindergarten or first grade (false negative errors), their placement in the regular school program or in inappropriate remedial or treatment programs can result in several undesirable consequences: (a) the academic problems tend to worsen as the child gets older until the proper intervention is provided and, as a result, the greater the achievement deficit, the more difficult it will be to catch up, (b) repeated frustration and failure in the regular program can lead to poor self-concept (Bingham, 1980; Butkowsky & Willows, 1980; Husak & Magill, 1979), sometimes referred to as the "failure syndrome," (c) this syndrome may also manifest itself in the form of serious emotional and social problems (Bryan & McGrady, 1972; Pope, Lehrer, & Stevens, 1980). In addition to these individual consequences, false negative errors are instructionally inefficient and it becomes increasingly difficult to prescribe remedial materials for multiyear achievement deficits (Buktenika, 1971; Cruickshank, Morse, & Johnson, 1980).

False Positive Errors (Type II Error)

The consequences of false positive errors are also serious. A normal child who is incorrectly classified as learning disabled will suffer unnecessary labeling and will be deprived of an appropriate educational program until a subsequent evaluation indicates the need for a decision reversal.

Relative Seriousness of Errors

The preceding considerations serve to emphasize the seriousness of false negative and false positive errors. A screening procedure can take into account the losses or costs of these errors so as to minimize their probability of occurrence. The determination of *relative seriousness*, that is, which error is more serious, is a judgment that the assessment team must make based on experience, the characteristics of the children, and a conscientious balancing of the aforestated consequences of the two types of error. Once this decision is reached, there ar strategies one can use to adjust the discrepancy-score criterion to achieve the desired results. Typically, the false negative error rate can be decreased by widening the range of acceptable performance in the direction of overidentification[2].

Utility Analysis

The process by which a discrepancy-score criterion is adjusted according to the costs associated with false negative (diagnostic miss) and false positive (false alarm) errors as well as the benefits to be gained from the effective and efficient delivery of professional services is called utility analysis. Since the details of this analysis are beyond the scope of this chapter and have been presented elsewhere (see Berk, 1976; Harber, 1981b; Wiggins, 1973), only a few comments pertinent to screening procedures will be noted (see also Chapter 8).

Although the preceding discussion emphasized the costs of false negative errors in terms of the individual child's achievement, motivation, self-concept, and emotional and social well-being, there are also other costs related to programming, professional services, and facilities when a strategy of overidentification is adopted. Certainly, diagnostic and instructional provisions must be made to accommodate those children screened as learning disabled. The various costs at all levels must be evaluated thoroughly and perceptively before a final decision is reached to alter the screening criterion.

In the case of an ability-achievement discrepancy score, if the decision is to minimize the false negative error rate, the magnitude of the particular score required for learning disability classification may be reduced. For example, given the results in Table 5.5 based on a z-score discrepancy of .80, if an assessment team wished to eliminate the 3% error rate, this could be accomplished by reducing the discrepancy-score criterion to .70. Adjustments of this kind are dependent on the distribution of discrepancy scores in the learning-disabled and normal samples and, therefore, will vary with each decision validity study.

One consolation in this analysis of consequences of misclassification resides in the multistage structure of the assessment process. Screening is only the first stage. Children who are initially identified as potential learning-disability cases are then referred for more comprehensive, individualized diagnostic testing. This second stage provides a check on the screening decision by either corrobo-

---

[2] A 2% ceiling on the number of children between 5 and 17 years of age in a state that could be identified with specific learning disabilities was specified in P.L. 94-142 (Section 611) and in the Rules and Regulations (U.S.O.E., 1977a) for its implementation. This restriction (p. 42502) was originally designed "to prevent overinclusion" (Bersoff, 1979, p. 105), that is, to limit the false positive error rate. That 2% cap was deleted in the subsequent Rules and Regulations (U.S.O.E., 1977b, p. 65082).

rating true negative decisions or detecting false positive decision errors. This type of error can then be corrected by assigning the particular children to the regular instructional program. Unfortunately, there is no opportunity to check on true positive and false negative decisions in this process. Consequently, to the extent it is instructionally feasible, one should *commit as few false negative errors as possible in screening for learning disabilities* (cf. Salvia & Ysseldyke, 1981, p. 534), as there is no systematic recourse for correcting those errors.

Problems of Labeling and Low Base Rate

Labeling

All screening procedures analyzed in terms of this decision model reduce to a dichotomous decision choice: learning disabled or non – learning disabled. The regulations of P.L. 94-142, in fact, mandate this classification and labeling of learning-disabled children by requiring state educational agencies to categorize all handicapped children by handicap and age in submitting their annual reports (U.S.O.E., 1977a, p. 42482). As Bersoff and Veltman (1979) indicated, "in order to meet this requirement it seems that all children receiving any kind of special help will have to have a label, if only to enable the state to fulfill the administrative requirements imposed by [the law]" (p. 18).

The advantages and disadvantages of labeling have been debated extensively (see Algozzine & Mercer, 1980; Gallagher, 1976; Goffman, 1963; Gorham, Des Jardins, Page, Pettis, & Scheiber, 1975; Hallahan & Kauffman, 1978; Hobbs, 1975a, 1975b; Jones, 1977; MacMillan, Jones, & Aloia, 1974; Reschly, 1979). Some of the most salient advantages are summarized by Algozzine and Mercer (1980):

> The primary objective that ultimately permeates the rationale for labeling exceptional children is that the label will directly or indirectly facilitate treatment. . . . The use of labeling to improve communications among researchers, establish prevalence estimates, determine etiologies, design prevention programs, place in special education, and obtain funds are examples of indirect and direct uses of labeling to provide or improve treatment efforts. (p. 289)

They also observed two key disadvantages of labeling:

> First, to the extent that a label fails directly or indirectly to lead to differentiated treatment for an individual child, it fails to serve a useful function. Second, labeling may actually be harmful to the child. When a child's perceptions and behaviors, as well as those of others, are altered by labeling in a manner which results in restricting the social, emotional, and/or academic growth of the child, labels are harmful. (p. 289)

Clearly, this second observation has caused the greatest concern, and, consequently, has received the most research attention.

Historically, however, the mountain of research on the harmful effects of labeling that has grown since the 1970s deals almost entirely with the label "mentally retarded" (see review by Algozzine & Mercer, 1980). Perhaps due in part to the recency of P.L. 94-142, there have been only a few experimental studies of the adverse effects of the label "learning disabled." Most of these have examined the effect of the label on teacher judgments and expectancies of children (Algozzine, Mercer, & Countermine, 1977; Algozzine & Sutherland, 1977; Foster & Ysseldyke, 1976; Jacobs, 1978; Mooney & Algozzine, 1978), rather than on the child assigned that label (e.g., Sutherland & Algozzine, 1979). An analysis of the results of these investigations by Ysseldyke and Algozzine (1979) suggests that the "LD label transmits negative expectations to teachers and other professionals likely to be working with handicapped children, and that the effects of the LD label are somewhat less negative than those of other handicaps" (p. 6). In other words, "learning disabled" is perceived as a more acceptable handicap than "mentally retarded" and "emotionally disturbed" but is considered less preferred than "normal." In addition to these findings, Bryan (1974, 1976) has demonstrated that learning-disabled children tend to be rejected by their peers.

Although the research evidence on the effects of labeling a child as "learning disabled" that has accumulated is far from complete or conclusive, all available signs point negative. When this trend is viewed in the context of the aforestated legal regulations and currect screening practices, there are only two inescapable conclusions: labeling is unavoidable; mislabeling is not. The primary concern rests with the latter. It is the mislabeling or misclassification of children that produces the most damaging consequences. Several years ago, Hobbs (1975a) indicated one precaution to minimize the potentially harmful effects of labeling is to "improve the classification system . . [and] the procedures for early identification of children with developmental risk" (pp. 232 – 233). It is hoped that the application of the classification decision framework advanced in the preceding pages will constitute one step in that direction, by supplying a mechanism to test the accuracy of an identification procedure or device.

Low Base Rate

Perhaps the issue that is most troublesome in the application of the decision model is the extremely low base rate. Stated succinctly, where the base rate of any handicapping condition or disease is low, say 10% or less, it is very difficult ot justify a formal screening procedure over non screening on *empirical* grounds[3] (cf. Metz, 1978). Current state-by-state estimates of the incidence of

---

[3]This problem is analogous to the study of "orphan" diseases such as Tourette syndrome, where the prevalence rate in the population is relatively low, say 100,000 or less (Shapiro, Shapiro, Bruun, & Sweet, 1978). Despite knowledge of this disease over 150 years ago (Itard, 1825), only recently have research resources been committed toward testing appropriate pharmacotherapeutic treatments. In these cases, incidence rate tends to serve as a rationalization for the wrong problem. It is neither synonymous with the importance of treatment nor a justification for nontreatment. (*Note*: Concomitants of Tourette syndrome include learning disabilities in mathematics and speech and language disorders [Shapiro, Shapiro, & Wayne, 1973].)

learning disabilities range from less than 1% to about 7%, and nationwide it is about 3%. The problem is that in a state with a base rate, such as 7%, special education administrators can presume that all of the children are normal (or non – learning disabled), and they would be right 93% of the time. The other 7% of the children can be considered as false negative errors. In other words, by doing nothing there will be 93% correct identifications and 7% false negatives. The justification for using a screening procedure under these circumstances would then be contingent upon obtaining decision validity estimates that exceed 93% accuracy with a corresponding reduction in the 7% error rate. Obviously this is a formidable task.

While the use of base rate – independent indices such as sensitivity and specificity circumvents this problem as far as estimating the absolute effectiveness of a screening procedure, the determination of relative effectiveness in conjunction with the consequences of misclassifications does not. Since a screening procedure should be defensible psychometrically as well as clinically, it seems advisable to evaluate all decision validity evidence against the alternatives in order to assess the procedure's value in each application.

Summary

The step-by-step procedure for determining the decision validity of a screening procedure is summarized as follows:

1. Specify criteria for selecting definite learning-disabled and non-learning-disabled samples
2. Estimate sample sizes according to the known base rate
3. Determine the most appropriate sampling method—random or specially composed
4. Select the two criterion groups
5. Apply the screening procedure to these groups
6. Designate the criterion for a severe learning disability
7. Count the number of learning-disabled children that met this criterion(n_1)
8. Count the number of normals that failed to meet the criterion (n_4)
9. Count the number remaining in each group (n_2 and n_3)
10. Compute the probabilities of correct decisions based on steps 7 and 8 — $p(TP)$ and $p(TN)$
11. Compute the probabilities of incorrect decisions based on step 9 — $p(FP)$ and $p(FN)$
12. Compute $p(C) - p(TP) + p(TN)$
13. Determine the incremental validity (IV) of the procedure
14. Assess decision validity in light of these indices
15. Compute the sensitivity of the procedure for the actual learning-disabled cases — $p(SENS)$

16. Compute the specificity of the procedure for the actual normal cases — $p(\text{SPEC})$

17. Consider reducing the criterion in order to minimize false negative errors and maximize sensitivity

18. Assess the decision validity of the screening procedure in terms of $p(\text{C})$, $p(\text{FN})$, $p(\text{SENS})$, and $p(\text{SPEC})$

References

Abrams, J.C. Learning disabilities. In G.P. Sholevar, R.M. Benson, & B.J. Blinder (Eds.), *Treatment of emotional disorders in children and adolescents.* Jamaica, NY: Spectrum Publications, 1980. Pp. 483 – 500.

Algozzine, B., & Mercer, C.D. Labels and expectancies for handicapped children and youth. In L. Mann & D.A. Sabatino (Eds.), *The fourth review of special education.* New York: Grune & Stratton, 1980. Pp. 287 – 313.

Algozzine, B., Mercer, C.D., & Countermine, T. The effects of labels and behavior on teacher expectations. *Exceptional Children,* 1977, *44,* 131 – 132.

Algozzine, B., & Sutherland, J.H. The "learning disabilities" label: An experimental analysis. *Contemporary Educational Psychology,* 1977, *2,* 292 – 297.

Berk, R.A. Determination of optimal cutting scores in criterion-referenced measurement. *Journal of Experimental Education,* 1976, *45,* 4 – 9.

Bersoff, D.N. Regarding psychologists testily: Legal regulation of psychological assessment in the public schools. *Maryland Law Review,* 1979, *39,* 27 – 120.

Bersoff, D.N., & Beltman, E.S. Public Law 94 – 142: Legal implications for the education of handicapped children. *Journal of Research and Development in Education,* 1979, *12,* 10 – 22.

Bingham, G. Self-esteem among boys with and without specific learning disabilities. *Child Study Journal,* 1980, *13,* 41 – 47.

Bruininks, R.H., Glaman, G.H., & Clark, C.R. *Prevalence of learning disabilities: Findings, issues, and recommendations* (Project No. 332189). Washington, DC: U.S. Office of Education, 1971.

Bryan, T.S. Peer popularity of learning disabled children. *Journal of Learning Disabilities,* 1974, *7,* 621 – 625.

Bryan, T.S. Peer popularity of learning disabled children: A replication. *Journal of Learning Disabilities,* 1976, *9,* 307 – 311.

Bryan, T.S., & McGrady, H.J. Use of a teacher-rating scale. *Journal of Learning Disabilities,* 1972, *5,* 199 – 206.

Buktenika, N.A. Identification of potential learning disabilities. *Journal of Learning Disabilities,* 1971, *4,* 379 – 383.

Butkowsky, I.S., & Willows, D.M. Cognitive-motivational characteristics of children varying in reading ability: Evidence for learned helplessness in poor readers. *Journal of Educational Psychology,* 1980, *72,* 408 – 422.

Cronbach, L.J., & Meehl, P.E. Construct validity in psychological tests. *Psychological Bulletin,* 1955, *52,* 281 – 302.

Cruickshank, W.M., Morse, W.C., & Johnson, J.S. *Learning disabilities: The struggle from adolescence toward adulthood.* Syracuse, NY: Syracuse University Press, 1980.

Cureton, E.E. A recipe for a cookbook. *Psychological Bulletin,* 1957, *54,* 494 – 497.

Darlington, R.B., & Stauffer, G.F. Use and evaluation of discrete test information in decision-making. *Journal of Applied Psychology,* 1966, *50,* 125 – 129. (a)

Darlington, R.B., & Stauffer, G.F. A method for choosing a cutting point on a test. *Journal of*

Applied Psychology, 1966, *50,* 229 – 231. (b)

Dawes, R.M. A note on base rates and psychometric efficiency. *Journal of Consulting Psychology,* 1962, *26,* 422 – 424.

Edwards, A.L. *The measurement of personality traits by scales and inventories.* New York: Holt, Rinehart and Winston, 1970.

Flom, M.C. Statistical considerations. In D.B. Carter (Ed.), *Interdisciplinary approaches to learning disorders.* Philadelphia: Chilton, 1970. Pp. 40 – 47.

Forness, S.R., & Esveldt, K.C. Classroom observation of children with learning and behavior problems. *Journal of Learning Disabilities,* 1975, *8,* 382 – 385.

Foster, G.G., & Ysseldyke, J.E. Expectancy and halo effects as a result of artificially induced bias. *Contemporary Educational Psychology,* 1976, *1,* 37 – 45.

Gallagher, J.J. The sacred and profane uses of labeling. *Mental Retardation,* 1976, *14,* 3 – 7.

Gallagher, J.J., & Bradley, R.H. Early identification of developmental difficulties. In I.J. Gordon (Ed.), *Early childhood education: The seventy-first yearbook of the National Society for the Study of Education* (Part II). Chicago: University of Chicago Press, 1972, Pp. 87 – 122.

Gillespie, P.H., Miller, T.L., & Fielder, V.D. Legislative definitions of learning disabilities: Roadblocks to effective service. *Journal of Learning Disabilities,* 1975, *8,* 660 – 666.

Girshick, M.A. An elementary survey of statistical decision theory. *Review of Educational Research,* 1954, *24,* 448 – 466.

Goffman, E. *Stigma: Notes on the management of a spoiled identity.* Englewood Cliffs, NJ: Prentice-Hall, 1963.

Gorham, K.A., Des Jardins, C., Page, R., Pettis, E., & Scheiber, B. Effect on parents. In N. Hobbs (Ed.), *Issues in the classification of children* (Vol. 2). San Francisco: Jossey-Bass, 1975. Pp. 154 – 188.

Hallahan, D.P., & Kauffman, J.M. Categories, labels, behavioral characteristics: ED, LD, and EMR reconsidered. *Journal of Special Education,* 1978, *11,* 139 – 147.

Harber, J.R. Asessing the quality of decision making in special education. *Journal of Special Education,* 1981, *15,* 77 – 90.(a)

Harber, J.R. Evaluating utility in diagnostic decision making. *Journal of Special Education,* 1981, *15,* 413 – 428.(b)

Hobbs, N. *The futures of children.* San Francisco: Jossey-Bass, 1975. (a)

Hobbs, N. *Issues in the classification of children* (Vols. 1 & 2). San Francisco: Jossey-Bass, 1975.(b)

Husak, W.S. & Magill, R.A. Correlations among perceptual-motor abilities, self-concept, and reading achievement in early elementary grades. *Perceptual and Motor Skills,* 1979, *48,* 447 – 450.

Itard, J.M.G. Mémoire sur quelques fonctions involontaires des appareils de la locomotion, de la préhension, et de la voix. *Archives of General Medicine* (Paris), 1825, *8,* 385 – 407.

Jacobs, W.R. The effect of the learning disability label onclassroom teacher's ability objectively to observe and interpret child behaviors. *Learning Disability Quarterly,* 1978, *1,* 50 – 55.

Jones, R.A. *Self-fulfilling prophecies.* Hillsdale, NJ: Erlbaum, 1977.

Kass, C., & Myklebust, H.R. Learning disabilities: An educational definition. *Journal of Learning Disabilities,* 1969, *2,* 377 – 379.

Kirk, S.A., & Elkins, J. Characteristics of children enrolled in the Child Service Demonstration Centers. *Journal of Learning Disabilities,* 1975, *8,* 630 – 637.

Klein, D.F., & Cleary, T.A. Platonic true scores and error in psychiatric rating scales. *Psychological Bulletin,* 1967, *68,* 77 – 80.

Lusted, L.B. *Introduction to medical decision making.* Springfield, IL: Thomas, 1968.

MacMillan, D.L., Jones, R.L., & Aloia, G.F. The mentally retarded label: A theoretical analysis and review of research. *American Journal of Mental Deficiency,* 1974, *79,* 241 – 261.

Meehl, P.E., & Rosen, A. Antecedent probability and the efficiency of psychometric signs, patterns, or cutting scores. *Psychological Bulletin*, 1955, *52*, 194 – 216.

Meier, J.H. Prevalence and characteristics of learning disabilities found in second grade children. *Journal of Learning Disabilities*, 1971, *4*, 6 – 19.

Mercer, C.D. *Preliminary review of early identification indices for learning disabled children.* Paper presented at the meeting of the Conference of the State of Florida Association for Children with Learning Disabilities, Tampa, October 1975.

Mercer, C.D., Forgnone, D., & Wolking, W.D. Definitions of learning disabilities used in the United States. *Journal of Learning Disabilities*, 1976, *9*, 47 – 57.

Metz, C.E. Basic principles of ROC analysis. *Seminars in Nuclear Medicine*, 1978, *8*, 283 – 298.

Mooney, C., & Algozzine, B. A comparison of the disturbingness of behaviors related to learning disability and emotional disturbance. *Journal of Abnormal Child Psychology*, 1978, *6*, 401 – 406.

Myklebust, H.R., & Boshes, B. *Minimal brain damage in children* (Final Report, Contract 108-65-142, Neurological and Sensory Disease Control Program). Washington, DC: U.S. Department of Health, Education and Welfare, 1969.

National Advisory Committe on Dyslexia and Related Reading Disorders. *Reading disorders in the United States.* Washington, DC: U.S. Department of Health, Education and Welfare, 1969.

National Advisory Committee on Handicapped Children. *First annual report, Subcommittee on Education of the Committee on Labor and Public Welfare, U.S. Senate.* Washington, DC: U.S. Government Printing Office, 1968.

Niesworth, J.T., & Greer, J.G. Functional similarities of learning disability and mild retardation. *Exceptional Children*, 1975, *42*, 17 – 25.

Patton, D.D. Introduction to clinical decision making. *Seminars in Nuclear Medicine*, 1978, *8*, 273 – 282.

Pope, J., Lehrer, B., & Stevens, J. A multiphasic reading screening procedure. *Journal of Learning Disabilities*, 1980, *13*, 98 – 102.

Public Law 94-142. Education for All Handicapped Children Act, S.6, 94th Congress [Sec 613(a)(4)] 1st session, June 1975. Report No. 94 – 168.

Reschly, D.J. Nonbiased assessment. In G.D. Phye & D.J. Reschly (Eds.), *School psychology: Perspectives and issues.* New York: Academic Press, 1979. Pp. 215 – 253.

Rickey, D.D., & McKinney, H.D. Classroom behavioral styles of learning disabled boys. *Journal of Learning Disabilities*, 1978, *11*, 38 – 43.

Rorer, L.G., Hoffman, P.J., LaForge, G.E., & Hsieh, K.C. Optimum cutting scores to discriminate groups of unequal size and variance. *Journal of Applied Psychology*, 1966, *50*, 153 – 164.

Salvia, J., & Ysseldyke, J.E. *Assessment in special and remedial education* (2nd ed.). Boston: Houghton Mifflin, 1981.

Satz, P., & Fletcher, J.M. Early screening tests: Some uses and abuses. *Journal of Learning Disabilities*, 1979, *12*, 56 – 60.

Sechrest, L. Incremental validity: A recommendation. *Educational and Psychological Measurement*, 1963, *23*, 153 – 158.

Shapiro, A.K., Shapiro, E.S., Bruun, R.D., & Sweet, R.D. *Gilles de la Tourette syndrome.* New York: Raven Press, 1978.

Shapiro, A.K., Shapiro, E.S., & Wayne, H.L. The symptomatology and diagnosis of Gilles de la Tourette's syndrome. *Journal of the American Academy of Child Psychiatry*, 1973, *12*, 702 – 723.

Silverman, L.J., & Metz, A.S. Minimal brain dysfunction 3. Epidemiology. Number of pupils with specific learning disabilities in local public schools in the United States. *Annals of* the *New York Academy of Sciences*, 1973, *205*, 146.

Stearns, M.S., Norwood, C., Kaskowitz, D., & Mitchell, S. *Validation of state counts of handicapped children* (Vol. 2). Menlo Park, CA: SRI International, 1977.

Sutcliffe, J.P. A probability model for errors of classification-I: General considerations. *Psychometrika*, 1965, *30*, 73 – 96.

Sutherland, J.H., & Algozzine, B. The learning disabilities label as a biasing factor in the visual-motor performance of normal children. *Journal of Learning Disabilities*, 1979, *12*, 17 – 23.

Taylor, H.C., & Russell, J.T. The relationship of validity coefficients to the practical validity of tests in selection: Discussion and tables. *Journal of Applied Psychology*, 1939, *23*, 565 – 578.

Thurlow, M.L., & Ysseldyke, J.E. Current assessment and decision-making practices in model LD programs. *Learning Disability Quarterly*, 1979, *2*, 15 – 24.

U.S. Department of Education. *To assure the free appropriate public education of all handicapped children* (Second Annual Report to Congress on Implementation of Public Law 94-142: The Education for All Handicapped Children Act). Washington, DC: Author, 1980.

U.S. Office of Education. Education of handicapped children: Implementation of Part B of the Education of the Handicapped Act. *Federal Register*, 1977, *42*(163), 42474 – 42518. (a)

U.S. Office of Education. Assistance to states for education for handicapped children: Procedures for evaluating specific learning disabilities. *Federal Register*, 1977, *42*(250), 62082 – 62085. (b)

Wallace, G., & McLoughlin, J.A. *Learning disabilities: Concepts and characteristics* (2nd ed.). Columbus, OH: Merrill, 1979.

Wiggins, J.S. *Personality and prediction: Principles of personality assessment.* Reading, MA: Addison-Wesley, 1973.

Wissink, J., Kass, C., & Ferrell, W. A Bayesian approach to the identification of children with learning disabilities. *Journal of Learning Disabilities*, 1975, *8*, 36 – 44.

Ysseldyke, J.E., & Algozzine, B. Perspectives on assessment of learning disabled students. *Learning Disability Quarterly*, 1979, *2*, 3 – 13.

Ysseldyke, J.E., Algozzine, B., & Richey, L. Judgment under uncertainty: How many children are handicapped? *Exceptional Children*, 1982, *48*, 531 – 534.

Ysseldyke, J.E., Algozzine, B., Shinn, M.R., & McGue, M. Similarities and differences between low achievers and students classified learning disabled. *Journal of Special Education*, 1982, *16*, 73 – 85.

Chapter 6

DETERMINING THE
DECISION VALIDITY
OF A DIAGNOSTIC TEST

Introduction

A S the preceding chapter noted at different points, the general decision model used to determine the effectiveness of a screening procedure can also be employed to appraise the value of a single diagnostic test. Unlike the standardized, norm-referenced tests usually chosen for screening in broad domains of content such as reading comprehension and mathematics calculation, diagnostic tests provide a limited-focus measurement of specific skill areas with the intent of pinpointing strengths and weaknesses. These tests are often called criterion-referenced or mastery tests (Berk, 1980a, 1984). At this diagnostic stage of assessment, the teacher or specialist makes decisions of mastery or nonmastery so that appropriate remedial or ameliorative programs can be prescribed.

Task-Analysis Model

This approach to dianostic testing is part of a diagnostic-prescriptive teaching model that emphasizes —

1. the identification of specific skill-development weaknesses (i.e., specific learning disabilities);
2. the use of criterion-referenced tests and informal measures that are instructionally sensitive and custom-tailored to the curriculum;
3. the prescription of interventions designed to remediate the skill weaknesses.

It follows closely the *task-analysis model* described by Ysseldyke and Salvia (1974) and espoused by Resnick, Wang, and Kaplan (1973) or the *behavioral model* of academic remediation proposed by Treiber and Lahey (1983). Mercer and Ysseldyke (1977) capsulize the model as follows:

Each child is treated relative to himself [or herself] and not in reference to a norm.

177

> Academic performance is a function of an interaction between enabling behaviors
> and the characteristics of the task. Children demonstrate skill development strengths
> and weaknesses. There is no need to deal with presumed causes of academic difficul-
> ties. There are skill hierarchies; development of complex skills is dependent upon
> adequate development in lower-level enabling behaviors. (p. 86)

Testing in this context is viewed as an integral part of the teaching-learning
process, where testing serves initially as a diagnostic tool, teaching then occurs
based on the results, and then retesting is employed formatively to monitor the
progress in skill development.

Ability-Training Model

The antithesis of the task-analysis model is the *ability-training model* or psychoeducational process model that concentrates on the diagnosis and remediation of *ability* weaknesses as opposed to *skill-development* weaknesses. Differential
diagnostic information is used typically to determine cognitive, perceptual-
motor, and psycholinguistic ability or process deficits that are presumed to
cause inadequate skill development. The ability-training model captures the
"majority position within the field of learning disabilities over the past 20 or 30
years" (Haring & Bateman, 1977, p. 130). Despite the model's popularity
among most authorities and practitioners in special education (Arter &
Jenkins, 1977), its basic assumptions lack philosophical, theoretical, and empirical support (Arter & Jenkins, 1979). These assumptions that have been presented and scrutinized by Arter and Jenkins (1979) are the following:

1. Educationally relevant psychological abilities exist and can be measured.
2. Existing tests used in differential diagnosis are reliable.
3. Existing tests used for differential diagnosis are valid.
4. Prescriptions can be generated from differential diagnosis to remediate
   weak abilities.
5. Remediation of weak abilities improves academic achievement.
6. Prescriptions can be generated from ability profiles to improve academic
   achievement, with no direct training of weak abilities.

From their review of all available evidence, the authors concluded that the "repeated failure to support. . . [these] assumptions . . . casts doubt on the
model's validity . . . [and] with the current instructional programs and tests,
this model is not useful" (p. 549).

This chapter consequently will deal with an application of decision analysis
to criterion-referenced test decision making according to the task-analysis
model. The purpose of this analysis is to ascertain the accuracy of mastery-
nonmastery classification decisions in order to answer the question: How effective is this test for diagnosing specific learning disabilities? The presentation is
organized according to some of the major topics covered in Chapter 5, including (1) rationale, (2) terminology, (3) selection of criterion groups, (4) correct

and incorrect decisions, (5) sensitivity and specificity, and (6) consequences of misclassification. In addition, the application of the model to a basic skills test and its advantages and disadvantages are discussed.

Rationale

The criterion-referenced tests developed by classroom teachers are used most often for making mastery-nonmastery decisions about individual achievement of instructional objectives. These individual decisions are based on data that identify a student's strengths (mastery) and weaknesses (nonmastery). While a teacher can employ this information in a variety of ways, the diagnostic decisions that serve as the guide for proper instructional treatment are of primary concern here. The subsequent program design and materials that are tailored to fit each child's needs depend on the diagnostic profile. The weaknesses in skill development (specific learning disabilities) revealed through this process should be the *correct* weaknesses.

It is, therefore, very important to know the accuracy of diagnostic decisions. Certainly a teacher would not intentionally prescribe the wrong instructional materials for any student. Moreover, a test that sorts most students into the wrong groups would be useless (e.g., 40% accuracy). If the scores on a test are used for mastery-nonmastery classification decisions, then the quality of that test becomes contingent upon the accuracy of those decisions. The degree of accuracy attained provides evidence of *decision validity* (Hambleton, 1980).

Inasmuch as mastery-nonmastery decisions can be made only be referencing each student's score to the score chosen as the mastery standard, the *accuracy of the decisions is a function of the standard.* The standard is the point of decision making. For example, if a student scores three on a five-item subtest and the standard is set at three, that student would be labeled a "master." However, if the standard is set at four, that same student would then be labeled a "nonmaster." The underlying question is: Which *standard* is producing the *correct classification* of the student?

Therefore, evidence of decision validity is related directly to the choice of a mastery standard. One standard on a given subtest might yield highly accurate decisions, whereas another standard, perhaps one score higher or lower, might yield considerably less accurate decisions. The first task, then, is to select the standard that corresponds to the largest number of correct decisions. Once this is completed, the degree of accuracy should be estimated. Procedures for accomplishing these tasks constitute the thrust of the remaining sections of this chapter.

Mastery Standard

The *standard*, or criterion level, of performance can be expressed as a number (4 out of 5 items), as a percentage (80%), or as a proportion (.80) of the items a student must answer correctly. The number (4) that is based on the cluster of items measuring an instructional objective is commonly referred to as the *cutting score.* It is the score that cuts the distribution of scores into two mutually exclusive categories: one category containing the scores from which mastery is inferred and a second category containing the scores from which nonmastery is inferred. Students who are called masters must score *at or above* the cutting score; those who are called *nonmasters* score *below* the cutting score.

Typically, the *percentage* and *proportion* correct have been used interchangeably with the term *cutting score.* The former two terms should be reserved more appropriately for the standard of mastery performance in the item domain. That is, if a student can answer correctly four items in the specific five-item sample, it is expected that he or she should be able to answer correctly about 80% of "all possible items" that could have been written to measure the objective. If that total population, or *domain,* happens to consist of 90 items, then 72 items or more should be answered correctly.

Standard Setting Methods

To date a variety of standard setting methods have been recommended for use with criterion-referenced tests (for references, see Chapter 2). Although the polemics over which methods are best and related issues are far from over, at present there seems to be consensus among experts on the topic that *all of the methods involve some form of human judgment.* A completely objective, scientifically precise method does not exist. Regardless of how complex and statistically sophisticated a method might be, judgment plays a role in the determination of the cutting score and/or in the estimation of classification errors (Berk, 1980b).

On the spectrum of practicability, the simplest method is to pull the standard from thin air. This is exemplified by the teacher or administrator who sets a standard such as 80% without any foundation or reason. The judgment in this case is capricious. It is the weakest and least defensible, although the most popular, approach. For its lack of any logical, experiential, or empirical justification, it has been characterized as the *cardiac approach* (Berk, 1979), i.e., I know in my heart that she is a master and he is a nonmaster. The deficiencies or problems associated with this approach are numerous. A few of these problems are described by the following:

1. *A student's mastery or nonmastery of an objective has no meaning.* If a student is labeled a master based on some 80% standard, there is no way of knowing whether he or she truly possesses the skills defined by the instructional objective. The relationship between the performance standard and mastery-nonmastery of the actual skills is indeterminable. If a student does well or poorly, there is no way to explain why.

2. *The percentage of students who master an objective has no meaning.* This information, which is simply an aggregate of the preceding classification data, is

supposed to indicate the overall achievement of a class or grade level, and often the effectiveness of the instructional program as well. If 70% of the students in one class mastered an objective, no explanation of this percentage in terms of true mastery is possible. Certainly anyone can attach any meanings that they wish. Negative inferences would be as unjustified and unfounded as positive ones.

3. *The standard does not reflect the difficulty of the items measuring a single objective or different objectives.* It is very likely that item difficulties will vary within an instructional objective and even more so across the different objectives that comprise the total test. Consequently, one set standard of 80% may be easily attainable for some objectives and highly unrealistic or unattainable for others.

CRITERIA FOR A DEFENSIBLE STANDARD SETTING METHOD. Clearly, any standard setting method that is recommended as a substitute for the cardiac approach must address these problems. In addition, it must be compatible with the characteristics of most teacher-made tests and the practical constraints under which they are constructed. In view of these considerations, a defensible method should —

1. be sensitive to different item difficulty levels;
2. be applicable to different subtest and test lengths;
3. be linkable to the performance of students who possess the skills that are measured by the test;
4. produce mastery-nonmastery classifications;
5. provide estimates of probabilities of correct classification decisions and decision errors;
6. be intuitively sound and conceptually simple;
7. be easy to compute.

Terminology

The correct and incorrect decisions that can result from a mastery-nonmastery classification have been assigned labels using the terms "mastery" and "nonmastery" instead of "positive" and "negative." This is for purposes of clarity. The clinical terminology is less appropriate in a classroom setting and, furthermore, tends to create confusion, especially in distinguishing between false positives and false negatives. The mastery-nonmastery analogue for the positive-negative classification language is compared:

Decisions Based on a Screening Procedure	Decisions Based on Criterion-referenced Test Scores
True positive	True mastery
True negative	True nonmastery

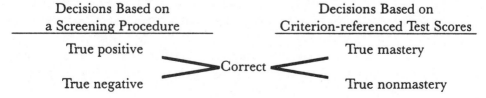

Correct

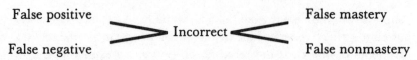

False positive   False mastery

False negative   False nonmastery

It should be noted that although "positive" has been associated typically with the presence of an undesirable characteristic, such as learning disability, it can just as easily refer to the presence of a desirable characteristic, such as mastery.

The correct and incorrect decisions that can result from a criterion-referenced test are depicted in Table 6.1. The structure of this classification model and its components are identical to that shown in Table 5.1 for a screening procedure; only the names have been changed.

Table 6.1

Predicted × Actual Classification
Decision Model for a Criterion-referenced Test

Actual Classification

		Mastery	Nonmastery
Predicted Classification *(Cutting Score on Test)*	**Mastery**	True Mastery n_1	False Mastery n_2
	Nonmastery	False Nonmastery n_3	True Nonmastery n_4

Selection of Criterion Groups

The foundation of this model and, in essence, the effectiveness of mastery and nonmastery decisions reduces to the samples of *actual* masters and nonmasters selected expressly for study. For the classroom teacher, this topic of sample selection translates into the following question: *Who should be able to master the objectives and who should not?* Two categories of students are of interest — those who would be *successful* (masters) and those who would be *unsuccessful* (nonmasters) on the objectives. For the majority of instructional programs for which tests are developed, these groups may consist of students who have and students who have not been exposed to the instruction, respectively. It is likely that most, if not all, students prior to instruction will perform poorly on the test. If this level of performance is not obtained, either the test is failing to function as expected or the objectives have been taught previously. When the latter appears to be the explanation, the justification for the instruction needs to be examined. In the case of the successful group that is tested after the instruction has been completed, performance should be quite high. That is, most, if not all, of these students should master the objectives.

These two groups of students chosen for the decision analysis are often referred to as *criterion groups*. Their selection is based on some criterion of current or future performance. This may be success in the instructional program in which the test will be used or success in a subsequent program, i.e., unit, course, grade level. The former often suggests summative decision making[1] at one point in time, whereas the latter denotes placement decision making[2] within a predictive context. Placement in a program that contains sequentially arranged units, each represented by an instructional objective, assumes that a student's success in any single unit is prerequisite for success in the following unit (see Glaser & Nitko, 1971). Therefore, a group of students that has successfully completed the entire program can serve as one of the criterion groups.

A clear definition of the criterion is essential. Three approaches for identifying criterion groups are described in this section: (1) preinstruction-postinstruction measurements, (2) uninstructed-instructed groups, and (3) contrasting groups. The first two approaches entail the selection of intact samples judged to contain both masters and nonmasters (Berk, 1976, 1978, 1980b). The last-named approach requires that the samples be composed by individually selecting each master and nonmaster (Livingston & Zieky, 1982). All the approaches are applicable to criterion-referenced tests used for diagnostic (or placement) decisions as well as summative decisions. The advantages and disadvantages of each approach are noted.

---

[1]*Summative decision making* is concerned with using test information to assign letter grades/pass-fail in a specific subject area or course. This use of test scores may occur periodically during the school year, such as every six weeks, and at the conclusion of the program. Previous decisions of mastery of the instructional objectives can be accumulated for each student to determine how many and which objectives were mastered during the instructional program. The results of a comprehensive test of all of the objectives may also be used. In order to determine a student's grade, his or her record of mastery can be compared with criteria specifying the number and type of objectives that should be mastered for an A, B, C, D, and F (see Chapter 3). A similar procedure can be employed to assess the pass-fail status of students for a set of objectives.

[2]*Placement decision making* is concerned with using test information to place a student in an appropriate instructional group within the classroom or assign him or her to a compensatory or remedial program. Test information that identifies which instructional objectives a student has already mastered as well as those that have not been mastered can facilitate placement at the appropriate point in the instructional sequence. The instructional materials and activities can then be prescribed according to the individual's needs.

Preinstruction-Postinstruction Measurements

The preinstruction-postinstruction method has been an integral part of mastery learning and diagnostic-prescriptive teaching for several years (Block, 1971; Block & Burns, 1976; Carroll, 1963, 1970). It involves *testing one group of students twice*, before (preinstruction) and after (postinstruction) the instruction. Students are commonly tested with the same set of items on the two occasions. Alternatively, a parallel or equivalent set of items can be used on the second administration.

ADVANTAGE. The advantage of measuring students before and after instruction is that it permits the teacher to examine individual, as well as group, gains. These data can be particularly useful in assessing progress from one unit to the next. Information on gains cannot be obtained from any other type of design.

DISADVANTAGES. One major disadvantage of the approach, however, pertains to the impracticality of administering the posttest. The analysis cannot be conducted until the instruction has been completed. Hence, any instructional application of the measure would likely be deferred until the following year. A second disadvantage concerns the amount of time allowed between the pretest and posttest. When the administrations are in close succession, it is possible for the students' performance on the pretest to influence their performance on the posttest. One way to obviate this problem of *testing effect* would be to develop an equivalent set of items. If this is unfeasible due to practical constraints or the extreme specificity of the objectives (i.e., no other items could be developed), it is recommended that the intervening period between the administrations be extended a reasonable length of time so that the carry-over effect of memory from the initial testing can be minimized. This extension should not be any longer than four months to avoid incurring the effect of *maturation*, since simply growing older could improve a student's achievement performance. This would confound the measurement of gain to which the teacher wishes to attribute the effect of instruction. Improvement as a result of instruction and maturation become inextricably mixed when several months pass before the posttest is administered. The analysis is intended to focus only on the change in performance due to instruction.

Uninstructed-Instructed Groups

The uninstructed-instructed groups approach is a form of the "known-groups" technique described in Chapter 5. Only during the past decade has this technique been applied to criterion-referenced measurement (Henrysson & Wedman, 1974; Klein & Kosecoff, 1976; Millman, 1974; Zieky, 1973). It involves *testing two separate groups of students at the same point in time*, one group that has not received instruction (uninstructed group) and a second group that has received instruction (instructed group). In this application of the technique, the trait of interest is *knowledge*. The acquisition of knowledge in most content domains is a continuous process. Learning to read, write, and solve mathematical problems occurs gradually throughout a person's formal schooling. Improvement in these areas is frequently accompanied by improvement in the other subject areas. Since students learn at different rates, at any given point in time the students within a single classroom would vary in the amount of knowledge they possess. Therefore, in general, it can be expected that students in an instructed group will possess *more knowledge* related to a set of instructional objectives and an uninstructed group will possess *much less*.

The uninstructed-instructed groups approach requires that the two groups be identified on the basis of *independent, informed teacher judgment*. Students in one classroom who have not received instruction or who are known to be deficient on the objectives to be assessed may serve as the uninstructed group. Conversely, students in another classroom who have received "effective" instruction on the objectives may comprise the instructed group. This group, in the judgment of the teacher, should have demonstrated *success* in the instructional unit. Whether this success pertains to a current or subsequent unit depends on the orientation of the test. Student performance on written assignments, quizzes, and other classroom tasks is often the available information a teacher must rely upon for guidance in making the judgment.

The students chosen for the instructed group should be as similar as possible to those in the uninstructed group in ability level and all other relevant characteristics. Although the groups will often be unequal in size, the proportional distributions of the characteristics should be equivalent. For example, if one group has 60% boys and 40% girls, this balance should be maintained in the second group. The only real difference that should exist between the uninstructed and instructed groups is exposure to the instructional treatment.

ADVANTAGE. The advantage of the uninstructed-instructed groups approach is practicality. The analysis can be conducted at one point in time, prior to instruction, if an instructed group of students is concurrently available. This can facilitate the immediate use of the test for mastery-nonmastery decisions during the program being taught.

DISADVANTAGES. One disadvantage is the difficulty of defining suitable criteria for identifying the groups. The more objectivity that can be incorporated into the process the better. Informed judgment as described previously is one step in this direction. At present, this seems to be an intuitively sound procedure for performing analyses at the classroom level. Another disadvantage that is inherent in the approach is the problem of assuring group equivalence. Since randomly assigning students to instructed and uninstructed groups is generally unfeasible and inappropriate, the test maker may need to explain differences in group performance that may not be attributable to the instruction, e.g., age, sex, ability level, socioeconomic background. Realistically, the best strategy to avert this charge from arising would be deliberately to control for possible extraneous factors in the initial selection of the groups and exercise caution in interpreting the scores.

CRITICISMS OF INTACT-GROUP APPROACHES. Perhaps the most common criticism of the preceding two intact-group approaches is that only rarely would the assumption of "instructed student equals true master" be satisfied completely (Hambleton, Swaminathan, Algina, & Coulson, 1978; Shepard, 1980). Usually there will be some instructed students who are clearly nonmasters and a few uninstructed students who may be masters of the objective. In addition, the base rate in both approaches is assumed to be 50%, which may not be an accurate representation of mastery in the population.

These assumptions are troublesome because they can markedly affect the choice of a mastery standard and the corresponding estimation of decision accuracy. Accuracy decreases to the extent that the equivalence of instructed students and masters and of uninstructed students and nonmasters is not real. Furthermore, the classification probabilities can be misleading and incorrect if the sample sizes do not reflect the incidence of mastery in the classroom or grade level.

Contrasting Groups

The contrasting-groups approach can be viewed as a refinement of the intact-group approaches inasmuch as it specifically addresses the aforementioned criticisms. Again based on teacher judgment, this strategy requires a teacher to choose only those students he or she is certain are either definite masters or nonmasters of the objectives measured by the test. By handpicking each student to compose the mastery and nonmastery samples, the borderline student who is too close to call a master or nonmaster is excluded. The composition of "definites" will tend to maximize decision accuracy at the cutting score.

ADVANTAGES. This process of criterion-group selection avoids the assumption of equating instruction with mastery. Therefore, it has the key advantage of including only those students judged to be definite masters and nonmasters in the respective groups. Another advantage is that the sample of masters reflects the base rate in the population. For example, if a classroom of 20 students constitutes the entire population, then the identification of 12 masters and six nonmasters provides proportional representation for that population, where the base rate is 60%.

DISADVANTAGES. Despite these important advantages of the contrasting-groups approach, there are several disadvantages that tend to diminish their impact. First, it is not clear at what point in the instruction a teacher should or could identify a definite group of masters and nonmasters. The number in each group will be quite disproportionate either prior to or after instruction; and the incidence rate may be very low during instruction. This identification problem must be resolved before one can recommend when the test should be adminis-tered to the two groups. Second, individually composing each group is logisti-cally more difficult and time-consuming than using intact groups, especially when populations other than a single classroom are considered. Third, the sample sizes drawn from one or two classes may be too small to yield reliable estimates of decision accuracy. If either sample contains less than 20 students, the classification probabilities can be very misleading. Finally, the difficulties of defining suitable criteria for identifying the students and of assuring group equivalence, which were mentioned already in the context of the uninstructed-instructed groups approach, also apply to contrasting groups.

Correct and Incorrect Decisions

Based on the classification model presented in Table 6.1 and the criterion groups of masters and nonmasters selected according to one of the preceding approaches, a cutting score can be chosen, and the probability of each type of correct and incorrect decision can be estimated. Although this criterion-groups method is far from perfect, as the foregoing discussion of disadvantages strongly suggests, it does supply the necessary ingredients for making better decisions than those that would probably result from many of the alternative methods. In particular, the method is conceptually, statistically, and computa-tionally simple, and its theoretical rationale grounded in decision theory is quite sound. In addition, the basic model has been applied successfully in psy-chology and medicine for many years.

In this section, the specific procedures for computing and interpreting in-dices of decision validity are outlined. It should be noted that all of the analyses and illustrative examples deal with subtest scores because criterion-referenced test decision making usually focuses on the mastery or nonmastery of an in-structional objective. The procedures, however, are just as applicable to any combination of subtest scores and to total test scores.

Distributions of Masters and Nonmasters

The n in each cell of Table 6.1 is simply a count of the number of students in the *actual* master sample or nonmaster sample who are *predicted* to be masters or nonmasters based on a particular cutting score, where:

n_1 = number of actual masters whose scores lie at or above the cutting score;

n_2 = number of actual nonmasters whose scores lie at or above the cutting score (false masters);

n_3 = number of actual masters whose scores lie below the cutting score (false nonmasters);

n_4 = number of actual nonmasters whose scores lie below the cutting score;

N = $n_1 + n_2 + n_3 + n_4$.

The *n* is computed by accumulating the specific frequencies at and above or below the cutting score. The following example will demonstrate the necessary steps.

SCORE THE SUBTEST. Suppose one objective or skill examined on a reading comprehension test was measured with five items. This five-item cluster, or subtest, first needs to be scored for each student in both criterion groups. The scores on this particular subtest *can* range from 0 to 5. The scores for the 10 students in each group are as follows:

Masters	Nonmasters
4	3
5	3
5	3
4	2
3	2
3	1
3	4
3	2
4	1
5	2

TALLY THE SCORES. A frequency distribution of these scores for each group can be obtained as follows:

1. List all of the different scores from highest to lowest. For the five-item subtest, that list ranges from 5 down to 1. (*Note*: Although it was possible to score 0, no one did, and consequently, it is not necessary to list the 0 or, for that matter, any other point at the top or bottom when there is no corresponding score.)

Table 6.2

Tallies and Frequency Distributions for
Masters and Nonmasters on Five-item Subtest

	Masters		Nonmasters	
Score	*Tally*	*Frequency*	*Tally*	*Frequency*
5	111	3		0
4	111	3	1	1
3	1111	4	111	3
2		0	1111	4
1		0	11	2

2. Tally the number of students at each score point, with one tally or slash mark alongside each score every time it occurs. These tallies provide summary information on how each group performed, i.e., how many students scored 5, 4, 3, and so on in each group. The tallies for the masters and nonmasters are listed in Table 6.2.
3. Sum the tallies for each score point in order to express them as frequencies. The frequency column to the right of each tally column represents the frequency distribution of subtest performance for the group.
4. Simplify the data in Table 6.2 by presenting only the frequency distributions of the masters and nonmasters, designated f_M and f_N, respectively. That format is shown in Table 6.3. This table supplies all of the information required to select the cutting score.

Table 6.3

Frequency Distributions for Masters (f_M)
and Nonmasters (f_N) on Five-item Subtest

Score	f_M	f_N
5	3	0
4	3	1
3	4	3
2	0	4
1	0	2

Selection of a Cutting Score

As stated previously, the cutting score is just one score that cuts the distribution of scores into two parts. Therefore, conceivably any score can be a cutting score. Suppose a horizontal line was drawn across the f_M and f_N distributions in Table 6.3 for each score point. This is illustrated in Table 6.4. Inasmuch as the line divides both of the distributions into two parts, four cells are created. These are the cells defined in Table 6.1. In other words, each n is the sum of frequencies in a cell based on a given cutting score.

As one can observe from Table 6.4, the n's change as the cutting score changes. The important question is: What cell composition is desirable? If the subtest is intended to differentiate between masters and nonmasters of a given objective, cells n_1 and n_4 should contain as many students as possible, and cells n_2 and n_3 should contain few or no students. That is, it is highly desirable that the master-master (n_1) and nonmaster-nonmaster (n_4) cells be filled to capacity.

Table 6.4

Possible Cutting Scores for Five-item Subtest

Score	f_M	f_N
5	3	0
4	3	1
3	4	3
2	0	4
1	0	2

Cutting Score = 5

Score	f_M	f_N
5	3	0
4	3	1
3	4	3
2	0	4
1	0	2

Cutting Score = 4

Score	f_M	f_N
5	3	0
4	3	1
3	4	3
2	0	4
1	0	2

Cutting Score = 3

Score	f_M	f_N
5	3	0
4	3	1
3.	4	3
2	0	4
1	0	2

Cutting Score = 2

Score	f_M	f_N
5	3	0
4	3	1
3	4	3
2	0	4
1	0	2

Cutting Score = 1

The cutting score that corresponds to this optimal combination of n_1 and n_4 is referred to as the *optimal cutting score*, i.e., where:

$$n_{max} = n_1 + n_4.$$

In Table 6.4, it is easy to determine that the sum of the upper left and lower right cells is optimal for the cutting score of 3. The n's for this cutoff are summarized in Table 6.5

Table 6.5

Predicted × Actual Classification Outcomes
for Five-item Subtest (N = 20; Base Rate = 50%)

Actual

		f_M	f_N
Predicted	M	10 (50%)	4 (20%)
	N	0 (0)	6 (30%)

OPTIMAL CUTTING SCORE (C_o). The optimal cutting score is the score on the subtest (or total test) that yields the highest number of correct mastery-nonmastery classification decisions (n_{max}) and the lowest number of classification decision errors (n_2, n_3). Cutting scores that are selected above or below c_o typically result in a reduction in correct decisions. The number of decision errors will also vary as a function of which cutting score is chosen. A further discussion of these characteristics related to c_o, however, is deferred until the next section on estimating the classification probabilities.

A SHORT-CUT PROCEDURE. So far, this section has presented a strategy for identifying the optimal cutting score; it has not outlined a step-by-step procedure. Given the preceding explanation, the procedure one can follow to select c_o is simple and short:

1. Inspect the f_M and f_N distributions in the form shown in Table 6.3 (or 6.4). (This eye-balling approach has also been called the "interocular perusal

technique.") *Search for the one or two cutting scores that appear to "pull apart" the two distributions in the opposite directions*, i.e., the largest number of frequencies in the upper left and the lower right. For the data in Table 6.3, the scores 3 and 4 would probably be nominated. Generally, for short subtests of between five and 10 items, there is rarely a clean break between the two distributions. Some overlap, with, it is hoped, only a few frequencies in the lower left and upper right areas, can be expected. The goal is to obtain zeros in those areas.

2. Take each of the nominated cutting scores and sum the upper left and lower right frequencies ($n_1 + n_4$). For the scores of 3 and 4 in the example, those sums are 16 and 15, respectively.

3. Select the optimal cutting score based on the sums.

Once the frequency distributions are set up for the subtests measuring the different instructional objectives, the preceding three steps can be completed for all of the subtests in only a few minutes. If one understands the process and its purpose, selecting c_o is rather mechanical and usually requires very little practice.

Probabilities of Masters and Nonmasters

Once the cutting score has been selected, evidence of the effectiveness of a criterion-referenced test can be obtained by expressing the cell frequencies in Table 6.1 as *probabilities* or percentages of the total sample (N). This involves dividing each n by N and multiplying by 100, or

$p(\text{TM}) = \dfrac{n_1}{N} \times 100 =$ probability of correctly classifying a master;

$p(\text{FM}) = \dfrac{n_2}{N} \times 100 =$ probability of incorrectly classifying a nonmaster as a master (false masters);

$p(\text{FN}) = \dfrac{n_3}{N} \times 100 =$ probability of incorrectly classifying a master as a nonmaster (false nonmasters);

$p(\text{TN}) = \dfrac{n_4}{N} \times 100 =$ probability of correctly classifying a nonmaster.

EXAMPLE. Using the n's in Table 6.5 for the c_o of 3, the probabilities are computed as follows:

$$p(\text{TM}) = \frac{10}{20} \times 100 = 50\%$$

$$p(\text{FM}) = \frac{4}{20} \times 100 = 20\%$$

$$p(\text{FN}) = \frac{0}{20} \times 100 = 0$$

$$p(\text{TN}) = \frac{6}{20} \times 100 = 30\%$$

INTERPRETATION. These various probabilities provide a set of statistical indices for evaluating the decision validity of a test. If certain probabilities are high, the use of the test scores for diagnostic decisions may be judged valid; if they are unsatisfactory, the use may be judged invalid.

Perhaps the best summary index of decision validity is the probability of correct decisions, $p(C)$, which is the sum of $p(TM)$ and $p(TN)$, or 80% in the example. This quantity measures how well the subtest (or total test) can classify *both* masters and nonmasters; that is, the overall degree of accuracy. For the five-item subtest then, the results indicate that about 80% of the students in a class (e.g., 24 out of 30 students) will be correctly labeled as masters and nonmasters of the particular objective. For such a short subtest, this is a high degree of accuracy. When the criterion groups are equal in size, which translates into a base rate of 50%, $p(C)$ values must exceed 50% (chance classification) in order to justify the diagnostic worth of a test. The greater the discrepancy between $p(C)$ and 50%, the stronger will be the justification for using the test for classification decisions (see Incremental Validity in Chapter 5). In this case the discrepancy is 30% (80% − 50%), clearly adequate for the intended use.

In addition to interpreting accuracy in terms of $p(C)$, a teacher *must* consider the magnitude of each type of decision error. Two types of error were estimated: $p(FM)$, the probability of mistakenly classifying a nonmaster as a master (a *false master*), and $p(FN)$, the probability of mistakenly classifying a master as a nonmaster (a *false nonmaster*). False masters are usually some of the students who score at the cutting score or within one or two scores above it; false nonmasters are those who score within a couple of scores below the cutoff. Therefore, the *decision errors are most likely to occur with students who score at or close to the cutting score*. One can place greater confidence in decisions about students who score far from the cutoff, either extremely high or extremely low.

With short subtests, of say, 5 to 10 items, however, it is often difficult to discern who is a false master and who is a true master based on the scores. The same difficulty also applies to distinguishing false nonmasters from true nonmasters. Typically, a teacher must rely on a student's response to the prescribed instructional materials or activities in order to infer a decision error has occurred. For example, a student who stands by a window dropping workbooks on passing pedestrians could be frustrated, bored, or just mischievous. This behavior strongly suggests that she is a likely candidate for "decision error of the day" (and also for the vice-principal's office). Clearly, the *probabilities* computed previously *provide a rough idea of how many errors and what kind of error will be made*; the specific identification and correction of those errors reside with the teacher.

A further illustration of this point can be found in the results for the five-item subtest. The computations produced a probability of 20% false masters. In other words, probably a few of the students in the class (e.g., 6 out of 30 students) will be treated as masters of the objective, even though they are not. Evidence of these errors is not obtained from the number of students (6 students); it is derived from student responses. For example, students may display frustration with a new and often more difficult assignment than the one previously "not mastered," or they may refuse to participate in the activities of the groups into which they were placed. These types of student response provide valuable feedback to the teacher, which can facilitate the correction of false mastery decision errors. The teacher can then assign appropriate materials to remediate each student's skill weaknesses or can place the students in appropriate work groups geared toward their skill levels. When false nonmastery decision errors occur, they can be corrected in a similar manner.

In addition to this analysis of error rates, it is especially meaningful to determine how well the subtest can identify skill weaknesses, that is, the specific areas of learning disability that warrant attention. This topic is examined next.

Sensitivity and Specificity

Perhaps two of the most useful indices of diagnostic effectiveness are sensitivity and specificity. They reveal how well the test detects strengths and weaknesses in a specific skill. Obviously, identifying specific learning disabilities is one major purpose of the criterion-referenced test. The index of specificity measures the extent to which this purpose is achieved.

Indices of sensitivity and specificity are computed from the cell frequencies in Table 6.1 on the basis of each actual sample of masters and nonmasters, independent of the base rate. *Sensitivity* is defined as

$$p(\text{SENS}) = \frac{n_1}{n_1 + n_3} \times 100 = \text{probability of correctly identifying a master in a sample of actual masters (or of detecting skill strengths in this sample)}$$

and *specificity* is expressed as

$$p(\text{SPEC}) = \frac{n_4}{n_2 + n_4} \times 100 = \text{probability of correctly identifying a nonmaster in a sample of actual nonmasters (or of detecting skill weaknesses in this sample).}$$

Example

Using the n's in Table 6.5 for the cutting score of 3, these two probabilities are computed as follows:

$$p(\text{SENS}) = \frac{10}{10 + 0} \times 100 = 100\%$$

$$p(\text{SPEC}) = \frac{6}{4 + 6} \times 100 = 60\%$$

Interpretation

These probabilities for the five-item subtest indicate that the optimal cutting score is perfectly sensitive (100%) for identifying masters and moderately specific (60%) for detecting nonmasters. In terms of diagnostic efficiency, this subtest is much better at pinpointing skill strengths than skill weaknesses. Of particular interest is the specificity index, as it is probably the best direct measure of whether any subtest can, in fact, diagnose specific learning disabilities. In this example, the results are not very impressive. However, given that the specificity index as well as all of the other indices of decision validity described in this chapter are a function of the cutting score, their values can usually be improved by adjusting the cutoff. These adjustments can be considered in conjunction with the relative seriousness of the error rates.

Consequences of Misclassification

Given the preceding explanations of correct and incorrect classification probabilities and sensitivity/specificity related to the optimal cutting score, suppose another cutting score was selected. How are the various probabilities affected by cutting scores above and below c_o? In general, the *probability of correct decisions will decrease with cutting scores above or below c_o*. The decrease above c_o will reflect relatively fewer correct (true) mastery classifications and more correct (true) nonmastery classifications; the decrease below c_o will reflect the converse. The decision error rates are inversely affected. *As the mastery standard is raised, the probability of false mastery errors decreases and the probability of false nonmastery errors increases*. The reverse trend occurs as the standard is lowered. Finally, the sensitivity and specificity probabilities are inversely related to the error rates, so as *false mastery errors decrease, specificity increases*; certainly a highly desirable combination for diagnosing specific learning disabilities. The relationship between false nonmastery errors and sensitivity is similar.

For clarification, the relationships between the location of the cutting score and these different probabilities are depicted in Table 6.6. They are briefly summarized here, with the most important effects emphasized:

1. Raise the cutting score above c_o — the probability of correct decisions decreases, *false mastery errors decrease*, false nonmastery errors increase, sensitivity decreases, and *specificity increases*

2. Lower the cutting score below c_o — the probability of correct decisions decreases, false mastery errors increase, *false nonmastery errors decrease, sensitivity increases*, and specificity decreases

Table 6.6

Illustrative Classification Probabilities as a Function of
Different Cutting Scores on Five-item Subtest

Cutting Score	Probability of Correct Decisions	Probability of False Nonmastery	Probability of False Mastery	Sensitivity (Masters)	Specificity (Nonmasters)
5	65%	35%	0	30%	100%
4	75%	20%	5%	60%	90%
3*	80%	0	20%	100%	60%
2	60%	0	40%	100%	20%
1	50%	0	50%	100%	0

*c_o

These relationships indicate that it is possible to reduce and eliminate either type of error. However, any reduction in one error rate must be weighed against the increments in the other error rate and overall classification accuracy. *Inter alia*, this process involves an analysis of the consequences of false mastery and false nonmastery errors.

Relative Seriousness of Errors

At this juncture in the presentation, the diagnostic decisions to be made based on the cutting score require some reconsideration. For example —

1. What are the consequences of mistakenly prescribing new or enrichment materials for a student who is not prepared to handle them (a false master)?
2. What are the consequences of mistakenly prescribing remedial materials/ activities for a student who has already mastered that content (a false nonmaster)?

The underlying question is, *What are the consequences of making a wrong decision?* These consequences can be assessed in terms of student motivation, student attitude, teacher time, availability of instructional materials, cost of materials, duration of the instructional sequence, content of the instruction, and the instructional objective to be mastered. Suppose consequences could be assigned pluses (benefits) and minuses (costs or losses). If the answers to questions 1 and 2 were compared, which type of decision error is more serious? Or, are the two types of error equally serious?

One assumption in the selection of c_o is the equal seriousness of the decision errors, regardless of their size. If this assumption is untenable and the relative seriousness of the errors is deemed unequal, steps should be taken to adjust the cutting score so as to minimize the probability of the more serious error occurring.

Adjusting the Cutting Score

A cutting score can be adjusted so that it is weighted in favor of a specific error rate reduction, the number of failures permissible, and/or any other criteria. This weighting can be accomplished in various ways. The simplest method is to adjust the cutting score up or down one or more score points contingent upon a *justifiable* reduction in the particular error rate and overall decision accuracy.

MAXIMIZING DIAGNOSTIC UTILITY. There are really only two criteria that signify the value of a criterion-referenced test for diagnosing specific learning disabilities: (1) minimize false mastery errors and (2) maximize specificity. Both of these criteria can usually be satisfied by raising the cutting score. This can be illustrated with the probabilities in Table 6.6 for the five-item subtest. First, suppose that the frustration encountered by a false master was judged more serious than the remedial instructional time wasted on a false nonmaster. Inasmuch as the false mastery error rate corresponding to c_o was 20%, a teacher wished to reduce that probability further. If the cutting score is raised to 4, the 20% could be reduced to 5%. However, in order to decrease the chances of false mastery errors by 15%, the chances of false nonmastery errors increase by 20% (from 0), and the overall accuracy decreases by only 5%. These trade-offs seem reasonable. In addition, by adjusting the cutting score from 3 to 4, the specificity for detecting nonmasters is increased to 90%. Such probabilities assure that a student with a weakness in a particular skill area will be correctly identified and that the weaknesses of different students with disabilities will be accurately detected. Therefore, in this example, a cutting score of 4 out of 5 items should be chosen instead of the c_o of 3 out of 5. (*Note*: The trade-offs would have been unreasonable for the cutting score of 5, where false mastery errors could be eliminated, but the costs were a 35% increase in the likelihood of false nonmasters and a 15% decrease in overall accuracy. Also, specificity would increase by only 10%.)

What happens if the trade-offs are unreasonable and no adjustment is possible? For the distributions shown in Table 6.7 for a different subtest, the c_o of 9 yields a 95% probability of correct decisions with only a 5% probability of false mastery errors. Obviously, it would be difficult to improve upon this accuracy even if there were some benefit to eliminating the 5% error. In this case, one can still consider error reduction, although no adjustment in the cutoff is made. This condition suggests that the judgments involved in weighting may not always result in a change in the cutting score. Therefore, the cutting score that is finally selected should be perceived as the best score for a particular decision application, deduced from a review of all available empirical and judgmental data.

Table 6.7

Frequency Distributions for an Eleven-item Subtest

Score	f_M	f_N
11	1	0
10	4	0
9*	5	1
8	0	3
7	0	3
6	0	3

*c_o

CASE OF 100% ACCURACY. On rare, but certainly welcome, occasions, a cutting score will produce 100% classification accuracy. However, that does not necessarily imply that there is only one optimal cutting score and there is no need for weighting. The distributions for a third subtest shown in Table 6.8 provide a case in point. The clean break in the two distributions at the scores 4 and 5 indicates that the subtest differentiates between masters and nonmasters with perfect accuracy. Following the definition of c_o stated previously, the scores 4, 5, *or* 6 can be selected. The choice of which single score to use for decision making is a function of weighting the seriousness of the errors as described before. Under these conditions a couple of rules of thumb seem appropriate:

1. If false mastery errors are judged more serious, select the highest score (6) in order to minimize any chance of that type of error and to set the highest standard for mastery.
2. If false nonmastery errors are judged more serious, select the lowest score (4) in order to minimize any chance of that type of error.

OTHER WEIGHTING FACTORS. The discussion of weighting up to this point has focused only on error rate reduction. There are also other grounds for adjusting a cutting score. One reason for raising the cutting score above c_o might be to establish higher standards in certain key content areas that students should strive to attain. Conversely, the cutting score might be lowered in other content areas in order to assess a "minimum," or "survival," level of mastery. The characteristics of the criterion groups that supply the data for the initial selection of c_o should be considered before these adjustments are made. For example, if the criterion mastery group is chosen because it typifies an acceptable minimum-level performance group in the school, c_o can be a very accurate and realistic minimum standard. Hence, no adjustment is needed.

Before leaving this topic, it should be emphasized that the foregoing guidelines for adjusting a cutting score for the reasons explicated are based entirely

Table 6.8

Frequency Distributions for a Nine-item Subtest

Score	f_M	f_N
9	5	0
8	4	0
7	6	0
6*	5	0
5*	0	0
4*	0	0
3	0	7
2	0	6
1	0	4
0	0	3

*c_o

on *judgment*. Perhaps even more noteworthy is the fact that the alternative formal and more complex analytic methods that use numerical values to represent the relative weighting of decision errors (e.g., false mastery errors are three times as serious as false nonmastery errors) are no less judgmental (see Berk, 1976; Harber, 1981).

Application of the Model to a Basic Skills Test

All of the foregoing procedures for selecting cutting scores and computing indices of decision validity are based on the assumption that a mastery standard can be set at any score point on the continuum. This assumption was demonstrated with Table 6.4 and is tenable for most content domains and test score uses. The exception is the case where basic, fundamental, or minimum essential skills are measured, predominantly in the primary grades.

100% Standard

The assumption that best fits the characteristics of basic skill domains is that *mastery is all or nothing*, i.e., either the student masters the instructional objective at 100% or he or she does not.[3] This assumption is meaningful for

---

[3]This is conceptually the same as the state model for setting standards described in Chapter 2. The procedure recommended here, however, is entirely judgmental, whereas the methods referenced in Chapter 2 are in the statistically complex, judgmental-empirical category.

objectives dealing with discrete pieces of information such as facts and terminology and with skills where perfect mastery is essential before one can proceed to acquire higher level skills. For example, few people could argue persuasively that total mastery of the objectives "Add single-digit numbers" and "Say the initial consonant sounds" is not essential for students to advance to more difficult arithmetic and phonics objectives, respectively. Although there are a few domains where substantial empirical evidence exists to verify a genuine learning hierarchy (Gagné, 1962; Glaser & Nitko, 1971), a teacher must teach and test in diverse content areas where such evidence is sparse or nonexistent. Therefore, it seems plausible at present that a teacher's content expertise, experience, and common sense constitute an adequate foundation for deciding at the classroom level which objectives are "basic" and which ones are not.

ADJUSTMENT FOR MEASUREMENT ERROR. Inasmuch as measurement error creeps into virtually every test score, it is recommended that the 100% standard be adjusted downward, particularly for short subtests, in order to account for this possible error. A cutting score of 4 out of 5 items or 7 out of 8 is still high enough to sort the true masters from everyone else and yet permit one careless error, for whatever reason, that even a true master might commit. Furthermore, it is likely that the difference between the false mastery error rate estimated using 4 out of 5, and the rate estimated using the 100% standard will be negligible. This is demonstrated in Table 6.6. where that error differs by only 5%.

Criterion-Groups Method

For objectives that fall into this basic skills category, this 100% standard approach is defensible in terms of the nature of the domain, the purpose of the testing, and the instructional decisions for which the scores are to be used. In contrast, it is likely that the criterion-groups approach proposed in the preceding sections of this chapter will produce a different solution to the same standard-setting problem. Often the variation in individual rates of learning and, therefore, in the acquisition of basic skills at the earlier grade levels precludes all instructed students who are measured at one point in time from attaining 100% mastery. Consequently, the procedures for choosing the cutting scores will inevitably yield a standard that is less than 100%. That standard, however, provides a *realistic performance level* for students based on their particular characteristics, as opposed to a level that each student is to strive toward and perhaps attain at some later date.

100% Standard Versus Criterion Groups

A teacher's choice between the "100% standard" approach and the criterion-groups approach to setting standards for basic skills tests seems to rest

on the answers to two key questions: (1) Are the assumptions underlying the
100% standard reasonable in the context of the specific objectives, the instruction related to those objectives, and the characteristics of the students? and (2)
Would the discrepancy between the more "realistic standard" and the 100%
standard be great enough to justify the additional work of the criterion-groups
method? The former question can be answered only by teacher judgment; the
latter can be answered by a hunch or by testing out the two approaches. Since
the 100% standard approach does not supply any evidence of decision validity,
the criterion-groups method with its resultant correct and incorrect classification probabilities can be perceived as one way to validate that approach. The
final determination of the best approach, however, will probably depend on
which notion of standard setting is judged most appropriate for a given decision appliction.

Reporting Evidence of Decision Validity

After the various analyses and adjustments of the cutting score have been
completed, several valuable pieces of information can be distilled from all of
that work:

1. *Mastery standard* (expressed as a cutting score and as a percentage)
2. *Probability of correct decisions*
3. *Probabilities of false nonmastery and false mastery decision errors*
4. *Probabilities of sensitivity and specificity*

They furnish evidence of the validity of mastery-nonmastery decisions. Inasmuch as these decisions are based on the subtest scores keyed to each instructional objective, the information should be reported by subtest. In addition, a
description of the samples employed, particularly grade level and class size,
and the method used to select the standard and estimate the classification probabilities should be indicated. An exemplary tabular format for displaying the
results for an entire test is presented in Table 6.9. The test measures introductory dictionary skills at grade 2.

Advantages and Disadvantages of the Model

Advantages

The major advantages of using the criterion-groups method for setting the
standard for mastery-nonmastery decisions are embedded in the seven criteria
for a defensible method proffered at the beginning of the chapter. They bear re-
peating in the context of all of the issues discussed thus far.

In general, the method is a potentially useful and attractive strategy for at-
tacking the standard-setting problem in a variety of test applications, because it

Table 6.9

Validity Evidence of Diagnostic Decisions Using the Dictionary Skills Test

Subtest	No. of Items	Cutting Score	Criterion	Correct Decisions	False Nonmastery	False Mastery	Sensitivity (Masters)	Specificity (Nonmasters)
						Classification Probabilities[*]		
1: Alphabetizing	8	6	75%	92%	4%	4%	83%	91%
2: Entry Words	14	11	79%	98%	2%	0%	88%	100%
3: Syllabication	17	14	82%	89%	9%	2%	75%	96%
4: Guide Words	7	5	71%	93%	7%	0	79%	100%
5: Word Meaning	6	4	67%	100%	0	0	100%	100%

[*]Based on criterion groups of 22 third-grade instructed and 24 second-grade uninstructed students.

is easy to understand, to use, to compute, and to interpret. It provides a mechanism for selecting the cutting score that maximizes the probability of correct classifications and minimizes the chances of false mastery and false nonmastery errors. The method facilitates the a priori estimation of classification probabilities so that the validity of the decisions to be made with the scores can be evaluated. Guidelines for adjusting the cutting score according to the consequences of the two types of error and other factors can also be considered within a decision framework.

However, the method's principal strengths lie in its data base (empirical component) and in its flexibility to accommodate diverse item and test characteristics. First, since the cutting score and the estimates of decision accuracy are empirically based on the performance of actual masters and nonmasters, they are sensitive to the following: (a) the difficulty and complexity of the instructional objective, (b) the actual instruction to which the students were exposed, (c) the abilities and background characteristics of the students, (d) the effectiveness of the items (i.e., difficulty and discrimination indices), and (e) the consequences of making incorrect decisions. Second, the nature of the analyses employed and the demonstrated utility of the method in personality assessment indicate that it can be used with most types of items and tests, including (a) dichotomous items (scored 0, 1) or multipoint items (scored 0, 1, 2, . . .), (b) subtests and tests of different lengths (e.g., 5 items to 100 items), (c) paper and pencil tests or performance tests, and (d) tests and scales measuring cognitive, affective, or psychomotor behaviors. Finally, the method can be applied to tests used with normal populations and also with special populations ranging from high risk infants (DeGangi, Berk, & Valvano, 1983) to the multiply handicapped (Berk & DeGangi, 1983; Gallagher & Bradley, 1972) to the gifted.

Disadvantages

The disadvantages of the method lie primarily in its subjectivity (judgmental component). There are two critical judgmental procedures that come at the beginning and at the end of the whole process: selecting the criterion groups and weighting the consequences of decision errors.

The problems associated with the selection of the criterion groups are threefold: (1) the fallibility of the success criterion, (2) the difficulty of estimating the true base rate, and (3) the inadequate sample sizes.

FALLIBILITY OF THE SUCCESS CRITERION. Teacher judgment provides the basis for selecting the criterion mastery and nonmastery groups. Regardless of how much information or what data (the external criteria) are incorporated into the decision or how systematic the execution of the procedures, the judgment of a single teacher furnishes the foundation for group selection and, consequently, the viability of all of the analyses that follow. Implicit in this selection is the presumption that the students in the two groups represent "live" masters and nonmasters of the objectives being measured. The equivalence of instructed students and true masters and uninstructed students and true nonmasters is certainly imperfect on both conceptual and empirical grounds. The alternative to the use of these intact groups is to handpick the masters and nonmasters from one or more classes to comprise the criterion groups. The selection of contrasting groups avoids this equivalence issue.

Ultimately, the groups that are chosen serve to define the "successful" and "unsuccessful" *type* of student operationally by approximating how most students would perform. It is in this way that the criterion-groups method confronts directly the issue of mastery or competency. The actual identification of students who possess this trait constitutes one feature that distinguishes the method from all others. This feature, however, turns out to be an advantage as well as a disadvantage of the method, depending upon one's perspective.

The task of operationally defining the criterion of success in academic and professional contexts has been fraught with problems ever since test scores have been used to predict future performance. Psychometricians have wrestled with objectifying the success criterion for nearly half a century. At this time, no completely objective procedure has been devised. Unless one defines the criterion solely in terms of another set of test scores, judgment plays a predominant role in the definition of success. Therefore, the criterion is always fallible; it contains one or more kinds of error to varying degrees. The goal is to reduce the potential sources of error (unreliability) and to minimize the magnitude of each identifiable error.

In the selection of intact groups, it is expected that a few students in each group may not represent true mastery or true nonmastery for whatever reason. Similarly, if instruction is ineffective, estimates of true mastery become inaccurate. These sources of error are ever present and irresolvable when using intact classes. The alternative contrasting-groups method suggested earlier can overcome these weaknesses. The added precision is attained, however, at the expense of practicability. In particular, administering tests to the same or even different intact classes is easier than administering them to specially composed groups.

Despite the obvious differences between the intact-groups and contrasting-groups approaches in regard to the selection process and test administration, the underlying foundation of both is the same — teacher judgment about student mastery and nonmastery. *Ergo*, a teacher might consider balancing precision with practicability in his or her own school setting in order to determine the most appropriate method. In view of the overall purpose and intended uses of the two approaches, the intact-groups strategy offers an acceptable compromise for most classroom level applications.

DIFFICULTY OF ESTIMATING THE TRUE BASE RATE. The sampling procedure described in the selection of criterion groups indicates that the intact groups (preinstruction-postinstruction or uninstructed-instructed) should be about equal in size, although disparities in class sizes are quite common. The rationale for this recommendation relates principally to the criterion-groups model and, to a much lesser extent, to convenience. Ideally, the proportion of true masters to true nonmasters in a classroom or school should be reflected in the instructed and uninstructed group sizes. That is, if it is known in advance that on a given set of objectives 90% of the students would be classified as masters, one could plan a decision validity study with, for example, 27 masters and 3 nonmasters. Such proportional representation at this extreme could produce very different estimates of classification probabilities than groups of near equal size, say 32 instructed and 28 uninstructed students.

Although it is highly desirable for the sample sizes in a validity study to be composed in accordance with the true base rate, the characteristic of mastery renders this task more difficult than is usually perceived. Unlike other population characteristics, such as those reported in a census, mastery is not static; at any point in time it fluctuates from test to test, subtest to subtest within a single test, class to class, and individual to individual. This variability limits the meaning of mastery to a specific test, sample, and decision application. For example, if the contrasting-groups approach is used to determine the base rate of mastery in a particular classroom, the resultant estimate of, say, 60% is interpretable only for the corresponding collection of objectives (or subtests) and the criteria employed by the teacher to select the mastery group. This base rate will then change as any one or more of these factors changes. Since the nature of mastery is immutable, a teacher must accept these restrictions on the estimation of base rate and exercise caution in the interpretation of that rate.

INADEQUATE SAMPLE SIZES. The declining class enrollments at all levels of the educational structure and subsequent public school closings nationwide are making it excessively difficult to obtain adequate sample sizes in order to assess test quality. In general, as the sizes decrease, so does the confidence a teacher can place in the results. To ascertain whether the test and its component subtests are functioning properly, consistent with the purposes for which they were developed, a teacher should try to acquire minimally about 20 students for each criterion group. When this is not possible and only five to 10 students are available, as is usually the case with special education classes, it is worth examining the data, but extreme caution should be exhibited in interpreting the distributions because they can be very misleading.

This sample size problem is lessened somewhat by using the 50% base rate requirement. If a true base rate were employed that was considerably higher than 50%, a much larger mastery group would be necessary to complement the low proportion of true nonmasters. This relationship was illustrated previously. In addition, where the base rate for mastery is extremely high, such as 90%, in order to maintain at least 20 students in the nonmastery group, 180 students would be needed for the mastery group.

JUDGMENTAL WEIGHTING OF DECISION ERRORS. One final disadvantage associated with the criterion-groups method is the judgmental and rather arbitrary weighting procedures a teacher can use to arrive at the final cutting score. The procedures delineated in this chapter admittedly depend upon the assignment of subjective value judgments to the classification probabilities. Given this nature of the weighting process (also called utility analysis), a teacher must decide whether to choose c_o and assume equal consequences of decision errors or to adjust the cutting score according to some judgments about those consequences. Considering the specific guidelines for making appropriate adjustments, along with the importance of the weighting factors to mastery-nonmastery classification decisions, it is advisable to incorporate all available judgmental information and insight into the selection of a cutting score. This advice seems reasonable in view of similar recommendations given by many psychometricians who have dealt with utility analysis in more sophisticated decision-theoretic approaches to standard setting.

Summary

The step-by-step procedure for determining the decision validity of a diagnostic test is summarized as follows:

1. Define the criteria for mastery of a set of objectives.
2. Determine the most appropriate strategy for selecting criterion groups — preinstruction-postinstruction measurements, uninstructed-instructed groups, or contrasting groups.
3. Select the two criterion groups.
4. Administer the test to these groups.
5. Score each subtest.
6. Tally the scores and sum the tallies by subtest.
7. Display the frequency distributions f_M and f_N.
8. Search for the one or two (cutting) scores that appear to "pull apart" the two distributions in the opposite directions, i.e., the largest number of frequencies in the upper left and the lower right.
9. Sum the upper left and lower right frequencies ($n_1 + n_4$) for each of those cutting scores.

10. Select the optimal cutting score (c_o) based on the largest sum (n_{max}).
11. Compute the probabilities of correct decisions based on cells n_1 and n_4 for $c_o - p(\text{TM})$ and $p(\text{TN})$.
12. Compute the probabilities of incorrect decisions based on the remaining students in each group (n_2 and n_3) $- p(\text{FN})$ and $p(\text{FM})$.
13. Compute $p(\text{C}) - p(\text{TM}) + p(\text{TN})$.
14. Compute the sensitivity of the cutoff for detecting actual masters — $p(\text{SENS})$.
15. Compute the specificity of the cutoff for detecting actual nonmasters — $p(\text{SPEC})$.
16. Consider raising the cutting score one or more points in order to minimize false mastery errors and maximize specificity.
17. Select the final cutting score.
18. Repeat steps 8 through 17 for each subtest and the total test, as appropriate.
19. Assess the decision validity of the test in terms of $p(\text{C})$, $p(\text{FM})$, and $p(\text{SPEC})$.

For comparison purposes, it is appropriate to summarize the methods for determining the effectiveness of a screening procedure according to the major characteristics or components of the decision model. A comparison of these characteristics for a screening procedure and those for a diagnostic test is shown in Table 6.10. The number of striking similarities through most stages of analysis should be evident. Perhaps the most important, as well as obvious, differences in the two applications of the decision model pertain to the type of decision error considered more serious and, subsequently, to the manner in which the criterion (for LD or mastery) is adjusted to minimize the error. These differences are indicated for the entry "Seriousness of Decision Errors." This characteristic is, in fact, the primary determinant of decision *effectiveness*, which is finally reflected in the evidence of decision validity.

MEMORY JOGGER

Table 6.10

Comparison of Decision Model Characteristics for Determining
the Effectiveness of a Screening Procedure and a Diagnostic Test

Characteristic	Screening Procedure	Diagnostic Test
Classification Decision	LD or non-LD	Mastery or nonmastery
Terminology	True positive True negative False positive False negative	True mastery True nonmastery False mastery False nonmastery
Selection of Criterion Groups	Random or specially composed	Intact or specially composed (contrasting groups)
Basis for Decision Making	Criterion for a severe learning disability	Criterion (cutting score) for mastery
Correct and Incorrect Decisions	p(TP) p(TN) p(FP) p(FN)	p(TM) p(TN) p(FM) p(FN)
Base Rate	1% – 7%	50% for intact groups; varies for contrasting groups
Seriousness of Decision Errors	Lower the criterion to minimize p(FN) and maximize p(SENS)	Raise the cutting score to minimize p(FM) and maximize p(SPEC)
Evidence of Decision Validity	p(C) p(FN) p(SENS) p(SPEC)	p(C) p(FM) p(SPEC)

References

Arter, J.A., & Jenkins, J.R. Examining the benefits and prevalence of modality considerations in special education. *Journal of Special Education*, 1977, *11*, 281 – 298.

Arter, J.A., & Jenkins, J.R. Differential diagnosis—prescriptive teaching: A critical appraisal. *Review of Educational Research*, 1979, *49*, 517 – 555.

Berk, R.A. Determination of optimal cutting scores in criterion-referenced measurement.
Journal of Experimental Education, 1976, *45*, 4 – 9.

Berk, R.A. A consumers' guide to criterion-referenced test item statistics. *NCME Measurement
in Education*, 1978, *9*, 1 – 8.

Berk, R.A. *Technical issues insetting standards for minimum competency testing.* Invited address at the
Regional Minimum Competency Testing Conference sponsored by the Basic Skills
Assessment Consortium and Educational Testing Service, San Francisco, April 1979.

Berk, R.A. (Ed.). *Criterion-referenced measurement: The state of the art.* Baltimore, MD: Johns
Hopkins University Press, 1980.(a)

Berk, R.A. Item analysis. In R.A. Berk (Ed.), *Criterion-referenced measurement. The state of the art.* Baltimore, MD: Johns Hopkins University Press, 1980. Pp. 49 – 79.(b)

Berk, R.A. Criterion-referenced tests. In T. Husén & T.N. Postlethwaite (Eds.), *International encyclopedia of education: Research and studies.* Oxford, England: Pergamon Press, 1984.

Berk, R.A. & DeGangi, G.A. *DeGangi-Berk Test of Sensory Integration: Manual.* Los Angeles: Western Psychological Services, 1983.

Block, J.H. (Ed.) *Mastery learning: Theory and practice.* New York: Holt, Rinehart and Winston, 1971.

Block, J.H., & Burns, R.B. Mastery learning. In L.S. Shulman (Ed.), *Review of research in education* (Vol. 4). Itasca, IL: F.E. Peacock, 1976.

Carroll, J.B. A model of school learning. *Teachers College Record*, 1963, *64*, 723 – 733.

Carroll, J.B. Problems of measurement related to the concept of learning for mastery. *Educational Horizons*, 1970, *48*, 71 – 80.

DeGangi, G.A., Berk, R.A., & Valvano, J. Test of Motor and Neurological Functions in High Risk Infants: Preliminary findings. *Journal of Developmental and Behavioral Pediatrics*, 1983, in press.

Gagné, R.M. Learning hierarchies. *Educational Psychologist*, 1968, *6*, 1 – 9.

Gallagher, J.J., & Bradley, R.H. Early identification of developmental difficulties. In I.J. Gordon (Ed.), *Early childhood education: The seventy-first yearbook of the National Society for the Study of Education* (Part II). Chicago: University of Chicago Press, 1972. Pp. 87 – 122.

Glaser, R., & Nitko, A.J. Measurement in learning and instruction. In R.L. Thorndike (Ed.), *Educational measurement* (2nd ed.). Washington, DC: American Council on Education, 1971. Pp. 625 – 670.

Hambleton, R.K. Test score validity and standard-setting methods. In R.A. Berk (Ed.), *Criterion-referenced measurement: The state of the art.* Baltimore, MD: Johns Hopkins University Press, 1980. Pp. 80 – 123.

Hambleton, R.K., Swaminathan, H., Algina, J., & Coulson, D.B. Criterion-referenced testing and measurement: A review of technical issues and developments. *Review of Educational Research*, 1978, *48*, 1 – 47.

Harber, J.R. Evaluating utility in diagnostic decision making. *Journal of Special Education*, 1981, *15*, 413 – 428.

Haring, N.G., & Bateman, B. *Teaching the learning disabled child.* Englewood Cliffs, NJ: Prentice-Hall, 1977.

Henrysson, S., & Wedman, I. Some problems in construction and evaluation of criterion-referenced tests. *Scandinavian Journal of Educational Research*, 1974, *18*, 1 – 12.

Klein, S.P., & Kosecoff, J.B. Issues and procedures in the development of criterion-referenced tests. In W.A. Mehrens (Ed.), *Readings in measurement and evaluation in education and psychology.* New York: Holt, Rinehart and Winston, 1976. Pp. 276 – 293.

Livingston, S.A., & Zieky, M.J. *Passing scores: A manual for setting standards of performance on educational and occupational tests.* Princeton, NJ: Educational Testing Service, 1982.

Mercer, J., & Ysseldyke, J.E. Designing diagnostic-intervention programs. In T. Oakland (Ed.), *Psychological and educational assessment of minority children.* New York: Brunner/Mazel, 1977. Pp. 70 – 90.

Millman, J. Criterion-referenced measurement. In W.J. Popham (Ed.), *Evaluation in education: Current applications.* Berkeley, CA: McCutchan, 1974. Pp. 311 – 397.

Resnick, L.B., Wang, M.C., & Kaplan, J. Task analysis in curriculum design: A hierarchically sequenced introductory mathematics curriculum. *Journal of Applied Behavior Analysis*, 1973, *6*, 679 – 710.

Shepard, L.A. Standard setting issues and methods. *Applied Psychological Measurement*, 1980, *4*, 447 – 467.

Treiber, F.A., & Lahey, B.B. Toward a behavioral model of academic remediation with learning disabled children. *Journal of Learning Disabilities*, 1983, *16*, 111 – 116.

Ysseldyke, J.E., & Salvia, J. Diagnostic-prescriptive teaching: Two models. *Exceptional Children*, 1974, *44*, 181 – 185.

Zieky, M.J. *Methods of setting standards for criterion-referenced item sets.* Princeton, NJ: Educational Testing Service, 1973.

Chapter 7

DETERMINING THE DECISION RELIABILITY OF A DIAGNOSTIC TEST

Introduction

ONCE estimates of the *accuracy* of classifying students as masters and non-masters have been obtained, it is essential to estimate the *consistency* of those classifications. As the former provides evidence of *decision validity,* the latter furnishes evidence of *decision reliability.* The common denominator in both procedures is the "decision" to be made with the test score; in this case, a mastery or nonmastery classification decision. Where the preceding chapter dealt with the methods for establishing the accuracy of classification decisions, this chapter focuses on procedures that a teacher can use to determine whether those decisions will also be consistent across repeated testings with the same test or with equivalent forms of that test. An index of decision consistency indicates the reliability or degree of confidence one can place in the diagnostic decisions.

The sequence of these validity and reliability analyses is extremely important. Without a priori validity evidence or a sound justification for setting the cutting score that differentiates masters from nonmasters, it seems pointless even to compute an index of decision consistency reliability. If it is not known whether the decisions based on the cutting score will be accurate, one possible interpretation of a high decision reliability index might be that the *test can consistently classify students into the wrong groups.* Consistent decision making without accurate decision making has questionable value.

This chapter presents one method for assessing the decision reliability of a criterion-referenced test used to diagnose specific learning disabilities. It is organized according to two main topics: (1) selection of the criterion group and (2) the p index. The proposed index is applied to the scores from a dictionary skills test. The specific advantages and disadvantages of the decision reliability estimate are also discussed. As in the preceding chapter, all of the analyses and illustrative examples in this chapter deal with subtest scores. Of course, the various procedures are just as applicable to any combination of subtest scores

211

and to total test scores.

Selection of the Criterion Group

The reliability of decision making should be estimated from data gathered at the point in the instruction when the decisions are to be made. Although diagnostic decisions based on individual skill strengths and weaknesses usually occur prior to instruction, they may be necessary after the instruction has begun. The criterion group, however, will typically be composed of students who have not been exposed to the instruction. This *nonmastery group* may be the same group employed in the decision validity study. It should consist of one or more classes of students for which the test was designed.

Test-retest Method

Computation of the decision reliability index described in the next section requires two sets of scores from *testing one group of students twice,* with a one- to two-week interval between the first and second testing. This is the same test-retest procedure described in Chapter 2, which was used to estimate a stability coefficient. The two test administrations should occur during the first couple of weeks when instruction is to commence, or soon thereafter. Feedback on the results of the first testing should be deferred until after the second testing has been completed. Giving students the correct answers to the items prior to the second test administration can greatly improve their performance on that testing. While this might be desirable for instructional purposes, it will confound the estimation of decision reliability. For the same reason, no formal instruction on the specific instructional objectives being measured should be conducted during the intervening period between the two testings. More will be said about these problems later in terms of testing effect.

STABILITY. The simplest testing procedure is to administer the *same test* to the *same students* on the *two occasions*. As indicated in Chapter 2, this framework produces a measure of stability. Although the stability of the test scores over time is being assessed, the reliability index for a criterion-referenced test focuses on the stability of the mastery-nonmastery decisions based on those scores.

STABILITY AND EQUIVALENCE. Alternatively, a parallel form or equivalent sample of items can be used on the second test administration. The decision consistency index estimated from equivalent test forms will reflect both the stability of the scores over time and their equivalence over item samples. Since two sources of error are being measured, the stability-equivalence estimate will typically be lower than the stability estimate based on only one test.

Whichever method is selected, the structure of the information that results is still identical. Repeated measurements with one test or equivalent tests yield two sets of scores on the same objectives. Given that it is usually quite difficult and very time-consuming for teachers to build equivalent test forms that are matched on content and statistical characteristics (i.e., mean, variance, and intercorrelation), the single test approach is generally preferable. The testing effect problem associated with the test-retest method, mentioned briefly in Chapters 2 and 6, will be discussed shortly in the context of reliability estimation. It is sufficient to note here that the advantages of the test-retest method far outweigh the disadvantages of a conservative estimation bias.

p Index[1]

Over the past decade more than eight different approaches have been devised for estimating the decision reliability of criterion-referenced tests (see review by Berk, 1980, in press; for additional references, see Chapter 2). Although they vary markedly in terms of their computational and interpretative complexity, fortunately the approach that is the most conceptually and statistically sound also happens to be the one that is the most practical for teachers. That approach will be described here.

In this section, the specific procedures for computing and interpreting the *p* index are outlined. Since the appropriateness of a statistic must be judged prior to its use, the crucial assumptions underlying the *p* index of decision consistency will be delineated next. Only if these assumptions are upheld should a teacher proceed to compute and to interpret the index.

Optimal Cutting Score Assumption

There are two fundamental assumptions associated with classification decision consistency: (1) students are classified as either masters or nonmasters of an objective based on a cutting score and (2) the consequences (or losses) related to all false mastery and false nonmastery decision errors are equally serious regardless of their size. These assumptions actually reduce to one issue: Was the optimal cutting score selected? If it was not, then one or both of the assumptions are untenable and an index of decision consistency should not be used. The conditions under which the assumptions will not be met are as follows: (a) when it is preferable to use two cutting scores — one to identify masters at the upper end of the score distribution, a second to identify nonmasters at the lower end, with a region of no-decision between the two cutoffs, (b) when

---

[1]The use of the term *reliability* to characterize the *p* index of decision consistency is actually inappropriate. This term is, in fact, a misnomer since the index is neither defined nor interpreted in the language of the standard psychometric reliability components of observed-score and true-score variance. The properties of the index suggest that the term *agreement index* provides a more accurate label. The reader should be cognizant of this distinction in terminology as he or she proceeds through the chapter, although *reliability* is still used in an effort to minimize confusion and maintain consistency in terminology with earlier chapters.

the *degree* of mastery or nonmastery of each student is felt to provide more meaningful information than simply the dichotomous, qualitative mastery-nonmastery classsification, (3) when a weighted cutting score is chosen in lieu of the optimal cutting score (and the two do not coincide). Unfortunately, at present there are no alternative indices of decision consistency that both satisfy any of these conditions and are also practicable for teachers.

Computation

SCORE THE SUBTEST. Suppose the subtest scores on the reading comprehension objectives from the uninstructed or nonmaster group of the decision validity study (see Chapter 6) were used as the data for the first test administration. The scores on this five-item subtest ranged from 1 to 3. After the subtest is administered a second time to the same students, it must be scored again.

In order to compute an index of decision reliability, both sets of subtest scores should be organized into two columns as illustrated in Table 7.1. This table displays the subtest scores of 10 students who were administered five items measuring one objective both at the beginning of instruction (Measurement 1) and two weeks later (Measurement 2). Inasmuch as these are preinstruction measurements for a test to be used for placement (diagnostic) decisions, the overall poor performance was expected. The optimal cutting score for this subtest, as determined previously in Chapter 6, is 4.

Table 7.1

Test-retest Data on Ten Students for Five-item Subtest

Student	Measurement 1	Measurement 2
1	4	5
2	3	2
3	3	4
4	3	3
5	2	4
6	2	2
7	2	2
8	2	3
9	1	2
10	1	2

COMPUTE THE INDEX. The p index is equal to the percentage of students consistently classified as masters and nonmasters on two measurements (Hambleton & Novick, 1973), or

$$p = \frac{mn + nn}{N} \times 100$$

where:

mm = number of students who are classified as masters on both meaure-
ments

nn = number of students who are classified as nonmasters on both
measurements

N = total number of students in the group

Computation of p using the optimal cutting score (c_o) of 4 and the subtest
scores shown in Table 7.2 is as follows:

$$p = \frac{1 + 7}{10} + 100$$
$$= 80\%$$

Only one student scored at or above the cutting score on both measurements;
seven scored below both times.

Interpretation

In that p is a percentage, its values can range from 0 to 100. The index indicates the degree to which students retain the same mastery or nonmastery status on the two testings. The maximum value of 100% occurs when all students
are consistently classified the same way on both occasions. A zero index signi-
fies no consistent classifications.

The p index measures the *overall* consistency of classification decisions. Subkoviak (1980, p. 152) noted two factors that contribute to that consistency: the
mastery-nonmastery composition of the group tested and the measurement
precision of the test itself. When there is a large proportion of masters or nonmasters in the group, as in the preceding sample, index values tend to be high.
In addition, the index is sensitive to the selected cutting score, test length, and
the spread of the scores. The position of the cutting score, in particular, has a
much more profound effect upon the magnitude of the index than either of the
other two characteristics. Higher values of p are associated with extremely high
cutting scores (e.g., 7 out of 8 items), and lower values occur with cutting
scores near the average score. The values also can increase as the number of
items increases and the spread of the scores increases. In practice, however, it is
not unusal to obtain p values of 75% or higher with subtests containing fewer
than 10 items and exhibiting relatively little score variance.

In addition to these factors, the specific test administration procedure employed will influence the p index. If the test-retest method is used, the index
will measure only the stability of the decisions. Where equivalent forms are

administered, both stability of the scores and equivalence of the item samples are measured. Inasmuch as the latter taps two sources of error, stability-equivalence estimates of p tend to be lower than stability estimates of p. This relationship between the two estimates, however, may be offset if there is a pronounced testing effect. Knowledge gained from the first testing, which improves the scores on the second testing, can lower the stability estimate of p. Testing effect is discussed further in the section on advantages and disadvantages.

Application to a Dictionary Skills Test

The p index was computed for each subtest of the 52-item introductory dictionary skills test analyzed in Chapter 6. The procedures used in this application are as follows:

1. Since the test was to be used for diagnostic decisions, only the performance of the 24 second-grade uninstructed students was of interest.
2. The requirements of the test-retest method were followed. Based on the first test administration, the subtest scores of the 24 students were obtained from the decision validity study (see Table 6.2). The test was readministered one week later to the same students. The students did not receive any information on their first performance nor formal instruction on the five objectives during that week. They were told simply, "You didn't do very well on the test, and I'd like to test you again." The subtest scores from the retesting were calculated from the answer sheets. These scores and the item-by-item results were given to the students. All of this scoring produced 10 sets of scores—two measurements for each of five subtests. These scores are assembled in Table 7.2.
3. The p index was computed for each subtest using the cutting scores determined previously (see Table 6.9).
4. The indices for all five subtests shown in Table 7.2 were extremely high, indicating the near perfect consistency of the classification decisions. The one inconsistency that occurred in subtest 1 might be attributed to guessing, in that the greatest fluctuation in individual scores from measurement 1 to measurement 2 was on the multiple-choice items in subtests 1, 3, and 5. The most stable subtest score performance was observed for subtests 2 and 4, which contained short-answer (completion) items. Furthermore, in view of the properties of the p index, it was not surprising to find such high proportions of agreement. The magnitude of the indices could easily be due to the almost total nonmastery composition of the sample and, consequently, to the large discrepancies between the students' overall poor performance and the high cutting scores. Even considering the small sample size and the amount of error or imprecision

Table 7.2

Test-retest Data for Five Subtests on the Dictionary Skills Test[*]

Student	Subtest 1 Meas. 1	Subtest 1 Meas. 2	Subtest 2 Meas. 1	Subtest 2 Meas. 2	Subtest 3 Meas. 1	Subtest 3 Meas. 2	Subtest 4 Meas. 1	Subtest 4 Meas. 2	Subtest 5 Meas. 1	Subtest 5 Meas. 2
1	0	0	0	0	1	0	0	0	0	0
2	0	0	0	0	0	0	0	1	0	0
3	3	2	1	0	0	1	0	0	0	0
4	5	6	2	2	0	0	0	0	0	1
5	1	0	0	1	9	11	2	2	0	0
6	3	2	0	0	0	0	0	0	0	1
7	3	3	1	1	1	2	0	0	2	2
8	0	0	4	6	16	2	3	4	0	0
9	8	8	2	3	0	17	0	0	2	2
10	4	4	0	0	2	0	0	0	0	1
11	1	2	0	0	0	3	0	0	0	0
12	2	1	0	0	7	0	1	0	0	0
13	3	3	0	0	2	9	0	0	0	1
14	3	3	0	0	0	2	2	3	0	0
15	2	3	0	8	6	0	0	0	0	0
16	8	7	7	0	0	5	0	0	0	0
17	0	1	0	1	1	1	2	2	1	1
18	3	2	1	3	6	1	0	0	1	0
19	5	4	4	4	1	7	2	0	1	2
20	3	5	3	0	0	0	0	0	1	1
21	0	1	0	0	1	1	0	0	0	0
22	3	4	0	0	0	3	0	0	0	0
23	3	5	1	2	3	1	0	0	0	1
24	5	5	0	0	3	6	0	0	0	0
c_c	6/8		11/14		14/17		5/7		4/6	
p	96%		100%		100%		100%		100%	

[*]Based on a criterion group of 24 second-grade uninstructed students.

typically found for that size (about 8 %), the indices still provide sufficient evidence that the decisions made by the teacher would be highly reliable.

5. Reviewing all the validity and reliability results summarized in Table 7.3 leads one to conclude that there is very convincing evidence of the quality of the dictionary skills test for making diagnostic decisions about the second-grade children. Both the estimated accuracy and consistency of these mastery-nonmastery decisions based on the selected subtest cutting scores were found to be exceptionally high.

Reporting Evidence of Decision Reliability

After the analysis has been completed, the p index should be reported to furnish evidence of the reliability of mastery-nonmastery decisions. Since certain key factors must be examined jointly with the index in order to interpret the results correctly, they should also be reported. These factors consist of the mastery standard (cutting score as a function of test length), the sample size, and the method used to estimate p (e.g., test-retest). Perhaps the most efficient way to present these different pieces of information is to expand the decision validity evidence table (e.g., Table 6.9) to include the decision reliability evidence. Such a table would supply all of the important technical characteristics related to the test and score use. An exemplary format displaying both validity and reliability evidence is shown for the application just described (see Table 7.3).

Advantages and Disadvantages of the Method

Advantages

There are several advantages to using the test-retest method for computing the p index. First, it is easy to understand, to use, to compute, and to interpret. Second, the method can be applied to most types of items and tests, including (a) dichotomous or multipoint items, (b) short or long subtests and tests, (c) paper-and-pencil tests or performance tests, and (d) tests and scales measuring cognitive, affective, or psychomotor behaviors. Finally, the testing procedure can be employed with samples representing virtually any populations of students for which a criterion-referenced test can be designed.

In addition to these advantages, it is worth noting that the p index itself is the most statistically sound estimate of decision consistency. Although the alternative x index (Swaminathan, Hambleton, & Algina, 1974), which takes into account the agreement that could be expected by chance alone, has received a preponderance of attention in the literature (see, for example, Subkoviak, 1980, in press,) it has numerous disadvantages that render it inappropriate for tests used for instructional decisions at the classroom level (Berk, 1980).

Table 7.3

Validity and Reliability Evidence of Diagnostic Decisions Using the Dictionary Skills Test

Subtest	No. of Items	Cutting Score	Criterion	Classification Probabilities[a]					
				Correct Decisions	False Nonmastery	False Mastery	Sensitivity (Masters)	Specificity (Nonmasters)	p Index[b]
1: Alphabetizing	8	6	75%	92%	4%	4%	83%	91%	96%
2: Entry Words	14	11	79%	98%	2%	0%	88%	100%	100%
3: Syllabication	17	14	82%	89%	9%	2%	75%	96%	100%
4: Guide Words	7	5	71%	93%	7%	0	79%	100%	100%
5: Word Meaning	6	4	67%	100%	0	0	100%	100%	100%

[a]Based on criterion groups of 22 third-grade instructed and 24 second-grade uninstructed students.
[b]Based on criterion group of 24 second-grade uninstructed students using test-retest method.

Disadvantages

There is one disadvantage of the test-retest method and one disadvantage of the p index, both of which need to be considered in interpreting p.

TESTING EFFECT. First, the magnitude of a testing effect that could result from administering the same test twice in close succession must be assessed. If the specific content being tested is not easily remembered (e.g., algebraic equations, phonics) or both testings occur near the end of instruction and the retest data are collected for review purposes, the effect will be negligible. On the other hand, a significant testing effect could be expected when (a) some items can be easily recognized on the retest, (b) teaching of the test content occurs during the intervening period between the two testings, or (c) errors on the first testing are corrected prior to the second testing.

Inasmuch as the knowledge gained from the initial testing tends to inflate the scores on the retest, typically only the status of nonmasters on measurement 1 will be altered on measurement 2. This can be illustrated by the performance of students 3 and 5 in Table 7.1. How does this affect the p index? Certainly if several nonmasters become masters, thereby reducing the total number of *consistent* decisions, the p index will be deflated. In other words, when a testing effect is suspected, the value of p will usually be lower than it would be without that effect (i.e., a conservative bias). Had students 3 and 5 not achieved the mastery score on the second testing, p would have been 100%. Therefore, the effect in this case deflated p by 20%. The teacher should be cognizant of this possible bias in interpreting p.

IMPRECISION OF THE p ESTIMATE. The disadvantage of the statistic p pertains to the precision of the p estimate for groups of 30 or less. When the group size used to compute p is small, there will be a large amount of error asssociated with p. That is, if p is computed from the scores of one class, that p could be quite inaccurate compared with an estimate computed from the scores of three or four classes. Consequently, if p is computed from data gathered on only a few students, caution should be observed in attaching undue weight to the resultant value, e.g., a high value could be very misleading. The accuracy of p can be improved by administering the test to several classes at a given grade level. A teacher would then be able to place greater confidence in the estimate and, if it happens to be in the 80s or above, in his or her decisions.

In summary, the disadvantages of the test-retest estimate of p can be overcome if the testing effect is negligible and the data used to compute p are gathered from three or four classes. Otherwise, the caveats mentioned in the preceding discussion should be considered in interpreting the p index.

Summary

The step-by-step procedure for determining the decision-consistency reliability of a diagnostic test is summarized as follows:

1. Select a criterion group for which individual mastery-nonmastery decisions will be made (preferably one or more classes of uninstructed students).
2. Administer the test twice to this group. An equivalent form can also be used on the second setting. There should be a one- to two-week interval between the measurements. During this period, no feedback should be given to the students on their initial test performance, nor should any formal instruction be conducted on the objectives being measured. These steps are intended to minimize the chances of a testing effect.
3. Score the subtest (or test) for each student on each testing.
4. Assemble the pairs of scores for the total group into two columns as shown in Tables 7.1 and 7.2.
5. Compute the p index using the subtest scores based on the optimal cutting score. First, count the number of masters on both testings, and then the number of nonmasters. Second, add these two numbers. Finally, divide this sum by the number of students and multiply by 100.
6. Evaluate this observed degree of decision consistency in the context of any possible testing effect and the possible inaccuracy of the value due to the group size.
7. Report evidence of decision reliability along with the evidence of decision validity to facilitate the correct interpretation of both types of information about test quality and score use (see Table 7.3).

References

Berk, R. A. A consumers' guide to criterion-referenced test reliability. *Journal of Educational Measurement*, 1980, *17*, 323-349; Errata, 1981, *18*, 131.

Berk, R. A. Selecting an index of reliability. In R. A. Berk (Ed.), *A guide to criterion-referenced test construction*. Baltimore, MD: Johns Hopkins University Press, in press.

Hambleton, R.K., & Novick, M. R. Toward an integration of theory and method for criterion-referenced tests. *Journal of Educational Measurement*, 1973, *10*, 159-170.

Subkoviak, M. J. Decision-consistency approachess. In R. A. Berk (Ed.), *Criterion-referenced measurement: The state of the art*. Baltimore, MD: Johns Hopkins University Press, 1980. Pp. 129-185.

Subkoviak, M. J. Estimating the reliability of mastery-nonmastery classifications. In R. A. Berk (Ed.), *A guide to criterion-referenced test construction*. Baltimore, MD: Johns Hopkins University Press, in press.

Swaminathan, H., Hambleton, R. K., & Algina, J. Reliability of criterion-referenced tests: A decision-theoretic formulation. *Journal of Educational Measurement*, 1974, *11*, 263-267.

Chapter 8

RECOMMENDED PROCEDURES
FOR SCREENING AND DIAGNOSIS

Introduction

EMBEDDED throughout the preceding seven chapters is the concern that current screening and diagnostic practices have not taken advantage of the available testing technology. Very often either technically inadequate instruments and procedures are used or the data from technically adequate devices are applied incorrectly or ignored in the decision-making process. In an attempt to set practices on a more defensible course, the various chapters in this volume present evaluations of the quality of the most popular norm-referenced and criterion-referenced tests and many of the procedures employed in screening and diagnosis for learning disabilities. In addition, guidelines for selecting and using test scores correctly are given, and methods for determining the quality of both tests and test-based screening procedures are described.

The purpose of this chapter is to synthesize the evaluation results, guidelines, and methods into a form that practitioners involved in screening and diagnosis can use. This form consists of step-by-step procedures that learning disability specialists, school psychologists, and classroom teachers can follow in executing the screening process, from test selection through decision making by the multidisciplinary team. The information produced at this stage can then be utilized in the diagnosis of individual skill-development strengths and weaknesses. The chapter is organized according to these two topics: screening and diagnosis. Concrete examples are provided to illustrate particular procedures, especially those requiring computations. In addition, the role of the multidisciplinary team in the identification process is examined.

Screening

Screening is the first stage in the assessment of children with learning disabilities. The method adopted for screening should be both effective and efficient. That is, the screening method should accurately identify those children

222

who exhibit learning problems, and that method should be executed with a minimum expenditure of time and effort, if possible. These criteria must be met so that children who need special instructional attention are not deprived of that attention any longer than is absolutely necessary.

All of the screening procedures recommended in earlier chapters are expressly designed to be effective and efficient. They are summarized in this section under six major steps:

1. Select the standardized ability and achievement test batteries.
2. Convert ability and achievement test scores into a common metric.
3. Compute ability-achievement discrepancy scores.
4. Determine which discrepancies are "severe."
5. Determine whether children with a severe discrepancy are learning disabled.
6. Incorporate discrepancy information into multidisciplinary team decisions.

Select the Standardized Ability and Achievement Test Batteries

Based on the recommendations given in Chapter 2 and the criteria for determining a reliable discrepancy score delineated in Chapter 4, the following procedure is suggested for selecting standardized, norm-referenced ability and achievement test batteries:

1. Evaluate the test batteries currently being used for screening or those administered as part of the district- or state-wide testing program.
   a. Use Tables 2.4 through 2.7 as a starting point.
   b. Evaluate the curricular validity of the achievement tests.
   c. Analyze available evidence related to sex, racial, and ethnic bias for both the ability and achievement tests.
   d. Determine whether the appropriate level tests are being administered to the children who have or are suspected of having learning disabilities; consider lower level (out-of-level) tests to match the children's functional levels.
   e. Identify the areas of possible achievement deficit among the seven areas specified in the *Procedures for Evaluating Specific Learning Disabilities* (U.S.O.E., 1977b) that are not measured by the testing program; the seven areas are the following:
      (1) oral expression
      (2) listening comprehension
      (3) written expression
      (4) basic reading skill
      (5) reading comprehension
      (6) mathematics calculation
      (7) mathematics reasoning

2. Consider adding or substituting technically adequate ability and achievement tests, where available, in the areas needed to fill in gaps in the coverage.
   a. Select ability-achievement test batteries that have been normed on the same standardization sample, such as the following:
      (1) Otis-Lennon School Ability Test (OLSAT) and Metropolitan Achievement Tests (MAT, 1978 edition) or Stanford Achievement Test (SAT, 7th edition)
      (2) Cognitive Abilities Test (CogAT) and Iowa Tests of Basic Skills (ITBS)
      (3) Test of Cognitive Skills (TCS) and Comprehensive Tests of Basic Skills (CTBS, Form U)
      (4) Short Form Test of Academic Aptitude (SFTAA) and California Achievement Tests (CAT-70)
         Alternatively, other battery combinations can be used if the norm samples are comparable. Determining comparability would require an examination of the demographic characteristics of the children in the samples. For example, if the California Achievement Tests (Forms C and D) have been used in a school district for several years, the test user would have to inspect the standardization samples of different ability tests to choose the battery that best matches the CAT in terms of date of standardization and the characteristics and representativeness of the sample.
   b. Select ability tests that are structured according to different types of ability such as verbal, nonverbal, and quantitative as opposed to tests that yield only a global ability index. For example, while the OLSAT produces only a single School Ability Index, the CogAT gives separate scores for Verbal, Nonverbal, and Quantitative batteries, the TCS provides scores for Sequences, Analogies, Memory, and Verbal Reasoning, and the SFTAA furnishes subtest scores in Language (Vocabulary and Memory) and Nonlanguage (Analogies and Sequences). The CogAT, TCS, and SFTAA also report indices for the total battery. Tests that partition ability as described previously can be more useful in combination with specific achievement subtests for estimating discrepancies than tests that supply only a total score or ability index (see step 4).
   c. Select achievement tests that cover as many of the seven areas of potential achievement deficit as possible. Most of the top-rated achievement test batteries, such as those mentioned in step 2a, contain subtests in language, reading, and mathematics that correspond to the areas of written expression, basic reading skill and reading comprehension, and mathematics calculation and reasoning, respectively. In

other words, five of the seven areas are usually covered. It should be noted, however, that all of the subtest items are in multiple-choice format, which is certainly not the optimal format to assess written expression. A writing sample format would be the most direct measurement approach. Similarly, alternative formats need to be considered to test validly and reliably oral expression and listening comprehension, the two areas not addressed by the achievement batteries. Unfortunately, the measurement problems in those areas have not been completely resolved (Mead, in press), and there is a scarcity of technically adequate tests of speaking and listening skills.

3. Based on the tests chosen according to the preceding guidelines, pair the ability and achievement tests that are either conormed or have comparable norm samples.

4. Match the ability test to the achievement test area in which the ability-achievement discrepancy score is to be estimated; the test performance comparison depends upon the kind of educational intervention contemplated. For example, a verbal ability test is a more accurate and content appropriate predictor of reading comprehension test performance than a nonverbal ability test. It is also more meaningful for judging the degree to which the ability-reading comprehension achievement discrepancy is remediable and/or compensatable (Hanna, Dyck, & Holen, 1979). When several ability tests are administered, the test on which the student scores the highest should not automatically be chosen as the ability test for all discrepancy analyses; the best ability-achievement test match should be the primary determinant.

    a. Match the verbal ability test with the verbally based achievement subtests (e.g., vocabulary, reading comprehension, capitalization, punctuation, usage, spelling).

    b. Match the quantitative ability test with the mathematics achievement subtests (e.g., concepts, problem-solving, computations).

    c. If neither a nor b is possible, use the global ability test or nonverbal test with each achievement subtest to estimate discrepancies. This alternative is less desirable for the reasons explicated previously.

Convert Ability and Achievement Test Scores into a Common Metric

Given the vast array of scores that are usually reported for standardized tests (for a review, see Chapter 3), it can be difficult to sort out which type of score is best for a particular use. Clearly, the requirements of discrepancy score computations leave very few options. Normalized standard scores are essential, and z- and T-scores are the most useful in determining a "severe" discrepancy. Interestingly, not all publishers report these specific standard scores; however, virtually all do report percentile ranks. For some of the intelligence tests, only deviation IQ scores are available. The procedure for converting percentile ranks and deviation IQ scores to *z*- or *T*-scores[1] is outlined as follows:

1. Locate the student's *national grade-based* percentile rank on the ability and achievement tests. In order to compare performance on the two tests, the same type of score must be chosen for both. National norms are preferable for this purpose to local norms because of the instability and peculiarities that typically characterize locally drawn grade-level samples.

   a. For ability and achievement tests administered *on grade level*, national grade-based percentile ranks can be obtained directly from the test reports of any of the tests mentioned in the preceding section. For other tests where only age-based percentile ranks or age-based deviation IQs are available, test users should request grade-based percentile ranks from the publisher. If this request is not met, then the test should not be used (see step 3).

      Example: Suppose the CogAT—ITBS battery combination was selected and Monroe received the grade-based percentile ranks of 47 on the Verbal Ability battery and 23 on the Reading Comprehension subtest (level 11, grade 5).

   b. For achievement tests administered *below grade level*, locate the student's *scaled score* first, and then convert that score, using tables in the appropriate test manual, to a national grade-based percentile rank for the on-level test. The percentile ranks must be derived from the *on-grade-level norm sample*. Scaled scores are reported for the MAT, SAT, CTBS, and CAT, but not for the ITBS. The publisher of the ITBS recommends the use of *their* standard scores that have been equated across grade levels (Hieronymus, Lindquist, & Hoover, 1982) instead of the use of separate scaled scores. The standard score on the out-of-level test can then be converted to an on-grade-level percentile rank. In other words, ITBS standard scores should be treated the same as the scaled scores on the other achievement test batteries.

      Example: Suppose Brunhilda was given the level 9 (grade 3) ITBS, although she was in grade 4. She received a standard (scaled) score of 110 on the Language Usage subtest. Based on grade 4 norms for that subtest, the score of 110 converts to a percentile rank of 34. Had the grade 3 norms been used inappropriately, the percentile rank would have been 57. Such a difference in normative scores between two grade levels can obviously create errors in discrepancy scores, which would render them worthless. It is crucial that scaled scores be referenced to on-level norms.

---

[1]Although *T*-scores may be used to determine ability-achievement discrepancies, preference is given here to *z*-scores because of the simplified formula that can be employed to compute reliable discrepancies (see Determine Which Discrepancies Are "Severe"). For a step-by-step presentation of this screening procedure based on *T*-scores, the reader is referred to Hanna et al. (1979).

Table 8.1

Conversion of Percentile Ranks into *z*- and *T*-Scores

Percentile Rank	z-score	T-score	Percentile Rank	z-score	T-score	Percentile Rank	z-score	T-score
99	2.33	73	66	.41	54	33	− .44	46
98	2.05	71	65	.39	54	32	− .47	45
97	1.88	69	64	.36	54	31	− .50	45
96	1.75	68	63	.33	53	30	− .52	45
95	1.64	66	62	.31	53	29	− .55	45
94	1.55	66	61	.28	53	28	− .58	44
93	1.48	65	60	.25	53	27	− .61	44
92	1.41	64	59	.23	52	26	− .64	44
91	1.34	63	58	.20	52	25	− .67	43
90	1.28	63	57	.18	52	24	− .71	43
89	1.23	62	56	.15	52	23	− .74	43
88	1.18	62	55	.13	51	22	− .77	42
87	1.13	61	54	.10	51	21	− .81	42
86	1.08	61	53	.08	51	20	− .84	42
85	1.04	60	52	.05	51	19	− .88	41
84	.99	60	51	.03	50	18	− .92	41
83	.95	60	50	.00	50	17	− .95	41
82	.92	59	49	−.03	50	16	− .99	40
81	.88	59	48	−.05	50	15	−1.04	40
80	.84	58	47	−.08	49	14	−1.08	39
79	.81	58	46	−.10	49	13	−1.13	39
78	.77	58	45	−.13	49	12	−1.18	38
77	.74	57	44	−.15	49	11	−1.23	38
76	.71	57	43	−.18	48	10	−1.28	37
75	.67	57	42	−.20	48	9	−1.34	37
74	.64	56	41	−.23	48	8	−1.41	36
73	.61	56	40	−.25	48	7	−1.48	35
72	.58	56	39	−.28	47	6	−1.55	35
71	.55	56	38	−.31	47	5	−1.64	34
70	.52	55	37	−.33	47	4	−1.75	33
69	.50	55	36	−.36	46	3	−1.88	31
68	.47	55	35	−.39	46	2	−2.05	30
67	.44	54	34	−.41	46	1	−2.33	27

2. Using Table 8.1, locate the *z*-scores that correspond to the grade-level percentile ranks for the ability and achievement tests. By converting scores to percentile ranks before transforming them into standard scores,

the z-scores become normalized. For each student, this process yields two z-scores for each pair of ability and achievement tests. (*Note:* T-scores may also be used.)

Example: Monroe's percentile ranks of 47 on the CogAT Verbal Ability battery and 23 on the ITBS Reading Comprehension subtest convert to z-scores of −.08 and −.74, respectively.

3. The deviation IQs reported for individually-administered intelligence tests such as the WISC-R and Stanford-Binet can also be converted to z- or T-scores. However, their deviation IQs are age based rather than grade based, and they are not usually normalized. These characteristics present two problems.

   a. First, as explained in step 1, a common metric and reference group are essential in order to compare the scores from an ability and achievement test. If age-based scores are given for the intelligence tests and grade-based scores are reported for achievement tests, the comparison cannot be made. Scores derived from different reference groups can be very misleading, especially for students who are much older or younger than their grade level peers (Hanna et al., 1979). Consequently, if a test such as the WISC-R is going to be used with an achievement test battery to estimate discrepancy scores, the test user should try to obtain grade-based percentile ranks from The Psychological Corporation or abandon that use of WISC-R scores.

   b. Second, if one decided to tackle the chore of estimating grade-based scores for the WISC-R (for details, see Hanna et al., 1979), the problem of converting *nonnormalized* deviation IQs into z- or T-scores still must be confronted. The conversion tables that are readily accessible are based on *normalized* deviation IQs (see Table 8.2). Therefore, the accuracy of conversions using those tables would be questionable.

   c. The difficulty of overcoming these problems suggests that a school psychologist may have little recourse. One alternative is to consider the recently published individually administered Kaufman Assessment Battery for Children (Kaufman & Kaufman, 1982), which was described briefly in Chapter 2. Since it consists of both intelligence and achievement components, discrepancy scores can be computed. Among the various scores reported for these components are national age-based percentile ranks. These ranks can be converted easily into z- or T-scores by using Table 8.1.

4. It should be emphasized that while all of the preceding conversions can be completed manually by teachers and psychologists for children suspected of having a learning disability, they also can be programmed for microcomputers as well as large computer systems. Computerized reports of test scores and their conversions to different metrics can be made

Table 8.2

Conversion of Deviation IQ Scores for WISC-R[a] and
Stanford-Binet[b] (Italics) into z – and T-Scores

Dev. IQ	z-score	T-score	Dev. IQ	z-score	T-score	Dev. IQ	z-score	T-score	Dev. IQ	z-score	T-score
169	4.60	96	144	3.93	79	119	1.27	63	94	− .40	46
	4.31	*93*		*2.75*	*78*		*1.19*	*62*		− *.38*	*46*
168	4.53	95	143	2.87	79	118	1.20	62	93	− .47	45
	4.25	*93*		*2.69*	*77*		*1.13*	*61*		− *.44*	*46*
167	4.47	95	142	2.80	78	117	1.13	61	92	− .53	45
	4.19	*92*		*2.63*	*76*		*1.06*	*61*		− *.50*	*45*
166	4.40	94	141	2.73	77	116	1.07	61	91	− .60	44
	4.13	*91*		*2.56*	*76*		*1.00*	*60*		− *.56*	*44*
165	4.33	93	140	2.67	77	115	1.00	60	90	− .68	43
	4.06	*91*		*2.50*	*75*		*.94*	*59*		− *.63*	*44*
164	4.27	93	139	2.60	76	114	.93	59	89	− .73	43
	4.00	*90*		*2.44*	*74*		*.88*	*59*		− *.69*	*43*
163	4.20	92	138	2.53	75	113	.87	59	88	− .80	42
	3.94	*89*		*2.38*	*74*		*.81*	*58*		− *.75*	*42*
162	4.13	91	137	2.47	75	112	.80	58	87	− .87	41
	3.88	*89*		*2.31*	*73*		*.75*	*58*		− *.81*	*42*
161	4.07	91	136	2.40	74	111	.73	57	86	− .93	41
	3.81	*88*		*2.25*	*73*		*.69*	*57*		− *.88*	*41*
160	4.00	90	135	2.33	73	110	.68	57	85	−1.00	40
	3.75	*88*		*2.19*	*72*		*.63*	*56*		− *.94*	*40*
159	3.93	89	134	2.27	73	109	.60	56	84	−1.07	39
	3.69	*87*		*2.13*	*71*		*.56*	*56*		−*1.00*	*40*
158	3.87	89	133	2.20	72	108	.53	55	83	−1.13	39
	3.63	*86*		*2.06*	*71*		*.50*	*55*		−*1.06*	*39*
157	3.80	88	132	2.13	71	107	.47	55	82	−1.20	38
	3.56	*86*		*2.00*	*70*		*.44*	*54*		−*1.13*	*39*
156	3.73	87	131	2.07	71	106	.40	54	81	−1.27	37
	3.50	*85*		*1.94*	*69*		*.38*	*54*		−*1.19*	*38*
155	3.67	87	130	2.00	70	105	.33	53	80	−1.33	37
	3.44	*84*		*1.88*	*69*		*.31*	*53*		−*1.25*	*37*
154	3.60	86	129	1.93	69	104	.27	53	79	−1.40	36
	3.38	*84*		*1.81*	*68*		*.25*	*53*		−*1.31*	*37*
153	3.53	85	128	1.87	69	103	.20	52	78	−1.47	35
	3.31	*83*		*1.75*	*68*		*.19*	*52*		−*1.38*	*36*
152	3.47	85	127	1.80	68	102	.13	51	77	−1.53	35
	3.25	*83*		*1.69*	*67*		*.13*	*51*		−*1.44*	*36*
151	3.40	84	126	1.73	67	101	.07	51	76	−1.60	34
	3.19	*82*		*1.63*	*66*		*.06*	*51*		−*1.50*	*35*
150	3.33	83	125	1.67	67	100	.00	50	75	−1.67	33
	3.13	*81*		*1.56*	*66*		*.00*	*50*		−*1.56*	*34*
149	3.27	83	124	1.60	66	99	−.07	49	74	−1.73	33
	3.06	*81*		*1.50*	*65*		−*.06*	*49*		−*1.63*	*34*
148	3.20	82	123	1.53	65	98	−.13	49	73	−1.80	32
	3.00	*80*		*1.44*	*64*		−*.13*	*49*		−*1.69*	*33*
147	3.13	81	122	1.47	65	97	−.20	48	72	−1.87	31
	2.94	*79*		*1.38*	*64*		−*.19*	*48*		−*1.75*	*32*
146	3.07	81	121	1.40	64	96	−.27	47	71	−1.93	31
	2.88	*79*		*1.31*	*63*		−*.25*	*47*		−*1.81*	*32*
145	3.00	80	120	1.33	63	95	−.33	47	70	−2.00	30
	2.81	*78*		*1.25*	*63*		−*.31*	*47*		−*1.88*	*31*

[a]where: $\overline{X}$ = 100 and SP = 15
[b]where: $\overline{X}$ = 100 and SD = 16

available at the classroom, school, and district levels for any designated population of students. Such reports can greatly facilitate the screening process.

Compute Ability-Achievement Discrepancy Scores

Once the score on each test is in standard score form, one only has to subtract the achievement score (z_{AC}) from the ability score (z_{AB}) to obtain the discrepancy score (z_D), or

$$z_D = z_{AB} - z_{AC}. \tag{8.1}$$

Example: Monroe's discrepancy score is computed as follows:

$$z_D = -.08 - (-.74)$$
$$= .66$$

As indicated in the previous section, computerized reports can be extremely helpful in screening large numbers of students. If all of the percentile ranks have been converted to z-scores, a simple program can be written to subtract specific ability-achievement subtest pairs of z-scores and then to report those discrepancies.

Determine Which Discrepancies Are "Severe"

The *Procedures for Evaluating Specific Learning Disabilities* (U.S.O.E., 1977b) use the expression "severe discrepancy between achievement and intellectual ability" (p. 65083) to define a specific learning disability. In Chapter 4 an attempt was made to define the criterion of *severe* operationally as the magnitude of the discrepancy needed to reach statistical significance. This definition was intended to provide some assurance that a discrepancy is real (a true difference) rather than a chance occurrence due to errors of measurement.

SELECTION OF RELIABILITY COEFFICIENTS. Without delving into the statistical formulas for the standard error of measurement of a discrepancy and the test of significance of the discrepancy that underlie the preceding criterion, it is possible for a classroom teacher or learning disability specialist to determine quite easily whether or not a given discrepancy score is severe. The simplest procedure is to compare the discrepancy (z_D) with the tabled value for a reliable discrepancy based on the known reliability coefficients of the ability test (r_{AB}) and achievement test (r_{AC}). Table 8.3 was prepared for this purpose. For each discrepancy then, only two pieces of information are required—two estimates of reliability. Since there are several types of coefficients frequently reported in the technical manuals of ability and achievement tests, a couple of points need to be considered:

1. Choose the same type of reliability coefficient for each test pair; a six-month stability estimate for the ability test and a K-R$_{20}$ internal consistency estimate for the achievement test measure different types of

MEMORY JOGGER

Table 8.3

Guidelines for Determining Whether an
Ability-achievement Discrepancy Is Severe

| Condition | Reliability Coefficent | | Discrepancy Score (z_{RD})* |
	Ability (r_{AB})	Achievement (r_{AC})	
1	.90 or above	.90 or above	.738
			1.042
			1.377
2	.90 or above	.85 – .89	.825
	.85 – .89 or	.90 or above	*1.165*
			1.540
3	.85 – .89	.85 – .89	.904
			1.276
			1.687

*p = .05
p = .01
p = .001

reliability and, therefore, are not comparable. Not all types of reliability evidence are reported for both ability and achievement tests. Typically, the K-R$_{20}$ coefficient is the most popular, with equivalence next. Stability coefficients, however, are more common for ability tests than for achievement tests. These restrictions will become evident as the different ability-achievement test combinations are examined.

2. The relationship between the reliability of test scores and the reliability of a discrepancy score can influence the choice of the type of reliability coefficient. In general, the higher the reliability coefficients of both tests, say in the .90s, the smaller the discrepancy score between the tests needed to be reliable; to the extent that the coefficient of either the ability or achievement test drops below .90, the discrepancy score required to reach significance (reliability) must be larger. This is demonstrated in Table 8.3. Under the first condition where the coefficients of both tests are .90 or above, a discrepancy score of at least .738 is needed; while under the second condition where one of the coefficients is between .85 and .89, a discrepancy must be at least .825 to be reliable. Among the various types of reliability defined in Chapter 2, the highest coefficients are often reported for K-R$_{20}$ estimates of internal consistency, due, in part, to the effect of speededness on the scores. In other words, by selecting K-R$_{20}$ coefficients, one can usually maximize the chances of detecting severe discrepancies because the values given are usually in the mid .90s. The

other types of coefficients are typically lower, especially stability estimates based on a lengthy time interval of, for example, six months or longer and stability-equivalence estimates.

These two considerations suggest that if it is desirable to identify as many real LD children as possible at the risk of committing a few false positive errors in the screening process, the K-R$_{20}$ coefficient may be the most appropriate. Alternatively, this goal can also be achieved by using another type of reliability and lowering the criterion for severe according to the probability levels. This method will be discussed shortly.

TABLED VALUES OF z_{RD}. In order to determine which ability-achievement discrepancies are severe, the following procedure is recommended:

1. Identify the reliability coefficients for each ability-achievement subtest pair.
2. Determine which condition indicated in Table 8.3 is appropriate for each pair of coefficients.
3. For a given condition, determine whether the corresponding discrepancy score (z_D) is equal to or greater than the *first value* in the table; when this happens, it means that a discrepancy that large would occur only 5 times out of 100 or less as a result of errors of measurement alone. For example, a discrepancy of .932 under condition 2 would exceed the criterion of .825; therefore, it is reliable. The other two values listed for each condition are the larger discrepancies necessary to satisfy the *.01* and **.001** probability levels, as opposed to the .05 level defined previously. The meaning in each case is the same; only the chances of obtaining an unreliable discrepancy at the designated magnitudes decrease, from 5 times out of 100 to 1 time out of 1,000.
4. Identify the achievement areas where the discrepancy scores met the criterion for severe.

The guidelines proffered in Table 8.3 are applicable to any ability-achievement test combination with reliability coefficients of .85 or higher. Subtest scores should not be used for individual decisions if the coefficient is below .85. Inasmuch as ranges of coefficients are presented for each condition, the reliable discrepancy scores were estimated for the lower coefficient in each range. In other words, if the actual reliability coefficient(s) for one or both of the tests exceeds the lower limit, the corresponding reliable discrepancy score will be higher than it should be. In condition 1, for example, if the coefficients are .92 and .94 instead of .90, the score of .738 is higher than necessary to reach significance at the .05 level. Only a discrepancy of .617 would be required. For Monroe, the discrepancy of .66 between verbal ability (CogAT) and reading comprehension (ITBS) would not be reliable according to the Table 8.3 criterion but would be reliable had the criterion been computed on the basis of the .92 and .94 coefficients.

Table 8.4

Reliable Discrepancy Scores (z-scores[a]) between the CogAT-Verbal and Reading/Language Subtests of the ITBS[b] for Grades 3 - 8

| Grade Level/ (Test Level) | Vocabulary | Reading | Language Skills | | | | |
			Spelling	Capitalization	Punctuation	Usage	Total
3/(9)	.595	.595	.572	.680	.756	.680	.467
	.840	*.840*	*.807*	*.961*	*1.068*	*.961*	*.659*
	1.111	**1.111**	**1.067**	**1.270**	**1.411**	**1.270**	**.871**
4/(10)	.595	.639	.617	.719	.719	.700	.495
	.840	*.902*	*.872*	*1.016*	*1.016*	*.989*	*.699*
	1.111	**1.193**	**1.153**	**1.343**	**1.343**	**1.307**	**.924**
5/(11)	.595	.617	.617	.791	.756	.700	.522
	.840	*.872*	*.872*	*1.117*	*1.068*	*.989*	*.737*
	1.111	**1.153**	**1.153**	**1.477**	**1.411**	**1.307**	**.974**
6/(12)	.595	.617	.595	.774	.774	.700	.522
	.840	*.872*	*.840*	*1.093*	*1.093*	*.989*	*.737*
	1.111	**1.153**	**1.111**	**1.445**	**1.445**	**1.307**	**.974**
7/(13)	.639	.639	.595	.841	.738	.700	.522
	.902	*.902*	*.840*	*1.188*	*1.042*	*.989*	*.737*
	1.193	**1.193**	**1.111**	**1.571**	**1.377**	**1.307**	**.974**
8/(14)	.639	.639	.595	.808	.719	.738	.522
	.902	*.902*	*.840*	*1.142*	*1.016*	*1.042*	*.737*
	1.193	**1.193**	**1.111**	**1.509**	**1.343**	**1.377**	**.974**

ɔ = .05
p = .01
p = .001

[b]Based on K-R$_{20}$ reliability coefficients from the fall 1977 standardization

If the values in the table are judged to be too stringent in a particular application, where the reliability coefficients differ markedly from the lower limits, there are two options: (1) request the publisher to prepare a table of values for all of the ability-achievement subtest combinations being used or (2) compute the reliable discrepancy score in each specific case. An example of the former for CogAT-ITBS subtest combinations is shown in Table 8.4. This table displays reliable discrepancy scores between the CogAT Verbal battery and each ITBS reading and language subtest. In the case of Monroe, one just has to locate the particular subtest (Reading) and grade level (5) to identify the reliable discrepancy (.617). Monroe's discrepancy of .66 exceeds the tabled value, and, therefore, can be considered severe. Similar tables were also prepared for the CogAT Quantitative battery and ITBS mathematics subtests (Table 8.5), the CogAT Nonverbal battery and selected ITBS subtests (Table 8.6), and the CogAT batteries and Tests of Achievement and Proficiency (TAP) subtests for the upper grade levels (Table 8.7).

Table 8.5

Reliable Discrepancy Scores (*z*-scores[a]) between the CogAT-Quantitative
and Mathematics Subtests of the ITBS[b] for Grades 3 – 8

Grade Level/	Mathematics Skills			
(*Test Level*)	*Concepts*	*Problems*	*Computations*	*Total*
3/(9)	.774	.841	.738	.639
	1.093	*1.188*	*1.042*	*.902*
	1.445	**1.571**	**1.377**	**1.193**
4/(10)	.825	.808	.700	.639
	1.165	*1.142*	*.989*	*.902*
	1.540	**1.509**	**1.307**	**1.193**
5/(11)	.791	.808	.719	.617
	1.117	*1.142*	*1.016*	*.872*
	1.477	**1.509**	**1.343**	**1.152**
6/(12)	.791	.774	.756	.639
	1.117	*1.093*	*1.068*	*.902*
	1.477	**1.445**	**1.411**	**1.193**
7/(13)	.774	.774	.738	.617
	1.093	*1.093*	*1.042*	*.872*
	1.445	**1.445**	**1.377**	**1.152**
8/(14)	.719	.825	.738	.617
	1.016	*1.165*	*1.042*	*.872*
	1.343	**1.540**	**1.377**	**1.152**

p = .05
p = .01
p = .001
[b]Based on K-R$_{20}$ reliability coefficients from the fall 1977 standardization

Table 8.6

Reliable Discrepancy Scores (z-scores[a]) between the CogAT-Nonverbal
and Selected Subtests of the ITBS[a] for Grades 3 – 8

Grade Level/ (Test Level)	p	Language Skills							Mathematics Skills			
		Vocabulary	Reading	Spelling	Capitalization	Punctuation	Usage	Total	Concepts	Problems	Computation	Total
3/(9)	.05	.639	.639	.617	.719	.791	.719	.522	.738	.808	.700	.595
	.01	.902	.902	.872	1.016	1.117	1.016	.737	1.042	1.142	.989	.840
	.001	1.193	1.193	1.152	1.343	1.477	1.343	.974	1.377	1.509	1.307	1.111
4/(10)	.05	.639	.680	.660	.756	.756	.738	.547	.808	.791	.680	.617
	.01	.902	.961	.932	1.068	1.068	1.042	.773	1.142	1.117	.961	.872
	.001	1.193	1.270	1.232	1.411	1.411	1.377	1.022	1.509	1.477	1.270	1.152
5/(11)	.05	.617	.639	.639	.808	.774	.719	.547	.774	.791	.700	.595
	.01	.872	.902	.902	1.142	1.093	1.016	.773	1.093	1.117	.989	.840
	.001	1.152	1.193	1.193	1.509	1.445	1.343	1.022	1.445	1.477	1.307	1.111
6/(12)	.05	.617	.639	.617	.791	.791	.719	.547	.756	.738	.719	.595
	.01	.872	.902	.872	1.117	1.117	1.016	.773	1.068	1.042	1.016	.840
	.001	1.152	1.193	1.152	1.477	1.477	1.343	1.022	1.411	1.377	1.343	1.111
7/(13)	.05	.660	.660	.617	.857	.756	.719	.547	.756	.756	.719	.595
	.01	.932	.932	.872	1.211	1.068	1.016	.773	1.068	1.068	1.016	.840
	.001	1.232	1.232	1.152	1.600	1.411	1.343	1.022	1.411	1.411	1.343	1.111
8/(14)	.05	.660	.660	.617	.825	.738	.756	.547	.700	.808	.719	.595
	.01	.932	.932	.872	1.165	1.042	1.068	.773	.989	1.142	1.016	.840
	.001	1.232	1.232	1.152	1.540	1.377	1.411	1.022	1.307	1.509	1.343	1.111

p = .05
p = .01
p = .001

[a]Based on K-R$_{20}$ reliability coefficients from the fall 1977 standardization.

Table 8.7

Reliable Discrepancy Scores (z-scores[a]) between the CogAT and Selected
Subtests of the TAP[b] for Grades 9 – 12

Grade Level/ (Test Level)	Verbal-TAP		Quantitative-TAP	Nonverbal-TAP		
	Reading Comprehension	Written Expression	Mathematics	Reading Comprehension	Mathematics	Written Expression
9/(15)	.572	.660	.680	.617	.680	.700
	.807	.932	.961	.872	.961	.989
	1.067	1.232	1.270	1.152	1.270	1.307
10/(16)	.572	.680	.680	.617	.680	.719
	.807	.961	.961	.872	.961	1.016
	1.067	1.270	1.270	1.152	1.270	1.343
11/(17)	.595	.639	.680	.639	.680	.680
	.840	.902	.961	.902	.961	.961
	1.111	1.193	1.270	1.193	1.270	1.270
12/(18)	.547	.617	.660	.639	.680	.700
	.773	.872	.932	.902	.961	.989
	1.022	1.152	1.232	1.193	1.270	1.307

[a] $p = .05$
  $p = .01$
  $p = .001$
[b] Based on K-R$_{20}$ reliability coefficients from the fall 1977 standardization

COMPUTATIONAL FORMULA. Other than referring to Table 8.3 or to Tables 8.4 and 8.5, the test user must resort to computing the reliable discrepancy scores. The formula is based on the reliability coefficient of each test and the z-score corresponding to the desired significance level. It is expressed as

$$z_{RD} = z\sqrt{2 - r_{AB} - r_{AC}} \tag{8.2}$$

where:

z_{RD} = a reliable ability-achievement test discrepancy in z-score form
Z = the z-score corresponding to the significance level for a one-tailed test of the learning disability hypothesis:
  H$_1$: The achievement test score of an individual will be significantly lower than his or her ability test score
  z-scores for three significance levels are 1.65 ($p = .05$), 2.33 ($p = .01$), and 3.08 ($p = .001$)
r_{AB} = reliability coefficient for the ability test
r_{AC} = reliability coefficient for the achievement test

The expression under the radical is known as the standard error of measurement of a discrepancy (or difference score). The decision of which significance level is most appropriate (.05, .01, or .001) is contingent upon how stringent a criterion one wishes to adopt for a severe discrepancy. It is advisable to start with the .05 level (substitute 1.65 into formula 8.2) before a decision validity study is conducted. Adjustments in the criterion can be considered later.

Example: Using the reliability coefficients of the CogAT Verbal battery (.92) and ITBS Reading subtest (.94) and the *z*-value of 1.65, one can determine whether Monroe's z_D of .66 is severe. These quantities are substituted into formula 8.2 as follows:

$$z_{RD} = 1.65\sqrt{2 - .92 - .94}$$
$$= 1.65\,(.374)$$
$$= .617$$

Clearly Monroe's discrepancy of .66 exceeds this criterion score of .617; therefore, Monroe has a severe ability-achievement discrepancy in the area of reading comprehension.

Although this example demonstrates the ease with which a teacher or psychologist can compute a reliable discrepancy score for one student, it makes little sense to proceed in this manner even with the aid of a hand calculator. In order to screen large numbers of students at a given grade level, formula 8.2 should be used to develop tables such as those presented previously. This task can be completed quickly with the assistance of a microcomputer.

Determine Whether Children with a Severe Discrepancy Are Learning Disabled

None of the procedures described up to this point has dealt with the label *learning disabled*. The children identified as having at least one severe discrepancy are not necessarily learning disabled. The criterion score used operationally to define severe must be validated with a group of children known to be learning disabled and another group of children who do not possess learning disabilities. That is, the procedure employed to estimate reliable discrepancy scores must now be subjected to the scrutiny of a decision validity study. Only then can one ascertain whether the children who exhibit severe discrepancies should be labeled as learning disabled. The decision validity evidence furnishes the justification for subsequent individualized diagnostic testing and decisions regarding the appropriate instructional treatment.

Since Chapter 5 delineates the complete framework for planning and executing a decision validity study, only a brief review of the major steps is outlined here. The steps are listed as follows:

1. Specify criteria for selecting "definite" learning-disabled and non-learning-disabled samples.
2. Select the samples in accordance with local estimates of the base rate.
3. Gather the ability and achievement test data for these samples.
4. Compute individual discrepancy scores for each test pair.

5. Count the number of children in the LD sample who had severe discrepancies.
6. Count the number of children in the normal sample who did *not* have severe discrepancies.
7. Count the number remaining in each sample.
8. Compute the probabilities of correct and incorrect decisions based on the results of steps 4 through 7.
9. Determine the incremental validity of the procedure in relation to the no-screening condition.
10. Compute the sensitivity of the procedure for the actual learning-disabled cases.
11. Compute the specificity of the procedure for the actual normal cases.
12. Evaluate the decision validity evidence from steps 8 through 11.

ADJUSTING THE CRITERION FOR SEVERE. Depending on the outcome of step 12, the criterion score for a severe discrepancy may need to be adjusted. This action is usually required when the false negative error rate is too high and the sensitivity index is too low. By adopting the reliable discrepancy score screening procedure advocated in the preceding section, it may also be necessary to adjust the criterion in order to avoid the overidentification of high ability students and underidentification of low ability students due to regression effect bias (see Chapter 4). The following guidelines are suggested:

1. If the criterion score for severe corresponds to the .05 level of significance (where $Z = 1.65$ in formula 8.2), the criterion cannot be adjusted to minimize false negative errors further, to maximize sensitivity further, or to minimize the underidentification of low ability students further (e.g., percentile rank below 50 on ability test); a smaller criterion would be unreliable (a chance level discrepancy).
2. If a more stringent criterion score for severe were used (e.g., .01, .001), then the criterion should be adjusted toward the .05 level to minimize false negative errors, to maximize sensitivity, and to minimize the underidentification of low ability students.
3. To minimize the overidentification of high ability students (e.g., percentile rank of 75 or above on ability test), the criterion score for severe should be adjusted so that it is more stringent for those students.
4. The actual degree of criterion score adjustment considered for these conditions should be determined by the corresponding effect on the classification probabilities in the decision validity study; the different trade-offs as they are reflected in the statistical indices will vary with each application.

Incorporate Discrepancy Information into Multidisciplinary Team Decisions

Among the numerous and diverse pieces of information used by the school-based multidisciplinary team for screening and placement decisions, the ability-achievement discrepancy should be considered foremost. This is exactly what the *Procedures for Evaluating Specific Learning Disabilities* (U.S.O.E., 1977b) stipulate as the basis for determining the existence of a specific learning disability:

> A team may determine that a child has a specific learning disability if:
>
> (1) The child does not achieve commensurate with his or her age and ability levels in one or more of the [seven subject] areas...when provided with learning experiences appropriate for the child's age and ability levels; and
>
> (2) The team finds that a child has a severe discrepancy between achievement and intellectual ability in one or more of the [seven] areas. (p. 65083)

Unfortunately, discrepancy scores are not given the priority that this second statement specifies, according to recent studies of team decision-making practices (Richey & Graden, 1980; Ysseldyke, Algozzine, Richey, & Graden, 1982). In fact, statements by team members which define a discrepancy are rather crude. Ysseldyke et al. (1982) provided a few examples:

> His IQ scores are average (i.e., 104), but he is two years behind in reading.
>
> She is functioning like an 8-year-old in reading, but she is actually 12 years of age.
>
> SRA scores were 1-3 years below expected grade level. (p.40)

Once the link between reliable discrepancy scores and learning disabilities has been established by means of a decision validity study, confidence can be placed in those scores for screening decisions. Of course, the degree of confidence will be tempered by the degree of accuracy in the classifications; however, the strategy for defining a severe ability-achievement discrepancy recommended in the preceding pages is far more sophisticated and defensible than the methods suggested by the previous statements and the alternatives evaluated in Chapter 4.

Summary

Some of the key steps in screening for learning disabilities are summarized in Table 8.8. These steps are viewed from the perspective of the classroom teacher who is frequently the primary referral source as well as a multidisciplinary team member, the learning disability specialist, or the school psychologist involved in LD identification. Although the example accompanying the procedure is for only one test battery combination and one child, the procedure may be applied to any battery combination and to any number of children. If the first three steps related to test selection have already been completed at the district level, only five steps remain in order to identify the area(s) of severe discrepancy.

MEMORY JOGGER
Table 8.8
Summary of Some of the Key Steps in Screening for Learning Disabilities

Procedure	Example
1. Select ability-achievement test batteries that have been normed on the same standardization sample	CogAT-ITBS
2. Select ability tests that are structured according to different types of ability	CogAT (Verbal, Quantitative, Nonverbal)
3. Select achievement tests that cover as many of the 7 areas of potential achievement deficit as possible	ITBS (covers 5 areas)
4. Match the verbal ability test with the verbally-based achievement subtests	Vocabulary, Reading, Spelling, Capitalization, Punctuation, Usage
5. Match the quantitative ability test with the mathematics achievement subtests	Concepts, Problems, Computations

6. Locate national grade-based percentile rank for each student on each test report

Scores for Melissa (grade 6):

Verbal = 62	Vocabulary = 41
Quantitative = 45	Reading = 32
Nonverbal = 51	Spelling = 37
	Capitalization = 26
	Punctuation = 21
	Usage = 30
	Concepts = 23
	Problems = 20
	Computations = 31

7. Convert each percentile rank to a z-score

Verbal = .31	Vocabulary = −.23
Quantitative = −.13	Reading = −.47
Nonverbal = .03	Spelling = .33
	Capitalization = −.64
	Punctuation = −.81
	Usage = −.52
	Concepts = −.74
	Problems = −.84
	Computations = −.50

8. Compute an ability-achievement discrepancy score for each appropriate test combination

Verbal-Vocabulary = .54	Quantitative-Concepts = .61
Verbal-Reading = .78	Quantitative-Problems = .71
Verbal-Spelling = .64	Quantitative-Computations = .37
Verbal-Capitalization = .95	
Verbal-Punctuation = 1.12	
Verbal-Usage = .83	

9. Determine which discrepancies are "severe" using Table 8.3 or other appropriate tables (e.g., Tables 8.4 and 8.5)

Severe discrepancies:
 Reading
 Spelling
 Capitalization
 Punctuation (very severe)
 Usage
Areas for remediation:
 Reading comprehension
 Language skills

Diagnosis

Once the screening procedure has identified the specific subject area(s) in which a child exhibits skill deficiencies, criterion-referenced tests should be used to pinpoint the skill-development weaknesses. Criterion-referenced testing constitutes the second stage in the assessment process. Only when this level of testing occurs can an instructional intervention be planned that is appropriate to each child's needs. The objectives-based framework for constructing the tests and the objectives-referenced, ipsative interpretation of the scores provide the essential ingredients for composing an individualized education program (IEP). As the Rules and Regulations for implementing P.L. 94-142 (U.S.O.E., 1977a) state,

> the individualized education program for each child must include:
> (a) A statement of the child's present levels of educational performance;
> (b) A statement of annual goals, including short term instructional objectives;
> (c) A statement of the specific special education and related services to be provided to the child, and the extent to which the child will be able to participate in regular educational programs;
> (d) The projected dates for initiation of services and the anticipated duration of the services; and
> (e) Appropriate objective criteria and evaluation procedures and schedules for determining on at least an annual basis, whether the short term instructional objectives are being achieved. (p. 42491)

The profile of mastery-nonmastery performance by objective can supply precise answers to (a), (b), and (e). Furthermore, it should guide the development of individual prescriptions and the statement of services required for (c) and (d).

In addition to the diagnostic and prescriptive value of criterion-referenced test data, the mastery-nonmastery results can also be used to check on the accuracy of the screening decision. For Monroe, who was initially labeled as learning disabled in the area of reading comprehension, the diagnostic testing in that area should confirm or disconfirm the LD classification. If Monroe's performance on the criterion-referenced test indicates that several reading comprehension objectives have not been mastered, that nonmastery performance serves as corroborative evidence of the true negative screening decision. On the other hand, if mastery of all of the objectives was demonstrated (convincingly), that level of performance should be interpreted as evidence of a false positive screening error, and corrective action should be taken. The verification of true positive and false negative screening decisions, however, is not possible with the test results. This limitation of the data was addressed in the screening process by adjusting the criterion for a severe discrepancy so as to minimize false negative errors.

Five of the chapters in this volume emphasized the importance of diagnostic testing with psychometrically defensible criterion-referenced tests for the preceding purposes. The procedures for implementing this type of testing program at the classroom level are summarized in this section under five major steps:

1. Select commercially developed criterion-referenced tests.
2. Construct criterion-referenced tests in content areas where they are needed.

3. Administer the tests to those children with severe ability-achievement discrepancies.
4. Score the tests.
5. Pinpoint skill-development weaknesses.

Select Commercially-Developed Criterion-referenced Tests

Based on the recommendations given in Chapter 2, the following procedure is suggested for selecting criterion-referenced tests available from commercial test publishers:

1. Evaluate the quality of the criterion-referenced testing systems or diagnostic-prescriptive packages currently being used in the school.
   a. Use Table 2.11 as a starting point.
   b. Evaluate the curricular validity of the tests.
   c. Analyze any reported evidence related to sex, racial, and ethnic bias.
   d. Conduct a judgmental review of the items for possible bias using the form in Table 2.10.
   e. Determine whether the appropriate level tests are being administered to the children who have or are suspected of having learning disabilities.
   f. Identify the areas of possible severe discrepancy that are not measured by the tests.
2. Consider adding or substituting technically adequate tests, where available, in the areas needed to fill in gaps in the coverage; most testing systems measure reading and mathematics skills and a few include language skills.

Construct Criterion-referenced Tests in Content Areas Where They Are Needed

If the preceding evaluation yields negative findings, the teacher must assume the role of test maker in order to obtain usable diagnostic tests. Although guidelines for building criterion-referenced tests are presented in Chapters 2, 3, 6, and 7, and in the numerous resources cited therein, a summary of the key steps involved seems appropriate in this section. The steps are as follows:

1. State instructional and behavioral objectives to define as precisely as possible the content area being measured.
2. Determine the number of items to be written for each objective (for details, see Berk, 1980b).
3. Develop a table of specifications to analyze the distribution of items against the taxonomic categories of the objectives.
4. Write the test items using the formats (selection and supply) that will best measure the objectives.

5. Review the items for their match with the objectives (item-objective congruence) and possible bias against girls and minority children especially (use Table 2.10).
6. Field test the items with criterion groups of masters and nonmasters to determine whether they are functioning properly (see Chapter 6 and Berk, 1980a).
   a. Compute difficulty and discrimination indices.
   b. Analyze the choice responses to multiple-choice items in order to detect internal flaws.
   c. Select the items that satisfy all judgmental and statistical criteria.
   d. Revise or replace those items that did not satisfy the criteria.
7. Set an appropriate cutting score (mastery standard) for each objective based on the field test results (see Chapter 6).
8. Determine the decision validity of the test (see Chapter 6).
9. Determine the decision reliability of the test based on the chosen cutting scores (see Chapter 7).

In addition to the specialized references given for the more technical steps, teachers should consult a basic measurement text such as Gronlund (1981, 1982) or Mehrens and Lehmann (1978) for general achievement test construction rules related to steps 1, 3, and 4.

After the test(s) has been developed, its technical quality must be evaluated in terms of the intended uses of the scores. In particular, the probability of true nonmastery decisions and the specificity index computed at step 8 and the p index computed at step 9 should be examined. This examination should reveal the degree to which each subtest can accurately and consistently identify nonmasters of the respective instructional objective. The diagnostic utility of the test for children screened as learning disabled is contingent on the outcome of the examination.

Administer the Tests to Those Children with Severe Ability-Achievement Discrepancies

Once criterion-referenced tests are available for the different content areas and grade levels, they should be administered according to the individual screening profiles. The testing should match the areas of severe ability-achievement discrepancy. Depending on the number of children labeled as LD and the achievement deficit areas identified in each case, the criterion-referenced tests can be administered individually or in a group setting by the classroom teacher. Alternatively, the learning disability specialist can administer the tests in either mode. Clearly, the responsibility for the test administrations and the schedule and method for conducting them must be decided in each school. Efficiency in executing the testing program is crucial, however, if the children are to receive the special services to which they are entitled as soon as possible.

Score the Tests

The scores on a criterion-referenced test can be tabulated manually or by computer. The commercially-developed tests usually require machine scoring in order to obtain a variety of test report formats. Regardless of how the test is scored, the individual or group report must furnish two levels of score information: subtest and item. Subtest raw scores supply the metric for inferring mastery or nonmastery performance on each instructional objective; item scores indicate the degree of mastery or nonmastery in terms of explicit behavioral objectives. Both types of scores are necessary in order to devise a diagnostic profile of the objectives that were not mastered and the specific skill deficiencies that contributed to that nonmastery (for details, see Chapter 3).

Pinpoint Skill-Development Weaknesses

An ipsative analysis of a child's diagnostic test score profile should indicate the skill-development weaknesses in each content area. These weaknesses should suggest the nature and duration of special services that are needed. Such services, which must be designated in the IEP, often take the form of remedial or ameliorative programs in the regular classroom setting with provisions for part-time special classes or resource room help (Poland & Mitchell, 1980).

Role of the Multidisciplinary Team

At the conclusion of the preceding section on screening, it was noted that the major legal responsibility of the multidisciplinary team was to determine whether a child has a specific learning disability based on a severe ability-achievement discrepancy in one or more of seven subject areas. Additionally, however, there are two other charges: (1) observing a child's academic performance in the regular classroom setting and (2) preparing a written report of the results of the evaluation (U.S.O.E., 1977b). Perhaps the best way to capsulize the mandated activities of the team is to list the specifications for the written report. The report must include statements dealing with the following:

(1) Whether the child has a specific learning disability;
(2) The basis for making the determination;
(3) The relevant behavior noted during the observation of the child;
(4) The relationship of that behavior to the child's academic functioning;
(5) The educationally relevant medical findings, if any;
(6) Whether there is a severe discrepancy between achievement and ability which is not correctable without special education and related services; and
(7) The determination of the team concerning the effects of environmental, cultural, or economic disadvantage. (p. 65083)

Despite these regulations on the proper operation of the team, there is an impressive corpus of research evidence now existing that seriously questions the effectiveness of the entire team decision-making process. Since the contribution of this book in improving the methods for identifying learning-disabled children depends ultimately on the effectiveness of the multidisciplinary team members who must use the test data and discrepancy scores for classification decisions, a review of the evidence related to team functioning appears essential at this point. Four pertinent topics are examined: (1) name of the team, (2) composition and participation, (3) use of assessment data, and (4) team effectiveness.

Name of the Team

The school-based multidisciplinary team has different names in different states (Pfeiffer, 1981a). It has been called the placement committee, the evaluation and placement committee, the planning and placement team, the assessment team, the school appraisal team, child study team, and the admission, review, and dismissal committee. The variety of names assigned to the team is not associated with differential functions. For the most part, individual assessment, classification, and placement are common team activities.

Composition and Participation

Although the Rules and Regulations (U.S.O.E., 1977b) state that the team must include the child's regular classroom teacher and at least one person qualified to conduct individual diagnostic examinations, such as a school psychologist or remedial reading teacher, the composition of any given team may also include a parent, learning disability specialist, principal, or other individuals from more than 30 different professional categories (Poland, Thurlow, Ysseldyke, & Mirkin, 1982; Thurlow & Ysseldyke, 1979; Yoshida, Fenton, Maxwell, & Kaufman, 1977, 1978a). Typically, the team consists of from five to 10 persons who are usually teachers (regular or special), school psychologists, and school administrators (Thurlow, 1980).

The diversity in team composition does not necessarily reflect the actual participation of the members. Although the regular classroom teacher is an important source of assessment and observational information on a child's performance and even though the teacher is the professional most responsible for implementing the placement decision, the teacher rarely participates in team deliberations. If he or she does participate, it is in a very superficial manner (Allen, 1980; Gilliam, 1979; Semmel, Yoshida, Fenton & Kaufman, 1978; Yoshida et al., 1977, 1978a, 1978b; Ysseldyke, Algozzine, & Allen, 1982). The unique information that the teacher possesses and his or her recommendations for placement are seldom presented or even requested. Yoshida et al. (1977) stressed that "regular education teachers, who are pivotal persons in operationalizing and implementing the PT [placement team] decisions, are low in participation and are generally not satisfied with the PT process" (p. 13). This minimal involvement also characterizes the role of parents in team decision making (Mitchell, 1980; Patton, 1976). By virtue of this disenfranchisement of teachers and parents from the process, the active participants are the school psychologists and administrators, although their roles as team members are not delineated, according to the various studies.

Use of Assessment Data

Among nine different types of assessment data collected for use in team decision making, a survey of 39 Child Service Demonstration Centers by Thurlow and Ysseldyke (1979) revealed that standardized, norm-referenced tests, past records, and observation were used most frequently for screening and placement decisions. Criterion-referenced tests and informal measures were employed most often for the purpose of instructional programming.

Given this emphasis on formal instruments, an analysis of the specific tests being used was also conducted by Poland et al. (1982), Thurlow and Ysseldyke (1979), and Ysseldyke et al. (1981). More than 30 different published tests and a variety of informal/center-developed devices were used by three or more centers. The four most popular tests were the Key Math Diagnostic Arithmetic Test, Peabody Individual Achievement Tests, WISC-R, and Wide Range Achievement Test. Interestingly, the evaluation of these tests reported in Chapter 2 indicates only the individually-administered PIAT and WISC-R satisfy the criteria for technical adequacy. Indeed, very few of the most frequently used tests are technically adequate.

Extending this data base even further, Richey and Graden (1980) investigated the relationship between the nature of the data presented at the team meeting and the placement decision. They found no relationship between statements supportive of ability-achievement discrepancies, WISC-R Verbal-Performance discrepancies, or federal definition criteria and the placement team decision. In other words, despite the considerable amount and types of assessment data discussed by team members (Shinn, 1980; Ysseldyke, Algozzine, Rostollan, & Shinn, 1981), those data have little or no influence on the actual decisions made by the multidisciplinary team. Ysseldyke et al. (1982) commented that "it looks as if decision makers used assessment data to support or justify decisions that are made independent of the data" (p. 42).

This disconcerting evidence is consistent with earlier observations about the team's unsystematic approach to gathering and analyzing the information (Goldbaum & Rucker, 1977; Morrow, Powell, & Ely, 1976). In addition, Ysseldyke and Algozzine (1981) demonstrated that classification decisions are more a function of naturally occurring pupil characteristics (e.g., sex, socioeconomic status, physical appearance) than of pupil performance data. All of these research findings point to one conclusion: *The abundance of test information available for screening and placement decisions is not being used by the multidisciplinary team.*

Team Effectiveness

The evidence that has accumulated on the effectiveness of team decision making is relatively sparse. Pfeiffer's (1981b) review of studies illustrating the difficulties that teams face indicated two problem areas adversely affecting team functioning: (1) the team's use of a loosely construed decision making-planning process (Horvath, 1978; Vautour, 1976; Yoshida et al., 1978a) and (2) the lack of interdisciplinary collaboration and trust (Fenton, Yoshida, Maxwell, & Kaufman, 1977; Hyman et al., 1973). In an extensive investigation of team effectiveness, Mitchell (1980; Ysseldyke, Algozzine, & Mitchell, 1982) found the following characteristics:

1. The purpose of the team meeting was stated about a third of the time; more often, meetings began with a statement such as "As you are all aware, Jason was referred for evaluation because of the difficulties he is having in . . ."
2. More time was spent describing a child's needs than generating alternative solutions to the problem (cf. Applied Management Sciences, 1979)
3. The roles of team members were never clearly defined, and never was a statement made encouraging participation by individuals
4. Parental input was requested occasionally during meetings, usually simply in verification of an observed problem
5. Least restrictive environment was never explicitly stated, nor was the concept employed in reaching a placement decision; the teams presented data, and then someone on the team recommended a placement (the efficacy of which was seldom discussed)
6. Decisions were made in a majority of the meetings, yet it was not possible to identify who made the decision or the specific nature of it; team members did not challenge the decisions. (pp. 30–32)

As if these impediments to effective team operation are not discouraging enough, Pfeiffer's (1981a) recent study of team members' perceptions led to the conclusion that "part of the problem is the antiquated and step-wise (linear) referral-evaluation system that is inefficient, cost-ineffective, and time consuming" (p. 332).

What these few investigations suggest is that the lack of structure (and a specific agenda) in the team decision-making process renders a team's effectiveness indeterminable at this time. Irrespective of who is on the team or what data are presented, there is no available evidence that any "team" decision about a child is correct and best for him or her.

Recommendations

This negative appraisal of the state of current multidisciplinary team practices should serve to stimulate a redirection of team activities. A school-based team can play a significant role in the screening and placement of learning-disabled children. Pfeiffer (1981b) contended that the team has the potential of providing the following benefits: (a) accurate assessment, classification, and placement decisions, (b) a forum for sharing differing values and perspectives,

(c) a source of specialized consultative services to school personnel, parents, and community agencies, and (d) resources for developing innovative programs and/or evaluating existing ones. In order to realize these benefits, however, much work lies ahead.

Several ideas are proffered here to initiate the redirection:

1. Develop a structure for the team meeting, including a definition of each member's role and an agenda specifying what is to be covered and the time allotment for each item.
2. Encourage regular classroom teachers, learning disability specialists, and parents to participate and to feel that they can make meaningful contributions to the process and to the decisions.
3. Select standardized, norm-referenced tests or extract data from tests that are technically adequate.
4. Use the test data, ability-achievement discrepancy scores, and other assessment information to guide screening and placement decisions; the data should not simply be discussed and then ignored in the actual decision making.
5. Base team decisions on the information presented; the decisions should be defensible in terms of that information as well.
6. Follow up the placement decisions to determine whether they are correct and in the best interests of the children.
7. If special team meetings are to be convened for the expressed purpose of designing IEPs, delay the preparation of instructional prescriptions until comprehensive diagnostic testing in the area(s) of severe discrepancy has been completed; use the profile of mastery-nonmastery performance by objective on criterion-referenced tests to guide the details of the plan.

Epilogue

This chapter summarizes the procedures recommended throughout the book for screening and diagnosis of children with learning disabilities. A two-stage assessment process is outlined. The first stage involves the use of standardized ability and achievement test batteries to determine severe individual discrepancies in performance. It is urged that the criterion for severe be validated with groups of learning-disabled and non-learning disabled children. The discrepancy information provides the foundation for the screening decisions. The second stage of assessment consists of diagnostic testing with criterion-referenced tests to pinpoint the specific skill-development weaknesses in the area(s) of severe discrepancy. The results of this testing can be employed to develop individualized education programs (IEPs) and to verify the accuracy of the screening decisions.

Finally, the role of the school-based multidisciplinary team is scrutinized.

The survey evidence on the team decision-making process that has accumulated indicates that team meetings are unstructured, some of the most important team members rarely participate in the decision making, assessment data are not used to arrive at screening and placement decisions, and it is not known whether any team decisions are accurate and best for the children. Despite these weaknesses, it is argued that the team can play a significant role in the screening and placement of learning-disabled children. However, a redirection of activities is essential before the potential benefits of the team process can be realized. Several recommendations are given to initiate this redirection.

It should be evident in this chapter that a deliberate effort has been made to devise screening and diagnostic procedures that not only are psychometrically and conceptually sound within the current state of testing technology but also satisfy all of the legal requirements of P.L. 94-142 and the subsequent rules and regulations for its implementation. Although some experts on learning disabilities have disputed the meaning and viability of many of those requirements, their arguments tend to arise from philosophical differences rather than from empirical evidence. By implementing scientifically defensible methods, such as those described in the preceding pages, the practitioners can actually test the law. Therefore, the effectiveness of the specific screening and diagnostic procedures could eventually determine the meaningfulness of the law. If the procedures are found to be ineffective, that may be perceived as evidence that the law does not work. The opposite result, however, seems to have a higher probability of occurring. Certainly, the procedures deserve serious consideration by both proponents and opponents of the law so that, at least, the accuracy of this prediction can be determined for the children's sake.

References

Allen, D. Participation of regular education teachers in special education team decision making. In J. E. Ysseldyke, B. Algozzine, & M. L. Thurlow (Eds.), *A naturalistic investigation of special education team meetings* (Research Report No. 40). Minneapolis: University of Minnesota Institute for Research on Learning Disabilities, August 1980. pp. 54-62.

Applied Management Sciences. *Study for determining the least restrictive environment (LRE) placement for handicapped children* (Final Report). Washington, DC: Bureau of Education for the Handicapped, U.S. Office of Education, November 1979.

Berk, R. A. Item analysis. In R. A. Berk (Ed.), *Criterion-referenced measurement: The state of the art.* Baltimore, MD: Johns Hopkins University Press, 1980. pp. 49-79.(a)

Berk, R. A. Practical guidelines for determining the length of objectives-based, criterion-referenced tests. *Educational Technology,* 1980, *20,* 36-41.(b)

Fenton, K. S., Yoshida, R. K., Maxwell, J. P., & Kaufman, M. J. *Role expectations: Implications for multidisciplinary pupil programming.* Washington, DC: Bureau of Education for the Handicapped, U.S. Office of Education, 1977.

Gilliam, J. E. Contributions and status rankings of educational planning committee participants. *Exceptional Children,* 1979, *45,* 466-468.

Goldbaum, J., & Rucker, C. N. Assessment data and the child study team. In J. A. C.

Vautour & C. N. Rucker (Eds.), *Child study team training program: Book of readings*. Austin, TX: Special Education Associates, 1977.

Gronlund, N. E. *Measurement and evaluation in teaching* (4th) ed.). New York: Macmillan, 1981.

Gronlund, N. E. *Constructing achievement tests* (3rd ed.). Englewood Cliffs, NJ: Prentice-Hall, 1982.

Hanna, G. S., Dyck, N. J., & Holen, M. C. Objective analysis of achievement-aptitude discrepancies in LD classification. *Learning Disability Quarterly*, 1979, *2*, 32-38.

Hieronymous, A. N., Lindquist, E. F., & Hoover, H. D. *Iowa Tests of Basic Skills manual for school administrators* (Forms 7 and 7/8). Chicago: Riverside, 1982.

Horvath, L. J. *The effects of parental requests on the selection of educational placements by child study team members*. Unpublished doctoral dissertation, University of Connecticut, 1978.

Hyman, I., Duffey, J., Carroll, R., Manni, J., & Winikur, D., Patterns of inter-professional conflict resolution on school child study teams. *Journal of School Psychology*, 1973, *11*, 187-195.

Kaufman, A. S., & Kaufman, N. L. *The Kaufman Assessment Battery for Children*. Circle Pines, MN: American Guidance Service, 1982.

Mead, N. A. Listening and speaking skills. In R. A. Berk (Ed.), *Performance assessment: Methods and applications*. Baltimore, MD: Johns Hopkins University Press, in press.

Mehrens, W. A., & Lehmann, I. J. *Measurement and evaluation in education and psychology* (2nd ed.). New York: Holt, Rinehart and Winston, 1978.

Mitchell, J. The special education team process: To what extent is it effective? In J. E. Ysseldyke, B. Algozzine, & M. L. Thurlow (Eds.), *A naturalistic investigation of special education team meetings* (Research report No. 40). Minneapolis: University of Minnesota Institute for Research on Learning Disabilities, August 1980. pp. 18-34.

Morrow, H. W., Powell, G. D., & Ely, D. D. Placement or placebo: Does additional information change special education placement decisions? *Journal of School Psychology*, 1976, *14*, 186-191.

Patton, C. V. Selecting special students: Who decides? *Teacher's College Record*, 1976, *78*, 101-124.

Pfeiffer, S. I. The problems facing multidisciplinary teams as perceived by team members. *Psychology in the Schools*, 1981, *18*, 330-333.(a)

Pfeiffer, S. I. The school-based interprofessional team: Recurring problems and some possible solutions. *Journal of School Psychology*, 1981, *18*, 388-394.(b)

Poland, S., & Mitchell, J. Generation of intervention statements by decision-making teams in school settings. In J. E. Ysseldyke, B. Algozzine, & M. L. Thurlow (Eds.), *A naturalistic investigation of special education team meetings* (Research Report No. 40). Minneapolis: University of Minnesota Institute for Research on Learning Disabilities, August 1980. pp. 63-73.

Poland, S., Thurlow, M. L., Ysseldyke, J. E., & Mirkin, P. Current psychoeducational assessment and decision-making practices as reported by directors of special education. *Journal of School Psychology*, 1982, *20*, 171-179.

Richey, L., & Graden, J. The special education team process: To what extent is it data based? In J. E. Ysseldyke, B. Algozzine, & M. L. Thurlow (Eds.), *A naturalistic investigation of special education team meetings* (Research Report No. 40). Minneapolis: University of Minnesota Institute for Research on Learning Disabilities, August 1980. pp. 48-53.

Semmel, D. S., Yoshida, R. K., Fenton, K. S., & Kaufman, M. J. *The contribution of professional role to group decision-making in a simulated pupil-planning team setting*. Washington, DC: Bureau of Education for the Handicapped, U.S. Office of Education, 1978.

Shinn, M.R. Domains of assessment data discussed during placement team decision making. In J.E. Ysseldyke, B. Algozzine, & M. L. Thurlow (Eds.), *A naturalistic investigation of spe-*

cial education team meetings (Research Report No. 40). Minneapolis: University of Minnesota Institute for Research on Learning Disabilities, August 1980. pp. 44-47.

Thurlow, M. L. What is a typical team meeting? In J. E. Ysseldyke, B. Algozzine, & M. L. Thurlow (Eds.), *A naturalistic investigation of special education team meetings* (Research Report No. 40). Minneapolis: University of Minnesota Institute for Research on Learning Disabilities, August 1980. pp. 9-14.

Thurlow, M. L., & Ysseldyke, J. E. Current assessment and decision-making practices in model LD programs. *Learning Disability Quarterly*, 1979, *2*, 15-24.

U.S. Office of Education. Education of handicapped children: Implementation of Part B of the Education of the Handicapped Act. *Federal Register*, 1977, *42*(163), 42474-42518.(a)

U.S. Office of Education. Assistance to states for education for handicapped children: Procedures for evaluating specific learning disabilities. *Federal Register*, 1977, *42*(250), 62082-62085.(b)

Vautour, J. A. C. *A study of placement decisions for exceptional children determined by child study teams and individuals.* Unpubilshed doctoral dissertation, University of Connecticut, 1975.

Yoshida, R. K., Fenton, K. S., Maxwell, J. P., & Kaufman, M. J. *Group decision making in the planning team process: Myth or reality.* Washington, DC: Bureau of Education for the Handicapped, U.S. Office of Education, 1977.

Yoshida, R. K., Fenton, K. S., Maxwell, J. P., & Kaufman, M. J. Group decision making in the planning team process: Myth or reality? *Journal of School Psychology*, 1978, *16*, 237-244.(a)

Yoshida, R. K., Fenton, K. S., Maxwell, J. P., & Kaufman, M. J. Ripple effect: Communication of planning team decisions to program implementers. *Journal of School Psychology*, 1978, *16*, 177-183.(b)

Ysseldyke, J. E., & Algozzine, B. Diagnostic classification decisions as a function of referral information. *Journal of Special Education*, 1981, *15*, 429-435.

Ysseldyke, J. E., Algozzine, B., & Allen, D. Participation of regular education teachers in special education team decision making. *Exceptional Children*, 1982, *49*, 365-366.

Ysseldyke, J. E., Algozzine, B., & Mitchell, J. Special education team decision making: An analysis of current practice. *Personnel and Guidance Journal*, 1982, *60*, 308-313.

Ysseldyke, J. E., Algozzine, B., Richey, L., & Graden, J. Declaring students eligible for learning disability services: Why bother with the data? *Learning Disability Quarterly*, 1982, *5*, 37-44.

Ysseldyke, J. E., Algozzine, B., Rostollan, D., & Shinn, M.R. A content analysis of the data presented at sspecial education placement team meetings. *Journal of Clinical Psychology*, 1981, *37*, 655-662.

Ysseldyke, J. E., Mirkin, P., Thurlow, M. L., Poland, S., & Allen, D. Current assessment and decision-making practicess. In W. M. Cruickshandk & A. A. Silver (Eds.), *Bridges to tomorrow* (Vol. 2): *The best of ACLD*. Syracuse, NY: Syracuse University Press, 1981. pp. 95-110.

APPENDIX A

Tests and Test Publishers[*]

Test	Publisher
Bender Visual Motor Gestalt Test	WPS
Brigance Inventory of Basic Skills	Curriculum Assoc.
California Achievement Tests	CTB/McGraw-Hill
Carrow Elicited Language Inventory	Learning Concepts
CIRCUS	Addison-Wesley
Cognitive Abilities Test	Riverside
Comprehensive Tests of Basic Skills	CTB/McGraw-Hill
Culture Fair Intelligence Tests	WPS Testing
Detroit Tests of Learning Aptitude	Pro•Ed
Developmental Test of Visual-Motor Integration (Beery)	Follett
Developmental Test of Visual Perception (Frostig)	Consulting Psychologists Press
Diagnosis: An Instructional Aid— Mathematics and Reading	Science Research Assoc.
Diagnostic Mathematics Inventory	CTB/McGraw-Hill
Diagnostic Reading Scales (Spache)	CTB/McGraw-Hill
Durrell Analysis of Reading Difficulty	Psychological Corp.
Fountain Valley Support System in Mathematics	Zweig Assoc.
Full-Range Picture Vocabulary Test	Psychological Test Specialists
Gates-MacGinitie Reading Tests	Riverside

---

[*]This is a list of the tests cited only in this book.

Test	Publisher
Gates-McKillop Reading Diagnostic Tests	WPS
Gilmore Oral Reading Test	Psychological Corp.
Goodenough-Harris Drawing Test	WPS
Gray Oral Reading Test	WPS
Henmon-Nelson Tests of Mental Ability	Riverside
Illinois Test of Psycholinguistic Abilities	WPS
Individual Pupil Monitoring System — Mathematics	CTB/McGraw-Hill
Iowa Tests of Basic Skills	Riverside
Kaufman Assessment Battery for Children	American Guidance Service
Key Math Diagnostic Arithmetic Test	American Guidance Service
Kuhlmann-Anderson Intelligence Tests	Scholastic Testing Service
Mastery: An Evaluation — SOBAR Reading and Mathematics	Science Research Assoc.
McCarthy Scales of Children's Abilities	Psychological Corp.
Memory for Designs Test	Psychological Test Specialists
Metropolitan Achievement Tests	Psychological Corp.
Metropolitan Readiness Tests	Psychological Corp.
Motor-Free Visual Perception Test	Academic Therapy Publications
Northwestern Syntax Screening Test	Northwestern University Press
Otis-Lennon School Ability Test	Psychological Corp.
Peabody Individual Achievement Tests	American Guidance Service
Peabody Picture Vocabulary Test	American Guidance Service
Prescriptive Reading Inventory	CTB/McGraw-Hill
Primary Mental Abilities Test	Science Research Assoc.
Purdue Perceptual-Motor Survey	Merrill
Quick Test	Psychological Test Specialists
Sequential Tests of Educational Progress	Addison-Wesley
Short Form Test of Academic Aptitude	CTB/McGraw-Hill
Silent Reading Diagnostic Tests	Out of print

Test	Publisher
Skills Monitoring System — Reading	Psychological Corp.
Slosson Intelligence Test	WPS
SRA Achievement Series	Science Research Assoc.
SRA Educational Ability Series	Science Research Assoc.
Stanford Achievement Test	Psychological Corp.
Stanford Diagnostic Reading and Mathematics Tests	Psychological Corp.
Stanford-Binet Intelligence Scale	Riverside
Test of Cognitive Skills	CTB/McGraw-Hill
Tests of Achievement and Proficiency	Riverside
Utah Test of Language Development	Communication Research Assoc.
Wechsler Intelligence Scale for Children — Revised	Psychological Corp.
Wepman Auditory Discrimination Test	WPS
Wide Range Achievement Test	Guidance Assoc.
Woodcock Reading Mastery Tests	American Guidance Service
Woodcock-Johnson Psychoeducational Battery	Teaching Resources Corp.

APPENDIX B

Addresses of Test Publishers

Academic Therapy Publications
20 Commercial Boulevard
Novato, CA 94947

Addison-Wesley Testing Service
2725 Sand Hill Road
Menlo Park, CA 94025

American Guidance Service, Inc.
Publisher's Building
Circle Pines, MN 55014

Communication Research Associates
Box 11012
Salt Lake City, UT 84111

Consulting Psychologists Press, Inc.
577 College Avenue
Palo Alto, CA 94306

Charles E. Merrill Publishing Co.
1300 Alum Creek Drive
Columbus, OH 43216

CTB/McGraw-Hill
Del Monte Research Park
Monterey, CA 93940

Curriculum Associates, Inc.
94 Bridge Street
Newton, MA 02158

Follett Publishing Company
1010 West Washington Boulevard
Chicago, IL 60607

Guidance Associates of Delaware, Inc.
1526 Gilpin Avenue
Wilmington, DE 19806

Learning Concepts, Inc.
400 East Anderson Lane #318
Austin, TX 78753

Northwestern University Press
Box 1093X
1735 Benson Avenue
Evanston, IL 60201

Pro•Ed
5341 Industrial Oaks Boulevard
Austin, TX 78735

The Psychological Corporation
7500 Old Oak Boulevard
Cleveland, OH 44130

Psychological Test Specialists
Box 1441
Missoula, MT 59801

The Riverside Publishing Company
8420 Bryn Mawr Avenue
Chicago, IL 60631

Scholastic Testing Service, Inc.
480 Meyer Road
Bensenville, IL 60106

Science Research Associates, Inc.
155 North Wacker Drive
Chicago, Il 60606

Teaching Resources Corporation
50 Pond Park Road
Hingham, MA 02043
Western Psychological Services
12031 Wilshire Boulevard
Los Angeles, CA 90025

Richard L. Zweig Associates, Inc.
20800 Beach Boulevard
Huntington Beach, CA 92648

AUTHOR INDEX

SUBJECT INDEX

A

Ability tests, 58, 62 (*see also* Specific test name)

Ability-achievement discrepancy
ability (or expectancy) component of, 126-131
achievement component of, 131
in definitions of learning disabilities, 5-6, 8-10, 21-22
in multidisciplinary team decisions, 22, 238-239, 246, 248
operational definitions of, 121, 125-136, 143-144, 230, 239
severe (*see* Severe ability-achievement discrepancy)

Ability-achievement discrepancy procedures
criteria for evaluating, 122-124, 130
evaluation of, 126-136, 143-144
recommended, 136, 143-144
selecting tests for, 123
selecting test scores for, 92, 101-103, 116-117, 122-123

Ability-achievement discrepancy procedures, categories of, 122 (*see also* Severe ability-achievement discrepancy)
ability-achievement *z*-score difference, 130, 132
expected-actual GE score difference, 130, 132
ratio of actual to expected GE scores, 130, 132
residual score, 130, 133-135, 144
true difference score, 130, 132-133, 136, 143-144
true residual score, 130-131, 135, 144

Ability-achievement discrepancy scores, 126-136
compared with criterion for severe, 230-237
ipsative interpretation of, 91-92, 121, 131
magnitude of, 122, 131, 133, 230
procedures for computing, 127-128, 132-135, 230, 240
reliability of (*see* Reliable discrepancy score)
statistical significance of, 122, 124, 132-133, 135, 230, 232, 236-237
strategies for defining, 131-135
validity of (*see* Valid discrepancy score; Decision validity)

Ability-training model, 178

B

Abnormal discrepancy score, 137-139, 141

Academic disorders, 10

Achievement tests, 59, 62 (*see also* Specific test name)

Age (*see* Chronological age; Mental age)

Age-equivalent scores, 29, 92, 97, 116 (*see also* Mental age)

Aphasia, 3, 5-6, 15

Armstead et al. v. Starkville, Mississippi Municipal Separate School District, 46

Assessment of learning-disabled children
definition of, viii-ix
two stages of, viii-ix, 169-170, 222-223, 240-242, 248

B

Bannatyne recategorization of WISC/WISC-R, 140-142

Base rate
of an abnormal Verbal-Performance discrepancy, 137-138
of learning disabilities, 155-158, 160-167, 171-172, 208
of mastery, 186, 191, 193, 204-205, 208

Behavioral model of remediation, 177

Bender Visual Motor Gestalt Test, 29, 59, 253

Bias
atmosphere, 47
construct, 47, 63
in criterion-referenced tests, 71, 242-243
decision-making, 47
examiner, 47
item, 45-57, 61-63
judgmental review for, 45-46, 62, 71, 242
linguistic, 47
predictive, 46-47, 63
racial or ethnic, 45-47, 61-62, 223, 242
relation to nondiscriminatory evaluation, 47-48
review form, 72
in selected ability and achievement tests, 61-62
in selection, 62-63
sex, 45-47, 61-62, 223, 242
standards related to, 47